Rivers of History

Life on the Coosa, Tallapoosa, Cahaba, and Alabama

HARVEY H. JACKSON III

The University of Alabama Press

TUSCALOOSA AND LONDON

Library of Congress Cataloging-in-Publication Data

Jackson, Harvey H.
    Rivers of history : life on the Coosa, Tallapoosa, Cahaba, and
Alabama / Harvey H. Jackson III.
        p.   cm.
    Includes bibliographical references (p.   ) and index.
    ISBN 0-8173-0771-0 (alk. paper)
    1. Rivers—Alabama—History.   2. River life—Alabama—History.
3. Alabama—History, Local.   4. Coosa River (Ga. and Ala.)—History.
5. Tallapoosa River (Ga. and Ala.)—History.   6. Cahaba River (Ala.)—
History.   7. Alabama River (Ala.)—History.   I. Title.
    F332.A17J33   1995
    976.1'5—dc20   94-32334

British Library
Cataloguing-in-Publication
Data available

Cover Illustration: Steamboat *William Jones* at Selma (c. 1855) by William F
(Courtesy Selma, Alabama, Public Library)

For my family:
Mama, Daddy, and Bill;
Kelly, Suzanne, and Will

Contents

Illustrations

Preface

> Eventually, all things merge into one,
> and a river runs through it.
>
> NORMAN MACLEAN
> *A River Runs Through It,* 1976

For me, things began merging back in 1989, when the mail delivered a letter from my longtime friend Tennant McWilliams. Enclosed was a copy of a letter Tennant had written to Malcolm MacDonald of The University of Alabama Press. Malcolm, it seems, was looking for someone to write a history of the Alabama River System. McWilliams had recommended me.

In touting my qualifications, Tennant bent the truth more than once when he told of how I had "spent most of [my] youth chasing alligators and observing submarines" along the rivers, but he was correct when he wrote of my long association with the streams and with the people who lived, worked, and played on them. My father's family was from Elmore County, and as a boy I spent many a happy hour on and in Lake Jordan, though at the time I do not think I understood that I was fishing and swimming in what had once been the Coosa River. My own home was in Clarke County, whose eastern border is formed by the Alabama, and to me places like Choctaw Bluff, Gainstown Landing, Old Claiborne, Packer's Bend, and Miller's Ferry were both physical and mental landmarks. The more I thought about a book about these rivers, the more I wanted to write it.[1]

A few days later a letter from Malcolm arrived. The project, as he envisioned it, called for a scholarly study written for the general public, a concept I endorsed and one I optimistically believed I could pull off. Too often historians (myself included) write with other historians in mind. I had reached the point in my career where I wanted to write a book for folks who simply liked history and enjoyed a good story. This was my chance to do it. And if my fellow historians found something of value in the effort, so much the better. So I prepared a proposal, the Press Committee approved it, and I set to work.

Early in my research I reread three older books that, to varying degrees, touched on the region and on the people I planned to write about—Carl Carmer's *Stars Fell on Alabama* (1934), Clarence Cason's *90° in the Shade* (1935), and H. C. Nixon's *Lower Piedmont Country* (1946). The influence of these authors, and of their contemporary W. J. Cash, remained with me as I gathered and organized material, pondered what I had found, and set about to tell the tale. Looking now on what I have written, I can see the many ways this book was shaped by their approach to regional studies, and it is with pride and gratitude that I acknowledge my debt to them.

What I have accomplished here also owes much to the old *Rivers of America* series published during the 1930s and 1940s. Both consciously and unconsciously, its books were my models. If that series were still around today, and if its editors wanted a book on the Alabama System, I would hope that this work might be considered for inclusion. I can think of no higher honor.

So I have written an older book, one that strikes me as being part of a tradition that goes back half a century or more. The style is mostly narrative, analysis is treated as part of the story, and the focus is on people rather than on institutions. Some of it might seem romanticized, hardly surprising since river life and lore have within them all the elements of romanticism. Yet at the same time I intended this to be a realistic treatment of the relationship between the citizens of this state and a river system that runs through it, a relationship that is critical to understanding the history of Alabama. In 1819, when Alabama entered the Union, its leaders designed a great seal that featured the state's waterways. In adopting this symbol they affirmed their belief that the future of Alabama lay with its rivers. It did, and it still does.

Like any book, this one could not have been written without the help of many people. At the top of this list are three lovely and knowledgeable ladies from different sections of the river system, who read the manuscript and critiqued it from their unique perspectives. Bette Sue McElroy of Gadsden, Kathryn Tucker Windham of Selma, and Kathy Painter of Monroeville did more than friendship requires, and I gratefully acknowledge the help they gave me.

Once this project began I discovered scores of river enthusiasts who were interested in my work and anxious to aid me. With David Haynes I traveled the lower Coosa and Tallapoosa; Edward Rozelle took me out to Embry Bend and helped me understand the Coosa before the dams were built; Judge William C. Sullivan told me tales of his lockkeeper grandfather; Charles Holliday talked to me about diving for sunken wrecks; state senator Doug Ghee took time from his busy schedule to explain pending environmental legislation; and William Harris became my guide to the Alabama River and to the steamboat *Orline St. John.* Among the many others who have helped me in various ways are Anne Jackson Bennett, William U. Eiland, Linda Derry, Julie Lyons, Viola Goode Liddell, R. A. Duke, Pete Conroy, Don Elder, Pauline Rozelle, Jim Cox, Joe Franklin, Elizabeth Hayes, John C. Hall, James L.

"Buddy" Estes, Connie Hines, Vern M. Scott, Truman Bass, Jerry Oldshue, Bernard Moseby, Larry McCullough, Annie Crenshaw, Charlotte Hood, Bill Tharpe, Yvonne Crumpler, Ed Hill, and Bryding Adams.

I have been fortunate to have had the support and encouragement of my colleagues in the history department at Jacksonville State University and of Dean Earl Wade. Department secretary Audrey Smelley was equally helpful, as was Reginna Horne, who was my graduate assistant in the last stages of the project. Jacksonville State University aided my work immensely through its faculty research grant program and through the resources of the Houston Cole Library. Library director William Hubbard allowed me to all but take up residence in the Alabama Gallery, and librarian Linda Cain cheerfully guided me to even the most obscure book and document. The rest of the library staff was equally helpful, and I am in their debt. I am also indebted to the Alabama Department of Archives and History and to its staff—especially Norwood Kerr, whose knowledge of that institution's holdings (and whose patience in helping me use them) made every trip to Montgomery a pleasure. Also helpful were the staffs of the Anniston Public Library, the Virginia Historical Society, Pocumtuck Valley Memorial Association, the Ralph Draughon Library at Auburn, the Selma Public Library, the Boston Museum of Art, the Amelia Gayle Gorgas Library of the University of Alabama, the U.S. Army Corps of Engineers, the Alabama Power Company Corporate Archives, the Birmingham Public Library, and the Birmingham Museum of Art. I also wish to thank Professor Sarah Wiggins, editor of the *Alabama Review*, for permission to reprint material from that journal.

Even with the help of these fine people and institutions, I could not have completed this work without friends who aided me both professionally and personally, and to whom I owe more than I can say here. Ed and Jane Weldon, Brad Rice, Suzette Griffith, Malcolm MacDonald, Leah Atkins, Melvin Herndon, and Ed Bridges have been sources of inspiration and support for which I am grateful. Jim and Lyra Cobb know what they have meant to me—better beach buddies never lived. Two friends, Phinizy Spalding and Bob Owens, did not make it to the end of this project with me. I miss them.

But in the final analysis, it has been my family who made it all possible. They read and reread the manuscript, told me stories and listened as I told them back, took to the highway with me, crossed every bridge on every river in the System, and rode the last ferry on the Alabama. They helped me in ways words can never express, and in gratitude I dedicate this book to them.

Rivers of History

INTRODUCTION

"Once There Were Rivers"

And a river went out of Eden to water the garden.

Genesis 3:10

We don't know what Alabama rivers were like before people came to change them. We only know that they were different then. But if we read closely, we can imagine how great that difference was.

* * *

In "the So[uth] West promontories of the Cherokee or Apalachian mountains in the Chicasaw territory," eighteenth-century naturalist William Bartram found the source of the Coosa, the longest branch of the Alabama. There the Oostanaula and the Etowah, crystal-clear mountain streams tamed by valleys, met and formed the river that physically and culturally shaped the region through which it flowed. Fed by the heaviest rainfall in the eastern continent, the Coosa moved south through land that hardly sloped at all. Unhurried by gravity, it went around obstacles rather than over them, and in the first two hundred miles of its meanderings, it cut a course more than twice as long as it would have needed had it flowed in a straight line. Years later settlers claimed that the Coosa curved to touch every farm in the valley.[1]

Toward the end of this stretch the bends became fewer; the country changed and with it the river. The land fell away, and rock ledges formed reefs, shoals, and rapids, separated by reaches where the stream collected itself before plunging ahead again. For another hundred miles the Coosa rushed across a ragged, irregular fall line that plagued navigation for centuries. Forced into a narrow channel by steep banks, the river raised a protesting roar that could be heard from miles away. For anyone who had seen the upper Coosa, it was as if nature had created the river twice.[2]

Mile after mile, the lower Coosa swept around islands and over falls, paused in pools, then rushed past reefs and rock gardens until, abruptly as it began, it was over. With one great surge the river raced through the last rapid, the Devil's Staircase, rested briefly where Wetumpka would be built, then began its meandering again. A state geologist in the nineteenth century was struck by the beauty of this section, with its "high banks and deep water," but those features signaled that the river's course was almost run. Fewer than twenty miles farther downstream the Coosa met its sister, the Tallapoosa, and together they ceased to exist.[3]

1

The Coosa was an old river before the Tallapoosa became a river at all. Rising south of its sibling's birthplace, the Tallapoosa began as a piedmont spring, grew into a branch, joined other branches to form a creek, and with other creeks feeding it, slowly broadened into a river. Though it never matched the Coosa, the Tallapoosa was no insignificant stream. Its bends were tighter and its banks narrower, but some of its reaches were over a hundred feet wide and fifteen to twenty feet deep. In the 1770s, William Bartram noted that its water ran "with a steady, active current" and was "very clear, [and] agreeable to the taste." The vegetation along its banks was lush, and in one spot Bartram enjoyed a "charming fruitful plain, under an elevated ridge of hills, the swelling beds or bases of which [were] covered with a pleasing verdue of grass." The richness of the land along the Tallapoosa and Coosa was matched by the richness of the waters, which Indian agent Benjamin Hawkins found teeming with "sturgeon, trout, perch, rock, red horse" and a trout "called the chub." Little wonder that the greatest concentration of Indian towns in what would become Alabama was along these streams.[4]

The Tallapoosa ran swifter as it flowed farther south, until it crashed over majestic falls near the place where the Indians built the town of Talisi. A few miles farther downstream the river hit a shelf of harder rock, turned sharply to the west, and headed to join the Coosa. The streams met at right angles, slowed on impact, deposited the soil they carried, and became the Alabama.[5]

Confined between banks that nineteenth-century geologist Sir Charles Lyell described as "enormous beds of unconsolidated gravel," the Alabama River flowed easily on a westward course. It formed a huge bend where one day Montgomery would be built and continued meandering along the northern boundary of the Black Belt, from whose sticky, chalky soil river plantations later rose. At times in this section the stream coursed through a "deep cut or trench, with perpendicular sides" that travelers claimed rose "to the height of sixty or eighty feet" and that were so regular that they reminded visitors of a canal. At other spots, usually in the bends, high bluffs on one shore looked across the river to "flat swampy margins" that were annually flooded. It was a varied landscape that over the centuries supported a varied population.[6]

Floods were as much a part of the river's character as its rapids, pools, bluffs, and swamps. Indians on the Coosa told of how every fifteen or twenty years a flood "overflow[s] the banks, and spreads itself for five and six miles in width." Such events were no less frequent on the Alabama, where accounts of water rising "64 perpendicular feet" or more were not uncommon, and even after the tide receded, according

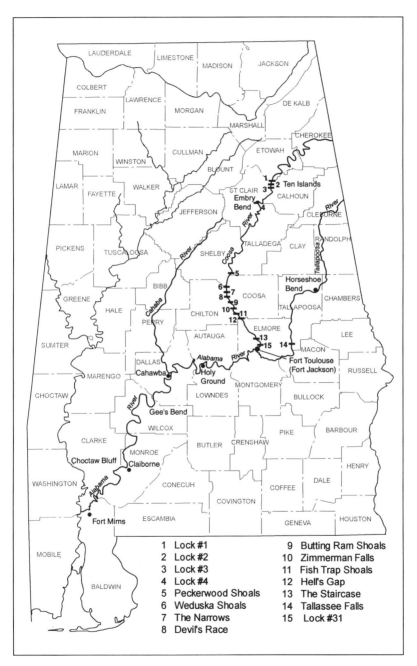

Landmarks on the Alabama River System

to one witness, "the water [continued] gushing out from millions of springs, and pouring in curious cascades into the main stream." Another rain, and the river was up again.[7]

As surely as the Alabama ran high in the spring, it dropped low in the summer and fall. Dry weather exposed gravel shoals and sandbars, which a summer downpour might turn into rapids; but as quickly as the river rose, it fell. The settlers who made their homes along the stream grew sensitive to its seasonal moods, though even the most experienced among them was unable to predict January droughts and July floods. The Alabama, it seemed, had a mind of its own.[8]

Early travelers were moved by the variety and pristine beauty of the river. A nineteenth-century Frenchman observed that at one moment the Alabama might be "fairly narrow, with here and there delightful little islands that look like bouquets of foliage placed there by a nymph to keep them from withering," while at another spot it would be so wide that he had "the feeling of being lost in one of those deserts of the ocean, seeing only the majesty of God." At night from the deck of a steamboat, Englishman Thomas Hamilton was "struck with the beauty of the stars reflected in the pure waters," and in the river he saw "the whole sky . . . mirrored with a vividness which exceeded everything of the kind [he had] ever witnessed."[9]

To some the Alabama and its valley were nothing less than an earthly paradise. Harriett Martineau, a visitor in the 1830s, was affected by the "shadowy and still" stream, where "dark-green recesses, with the relief of a slender white stem, or dangling creeper here and there" created an exotic atmosphere she compared to India and Ceylon, a jungle scene where some vines rose "like a ladder, straight from the water to a bough one hundred and twenty feet high." "The softness of the evening light on the water" complemented this melancholy "profusion of verdure" and created a world Martineau found "so bright, and yet not dazzling" that it was "as if the atmosphere were purified from all mortal breathings."[10]

Along the shore, between "considerable creeks" whose "serpentine courses" carried them to the Alabama, lay what Bartram described as "a pleasing sylvan landscape of primitive, uncultivated nature." Here were "undulating" prairies, "gently swelling knolls perceptible at a distance, but which seemed to vanish and disappear as [travelers] come upon them." The scene seemed so ancient that visitors believed the prairies "never to have been covered with woods." It was an impressive sight, and "when clothed with the vegetation of spring-time," the landscape looked "like a flower garden." Even where there were trees, there was little or no undergrowth, and "a deer could be seen a quarter of a mile through the woods." This land would be the Camelot of Alabama's cotton kingdom, and many would swear that "a more fertile and beautiful tract of country . . . does not exist in our state."[11]

The Alabama continued its circuitous route westward, past the bluff where Selma would someday sit, and then turned abruptly south to meet its last large tributary—the Cahaba. Born in the Appalachian foothills, fed by clear creeks and branches, the Cahaba, according to an early survey, flowed swiftly over "a beautiful bottom of solid rock" and between "considerable bluff[s]," tumbling down shoals and low falls as it went. In this rugged environment, the vegetation "interspersed with [the] rocky surface" was a "luxuriant" mixture of "mulberry, sugar tree, maple, white and red oak, post oak,——Ash, lind, and maiden [hair fern]." And in the spring there was the lily that would bear the river's name.[12]

The Cahaba left its rapids behind at the line where the Coosa and Tallapoosa abandoned theirs. After its last fall, not even three feet high, the river entered the coastal plain where it flowed slowly over a sand and gravel bottom, twisting and turning between low banks that an early settler remembered were covered with "pretty magnolias and bays with their milk-white flowers." The area the Cahaba drained seldom supplied enough water in the summer to keep its level up, and by July parts of it were easily waded. When the rains did come, the Cahaba rose rapidly, and low banks could not contain it. To those who lived in its valley, the Cahaba was a river of extremes, and it gained a reputation for excesses that it did not entirely deserve.[13]

With the addition of the Cahaba, the Alabama River was complete. Smaller streams joined later, but they brought little to distinguish them. Flowing slowly southward, the river grew sluggish with size and cut larger bends, wide and sweeping to accommodate its bulk. Tall bluffs still loomed above it, revealing what the river had cut through to reach its bed—clay, soapstone, white limestone, and in a few cases a black substance that early settlers believed was coal until burning proved them wrong. In the strata were marine fossils, "collateral proof," according to a Methodist bishop, "of the flood & therefore of the truth of the Bible." As the river wound its way farther south there were fewer bluffs and more swamps and canebreaks. Here thick fogs often rose from the water, and cypress with a palmetto undergrowth dominated a woodland "intersected with lakes, marshes and crooked draws" that travelers complained were "much infected with mosquitoes." It was as if one had entered the tropics, and the change meant that the Alabama was almost over.[14]

Some three hundred miles after it was created by the union of the

Coosa and Tallapoosa, the Alabama River joined the Tombigbee and disappeared. The juncture was haphazard, with streams merging through swamps and cutoffs into the ill-defined channels of what would become rivers called Mobile and Tensaw. Denied access to an ocean, gulf, or bay, in a sense it was an inglorious end. And yet the end was fitting, for it made the Alabama an Alabama river. It would share its name with the state, and no other state could claim it.[15]

* * *

This was how the rivers flowed when our story begins. They flowed like this for many years. But not forever.

ONE

The Alabama Invaded

Every careful student of the route of DeSoto will agree with Professor
Wyman that DeSoto crossed the Alabama River much higher up than
Pickett and Meek have stated, and if so, the battle of Mauvilla was
fought not at or near Choctaw Bluff in Clarke county but further up
the river.

M. in Montgomery *Advertiser*
reprinted in the *Clarke County Democrat*,
June 15, 1893

"Then how will you reconcile the statement of DeSoto's historians that
Mauvilla was only about 85 miles from the sea at Ochuse—Pensacola?"

Reply to M., *Clarke County Democrat*
June 15, 1893

In October of 1540 at the Indian town of Mabila, on or near the
Alabama River, soldiers of Hernando de Soto clashed with the forces of
chief Tascaluza. The battle raged for several hours, and when it was over
one Spaniard calculated that between twenty-five hundred and five
thousand Indians were dead and hundreds more were wounded. If this
estimate is accurate, it was the bloodiest battle fought on North American soil until Union and Confederate armies met at Shiloh in 1862.[1]

For generations of Alabama school children, the battle of Mabila was
the first great "event" in the state's history. Yet despite its significance,
the site where it occurred remains a mystery. This is unfortunate, for if
researchers could determine the specific location of the battle, then de
Soto's route might be traced with more certainty, for Mabila could
serve as a point of reference to verify locations mentioned in the often
imprecise accounts left by chroniclers of the expedition. Finding
Mabila would greatly narrow the options facing archaeologists and
enable them to concentrate their efforts. The result might be new and
important discoveries that would enlarge our understanding of Alabama Indians and their early contact with Europeans.

Though no one can say for certain where Mabila was, there has been
no shortage of opinions as to where it might have been. Among early
historians the most popular site was near the Alabama River in present-
day Clarke County, and local citizens, proud of this distinction, were
quick to take issue with anyone who was so bold as to suggest that the
Spaniards had not visited their region. Fears that another location
might present a better claim were calmed in 1939, when a national
commission established to mark the four-hundredth anniversary of the

de Soto expedition published a study that recreated the route taken by the invaders and put Mabila safely in Clarke. Residents of the county were overjoyed, and soon they confirmed their title by naming a local Boy Scout camp after the battle. The issue seemed settled.[2]

It was not. With the approach of the 450th anniversary of the Spanish campaign, scholars began to try once again to trace the route and locate the places that were visited—including Mabila. The effort divided the academic community. To the distress of Clarke County citizens, one cadre of anthropologists, archaeologists, and historians concluded that Mabila was not in their county but farther north, perhaps at the point where the Cahaba River joins the Alabama. Another group of researchers argued that earlier calculations were correct and that Clarke's claim was valid. The result was a standoff, with both sides aware that until confirmed by archaeological evidence, everything was theory. Amid all this controversy, one thing was clear. Scholars were not the only ones interested in the location. The reaction of Clarke County residents to the possibility that their historical markers would be ripped up and replanted in Dallas County revealed how much it meant to a community to know that history had touched it.[3]

Despite deep divisions between de Soto devotees over where to find Mabila, there was consensus on other points. All sides agreed that de Soto's expedition traveled down the Coosa River valley and along at least some of the Alabama. They also agreed that de Soto and his men were among the first and probably also the last Europeans to see the Indian river civilizations at their height.[4]

Indians had lived along the rivers for centuries before the Spaniards arrived. Drawn to the rich vegetation and animal life close to the streams, hunting and gathering groups wandered in, settled, and in time developed farming communities capable of sustaining large populations. Theirs was a seasonal way of life, and the rivers played an important part in it. Spring floods deposited rich soil on their fields and regenerated the land, so they did not need to move their villages frequently or far. Planting schedules were dictated by receding waters; and while the crops matured, the community turned to the river for food.[5]

Early on the Indians began altering the streams to serve their purposes. They built weirs by piling tons of rocks in a V shape with the point upstream, to divert the current and force spawning fish into reed traps and nets. These man-made obstructions required the same high degree of engineering skill, energy, and community organization that mound building demanded, and today they might be considered in the same category were not most lost beneath the waters of power company lakes. Weirs also created pools and eddies where schooling fish were easily poisoned with the pounded pulp of buckeye and the root of devil's shoestring that the Indians spread on the water. In this season they also hunted waterfowl that migrated along the river route, and they stalked animals in the swamps and canebreaks near the shore.[6]

Spring gave way to summer, a time of fewer fish and game but a season when Indians could depend on a variety of edible plants, including the "horticultural trinity" of maize, beans, and squash. During these more leisurely months, the tribes held contests and celebrations, including the Green Corn Festival or Boosketah (busk) that marked the point in the agricultural cycle when the crop matured. This pattern of activity was common to farming people in a warm climate, and it characterized life in the river valleys long after the Indians were gone and cotton had been crowned king. Fall brought not only the harvest but also better fishing and the return of migratory birds. This was the best time for hunting, as deer and turkey were fat and plentiful. Much of the fall bounty was stored in public granaries, for winter was a period of stress for the community. Sufficient supplies in the final weeks before the fish and birds returned in the spring were essential to the survival of the weakest members of the tribe—particularly the young and the old. As it was for the animals they hunted, winter was the critical season.[7]

The rivers drew tribes and towns together. In dugout canoes, Indians visited neighboring settlements, often for trade and sometimes for war; and through these contacts the river civilizations grew. The rapids on the Coosa and Tallapoosa made it difficult for these streams to become great avenues of communication and commerce, so north-south trade in the area depended heavily on woodland trails. Still, trading tribes knew the value of the rivers and used them when they could. Commerce passing through the region on an east-west axis was not so fortunate. For these travelers, the streams were obstacles to be crossed, so fords were their most important features. As this regional trade grew, control of these strategic spots was critical. The Indians soon recognized their importance; in time others would recognize it as well.[8]

What de Soto found when he arrived in the valley of the Coosa and Alabama rivers was a mature Indian civilization, organized around planned permanent towns and ceremonial centers, governed through a heirarchial social, political, and religious system, and linked to similar civilizations by an extensive regional trading network. Their population growing and communities expanding, the Coosa and Alabama Indians were an energetic people with a sense of self-worth that easily matched that of the Spanish. They were masters of a vast domain and a force with which to be reckoned.[9]

In September of 1540, de Soto, with about six hundred men, a few priests, assorted camp followers, perhaps 250 horses, some dogs, and a large drove of pigs, entered the territory of Coosa, somewhere near the modern juncture of Alabama, Georgia, and Tennessee. From there they pressed southward, down the valley, along a stream described as "large, swift, and hard to enter" and "no small venture" to cross. Here they "found some muscles that they gathered to eat, and some pearls," which encouraged dreams of greater wealth deeper in the interior. They also found flourishing towns and villages, from which they took supplies, porters, and hostages. Some Indians resisted, while others greeted the Spaniards courteously and offered to help however they could. But the natives always told the invaders that the riches they sought were farther on and made every effort to hurry de Soto and his men along their way.[10]

After weeks of marching near the river, the army reached the town of Atahachi, possibly at the junction of the Coosa and Tallapoosa. This was the seat of paramount chief Tascaluza, who the Spaniards had been told could provide supplies, porters, and women and could guide them to the wealthy cities to the west. The invaders entered the town and found Tascaluza "full of dignity," seated on a cushion atop a mound. De Soto spelled out his needs; the chief offered some help, then revealed that more supplies—and one hundred women—waited at Mabila, a town farther west. It had been a long journey, and with only the priests in the party pledged to celibacy, the inducement worked. Taking a less-than-enthusiastic Tascaluza with them, the Spanish army resumed its march down the Alabama River.[11]

During the week that followed the soldiers, stock, shackled porters, de Soto, and Tascaluza (with an attendant carrying his sunshade) made their way along a "craggy" gorge, where steep banks often towered a hundred feet above a winding river that they estimated was over four hundred feet wide. When they finally reached their destination the commander sent a party ahead to "discover the temper of the Indians," and it returned to report that the natives were collecting weapons and strengthening the town. The European arrival had united the region. Not only were Indians loyal to Tascaluza gathered at Mabila, but natives had come from all along the Coosa-Tallapoosa valley. The tribes of the river region were prepared to repel the invaders.[12]

Mabila was a fortified town built on a level plain, in the vicinity of the river that marked the frontier between Tascaluza's chiefdom and its neighbor. This was as far as the royal traveler intended to go. When de Soto, the chief, and a small detachment of soldiers entered the town, Tascaluza slipped away from the group and into a house where Indians waited, armed and ready. De Soto called for him to come out, but

Tascaluza responded that if the Spanish commander "wished to go in peace, he should quit at once, and not persist in carrying him away by force from his country." With those words the issue was drawn.[13]

A brief skirmish followed as the invaders tried to seize the chief, but they failed and were soon driven from the town. Outside the stockade they joined the main Spanish force and at a given signal "commenced a furious onset" which breached the walls and brought them into the center of Mabila. Tascaluza's men fought bravely, and the outcome was in doubt until de Soto's cavalry joined the fray. In the confusion that followed, soldiers began setting buildings on fire, and Indian resistance crumbled. Some tried to fight and were killed; others fled "headlong into the flaming houses, were smothered, and, heaped one upon another, burned to death." It was a slaughter. Even if the casualty figures reported later were exaggerated, there is little doubt that it was one of the bloodiest battles between Indians and Europeans ever fought in North America. But though they were the victors, the Spaniards had learned a lesson. No longer would they assume that the Indians were theirs to command. It was a wiser captain who led his battered army away from the land of Tascaluza.[14]

While the battle of Mabila was a turning point for the de Soto expedition, the expedition itself was a turning point for the Indians. Some twenty years later a Spanish party from Ochuse, on Pensacola Bay, arrived in the river region to find the Indian population so depleted and their society so disrupted that it bore little resemblance to that which de Soto's chroniclers described. What this expedition saw may have been early indications of a biological disaster of incredible proportion. The Europeans had brought diseases, especially smallpox and measles; and the Indians, with little or no resistance, perished by the hundreds. Over the next century and a half, epidemic after epidemic swept through the valley, and each time the tribes were decimated. Without concrete figures on the Indian population at the time the viruses hit, it is difficult to know how many died. But if it was true, as some claim, that over a million Indians lived in the southeast when de Soto invaded, later counts suggest a holocaust unrivaled in American history. By the eve of the American Revolution, the natives numbered less than a hundred thousand.[15]

It is hard to conceive, much less comprehend, the cultural impact this depopulation had on the Indians. When the epidemics struck, the weak—especially the young and the old—succumbed first. The loss of the young was a devastating blow to the future of the tribes, for it depleted the generation that was expected to maintain and perpetuate tribal traditions. But given the course of the disease, there was little for them to maintain. In an oral culture, the loss of older members meant the loss of the collective memory on which the culture depended. If the death of the young threatened the future, the death of the old erased the past. Without this reservoir of ancient knowledge from which to draw, tribal customs were abandoned, and those practices that did continue had little substance to support them. Looking back, we can see the results. At the end of the eighteenth century, Indian agent Benjamin Hawkins inquired as to the purpose of five mounds situated on the left bank of the Alabama, just below the confluence of the Coosa and Tallapoosa. Their location indicates that they may have been part of Atahachi, Tascaluza's principal town, and one may have been the very mound on which the chief sat when he greeted de Soto. Because none of the local Indians could tell Hawkins about the great tribe that built them or explain their ceremonial significance, the agent concluded that they were nothing more than a place of refuge from floods. By that time he was probably right.[16]

During this period the Indians also underwent a political transformation as disease-ravaged tribes reorganized and some village sites were abandoned. Unfortunately, we know little of what actually occurred in these years or how the natives coped with the transition. This era, between the departure of the Spanish and the arrival of the next wave of Europeans over a century later, is Alabama's "dark age," a time when the historical record is virtually blank and is not likely to be filled. What we do know, however, is that when the next invaders arrived, they found a river region that was very different from the one "discovered" by de Soto.[17]

By the middle of the seventeenth century, the Indians were at last bringing order out of the chaos left by the epidemics. Increasingly resistant to the diseases, their population growing, and their society more stable, the river tribes created a new and vibrant culture to replace the old. Important in this revival was a restored regional exchange system. Over woodland trails and navigable streams the natives swapped not only trade goods but ideas, which may have been the most important commodities of all. To reverse their political disintegration the Indians formed a series of river chiefdoms, with an organizational structure that was somewhere between that of a tribe and a state. At that moment, the future must have looked bright indeed. But what they did not know, could not have known, was that this revival would invite a second European invasion, one that brought with it an economic system that proved as destructive to their way of life as the epidemics that were brought before.[18]

The new chiefdoms were large enough to make commerce with them worthwhile, yet too small to effectively resist foreign intrusion or force trade concessions in their favor. They were ripe for exploitation, and in the late seventeenth century the exploiters arrived. Charleston was founded in 1670, and by the next decade traders headquartered there were moving into the Alabama-Coosa-Tallapoosa valley. French outposts on the gulf coast soon heard of how these Englishmen came into the villages with their "packhorses loaded with all the apparatus of guns, muskets, powder, lead and a great deal of other merchandise," ready to barter. More than anything else the traders wanted Indian slaves, for labor was scarce in Carolina, and prices were high. The Indians wanted what the Englishmen had to exchange, and it was not long before reports filtered out of how the natives would "go and make [slaves] of their neighbors with whom they engage in continual war, killing the men, carrying away the women and children whom they sell to the English, each one for a gun." This practice, according to the account, "has brought great destruction in the neighboring nations." Once again, Europeans were creating havoc along the rivers.[19]

In time African chattel drove Indian chattel from the market, and the slave catchers disappeared; but by then changes were set in motion that would not be reversed. Deerskins became the Indians' new medium of exchange, and that trade quickly grew to phenomenal proportions. Over forest trails that crossed the upper Coosa above the rapids and the Coosa-Tallapoosa near the place where those streams joined to form the Alabama, pack trains carried bundles of skins to Charleston, some twenty-seven days away. From there they went to England to fill a seemingly insatiable desire for buckskin breeches. Without powerful tribes or geographic barriers to hinder them, English traders became a prominent feature of the frontier scene. Their strategy for success was simple enough. As Thomas Nairne, Carolina's first Indian agent, observed, their trade "attracts and maintains the obedience and friendship of the Indians" because the Englishmen knew "they Effect them most who sell best cheap."[20]

The Charleston traders not only sold cheap, but also sold what the Indians wanted—cloth, arms and ammunition, metal goods, and rum. Each commodity played a part in altering the natives' way of life. Cloth and metal goods soon replaced their own crafts, and many Indians eventually lost their knowledge of and respect for recently revived skills. Guns were obviously superior to traditional weapons, and warriors went to great lengths to obtain them; but without the technology to produce ammunition or repair muskets, Native Americans became all the more dependent on the white men. As for rum, the tribesmen were so "passionately fond" of it that the image of the "drunken Indian" became fixed in the European mind. All the advances that had brought an end to the Indian's "dark age" were slowly crumbling away.[21]

English domination of the interior trade did not go unchallenged. In 1699 the French, who had explored the Mississippi Valley a decade earlier, stationed a garrison at Biloxi, and three years later they planted another at Mobile, a five-day float downriver from the Coosa-Tallapoosa chiefdoms. Though a permanent colony would not be founded there for nearly a decade, this incursion reflected the belief among some French officials that their government needed to act to check English advances. The arrival of the French also marked the beginning of European competition that eventually had an effect on the tribes even greater than the disruption caused by the Indian slave trade. Soon different chiefdoms agreed to military alliances with opposing sides in return for supplies and were thus drawn into conflicts in which they historically had no part. By mid-century England and France were at war, and so were their Indian allies. Two decades later there was yet another conflict—the American Revolution. The British won the first; the Americans won the second; the Indians lost both.[22]

Even as the French debated what course to follow, the advantage shifted in their favor. For some time Indians had complained to officials in Charleston of how English traders, when they gained control of a market, began cheating local tribesmen who now had no alternative but to deal with them and physically assaulting, even murdering, those who protested. The worst abuses apparently were heaped on some of Carolina's oldest allies, the Yamasee, who lived on the colony's southern frontier. Finally the Yamasee could take no more, and on Good Friday, April 15, 1715, they struck back. In the weeks that followed Indians killed traders and destroyed settlements throughout Carolina. As word of the uprising spread, other Indians, who felt equally exploited, joined the revolt, and soon the backcountry was illuminated by burning outposts. In the chaos, surviving traders fled from the interior, and the English presence in the Alabama-Coosa-Tallapoosa valley simply vanished. What the French had dreamed of doing, the Indians had accomplished.[23]

Though the English struck back and defeated the Yamasee, the network of trading houses and commercial agreements developed over the previous quarter century lay in ruins. Indians from the valleys of the Alabama, Coosa, Tallapoosa, and Chattahoochee, well beyond the reach of Carolina revenge, seized the moment and forged an alliance stronger than the river chiefdoms and better able to protect their interests—a confederation that came to be known as the Creeks. At the same time French interests and ambitions were working against Indian unity. Moving quickly to take advantage of English setbacks, their representatives formalized an alliance with the villages south and east of the Alabama River. These Indians would be known as the Lower Creeks. In years to come, when they looked for friends, they looked south toward Mobile and Pensacola.[24]

But the French had their eyes on an even bigger prize. The strategic fork of the Coosa and Tallapoosa—the "key to the country" according to imperial planners—lay within their grasp. Located at the border between the Upper and Lower Creeks, this site marked the juncture of two important trading paths and the beginning of clear navigation south. Luckily for officials in Mobile, the Alabama Indians, who lived at the forks and for whom the river was named, were as anxious to have the French in their neighborhood as the French were anxious to be there. The Yamasee War had disrupted trade, and the Indians needed a new source of arms, ammunition, and other supplies. An Alabama delegation went down the river to Mobile and invited the French to erect a fort in their territory, even promising to build it at their own expense. The offer was too good to refuse. In July of 1717, twenty soldiers under Lt. de La Tour Vitral left Mobile, rowed up the river to the forks, and on a high, level spot that dominated both the Coosa and Tallapoosa, built the fort that was sometimes called Post aux Alibamons, at other times Fort des Alibamons, and on official occasions, Fort Toulouse. The English, when news reached them, called it the "mischievous French garrison *Alebamah*."[25]

Located within a "musket shot" of two Indian villages, the stockade of Fort Toulouse was visible proof of France's intent to control the region. The English realized this, and before the summer was out their representatives were back on the Tallapoosa seeking to repair ties between the Upper Creeks and Charleston and restore their influence in the area. As for the natives, they enjoyed this competition for their favor, and whenever possible they used it to their own advantage. Thus began four decades of forest diplomacy, a time when the attention of England, France, and the Creeks was focused on the forks of the Coosa and Tallapoosa rivers.[26]

Even with the French at Toulouse, the English soon regained their commercial advantage among the Upper Creeks. When Carolina traders arrived on the Tallapoosa in the late summer of 1717, de La Tour had no presents with which to counter enemy enticements. Scraping together what personal items he could use as gifts, the French commander made an acceptable showing, but that was all. Before the year was out the English had reestablished trade with the Coosa-Tallapoosa tribes, and Englishmen were living in their villages. Troops from

Toulouse could do little to dislodge them. As Edmond Atkin, future British superintendent for Indian affairs for the Southern District, observed, the rapids on the Coosa and Tallapoosa put "a stop to the French Water Carriage" and protected English outposts from upriver invasions. Looking to the future, Atkin noted that these natural barriers would eventually "contribute greatly to the Security of any Fort which we may hereafter build higher up, on, or between those Rivers." Since the Coosa was "full of those Water Falls," the Indians along its banks were targeted by English merchants, and English goods soon covered the area like spring floods.[27]

Conditions downstream from Toulouse also contributed to the success of this English invasion. Under the best of circumstances the trip upriver was a difficult one, and when the Alabama was low, the larger boats—such as those described as forty feet long, nine feet at the beam, and manned by twenty-eight oarsmen—simply could not make it. Obviously pleased at how nature conspired against the French, Atkin reported that "in dry Season, the Boats, on account of Sand Bars in the River, cannot go up so far as the Fort, without having small Boats sent down to lighten them." As an alternative, officials in Mobile and Pensacola developed forest paths into avenues of commerce like those the traders used to bring their goods from Charleston. But this took time, and time was on the side of the English.[28]

French efforts in the region were also hindered by a policy that made shortages a fact of life at Toulouse. Officials believed that if "the Indians . . . [found] a market for their products" at the fort, they would develop closer ties to the troops stationed there. To encourage this relationship they sent "nothing but flour for the subsistence of the garrison," so the soldiers would have to turn to "trade in order to get a living." But the policy also meant that the soldiers lacked other essentials as well, and at times they were even reduced to bartering brandy with the Indians for English goods. French traders fared little better, for though they had more supplies, their resources never matched those of the competition. So it was that in this commerce, where status and power were measured by what a man had to trade, the English enjoyed every advantage. And so it was that even when the waters ran high, French boats had little reason to ply the Alabama.[29]

For over four decades Toulouse guarded the forks of the Coosa and Tallapoosa. To travelers who approached by water the fort was almost invisible until the boat was upon it and then could only be seen up the gully that formed a ramp to the crest of the bluff. Over the years French officials strengthened the site by adding a dry moat, enlarging walls and bastions, and sending additional ordnance, so that by 1732, Toulouse boasted "2 cannons, 2 cast-iron and 2 iron *pierriers* [swivel guns], and 7 *pierrier* breech-blocks." Despite this imposing appearance, all was not as it seemed. Though the spot was high, the rivers still broke from their banks and flooded the plain and the fort. Each freshet made the stockade more difficult to maintain, and by 1748 it was so dilapidated that they gave it up and built another fort some 100 feet to the south. Completed in 1751, this second Toulouse seemed to signal a renewed French commitment to the region. But those close to the scene knew there were still problems. Construction had cost some thirty-thousand livres, almost one-half of Louisiana's annual military budget. After the remaining funds were spread over the entire province, there was little left for presents and other inducements critical in negotiations with the local tribes.[30]

Still, the very fact that the new fort was built caused the English to pause and reevaluate the situation. That assessment in turn gave the appearance, at least, that French influence was growing, and the adversaries were approaching a balance of power. Now the advantage shifted to the Indians, who skillfully played one side against the other, much to the chagrin of the Europeans. Soon the French complained of how the Alabama Indians, whom they considered their allies, insisted that they trade with them on the same terms that the English offered, while Edmond Atkin denounced the Alabamas for taking English goods and selling them to their competitors. Meanwhile South Carolina governor William Lyttleton noted with disgust that it had become "a fix'd principle with [the Creeks] to observe neutrality between us and the French [so] that they may get supplies of goods and presents from both." This situation was exactly what the Indians wanted.[31]

Unfortunately for the natives, these conditions did not last long. By 1756 England and France were officially at war, and once again the advantage shifted to traders from the east. French supplies that got by the British navy usually found their way to other destinations, so the garrison at the forks had less and less to offer the Indians in return for their loyalty. In September of 1759 English merchants, now the region's main source of trade goods, forced the Alabama tribe to limit contact with Toulouse and to fly "the Suit of English Colours" on public occasions. By the end of the year these same Indians, once France's most dependable ally along the river, were dealing exclusively with the English. Despite its bold appearance, Post aux Alibamons was little more than a French island in a sea of English influence.[32]

French reversals in other quarters, however, doomed Toulouse. Losses in Canada were especially disheartening, and as their fortunes waned peace negotiations began. In February of 1763 the Treaty of Paris ended hostilities, and England became master of the Alabama, from the headwaters of the Coosa and Tallapoosa to Mobile Bay. Soon after the treaty was announced the cannons at Toulouse were spiked, and surplus powder was thrown into the river. Then the French garrison and many of the residents of the village that had grown up under the guns of the fort began an overland trek to Mobile.[33]

There may have been many reasons for the decision to withdraw by land and not by water, but the fact that the French marched south says something fundamental about the relationship between Toulouse and the Alabama River. If surviving records tell the whole story, the river was less a factor in the maintenance of the outpost than one might imagine. Though French boats carried goods to and from the fort, Toulouse never became a trading center, so the Alabama never became a significant avenue of commerce. A scarcity of goods and supplies, largely the result of a policy that limited what was sent to the garrison, drove the Indians into the arms of the English, whose quantity, quality, prices, and aggressive trading practices guaranteed that there would be little for the French to send downstream. Mobile never became a rival to Charleston, and the Alabama would have to wait for its moment of glory.[34]

Not long after the war ended, an English expedition made its way up to the fort. The commander surveyed the site, concluded that it had scant commercial or strategic value, and departed. A short time later, with little fanfare, Toulouse was abandoned. No one, neither Indians nor traders, needed or wanted it, so officials simply "declined sending from Mobile a garrison to Alabama." The "key to the country" was left to rot on the bluff above the river.[35]

TWO

Englishmen, Indians, and Americans

The trader obliged me with his company on a visit to the Alabama, an
Indian town at the confluence of the two fine rivers, the Tallapoose
and Coosau, which here resign their names to the great Alabama. . . .
This is perhaps, one of the most eligible situations for a city in the
world; a level plain between the conflux of two majestic rivers, which
are exactly of equal magnitude in appearance . . . and spreading their
numerous branches over the most fertile and delightful regions, many
hundreds miles before we reach their sources in the Apalachean
mountains.

WILLIAM BARTRAM, 1775

Between the arrival of the first Carolina traders at the forks of the
Coosa-Tallapoosa and the evacuation of the French from Fort Toulouse, European knowledge of the Alabama River region grew at a
phenomenal rate. The imprecise maps of earlier centuries were replaced
by increasingly accurate representations of the rivers and the land
through which they flowed. This cartography was an important source
of information for commercial and military planners, but it served
another role as well. Knowledge of trails, streams, and towns in the
interior was evidence that frontier imperialists had been on the land,
and it was theirs. To have a better claim, one had to have a better map.[1]

By the 1760s English maps revealed how far that nation had come in
understanding the complex pattern of streams and tributaries that
made up the Alabama River System. The courses of the Coosa and
Tallapoosa were more accurately defined, especially in the lower sections, and the twisting path of the Alabama revealed an attention to
detail that confirmed past exploration and invited more. Finally the
Cahaba made its appearance. Flowing through land controlled by the
Choctaws, who were French allies, this smaller stream had been all but
ignored by English imperial planners until the 1750s, when the ever-
watchful Edmond Atkin alerted the Lords Commissioners for Trade
and Plantations that the Cahaba was "unpossessed," and how, "if a
Blockhouse were built . . . to which such of the Choctaws . . . might
withdraw, our Traders might trade with them in all Security." But when
the Treaty of Paris gave the whole Alabama region to England, Atkin's
blockhouse was unnecessary. The only opposition English traders faced
was the Indians themselves.[2]

The Treaty of Paris also gave Florida to the British and with it
Mobile. Now the Alabama-Coosa-Tallapoosa was an English river system, and the wealth of the Indians above the fall line could be traded

south as well as east. Although deerskins still went to Charleston and Savannah, during the next decade more and more goods were carried to points below the falls where they were loaded on canoes and flats bound for Mobile and from there for England. Pensacola was the capital of West Florida and its market center, but the Alabama trade made Mobile so important that three members of the colony's first council chose to live there instead.[3]

After years of being able to play one European interest against another, the Indians were apprehensive about the future. Rumors spread "that the English intended first, totally to surround them and next, to extirpate them from the face of the earth by cutting off their trade," and there was talk of a "general insurrection" like the Yamasee uprising of 1715. To counter these rumors, John Stuart, the new superintendent for the Southern Indian Department, made sure the natives were well supplied, probably what the rumor mongers wanted in the first place, and the decade of peaceful commerce that followed was a testament to his success. Finding the tribes in the region tired of war, the superintendent was able to end the ongoing feud between the Creeks and Choctaw, and through his good offices tensions eased. By the mid-1770s John Stuart and the English nation he served were held in high esteem all along the rivers.[4]

This peaceful interlude did not last. In 1775 disagreements between Britain's North American colonies and the mother country broke into open rebellion, and for both sides—Whigs and Loyalists—the disposition of the Indians in the Coosa-Tallapoosa-Alabama valley was of critical concern. Assuming the natives were their allies, the English sought to keep them out of the fighting until the tribes could be united in a coalition that would control the frontier. Rebelling colonists countered with a policy they cynically, but accurately, described as "rum and good words," which was designed to undermine British efforts and keep the tribes neutral. Both approaches were based on the belief that the Indians would follow the side that could best provide the trade goods upon which the natives depended. Neither seemed fully to appreciate that another factor had been introduced into the equation and that in time this new element would become more important to the Indians than anything that the merchants could supply. In the summer of 1775, naturalist William Bartram was on the southern frontier studying regional flora and fauna when he "met a company of emigrants from Georgia; a man, his wife, a young woman, several young children, and three stout young men, with about a dozen horses loaded with their property." Inquiring as to their destination, Bartram learned that "their design was to settle on the Alabama." This area was Indian territory, and these were not traders—they were farmers and drovers, and they were the future.[5]

Bartram entered the Coosa-Tallapoosa-Alabama valley from the east and arrived at Talassee at the falls of the Tallapoosa in July of 1775. As he followed the river south, through the heart of the Creek nation, he was "continually in sight of the Indian plantations and commons adjacent to their towns." In places he found the stream "three hundred yards over, and about fifteen or twenty feet deep," with water "very clear, agreeable to the taste, [and] esteemed salubrious;" but since it "ran with a steady, active current," the party chose not to use it for their travels. Bartram wanted to study the natural surroundings at his leisure, and the river would have hastened their journey. So they turned away from the Tallapoosa and headed south, along "the great trading path for West Florida" and Mobile.[6]

During the next four months the naturalist wandered through the lower South, and by late fall he was back in Creek country, at the confluence of the Coosa and Tallapoosa. Surveying the location, Bartram declared that with its "two majestic rivers . . . of equal magnitude in appearance," the bluff was surely "one of the most eligible situations for a city in the world." But all he found there were rusted cannons, "half buried in the earth," and "two or three very large Apple trees"— the only "traces of the ancient French fortress, Thoulouse." Bartram's stay was brief. From the forks he made his way up the Tallapoosa to where it was crossed by the trading path that led to Augusta; there he joined a caravan heading east.[7]

Though Bartram's account gives little indication that an American revolution was underway, the struggle had an impact in the Alabama River region. Shocked by American victories over the Cherokee in Carolina and confused by British caution, many Indians remained neutral or drifted to the American side. A handful of Scottish merchants and their Indian allies were active Loyalists, but their role was never what the British hoped it would be. After the death of Superintendent Stuart in March of 1779, the Southern Indian Department was never the same. That year Spain joined the war against Britain, and pressure on English Florida increased. In March 1780, Mobile fell to Spanish forces, and in May of the following year Pensacola was taken. Two years later the American Revolution was over. But the treaty that ended the war failed to resolve the ownership of the Alabama River. Both the United States and Spain claimed the stream and the land it drained. So did the Indians.[8]

Thomas Brown, Britain's last Indian superintendent, realized the natives' dilemma, and before he withdrew he advised his Creek friends to "enter into a negociation with the Spanish Governor of Pensacola," who Brown knew was "jealous in the extreme of the encroachments of the Americans." From the governor the Indians could obtain "a supply of such arms and ammunition as would enable them to defend their territories." The British superintendent was well aware of the Americans' insatiable appetite for land and believed Spain was the natives' only hope. Alexander McGillivray, newly elected "King and Head Warrior of all the [Creek] Nation," agreed. Son of a Scottish trader and a half-French, half-Creek princess of the prestigious Wind Clan, McGillivray understood the threat the Indians faced. Reared among the Creeks on the Tallapoosa, educated among Englishmen in Charleston, and a Loyalist during the Revolution, he heeded Brown's advice and for the next decade worked with the Spanish to "frustrate the american Schemes" in the region. His was a difficult task, but McGillivray was a remarkable man.[9]

To accomplish this goal, the Creek leader maintained that Mobile, not Pensacola, should be the port of entry into the interior. From there, with boats designed for river commerce, he believed that he "could Supply [his] People by Water Carriage [which was] preferable to pack horses." This would give the Creeks easy access to the arms and ammunition they needed to resist the American invasion that was coming from the east. But McGillivray had more than convenience on his mind when he made the proposal. If Mobile eclipsed Pensacola as West Florida's major trading center, the Alabama River would become the most significant commercial artery in the region. And if that occurred, the forks of the Coosa and Tallapoosa that William Bartram had declared to be "one of the most eligible situations for a city in the world" would become the hub of inland trade. And on that site, near the ruins of Fort Toulouse, was Alexander McGillivray's plantation, Little Talassee.[10]

Virginian John Pope visited Little Talassee in 1791 and saw how well McGillivray's plan was working. He observed that Indians from above the falls, attracted by the chief's reputation and the fact that the site was "nearer to the Hunting-Grounds from whence they may have Water-Carriage," had turned the plantation into a center for the "Peltry-Trade." But there was more. Pope discovered that the "fertile Grounds upon the . . . Rivers" had been "settled . . . by Corn, Hemp and To-bacco-Makers" who chose this location because it had "better Navigation to *Mobile* than to *Pensacola*." Just as McGillivray had envisioned, Little Talassee was becoming a diversified economic center, with the Alabama River as its commercial corridor. Everything was falling into place, and Pope predicted that as products from forest and field flowed downstream, Mobile would "'ere long surpass *Pensacola*, in Population, Trade and Buildings."[11]

It is important to note, however, that Little Talassee and many of the farms Pope found along the rivers reflected the values of whites more than those of Indians. They seemed to herald the coming of the plantation system rather than the preservation of native culture. According to Frenchman Louis LeClerc Milfort, who lived with McGillivray in the mid-1770s, even that early the Creek leader "had in his service about sixty Negroes, each of whom lived in a private cabin, which gave his place the appearance of a small village." In nearby fields and in the woods, a later visitor found "large Stocks of Horses, Hogs, and horned Cattle," their "respective Ranges" managed by "two or three White Men." The prosperity McGillivray enjoyed was evident in his residence and on his table, which Pope was pleased to find "smokes with good substantial Diet, and his Side-board displays a Variety of Wines and ardent Spirits." Presided over by Mrs. McGillivray, whom the guest considered "a Model of Prudence and Discretion," the scene was so impressive that Pope was left wondering if "they order Things better in France?" Or, he might have added, in Charleston, Savannah, or Mobile.[12]

Although he lived like a white man, McGillivray did so as a Creek, not as an American. His first loyalty was to his Indian nation, and he proved that loyalty time and again. Always testing the wind, he knew the Americans were coming; like it or not, he would have to deal with either Georgians, who regarded the Indians as an impediment to be removed, or the government of the United States, which hoped to avoid a conflict with the Creeks or their Spanish allies. Choosing the latter (but being careful not to break his ties with Spain), McGillivray visited President Washington in New York in November of 1789 and the following August signed a treaty that declared the United States protector of the Creeks within its borders. To appease the Georgians, their state received a small cession, but the rest of the land was "absolutely guaranteed" to the Indians. Americans on the frontier felt betrayed, and the state of Georgia denounced the treaty. In the Creek nation Alexander McGillivray was hailed a hero.[13]

McGillivray never enjoyed the fruits of his "victory" over Georgia's land-hungry frontiersmen. Seldom a well man, he disregarded "an hibitual Head-Ache and Cholic" to remain active, and it may have been this determination that proved his undoing. It was cold and raining in early 1793 when McGillivray traveled to Pensacola to confer with merchant William Panton, his friend and sometimes business partner, about America's growing influence among the Creeks. Already sick when he arrived, his condition worsened, and on the evening of February 17, he died. Efforts to fill the void began immediately, but they were never completely successful. The Alabama region would not see his likes again.[14]

Significantly, McGillivray died still trying to steer his Creeks on a course between the interests of America, Spain, and the Indian traders. His vision for the future, though never fully articulated, seemed to have included an Indian state whose heart would be the forks of the Coosa and Tallapoosa and whose outlet to the greater world would be down the Alabama. Now that vision lay with him in the grave. Spain kept Mobile, but two years after his death it surrendered all claims to the disputed Alabama land. Now most of the Creek nation, Upper and Lower, lay within the boundaries of the United States, and though that nation had "absolutely guaranteed" the land to the Indians, Americans moving west believed the matter was far from settled. Unfortunately for the Creeks, the frontiersmen were right.[15]

Long before the Revolution, colonists in the east had heard of the Alabama region, a "very pleasant Country . . . full of Hills and Vallies" where the land was "fatter than many other Provinces." Now that the land was part of the United States, there were many who wanted a share of it. By the 1790s the occasional immigrant had become a steady trickle of settlers, which promised to become a stream, and the stream, in time, a flood. To avoid the Upper Creeks on the Coosa and Talla-poosa, the invaders followed routes that ran south of the fall line and took up land along both sides of the lower Alabama, where fewer Indians lived. Believing trees were a sign of fertility, they rejected the "bald prairies" that would later be the heart of the Black Belt and chose instead the heavily wooded ridges and bottom lands not far from the river. There they set to subsistence farming, raised their families, and looked to the future.[16]

In the east American policymakers appointed a government agent to oversee relations between the tribes and this growing white population and to minimize contact between the two. At the same time, the agent was charged to reduce the influence of Indian traders, whom American officials believed had seduced the natives from their primitive indepen-dence with presents and trade goods supplied on credit. Eastern ide-alists were convinced that if this dependence on the merchants was ended, the Indians would turn to agriculture and craftsmanship, which would set them on the path to civilization and eventual "American-ization." An unspoken, but equally important, assumption behind this plan was the conviction that Indians involved in agriculture needed less land for their support, and it would be easier for whites to persuade them to sign over the vast hunting reserves they claimed. For settlers moving into the Alabama River valley, this consideration was the most important of all.[17]

The man chosen as agent to the Creeks was Benjamin Hawkins, an experienced frontiersman, who agreed with those who sent him that most of the skills that once made the Indians self-sufficient still survived and that an independent agricultural society was possible if the natives could be weaned from the traders. Among the Indians, especially the Upper Creeks, there were many who agreed that the traders had corrupted the tribe's traditional value system, and Hawkins might have found allies among them if he had concentrated his efforts on that problem alone. But not every aspect of Indian culture fit into Hawkins's scheme. He considered tribalism and the influence of the powerful clans as impediments to individual accomplishment as well as to his plan to make the Creeks a nation of independent farmers. Thus his efforts were often at cross-purposes, for when he sought to alter the traditional role of tribe and clan, he created enemies among the very Indians who otherwise might have supported him. The settlers, however, cared little for tradition, tribalism, or even traders. They only wanted land.[18]

Hawkins arrived in the Coosa-Tallapoosa region late in 1796 and during the months that followed conducted a careful inspection of the territory under his jurisdiction. In the spring he made his way along the Tallapoosa so he "might have a view of the Indian fields [and] their mode of culture." He noted how many natives lived by their tracts on "the margin on the river" while the crops grew, and found them to be a pleasant people, who "show in a particular manner their hospitality to all travellers, by calling to them and giving them excellent melons, and the best fare they possess." Along the way the agent also observed how the stream, "after tumbling over a bed of rock for half a mile . . . is forced into two channels . . . [and] fish are obstructed here in their attempts to pass. . . . From appearances," Hawkins concluded, the fish "might be taken in the season of their ascending the rivers," but he found no evidence that "attempts have hitherto been made to do so." Still, farming had not been forsaken, so Hawkins was hopeful for the future.[19]

Hawkins also saw evidence of how far the Indians, and the Alabama region itself, had come since the days of Tascaluza and de Soto. At almost every location he visited, the Indian agent noticed the remains of ancient mounds, some conic, some circular, and he found it curious that the Indians who lived nearby knew nothing of their origin or purpose. At the forks of the river Hawkins wandered through the ruins of the "old French fort Toulouse" and found "5 iron cannon, the trunnions broke off," rusting amid the silt and debris left when "the flood of last January flowed over this high ground. . . . A few brick bats and the cannon [were] the only remains of the French establishment." Upriver he found "the remains of the Old Tallassee," seat of the McGillivrays. All that was left to remind visitors of the great inland trading center that its owner once envisioned were "some large apple trees . . . and a stone chimney."[20]

Despite his many references to things that interested him personally, Hawkins never lost sight of the reason for his tour—to assess the potential of the land and the potential of the people. In some cases he found towns with flourishing fields, but others, those in "low and unhealthy . . . situation[s]," were less productive. He paid attention to the condition of the soil, finding it "very rich . . . on the narrow flat margins of the river" but "too poor and broken for culture" in "the uplands." Near the Coosa, Hawkins was shown a large cave in which "some of the rooms appear as the work of art," but he was more impressed when he found that "in several parts of the cave saltpeter is to be seen in cristals." He also took care to identify sites for future industrial development and was especially pleased to find "a fine mill seat" on a stream not far from the river. The trip convinced him that the land of the Upper Creeks was well suited for agriculture and for the sort of manufacturing an agricultural society promoted.[21]

Of the thirty-seven Creek towns Hawkins identified, twenty-five were on the waters of Coosa and Tallapoosa. These were the Upper Creeks, and their population concentration was one reason whites were settling farther downstream. McGillivray's plan, had it worked, would have minimized the division between these two groups, for Upper Creek trade would have flowed south and joined that of their Lower Creek brothers in Mobile. But when McGillivray died, and there was no one to carry on the effort, the Indians returned to old patterns and practices. The Lower Creeks near the Alabama River continued to trade downstream, which was the most "convenient market for their products." While this trade did keep them in close contact with the Spanish, agent Hawkins noted that it also enabled them to taste "the sweets of civil life," which he felt might ultimately work to his advantage. The Upper Creeks, however, did not follow this course. Separated from the south by the falls and rapids of the rivers, wary of American encroachments from the east, they became more isolated, more insular, and more resistant to change. And change, of course, was what Benjamin Hawkins wanted.[22]

The Lower Creeks on the Alabama, less numerous and less concentrated than their northern neighbors, seemed more amicable to the Indian agent's plan, but Hawkins was not optimistic that his reforms would take hold in that region. The problem was the land. Although the river bottoms were rich, the agent feared that since "the annual floods always in the spring rise from 3 to 10 feet," the margins of the stream could never be fenced off into individual farms for the Indians. Inland seemed no better. "The land bordering on the swamp for a mile back," he noted, was "poor stiff clay," and beyond that was "broken pine barren, [with] veins of reeds in the branches and cypress ponds." While this "pine and underbrush" was "said to be good for cattle," Hawkins was not convinced. The farther south he went, the less enthusiastic he became. At the end of the Alabama, where it joined the Tombigbee, he found a waterway "intersected with lakes, marshes and crooked draws and much infected with mosquitoes." Some white settlers were already there, "liv[ing] on the pine lands bordering on the rivers," but the agent saw little to recommend that location or their way of life. Benjamin Hawkins would concentrate his efforts farther north.[23]

Hawkins's attempt to extend American influence over the tribes and bring them into the world of whites set the stage for yet another clash of cultures in the Alabama region. The United States government's plan for the Indians called not only for the introduction of crops, livestock, and technology to make the natives into self-sufficient farmers but also for Indians to adopt white men's values—especially "the value of labor," which the agent noted "they are totally unacquainted with." In his efforts to determine if this transformation was taking place, Hawkins assumed that changes in lifestyle were evidence of a change in attitude; therefore individual farms, fenced fields, neat houses, and cottage industries became gauges by which he measured success. These accomplishments, he believed, would make the natives more like whites with each generation, and in time they would be absorbed into the frontier melting pot and become indistinguishable (at least in their activities) from other Alabamians.[24]

The magnitude of his task was soon apparent. The natives, according to Hawkins, had been "accustomed for several years past to receive presents from Great Britain or Spain sufficient to clothe all the idlers in the nation," and as a result they had reached the point that they would "demand anything they want[ed] from a white man, and feel themselves insulted, when refused." Never once, he caustically commented, did those who supplied and indulged the Indians make any "attempt to better [their] condition." Instead foreign agents and renegade merchants had reduced the once-independent warriors to "beggars" interested only in trade goods and presents. Having accepted this relationship for so long, the Indians "view[ed] with surprise" any effort to offer instead "instructions in the useful branches of mechanics and agriculture."[25]

Benjamin Hawkins was determined to turn what he felt was "a proud and haughty, begging, spoiled, untoward race" into vigilant, careful, economical citizens, and he hoped whites in the region would help him. He was encouraged by the success of Robert Grierson, a trader-stockman-planter on the upper Tallapoosa, who married an Indian woman and with her had five children. Hawkins observed how Grierson, "by steady conduct, contributed to mend the manners" of the natives in his vicinity, and to the agent, this was a shining example of what could be accomplished. Soon others—whites and Indians—were following, or seemed to be following, the same course, and as time passed Hawkins was convinced he was making progress. Toward the end of 1798 he proudly wrote John Habersham of Georgia that finally the "Creeks are alarmed at their poverty," and finding they could not get presents, they were asking for ploughs. Though there were still traders among the Indians, many of whom were supplied from Pensacola and Mobile, Benjamin Hawkins believed that their influence was waning and that the age of the farmer was at hand.[26]

Even as Hawkins was trying to transform the Indians into yeoman farmers, another force was at work that would, in a short time, turn some yeomen, mostly white yeomen, into planters. On the farms praised by the Indian agent, the crop he seemed to mention more and more frequently was cotton. The plant had been raised in the area as early as 1772, and over the next two decades its cultivation spread. Soon most farms in the valley included a cotton patch somewhere on the place. Eli Whitney's invention eventually arrived, and by 1796 Robert Grierson owned a "treadle-gin" made in Rhode Island. On Hawkins's recommendation Grierson "set up a manufactory of cotton cloth" and paid Rachel Spillard, "an active girl of Georgia . . . 200 dollars per annum . . . to superintend the establishment." With "11 hands, red, white and black, [employed] in spinning and weaving" and others "raising and preparing the cotton for them," by 1799 Grierson's operation was one of the largest in the river region and the one in which Hawkins took the most pride.[27]

Many of the plantations and farms on which cotton was grown used Negro slaves. Blacks in bondage had been part of the region's labor force for decades, but not until after the Revolution did slaves arrive in numbers large enough to signal the change that was coming. At this point, early in the development of the plantation system, the seasonal demands on its peculiar institution were so ill defined that at times the bondsmen seemed able to dictate their own routines. Two of the largest slaveholders in the Creek nation, Mrs. Charles Weatherford and Mrs. Alexander Durand (sisters of Alexander McGillivray), could not control their chattel, and this contumacy affected discipline at neighboring plantations. In December of 1796, Hawkins reported being "visited by the negroes from the town above me, on their way to Mrs. Durand's to keep Christmas," which they did with "a proper frolic of rum drinking and dancing" that attracted Indians and whites as well. Hawkins expressed no particular surprise at this, for in his opinion most slaves did "nothing the whole winter but get a little wood," while in the summer they did little more than cultivate "a scant crop of corn barely sufficient for bread." As far as the agent was concerned, they seemed to do only what they wanted to do and as a result were "an expense to their owners." But this liberty would not last. Cotton and the cotton gin brought with them a seasonal routine that forced labor and laborer into a cycle difficult to break and difficult to endure.[28]

Cotton also brought people. What had been a slow, disorderly migration into the lower Alabama River Valley picked up markedly in the early 1800s. Despite the region's growing population, and its inclusion in the newly created Mississippi Territory, it was still a raw frontier. Settlement was scattered; civil government was seldom evident and usually ignored; the benefits of civilization were few; and except for the wanderings in and out of the eccentric but effective evangelist Lorenzo Dow, there was little semblance of religion. Ministers were so scarce that older settlers remembered how "young people were accustomed to marry themselves, that is they paired off, like birds, and lived together as husband and wife." As more immigrants moved in, ferries and ferry settlements appeared at key points on the stream. One of the earliest was built by Samuel Mims at the cutoff that joined the waters of the Alabama and Tombigbee; and Mims's home, near this strategic spot, became a social and commercial center. Later, when tensions between Indians and whites increased, Mims would fortify the location, and Fort Mims would replace Mims Ferry as a point of reference and refuge.[29]

The Creeks were aware that this "brisk migration," as an early Alabama historian described it, was crossing territory that was theirs by treaty. But since few whites stopped and settled on land south and east of the Alabama River, Indians and whites seldom came in contact. Most of the immigrants who took up land near the Alabama chose the western side of the stream, in what is present-day Clarke County. Here the Indians were few, and frontier farmers felt more secure. The pattern of settlement was soon set. Creeks would hunt and farm on the east bank of the river, while whites cleared land and raised crops on the west. The

Alabama would be a barrier between the two, effectively separating and protecting them from each other.[30]

Even as this physical division between Indians and whites was developing, forces were at work to destroy it. In 1805 the Lower Creeks agreed to allow the government to build a horse path by which mail could be carried through their country. It crossed the Chattahoochee River at Fort Mitchell, touched the Alabama below the forks of the Coosa and Tallapoosa, then turned southwest and met the river again near Mims Ferry. But what the Lower Creeks allowed, the Upper Creeks refused. Three years later when Hawkins tried to get permission for mail to be carried by horse along the Coosa, he was rejected. Events suggest that the Upper Creeks were wise to do so, for though government officials assured the natives that they had no designs on their land, soon after the mail road through Lower Creek territory opened in 1806, it was apparent that the postal service would be a minor user. By 1811 the horse path had become the Federal Road, and it was "filled from one end to the other" with Georgians and Carolinians heading toward the Alabama.[31]

The country was growing. In 1801 the lower Alabama claimed some 500 whites and about half that number blacks. By 1810, Washington County alone counted 733 whites and 517 blacks, and two years later the population was sufficient to justify creating Clarke County in the forks of the Alabama and Tombigbee. During this time the Federal Road became so crowded that the immigrants found security in numbers, and highway robberies actually decreased. Meanwhile, problems in the more settled areas were on the rise, due, in no small part, to tensions between expanding settlements and the Indians who believed the land was theirs. Soon the westward movement became eastward as well, as settlers in Clarke and Washington counties moved back across the river to the rich lands they had passed through on their first migration. Pushed now from both sides, the Indians grew uneasy. With the British and French gone, and the Spanish unable or unwilling to help, there were no allies to whom they could turn. It seemed the Creeks had only themselves, but for some among them, that was enough.[32]

THREE

The War for the Alabama

It was the twelfth day of November, a day to be remembered in
Alabama Indian border strife, when on the beautiful Alabama in that
noted river bend, with nine American spectators on one bank and
sixty-one on the other, and how many concealed Indians in the dense
canes none knew . . . this conflict of three against nine was waged.

Account of the "Canoe Fight"

H. S. HALBERT and T. S. BALL, 1895

It was the strong-hold of the Indians, in a position of great strength,
had been partially fortified by Weatherford, and consecrated by the
Shawnee prophets, who assured their followers that if the white men
dared to tread upon it the earth would open and swallow them
up! . . . It stood upon a lofty bluff, just below what is now Powell's
Ferry, in the county of Lowndes. . . . The fanatics and prophets of
the tribe made it the scene of their sorceries and incantations.

Description of the Holy Ground

J. F. H. CLAIBORNE

Life and Times of Gen. Sam Dale

Between August of 1813 and March of 1814, frontiersmen and Indians in
the river region fought what has come to be known as the "Creek War."
It was part of a larger conflict, the War of 1812, waged between the
United States and Great Britain over often ambiguous matters like
maritime rights and territorial sovereignty. On the frontier, however,
things were more clearly defined. For everyone involved, the struggle
was for survival, and victory would be decided in battle, not
at some postwar conference between diplomats. That realization was
why they fought with desperate, reckless courage; why they asked no
quarter and expected none in return. Both sides had everything to gain
and everything to lose.[1]

As the conflict wore on it became increasingly apparent how gains
and losses would be calculated when there was peace again. Frontiersmen and Indians alike knew that the victor would confirm victory
by occupying the land drained by the Alabama River and its tributaries.
Each understood that this was a contest to determine who would live
along the streams, farm the river bottoms and ridges, build towns and
cities on the bluffs. Call it what you will—the Creek War or the War
of 1812—by the time it was over, it had become the war for the Alabama.[2]

From the time they first arrived, frontiersmen considered the Creeks
an obstacle between themselves and the land they intended to enjoy.

The natives were something to be removed—either through Americanization or expulsion or annihilation. Any of these options was acceptable so long as it eliminated the danger of Indian attack and opened tribal land for settlement by whites. Once these things were done, more immigrants could come, and, safe in numbers, their race would dominate the region. The idea that Indians might remain in Alabama as Indians was not something frontiersmen cared to consider.

Some Indians, particularly the Lower Creeks and mixed bloods in the region, wanted to reach an accommodation with the Americans and saw Hawkins's plan as a means to that end. From the start they were amenable to the innovations necessary for Americanization and were willing to work with the whites. Among the Upper Creeks, however, there was resistance. Suspicious of government efforts to build a federal road through their land and concerned that demands by Tennessee settlers to send goods down the Coosa would bring more whiskey into the valley, their attitude hardened. This position became clear in the fall of 1807. At a meeting at Tuckabatchee, a Tallapoosa town that served as the capital of the Upper Creek nation, tribal representatives denounced white intrusions and warned that further encroachments might well bring reprisals.[3]

In the wake of this conference, dissenting Creeks began to criticize Indians who accepted the role Hawkins designed for them. Most vehement in this denunciation were the "prophets," leaders of a faction that came to be known as the Red Sticks, whom assistant agent Alexander Cornells described as "enemies to the plan of civilization and advocates of the wild Indian mode of living." For them, Americanization implied, and not too subtly, that the customs and values on which their culture rested were fundamentally flawed. Refusing to accept this idea, Red Sticks reaffirmed Creek traditions but expanded them to include religious practices adopted from tribes farther north. Over the next few years, their influence and their following grew. Hawkins could do little to stop them and soon lamented how even "the most industrious and best behaved of all our Indians" had succumbed to this "fanaticism." The whole plan for the Americanization of the Indians was in jeopardy.[4]

Benjamin Hawkins became all the more uneasy when Tecumseh appeared at Tuckabatchee in the fall of 1811. In the Indian Territory north of the Ohio River, this Shawnee chief and his prophets had woven native nationalism and mystical religious beliefs into a force powerful enough to inspire the tribes to oppose the rising tide of white settlement. Now Tecumseh wanted the Creeks to join them. Hawkins and his men were not at the meeting where the Shawnee made his appeal, but they soon learned what he had said. Reports indicated that

Tecumseh urged the Creeks to rid the tribe of alien influences and promised the Red Sticks that if they would "sing 'the song of the Indians of the northern lakes, and dance their dance'" this would "frighten the Americans, their arms will drop from their hands, the ground will become a bog, and mire them, and you may knock them on the head with your war clubs." The call was clear, and even though the religious mysticism in which it was clothed struck Americans as strange, even ridiculous, they feared that it would be enough to send the Creeks into battle.[5]

Reports from the scene also indicated that Tecumseh promised the Indians that they could expect aid from the British in Canada and from the Spanish in Pensacola; so when the United States, angered over interference with its commerce and insults to its sovereignty, declared war on Great Britain that following summer, everything the settlers believed, and feared, seemed to be coming to pass. By their frontier calculus they reasoned that the English in Canada had incited Tecumseh, who in turn incited the Creeks, and therefore the English and the Red Sticks were allies. Now that this alliance was revealed, they assumed it would only be a matter of time before the war reached them.[6]

Ironically, Americans along the river had cause to welcome a wider conflict. Most of them were "settlers on the public lands without any authority of government," and as militia colonel James Caller explained, they had feared for some time that "they would receive no support from the U.S. troops" if the Indians moved to oust them. Now, if the Creeks attacked it would not be as injured parties defending their land from squatters but as allies of Great Britain, and authorities might be more inclined to protect the white intruders. The settlers along the Lower Alabama could not be sure, however, so they fell back on their own resources and began building forts at central locations where they could flee if an attack came. On the western side of the river they built forts Madison, Sinquefield, and White, Landrum's Fort, and Glass Redoubt, while on the other side, down near the cut-off, was the stockaded home of ferryman Samuel Mims, and about two miles below it was Fort Pierce. The number of forts suggests how large the population of the region had grown; the speed with which they were erected reveals the anxiety those people felt.[7]

For the rest of the year an uneasy calm settled over the area. Then, early in 1813, word arrived that Gen. James Wilkinson, who held the distinction of being both the commander of the United States garrison at New Orleans and a paid agent of Spain, had landed below Mobile with some six hundred men. From there Wilkinson marched to the city and told Commandant Cayetano Perez that he had come to remove the

Spanish troops from what he declared was "a post within the legitimate limits of [the United] States." It apparently made little difference to Wilkinson (and none to upriver settlers) that the United States and Spain were not at war or that Madrid's claim to Mobile was at least as strong as Washington's. The commandant had no choice but to surrender, and the Alabama River's outlet to the sea was in American hands. General Wilkinson's conquest, accomplished "without the effusion of a single drop of blood," has become a footnote in most accounts of the War of 1812, but it changed the course of Alabama history.[8]

After the fall of Mobile, Spain understandably became interested in the disposition of the Creeks, and when a Red Stick delegation sought aid at Pensacola in the summer of 1813, officials welcomed them and supplied much of what they wanted. At this time the Indians supposedly told the Spanish that war was imminent and that they planned to return to Whet Stone Hill, near the Alabama River at the present site of Lowndesboro, where they would distribute arms to several hundred warriors. This force, according to American intelligence, was ready "to move down the river to break up the half-breed settlements and those of the citizens at the forks." It is not clear just how encouraging the Spanish actually were, but to Alabama frontiersmen the evidence spoke for itself. The Creeks had visited Pensacola, and they were returning ready for war.[9]

Aware that if these supplies were distributed among the Red Sticks, the balance of power along the Coosa-Tallapoosa-Alabama valley would shift dramatically, settlement leaders assembled a motley "army" of whites, Indians, and mixed-bloods and set out to intercept the pack train. Led by Colonel Caller, who cut a dashing figure in "a calico hunting shirt, a high bell-crowned hat and top boots," they marched east to Sizemore's Ferry on the Alabama where they spent the night; the next day they crossed the river in canoes, with horses swimming alongside. Then the troops marched east to the Pensacola Road, where they found the Indian caravan near Burnt Corn Creek. Surprise was total, and the Creeks fled in disarray. Then, in the flush of victory, the untrained troops broke ranks and began looting the Creek packhorses. At this moment the Indians counterattacked, and most Americans took to their heels. In what one early Alabama historian called "a disgraceful rout," some of the survivors fled back to Sizemore's Ferry while others ran into the woods. Caller got away with only "his shirt and drawers." Though Americans had just two killed and fifteen wounded, the humiliation of the defeat was such that for years afterward veterans would deny having ever been at Burnt Corn.[10]

News of the "battle" quickly spread through the lower Alabama region, and settlers began making their way to their neighborhood forts. By mid-August Mims's stockade was reported to have over three hundred refugees packed within its walls, and conditions in smaller outposts were just as crowded. But inside Fort Mims things were calm, for most of the occupants, including garrison commander Maj. Daniel Beasley, believed the Indians would not attack a fort as large as theirs. Advised earlier in the month to strengthen his defenses, the major had reportedly "turned a deaf ear to all idea of danger" and in the weeks that followed ignored warnings from experienced woodsmen that Indians were in the vicinity. Discipline relaxed, pickets kept an irregular watch, and sand drifted against the open gates of the fort. Mims was a disaster waiting to happen.[11]

Early on the morning of August 30, Beasley wrote Gen. Ferdinand L. Claiborne that he had "made the fort much stronger," and a short time later that day he wrote once again to assure the general that the fort could hold out "against any number of Indians." He may have written the second message because he forgot he had written the first, for according to eyewitnesses, by mid-day "Major Beasley was drunk." He was in that condition when Beasley received his last warning. Scout James Cornells rode up to the gate and called out that the Indians were approaching. Outraged, the major roared that Cornells had only seen "a gang of red cattle" and ordered him arrested. The scout retreated, but as he left he shouted that Beasley's cattle would "give him a h—ll of a kick before night." The Red Sticks were already in place when Cornells rode away. When the drum called the garrison to its noon meal, they struck.[12]

Leading the attack was the man Creeks called Red Eagle and settlers addressed as William Weatherford. The mixed-breed son of a Coosa-Tallapoosa trader and the daughter of a Tabacha chief, Weatherford was known and respected throughout the region. Since his brother, half brother, and a number of other relatives had sided with the Americans, whites expected him to do the same, and they were confused and angered when he did not. Red Eagle, according to his aunt who was a refugee at the fort and survived to tell the tale, "came in the gate at full run, at the head of his warriors, [and] jumped a pile of logs almost as high as his head." Behind him came the Creeks. Fighting was fierce, but the outcome was never really in doubt. Ten days later a burial party under Maj. Joseph Kennedy arrived to find that the bodies of "Indians, negroes, white men, women and children lay in one promiscuous ruin." Kennedy's men buried 247 of them in two large pits; then, according to the major's report, "the soldiers and officers, with one voice, called on Divine Providence to revenge the death of [their] murdered friends." It was the worst Indian "massacre" in American history.[13]

News of the fall of Fort Mims created panic across and up the Alabama. Settlers who had hesitated earlier now rushed to neighborhood stockades, leaving farms and fields just as the harvest was coming in. The fear was so great that refugees at Fort Madison, on a ridge running parallel to the river, raised a tall pole in the middle of the fort and built a scaffold on top where they burned "fat pine" all night. It was a primitive but effective search light for frontiersmen who could find deer in the dark by firelight reflected in their eyes. Now their skill at "fire hunting" was used against another prey. Meanwhile news of an attack on nearby Fort Sinquefield and reports of the massacre of members of two local families raised tensions to a new level. Whites along the river were paralyzed with fear, for the Red Sticks seemed to be everywhere.[14]

But relief was on the way. In October General Claiborne crossed the Tombigbee at St. Stephens with an army raised to put down the Red Stick uprising. Among these troops was the veteran frontiersman Sam Dale. Forty-one years old, Big Sam as he was called, stood over six feet tall, his 190 pounds spread over "a large, muscular frame . . . [with] no superfluous flesh." Earlier Dale had distinguished himself in Georgia's Indian wars, and he might have stayed in that state had he not become involved in a plan to smuggle coffee and slaves from Spanish Pensacola. The scheme was uncovered, officials ordered him arrested, and he fled—across Alabama and into Mississippi, where he was when the war broke out. Identified by the double-barreled shotgun he carried, an unusual weapon on the frontier, he knew the Alabama River region and its people well. So Claiborne made Dale his scout and sent him ahead with a band of men to find a safe spot to cross the Alabama.[15]

The advance party reached the river without incident and camped across from Weatherford's Bluff, near where Red Eagle's brother John had operated a ferry. Then, on the morning of November 12, 1813, as they pushed off for the other side, Dale looked up the river and saw eleven warriors in a large canoe floating downstream. Spoiling for a fight, Big Sam and three comrades paddled to meet the enemy. In the boat with Dale was Jeremiah Austill, nineteen years old, tall, "very sinewy," and despite his youth considered "a much more than ordinary man"; the "stout and finely proportioned" James Smith; and an "Indian negro" slave named Caesar. The Americans moved out into the Alabama and fired on the Indians. Two of the natives slipped into the water and swam for shore, while the nine who remained turned toward their white attackers, and the canoes closed for battle.[16]

The river swings wide below Weatherford's Bluff, and in the fall the water is usually low and slow. Still, the Alabama's current is strong wherever it flows, so the outnumbered Americans knew that it was critical to maneuver into place and maintain that position. As they pulled alongside the Creeks, Caesar grabbed the other boat and held it fast. Then, their rifles swinging, fighting hand to hand to the cheers of fellow frontiersmen on the shore, Dale, Austill, and Smith clubbed their way to victory. For future generations of Alabama students, this was the famous "canoe fight."[17]

Along the river valley the victory was more important in symbol than in substance. In itself it did little to permanently secure the stream and the ferry crossing; yet it was a potent tonic for settlers demoralized by events at Burnt Corn and Fort Mims. Though the Indians were still feared as foes, the canoe fight was seen as proof that natives were "not a match even handed for the bold and hardy pioneer white man." Their place in history secure, Dale, Smith, Austill, and Caesar took the dead warriors and, in the flowing phrases of the state's first historian, Albert J. Pickett, "cast them into the bright waters of the Alabama, their native stream, now to be their grave."[18]

Claiborne's main force arrived at the river on November 16, 1813. The next day they ferried across, and on Weatherford's Bluff, in "the best part of the enemy's country," they built a post that the general named for himself—Fort Claiborne. From this strategic spot, Claiborne reported, they could "cut the savages off from the river, and from their growing crops . . . [and] render their communication with Pensacola more hazardous." The fort could also serve as a supply depot for the army under Gen. Andrew Jackson, moving south from Tennessee. Plans for the American offensive were taking shape. Two armies, one marching down along the Coosa and the other making its way north along the Alabama, would sweep through the heart of the Creek nation, destroying settlements and demoralizing survivors. The rivers would be the line on which the campaign was fought.[19]

Though Jackson's soldiers needed little to inspire them to revenge and retribution, reports that Indians at Mims dismembered, disemboweled, and burned alive men, women, and children gave them an added incentive in the struggle. As his army of frontiersmen marched south that fall, fighting occurred with savage regularity. At Tallussahatchee, a village between the Coosa and Tallapoosa, Tennessee troops under Gen. John Coffee "retaliated for the destruction of Fort Mims" and reported that "not one of the warriors escaped to carry the news." Moving down the Coosa to Ten Islands, where easy navigation ended and the shoals and rapids began, Jackson paused, built Fort Strother, and then led troops south, to Talladega, to rescue friendly Creeks whose town was under siege. Again, Indian casualties numbered in the hundreds. Aware of the odds against them, residents of the town of Hillabee tried to surrender and were attacked anyway—it was, according to an early historian, "a massacre and not a battle." On through November, December, and into the new year, the list of American victories grew, but many brought no glory to the victors.[20]

These defeats left the Indians badly shaken. Men, women, and children had been killed, towns and villages razed, and crops destroyed. It was a lean winter for the survivors. But Jackson's policy was one of total war, intended to break the will to resist. In some cases the strategy backfired, for after the Hillabee massacre escaping warriors fled south, joined the main Red Stick force, and in subsequent battles fought with the same vindictive fierceness shown by Americans revenging Fort Mims. In most cases, the effect was as intended. It is easy to imagine the impact on the natives when towns like Autossee, with four hundred houses, "fine specimens of Indian architecture," were put to the torch. A way of life went up in flames with the buildings, and the Indians seemed to sense that they faced cultural as well as physical extermination. Now their struggle became more desperate and, as some among them surely knew, more hopeless.[21]

As Jackson moved relentlessly toward the forks of the Coosa-Tallapoosa, Claiborne focused his attention north, to Ikanatchaka, an Indian village on the south bank of the Alabama, in modern Lowndes County. This was the Holy Ground, seat of the tribe's most powerful prophets. Located on a peninsula formed by a creek and the river, the fifty-acre site was protected by ravines and by a barrier of finely split fat pine, which extended across the neck of land. The prophets had blessed the wood and told the people that if they set it ablaze when the enemy attacked, those who tried to cross it would fall dead. Claiborne was convinced that the Holy Ground was the key to Creek military operations, so in December he took his soldiers, along with a detachment of friendly Choctaws under Chief Pushmataha, and marched north.[22]

The battle took place two days before Christmas, 1813. Claiborne's army advanced; the Indians fired, then waited for it to cross the burning barrier and fall. When the army broke the magic line and continued on, the Indians withdrew in disarray. Only Weatherford, with a small force of men who reportedly put little stock in the prophets' promises, held their ground. They were not enough. The fighting ended quickly as the retreat became a rout. The Indians left behind twenty-one dead. American casualties consisted of one killed and some twenty wounded.[23]

Weatherford and his men were the last to withdraw, and from his flight comes yet another of the heroic episodes that enable Alabamians to make an epic out of what was in reality a dirty, vengeful war. Accounts tell of how the Creek leader mounted his horse, Arrow, and made his escape by leaping off a twelve-foot bluff into the Alabama. He and Arrow swam the stream, and according to one of the men who chased him, when they reached the other side, Weatherford "dismounted, unsaddled his horse, wrung the water out of his blanket and other articles, then again resaddling, he mounted and rode off"—all in full view of the Americans. Gen. Thomas S. Woodward, whose *Reminiscences* of the war debunked many jealously protected Alabama "myths," claimed that the leap never occurred and that Weatherford escaped down a ravine. But Alabamians believed and continue to believe it happened.[24]

General Claiborne let Pushmataha's Choctaw collect the spoils of war from the Holy Ground, and scalps from the dead Creeks were raised on poles and carried to Choctaw villages as symbols of their victory over the Red Sticks. Then, after dispatching an expedition to wipe out remaining pockets of resistance, he turned his troops south. A short time later they ferried the Alabama, then crossed Clarke County to the Tombigbee and to St. Stephens, where the general was honored with a parade and a tune written for the occasion, which the composer proudly entitled "Claiborne's Victory." Behind him the triumphant commander left a river valley free from hostile Indians and the fort at Weatherford's Bluff. General Claiborne had won the lower Alabama.[25]

Meanwhile Jackson steadily moved south, keeping pressure on the enemy despite the Indians' often fierce resistance and his own supply problems. In early March news reached him that the remaining Red Sticks had gathered at a horseshoe-shaped bend in the Tallapoosa where they waited, protected by a trench and breastworks before them and the river to their flanks and rear. With his army of hardened veterans, reinforced by Cherokee allies, Jackson marched to Horseshoe Bend for a battle both sides knew would be decisive. The American attack came on March 27. Trapped within the bend that had protected them, the Creeks fought and died bravely. Afterwards, one of Jackson's men wrote his wife that "the Tallapoosa might truly be called the River of blood," for hours after the fighting had ceased, the stream still ran so red "that it could not be used." Some survivors tried to swim to safety, but exhausted from the fight, they lacked the strength to make it across a river swollen and chilled by spring rains. As many as a thousand Creeks may have fallen at Horseshoe Bend, and with them perished the Red Stick cause.[26]

The bitter, bloody struggle brought out the worst on both sides. Americans, outraged by the scalps of whites that they found on a pole in the center of the Holy Ground, after that battle showed little remorse at the way the Choctaw treated the bodies of fallen Creeks. Accounts of atrocities at Mims, some told by the Indians themselves, left little room for sympathy. Yet whites were no better. One volunteer told of how Tennessee soldiers made bridle reins from strips of skin cut from Creek bodies, and in one case a soldier approached an elderly native who was sitting on the ground pounding corn and shot him so "he might be able to report when he went home that he had killed an Indian." Another soldier told of how, after Horseshoe Bend, an American killed a "little Indian boy" with the butt of his musket, and "when reproached by an officer for barbarity in killing so young a child," he justified the act by observing "that the boy would have become an Indian some day."[27]

The fate of William Weatherford—the hated and feared Red Eagle—stands in dramatic contrast to that of his followers. During the war Weatherford had, by his own admission, "done the white people all the harm [he] could," and settlers wanted their revenge. But rather than try to escape when he knew his cause was lost, the chief instead rode to Jackson's headquarters and surrendered. The general, "awed and impressed" by this boldness, held back troops who would have killed him, and after a brief interview in which Weatherford expressed regret that he was not able to prevent the massacre of women and children at Fort Mims, General Jackson allowed him to depart. White Alabamians heard of what happened and concluded that if their leader could be magnanimous in victory, so could they. Following the general's lead, they let their former enemy go in peace.[28]

Weatherford did not return to the Creeks. He settled instead on family land in south Monroe County, not far from the site of Fort Mims. In later years he explained this decision with cryptic simplicity: "[my] old comrads, the hostiles, ate [my] cattle from starvation; the peace party ate them from revenge; and the squatters because [I] was a d——d Red-skin. So, I have come to live among gentlemen." Opting for class over race, he became one of them—a frontier aristocrat with a river plantation worked by some three hundred slaves. In time, forgiven for his trespasses and praised for his "bravery, honor, and strong native sense," William Weatherford, the Red Eagle, was enshrined as Alabama's good Indian. The Creek chief lived out his days in a manner almost indistinguishable from other frontier planters, an example to former followers of how things might have been if they had listened to Hawkins. But to his white neighbors, Red Eagle was something else. He was one of the spoils of war, and as such, he and his exploits belonged to the victors.[29]

Sam Dale was Alabama's Creek War hero, and his reputation along the river was equal in its place and time to that of Boone in Kentucky.

He also settled in Monroe County, which he represented in the legislature. He and Weatherford became friends, and when Red Eagle was married, Dale stood as a groomsman. Eventually a grateful state awarded Big Sam the rank of brigadier general. He later moved to Mississippi, where he died in 1841. But despite an active life and outstanding career, Dale's place in history remains tied to that November day on the Alabama River, when white men in a canoe fought red men in a canoe, while Caesar, a black man, held the two together. Of such much-needed heroes are made, and for the sake of heroes we should appreciate all the more the strength of Caesar's grip.[30]

FOUR

Settling the Alabama

I said if he wanted to take a broad view of the thing, it really began
with Andrew Jackson. If General Jackson hadn't run the Creeks up
the creek, Simon Finch would never have paddled up the Alabama,
and where would we be if he hadn't?

> HARPER LEE
> *To Kill a Mockingbird*, 1960

The rich lands, on the sides of the [Alabama] river, are far superior
to any I have ever seen in any country, and I have no doubt will
prove a source of immence wealth to those who may hereafter be
doomed [to be] the cultivators.

> "Major HOWELL TATUM's Journal"
> August 1814

It is good to be shifty in a new country.

> JOHNSON JONES HOOPER
> *Adventures of Captain Simon Suggs,*
> *Late of the Tallapoosa Volunteers*, 1845

If credit must be given to one man, give it to Andrew Jackson. In
August of 1814 representatives of the defeated Creeks gathered at the
site of old Toulouse, where Jackson's army had built a fort that its
general, with the same frontier vanity that inspired Claiborne, had
named for himself. There the victorious commander told the Indians
what their fate would be; it was all they feared and more. By the Treaty
of Fort Jackson the Creeks lost over half their former land, including
most of the territory west of the Coosa and south of the Alabama.
Then, in a move applauded by fellow frontiersmen, Jackson stripped his
Indian allies of much of their land as well. Nearly three-fifths of the
future state of Alabama was soon open to settlement, and a new disease,
"Alabama fever," began to spread. Harper Lee was right.[1]

Soon after the treaty was signed General Jackson ordered Howell
Tatum, his topographical engineer, to descend the Alabama and
"ascertain the courses and distances" from junction to junction, for it
was an American river now. Tatum set out in August, a low-water
month when shoals and islands were exposed, but he had little trouble
with these obstacles. From what he observed he was sure that during
the wetter months the stream could be "navigated with large keel boats,
with tolerable ease and expedition." These boats would have plenty to
carry. All along the route were abandoned farms and plantations—
"improvements" made by dispossessed Indians—which convinced
Tatum that the land was "capable of producing, in great abundance,

every article necessary to the sustenance of man, or beast." All that was needed was the people.[2]

They were coming. Even as Tatum made his survey, settlers were arriving in ever-increasing numbers. Some were veterans of the Creek War who had coveted the land when they marched through it with Jackson and Claiborne; others had simply heard the talk and were willing to take the risk to see it for themselves. They were followed (sometimes accompanied) by merchants and peddlers, who set up shop and served the limited needs of frontier people and their frontier communities. Speculators were there already, with land to sell and credit to offer; and of course there were professional men, a breed that ran high in lawyers, for there were deeds to record, suits to file, and adversaries (many adversaries) to defend or prosecute. To all these people, this was the land of opportunity, and the able, energetic, lucky, and (perhaps above all else) "shifty" among them made the most of it.[3]

As the population of the region grew, advocates of systematic settlement (planners in Washington, far from the scene and untroubled by actual knowledge) expressed dismay that during the war squatters had crossed the Alabama from the west and cleared farms in what was then Indian land and was now Monroe County. Since the encroachers had no legal title to their holdings, defenders of the law decided to dislodge them. Deciding was one thing; doing it quite another. With a tenacity characteristic of Alabama frontiersmen, the unauthorized settlers, who by 1816 were estimated to be over thirty-five hundred, refused to leave. They pointed instead to what they considered a higher authority and wrote officials that "general Jackson encouraged us to Settle on the allebarmer." On Jackson's word (which their letter implied should have been enough for anyone) they had "sold there Carages[,] waggon & &," and now they were stranded; "how to get back god only knows."[4]

Not that they intended to go back, even if they had the means. Convinced, perhaps rightly, that speculators were behind efforts to remove them, they petitioned for protection, arguing that if they were not allowed to buy their property, groups like "the Yazzo Company will Purchase all the good land from the Head to the Mouth of the allebarmer," and politicians would have to explain how they allowed a situation to exist where people who "fought Brave to obtain this Cuntry . . . Now Cannot Injoy it." Politicians did not want to explain it. With western interests in Washington growing, Congress was sensitive to the settlers' plea. It moved quickly to stop the evictions, then made provisions for those who came into the region before February 1816 to purchase their claims. One wonders how many actually did. Most frontier squatters, according to one historian, were "improvident by nature, [and] did not come to seek wealth but merely to gain a subsistence or to enjoy the freedom of the forest." But if this motive was so, these first frontiersmen were soon followed by another wave of settlers, and among them were the men who would turn farms into plantations, villages into towns, and towns into cities. The "golden age" of the Alabama River valley was at hand.[5]

As word of the Alabama land drifted back east, the effect was both excitement and uneasiness. In Hillsborough, North Carolina, James Graham complained that "the *Alabama Fever* rages here with great violence and has carried off vast numbers of our citizens." Indeed, he lamented, "some of our oldest and most wealthy men are offering their possessions for sale and are desirous of removing to this new country." Although "apprehensive" that if the trend continued it would "almost depopulate" the region, Graham was intrigued by the opportunity and resolved that the next year he would go west to "satisfy myself respecting the advantages and inducements which that country is said to afford." He was not alone, for the postwar trickle of immigration into Alabama was about to become a flood.[6]

At the land office in Milledgeville, Georgia, in August 1817, the first Alabama land went on sale—a tract near the headwaters of the river that would soon be the site of Montgomery. Purchased largely by wealthy Georgians, who concentrated their acquisitions along the stream, this property became the core holdings of the upper Alabama's first planters. During the last five months of that year sales totaled nearly $800,000, and in 1818 new purchases pushed the figure to almost $1,000,000. The less wealthy or less well connected bought land farther back from the river, where in time they would raise plantations from the rotten limestone soil whose color gave its name to Alabama's Black Belt. Arriving through the fall and winter, their numbers were so great that before the first season's crop was made there was a real threat of starvation, and at Fort Claiborne flour sold for an inflated $20 a barrel and corn at $5 a bushel. And still they came, victims of "*Alabama Fever.*"[7]

Many who arrived in that initial wave of immigration did not come voluntarily. Planters, and some who hoped to be planters, brought slaves, so from the beginning the south's peculiar institution helped shape the region's character. As for the masters, most were not wealthy men by eastern standards, and despite efforts to picture them as aristocrats, ambition and drive more than education and refinement made them what they were. But whatever their origins, they knew what the plantation system was like in older areas and were determined to have it for themselves along the Alabama. For these men, as Major Tatum had predicted, the land would "prove a source of immence wealth," wealth made possible by the labor of "those who may hereafter be doomed [to be] the cultivators."[8]

In a very real sense, these immigrants were colonists, entering a new world from an old and bringing with them a vision of what they wanted to create. What is remarkable is that in the brief time between settlement and the Civil War, many came close to making that vision a reality. The course they followed was not unlike that followed by Englishmen who settled the Atlantic coast two centuries before. First they simplified eastern ideas and institutions, stripped them down to their essentials, so that government, church, and society could function as practically and efficiently as conditions required. Then, in time, as population and prosperity allowed, they began to elaborate on what they had created. They added offices and duties, paid heed to ceremonies and codes of conduct, and in the process left behind the simplicity of frontier farmers for the civilized life of planter and merchant. And finally, the wealthiest and most successful among them set out to replicate the world of the wealthiest and most successful of their eastern counterparts by copying, as best they could, the life of the tidewater and the low country planter. In short, they created the Old South but did it in so short a time that the frontier remained clear on the horizon behind them—silhouetted but never out of sight.[9]

What brought these men to Alabama, what promised to make them wealthy and powerful, was cotton, and Black Belt land did not disappoint them. Running in a rich crescent that began east of the Coosa-Tallapoosa junction, following the Alabama to the place it met the Cahaba, and finally curving northwest toward Mississippi, the Black Belt was over four thousand square miles of scrubby woods, prairie, and canebrake that became the heart of the plantation district. Initially settlers avoided it, believing land with so few trees and such lime-tainted water was good for little more than pasture. Then, the story goes, planters in the Cahaba River region decided to put one of their slaves on a remote plot, alone, with just enough to sustain himself until he could plant and harvest a crop. Scoffers expected to find him dead when they returned to his cabin that fall, but instead he met them, fat and fine, with corn in the crib and cotton ready to be picked. A Black Belt land rush followed. The story may be apocryphal, but the population along the Alabama grew so fast that some believed the region would soon dominate the whole Mississippi territory.[10]

The farmers and planters with easy access to water transportation had the advantage over their neighbors. Roads, even the Federal Road, were muddy, rutted trails, any one of which could have been the one described by the Alabama poet who posted this bit of doggerel on a byway:

> This road is not passable
> Not even jackassable.
> So when you travel
> Take your own gravel.

It followed, therefore, that when the cotton had been picked, ginned, and baled, traffic on the Alabama increased dramatically. At plantation landings slaves loaded the staple onto flat-bottomed boats for the journey to Mobile. Crudely built, their seams caulked with pitch, they could carry up to a hundred bales. Once they reached their destination they were broken up, and their lumber was sold, while the crew returned home by land. Travel upstream was difficult and slow. A schooner, poled and sailed, might make it as far as Fort Claiborne, but from there it was by keelboat and poles. Under even the best of conditions the trip from Mobile to Fort Jackson might take two months. As a result, river trade was largely a one-way commerce. Flour, whiskey, and other "necessities" still came overland from Georgia and Tennessee, but at prices that made them luxuries for most.[11]

River residents lived by the dictates of the weather, cotton, and the Alabama. On Charles Tait's Wilcox County plantation, January was a month for fertilizing with rotten leaves and barnyard manure; in February the land was plowed and harrowed; then in March, with an eye out for a late frost, the fields were planted. April through June were given over to chopping (thinning) and weeding, and by July the crop was laid by. In the future, when the country had matured, late summer would be the time for revivals, political rallies, and elections, as well as the time when assaults and murders increased, for southern activities were as varied as southerners. Then in the fall the cotton bolls opened, and picking began. By November, with the average worker picking from 100 to 120 pounds a day, the crop was in, ginned, baled, and ready to ship.[12]

Most of the time the river was ready. As if nature scheduled its cycles especially for the planter, winter rains usually came just when the processing was done, and flatboats loaded with cotton floated the swollen stream to market. But sometimes the rains were late, and the river was still low when the harvest was in. Although this created problems all along the valley, concern was greatest on the shallower upper Alabama, where low water revealed channel-blocking snags, sandbars, and gravel shoals that were difficult for clumsy flats to avoid. In such cases, cotton would have to be stored until the river rose, a recourse that added to the planter's expense, stretched his credit, and threatened to occupy hands at the very time they were needed for planting. The planter had little choice, however. The river was one more force of nature with which he had to contend, and until it could be mastered, planters had to live by its rules.[13]

During this era the Alabama's river towns were born, and it was a fitful beginning. Initially there seemed little need for towns, at least not as centers for the cotton trade. Most river plantations had their own landings, which also served the needs of neighbors. But circumstances other than river commerce brought these towns into being, and as these circumstances changed, so did the towns. Though the river was a factor, the river alone could not sustain them. Thus it was that settlements on the Alabama were never purely *river* towns. To survive and prosper, they had to be something else, something more.

The first of these settlements was Claiborne, on the bluff where the general raised a fort during the Creek War and where a branch of the Federal Road crossed the river. There schooners from Mobile transferred goods to keelboats for the trip upstream and loaded cotton for the trip south. Local merchants acted as factors in the commerce, stocked their stores with merchandise from the port city, and carried on a "brisk retail trade [in] the settlement and its vicinity." Blessed with what its newspaper, the *Alabama Courier*, described as "natural advantages that will always insure its prosperity," by 1819 Claiborne was a "considerable village" with "two thousand inhabitants, thirty stores, two female seminaries and a grammar school," details the editor offered as "ample proof of the eligibility of the site for a town and the capacity of a neighboring county to support it."[14]

Further upstream other settlements were getting started. After the war a man named Thomas Moore came down from Tennessee and settled what was soon called Moore's Bluff. By 1817 he was gone, replaced by three Scotsmen who set up a store to serve travelers through the area and settlers who lived nearby. At about this time speculators from back east, mostly Georgians, took an interest in the location, bought a large part of it, and set up the Selma Land Company to oversee the sale and distribution to the horde of settlers they knew would come. On the bluff they laid out the town; set lots aside for churches, schools, a public square, and a cemetery; and auctioned off what they could of the rest. One hundred and one lots were sold, for a total of nearly $38,000. Not surprisingly the highest price went for a riverfront location, the future site of the St. James Hotel. Selma was begun.[15]

Selma did not prosper in these early days, despite investors' success in getting the legislature to incorporate the town and authorize a public

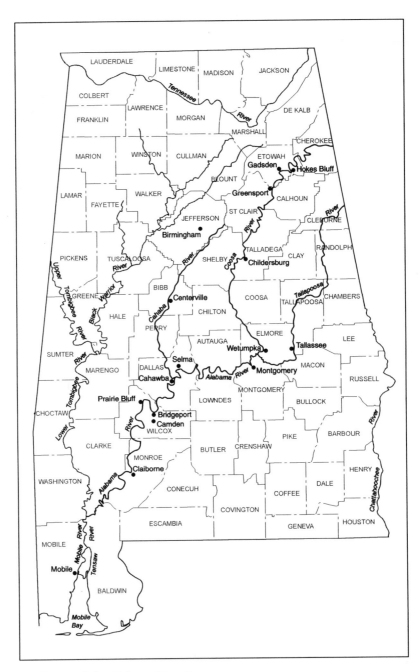

Towns of the Alabama River System

road leading to a public ferry. It was a short road and scant inducement to travelers, so little was gained from the free ferry. Yet this legislative attention reveals something significant about the venture. Powerful men supported Selma—William Rufus King, Dr. George Phillips, and Reuben Saffold to name only a few—and through their efforts Selma survived. Its day was yet to come, but come it would.[16]

In a sense, early Selma was a reflection, a pale reflection but a reflection nonetheless, of activity going on farther upriver, near Chunnanugga Chatty (the "high red bluff") in Montgomery County, where the Federal Road curved close to the river. Here a group of Georgia investors laid out the Town of Alabama and in August of 1817 advertised the sale of lots on a site they described as "high and commanding, . . . entirely removed from swamps[,] lagunes[,] and morasses," where "the purity of the water, the salubrity of the air, and the contiguity of a Mineral Spring to the Town Spring, will ensure to its inhabitants the most perfect health." But there was even more to recommend the spot. "In point of commercial advantages," the announcement boasted, "this town cannot be surpassed." Not only had "the fertility of the surrounding country . . . been tested" and found excellent, but the town itself "stands at the nearest eligible site to the head of navigation on the Alabama, and is only ten miles by land to the junction of the Coosa and Talapoosa rivers."[17]

So promising was the location that Alabama Town's promoters were faced with competition from a group of investors led by a transplanted northerner named Andrew Dexter. Nearby Dexter's company laid off the town of New Philadelphia, which locals took to calling Yankee Town, and a fierce rivalry between the two ventures commenced. The Georgians tried to block Dexter's settlers from the river, and in retaliation the Yankees began intercepting immigrants and enticing them to settle in New Philadelphia. The tactic met with some success, and in the winter of 1817–18 a New York visitor reported that on its "high and pleasant place," Yankee Town "bids fair to flourish." But there was not enough immigration to support two ventures, much less satisfy the inflated expectations of investors. Finally, in 1819, with prospects shrunk all the more by a national panic and depression, the rivals agreed to merge. They put the courthouse on the line that divided them and named the town Montgomery. Even with the union the new settlement could boast only about sixty or so dwellings, over half of which were log. It was a frontier village, populated by men whose priorities were such that guardians of the public morality found it necessary to prohibit a host of Sabbath trespasses, including "gaming, fiddling, or other music for the sake of merriment." But though it and its people were rough around the edges, Montgomery was a growing settlement, which at the moment, Selma was not.[18]

No small part of Montgomery's initial progress was due to the rapid growth of the country around it. Land upstream from the village, in and near the forks, was remembered as "the favorite portion of the county of the early settlers," who raised their cotton on the high "levels" along the rivers. To serve them a "Gin shop" was established in the town, and the "rudely constructed" machines it produced were soon giving "very good satisfaction" to planters in the region. Naturally, as if gravity pulled it, cotton moved from field to gin to cribs and warehouses and finally to the water. And whether it was floated down or brought overland by wagon, Montgomery was the spot where it was loaded and shipped to Mobile.[19]

Settlement upstream from Montgomery could go only so far. The falls of the Coosa and of the Tallapoosa were near the fork, which discouraged both navigation and immigration. But the principal reason why many whites headed south was that most of the territory between the Coosa and the Georgia line still belonged to the Creeks. The area had been favored by the Indians since before de Soto, and if there was any justice in the Treaty of Fort Jackson, it was that the tribe had been promised this historic land. Despite what the treaty said, however, some early settlers carved out farms on the Indian side of the river, and there they remained. Other immigrants who stayed in the neighborhood had more than farming on their minds. The Indians, defeated and dejected, were ripe for exploitation, and there were whites who were ready to make the most of the situation. As settlers from the west poured in, reports of cheated, drunken, and debauched Indians increased, and everyone knew that immigration and the Indian's decline were directly related.[20]

As a result of Alabama's population explosion, the territory was admitted into the union in 1819. While territorial leaders had been united in their desire for statehood, state leaders were deeply divided over a site for the new seat of government. One group hoped to put the capital at Tuscaloosa on the Black Warrior River, but another, led by territorial governor William Wyatt Bibb, wanted it on the Alabama, nearer his and his fellow Georgians' holdings. Bibb's choice, and that of the Alabama River faction, was a spot on the west bank of the stream, near its junction with the Cahaba River—a site that offered enough to settlers on the smaller stream to get their support. With all the overblown exuberance of the booster he was, Bibb promised that the city built at this location, "situated on a river capable of being navigated by boates of great burthen, and supported . . . by the abundant pro-

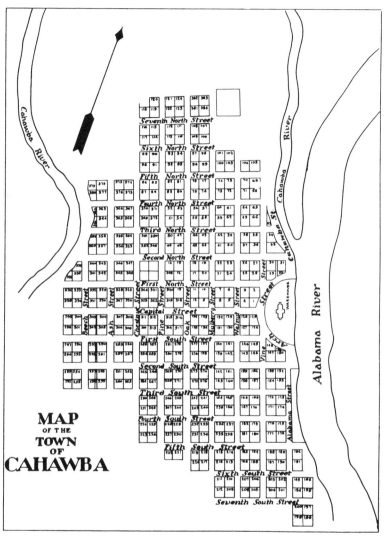

An Early Plan of Cahawba, before the first sale of lots in May 1819
(From *Three Capitals: A Book about the First Three Capitals of Alabama*
by William H. Brantley, 1947; reprint, The University of Alabama
Press, 1976)

duction of an extensive and fertile back country," would one day "vie with the largest inland towns in the country."[21]

Bibb proposed to name the town Cahawba—one more effort to assure critics that the location was for the benefit of more than the Alabama River faction. But critics were not convinced, and Bibb did not get everything he wanted. Although he was able to push the site selection through the legislature and obtain authorization to begin the town, his enemies added a provision to the state constitution directing the assembly to meet in Cahawba only until 1825, at which time it would select a "permanent Seat of Government." Both sides did agree on one thing, however. They adopted a great seal for the state's official use, and highlighting it were what they considered Alabama's most significant features—its rivers.[22]

There was good reason for the Alabama River faction to seek support from settlers in the Cahaba valley, for since the Creek War that district had grown rapidly. Men attached to Jackson's army explored the area and returned home with stories of "one of the most beautiful small rivers they had seen" and of a land "checkered and diversified" by open prairies and dense woodlands and drained by "springs and creeks . . . abundantly supplied with excellent seats for water works of, almost, any kind." Frontiersmen, even those considered "good judges," were inclined toward boast and exaggeration, but if the region was not "the Acadia of America" as some claimed, settlers who went to see for themselves were more than satisfied with what they found.[23]

The family of seven-year-old Angeline Elizabeth Eiland was among the immigrants. Years later, widowed and living in Texas, she remembered fondly the "beautiful river, the pretty magnolias and bays with their milk-white flowers," the tall palmetto, and the "fine and stately" cypress that gave a tropical character to the lower Cahaba. She recalled the days of keelboats and cotton flats and of how "old Alabama was full of energy." And she remembered the open, undulating land. Texas had its prairies, but they could not "compare with those coming out of Perry into Moringo, between Woodville and Marion, and on to Wilcox to Prairie Bluff on the Alabama River." Before she left the Cahaba valley, that land was covered with cotton.[24]

Once the site of the state's first capital was confirmed, everything seemed to fall in Cahawba's favor. The legislature set aside over sixteen-hundred acres for sale to support the project; the district land office was moved there; and Cahawba's staunchest supporter, William Wyatt Bibb, was chosen governor. A glorious future seemed assured. The town plan was drawn anticipating greatness. Broad streets were laid out in a grid pattern on the bluff, where large lots were surveyed for sale.

But for investors studying the plat, the feature that set the plan apart and made the city just a little more grand, a little more special, was Arch Street. Drawn along the palisade line of an ancient Indian town, the thoroughfare rose from the river's edge and curved gently up the bank so wagons could reach the top with ease. At the crest it began a similar curved, gentle descent back down to the Alabama. Lots inside the arch, closest to the river, were set aside for warehouses, to hold the bounty of the Black Belt. In time, they were built, but Arch Street did not work out quite as planned; in the end, neither did Cahawba.[25]

Attracted by its political importance and its economic promise, visitors crowded into the capital. Ferries operated on both rivers to handle the flow, hotels opened, construction of state buildings began, and courts held sessions. Soon there were stores and shops, the *Cahawba Press* appeared, and land sales continued brisk. Then as fast as it began, it ended. The long arm of economic panic reached the Alabama frontier in 1819, and in the face of "pecuninary embarrassment" many could not pay their debts and asked the legislature for relief. Then, in the summers and autumns of 1821 and 1822, a "bilious remitting fever" struck the town, caused, some believed, by the "heat and moisture" that lingered after the "heavy rains in the Spring," when "the rivers [were] swollen in an unprecedented manner." As the death toll rose, some of Cahawba's "hard drinkers" (and the capital had its share) sought "to keep themselves above fever heat" with a daily pint of brandy or whiskey. Those among them who survived (the disease and the cure) credited this remedy. Others, however, chose to leave until the weather turned cool, which course may have been the more prudent. In time the land dried out, and with frost the fever passed; but many legislators remembered Bibb's promise of the excellent "prospect of health" at Cahawba and began to support a move to a friendlier climate.[26]

Meanwhile, the Cahaba valley was attracting its share of adventurers among them Mrs. Sarah F. Williams Willis Chotard, a "glamorous Frenchwoman" who appeared in Alabama around 1820. Through a series of circumstances, including two marriages (the second to a San Domingo refugee), Mrs. Chotard (who was actually a Virginian) was granted some fifteen-hundred acres in either Alabama or Mississippi—the choice was hers. She looked first at Claiborne, but when it was ruled that her grant was for rural land, not town lots, she shifted her attention to the falls of the Cahaba, where a major east-west migration route crossed the river. Here she believed she could build a commercial center so immediately successful that it would be designated the permanent state capital when the legislature made its choice in 1825. To emphasize the advantages of the site, she named her town Centerville. In 1821, it got a post office, and the next year the founder appeared on the site, with a surveyor, to lay off lots and evict squatters.[27]

As much the promoter as any speculator in the region, Mrs. Chotard made a "liberal offer" of town lots to General Jackson (whom she apparently knew) in hopes that he would endorse her scheme. The general declined the offer, though he softened the blow with the wish that her "town will grow and prosper like the rose." She took the refusal in stride and continued on, but things did not go as planned. Though the surveyor laid out an appealing village, with broad streets, large lots, and connecting alleys, buyers did not come, and by the end of 1823 only 23 of the 265 plots were sold. It was a grand failure, but Mrs. Chotard never knew. In 1824 she died in Cahawba. Centerville continued without her, but it never became the metropolis of her dreams. In later years uncertainty about her background fed legends of how she had met the man she married at a ball after the Battle of New Orleans, how he was one of Jackson officers, and of how she had been Jackson's French interpreter when he was in Louisiana. None of these could be verified, but the telling added to the mystery that surrounded the woman who wanted to build a city on the Cahaba.[28]

As the population of the region grew, more and more cotton was shipped by flatboat down to Mobile, but still only an occasional keelboat brought goods back. Then, in 1821, this unbalanced commerce began to change. In October the steamboat *Harriet* came up the Alabama, past Claiborne and Cahawba, under Selma's bluff, and on to Montgomery. The river had been overcome. Citizens along the stream greeted the *Harriet* as they might a circus—something sent solely to excite and entertain them—and her arrival occasioned celebrations all along the way. But in the crowds, and looking down from warehouse windows and brokers' offices, were those who also understood the opportunity this new wonder offered them. Andrew Jackson opened the Alabama land for those brave and resourceful and cunning enough to exploit it; the steamboat opened the Alabama River.[29]

The voyage of the *Harriet* was a temporary tonic for a region trying to cope with an economic depression and at the same time hold fast to the symbol of its importance—the state capitol. Even as Cahawba was created there were politicians lobbying to move the capitol elsewhere. Things got no better after buildings were up and government was functioning. The town was never a favorite spot among legislators, especially those from the north, and these critics quickly seized on anything that cast doubts on the wisdom of selecting this location. The death of Governor Bibb in 1820, the result of a fall from his horse, ended the career of one of Cahawba's most powerful advocates and may have eventually allowed "removers" to tip the balance in their favor. But nature was also on their side. In 1822, according to local physician J. W. Heustis, a rainfall unprecedented across the state drove the river from its banks, and outlying areas of the town were flooded. Stories of the deluge grew with the telling, and soon it was believed that Cahawba had been inundated and that legislators had to take rowboats to the state house. These exaggerated accounts supported the removers' contention that the site was unhealthy and dangerous; and as the stories spread, Cahawba's future as the seat of government became more and more doubtful.[30]

The Alabama River valley enjoyed one more moment in the spotlight before its jewel, the capitol, was snatched from its grasp. In 1825 the state was visited by the Marquis de Lafayette, who was making a grand tour of the nation he had helped free from colonial rule. Everyone wanted to pay tribute to the aging hero of the Revolution, in part because he was truly loved and respected by the American people but also because this promised to be the most important social event in the life of the young state. It was an opportunity for towns to put on a reception that would reflect, if not magnify, their importance, and in the climate of boosterism that warmed Alabama, this was a serious matter indeed.[31]

Accompanied by a retinue that included his dog Quiz and his secretary Levasseur (who later published a record of the visit), Lafayette followed the Federal Road into Alabama and on April 3 arrived in Montgomery. There the party was greeted "by the inhabitants of [the] village" (Levasseur knew the difference between a town and a village, and Montgomery was still the latter) and by Gov. Israel Pickins, up from Cahawba with "a large concourse of citizens, who had assembled from great distances to accompany him." Montgomery's finest home, that of John Edmondson, was stocked with French wine and food and given over to the general. In the evening a "grand ball" was held on the second floor of a large brick building, above the prying eyes of the masses not invited. Music was provided by a band brought from New Orleans (Montgomery, indeed Alabama, had no group deemed suitable), and a good time apparently was had by all—including the general. Among the revelers was Samuel Dale, in full uniform, who claimed to have ridden 250 miles to see the show and be part of it.[32]

Not long after midnight Lafayette left the party and, accompanied by "all the ladies of Montgomery," went to the river where he boarded a steamboat that Levasseur identified as the *Anderson* for the next phase of the trip—and a much-deserved rest. About two o'clock in the morning they headed downstream, to the salute of artillery on a shore illuminated by large fires built to light the way. By morning the boat was well down the river, and at noon it arrived at Selma, where "an immense concourse of people . . . assembled at the landing, . . . rent the air with shouts as the hero walked out on the plank to land." Escorted by Col. William Rufus King, who chaired the committee that planned the event, Lafayette entered Woodall's Hotel, where "lunch was enjoyed with great gusto"—accompanied by numerous toasts, which the general apparently enjoyed as much as the meal. But the party could not linger long, so after Selma had received its hour, the group again boarded the *Anderson* and headed downstream.[33]

Cahawba anxiously waited. Fears that the capitol would be moved had depressed its citizens, and Lafayette's visit promised to give them at least one opportunity to play the role to which they believed their political position entitled them. They were especially nervous because they had already endured one embarrassing false alarm. It seems that the folks who had been arranging things up at Selma had decided to fire a cannon to alert everyone when the *Anderson* approached and fire it again when the boat departed. A few days before the general was expected, some young men from the town learned of the plan and "wishing to have a little sport" smuggled a cannon into a canebrake near the landing. Though Lafayette and his entourage were still in Montgomery, the pranksters fired the piece and announced the party's arrival with a resounding roar. Residents rushed to the river, only to find that they had been fooled. Meanwhile, outside of town "country people" got word that the general was approaching and set out toward Selma to "get a peep at the great Frenchman." As they approached the town someone fired the cannon again, and rural residents assumed it was the signal for the boat's departure. Immediately some of them "turned their course" and headed for the capital with word that Lafayette would soon be there. At Cahawba "a large multitude" gathered on the banks of the river, where they waited late into the night for the boat to arrive. Then, bitterly disappointed, they went home.[34]

This time, however, the *Anderson* appeared. The town was ready, but preparations had not been easy. All, it seemed, wanted their share of the general. The "gentlemen" of Cahawba, who included the state's political figures, wanted only invited guests to have dinner with Lafayette. This exclusion did not sit well with common folks who also wanted to dine with the great man, and, in the democratic climate of frontier Alabama, believed they had every right to do so. Meanwhile, the "ladies" of the town wanted more than a meal with speeches and toasts. They wanted a ball, which would "give them an opportunity to pay their respects to him"—and show off like everyone else. What

Lafayette wanted was probably a good night's sleep, but no one, at least no Alabamian, seems to have asked him.[35]

Determined "not to be outdone by the capital of Georgia," which reportedly spared no expense to entertain the general, citizens of Cahawba decided to do all three. There would be a public barbecue for those who could not afford to pay five dollars for the dinner—a sum that comfortably drew the line between the haves and have-nots. Lafayette would first attend the dinner, but after "a few toasts" he would leave for the less formal gathering. There he would give a toast (the more toasts the better, it seems) and then return to the exclusive celebration, where by that time the dishes would have been cleared away and the dancing begun. Apparently it worked. Levasseur recorded that Cahawba's arrangements were "remarkable for their elegance and good taste," and everyone seemed to have a fine time. At eleven o'clock the exhausted general took his leave, boarded the steamboat, and as it headed south, headed to bed.[36]

The final stop on the Alabama was Claiborne, where citizens anxiously waited to pay their respects and showcase their accomplishments. They were almost disappointed. A tight schedule and fatigue threatened to make the visit little more than a stop for fuel; but finally Lafayette "was induced by the intreaties of the inhabitants to remain a few hours," and Claiborne had its moment of glory. Speeches were made, toasts drunk, and Levasseur noted that the man appointed to speak for the citizenry "acquitted himself with an eloquence we were astonished to meet in a spot, which, but a short time before, only resounded with the savage cry of the Indian hunter." The general was able to excuse himself from attending a ball in his honor held at the Masonic Lodge, but the event was "reportedly splendid indeed" even without him. As their visitor steamed away, the people of Claiborne congratulated themselves on a job well done.[37]

Lafayette went downriver to Mobile and then to New Orleans, leaving the Alabama River valley with just cause to be proud, and the state with a bill of nearly sixteen thousand dollars. The whole thing had been a marvelous diversion, but it was over; and back in Cahawba, politicians again turned their attention to the question of a permanent location for the capitol. Heavy rains that year brought new flooding, which advocates for removal exaggerated to the point that later generations would believe that the town had been entirely cut off from the outside world. Assemblymen whose interests lay outside the Alabama River region united and heaped such abuse on Cahawba that even its friends acknowledged the inevitable. Removal supporters proposed Tuscaloosa as the new site. Alabama River advocates countered with Montgomery. Then the final vote was taken, and by a majority of one the Alabama River lost. On December 13, 1825, Cahawba ceased to be the capital of Alabama. From Montgomery to Claiborne, citizens wondered what the future held for their region and for themselves.[38]

FIVE

The Age of the Alabama:
Life along the River

Montgomery is near the head waters of the Alabama River, and at
the limit of Steam Boat Navigation. It is the Depot of the cotton
which is raised for many miles around it, and is a rapidly increasing
and very thriving town. Boats sometimes ascend the river to
Wetumpka some miles above, but nothing can interfere with the
growth of Montgomery, which will before long be second only to
Mobile in the State of Alabama.

> JOHN H. B. LATROBE
> *Southern Travels:*
> *Journal of John H. B. Latrobe,* 1834

The scenery on the Alabama river is beautiful & in many places very
wild & romantic. The river is lined for miles with high bluffs and is
not unlike the Hudson R at the Highlands with the exception of the
rocks which line its banks. Some of these bluffs are 200 feet high &
it is an amusing sight to see the cotton come sliding down the steep
banks. Owing to the many water courses & violent rains this river
rises very rapidly & very high. During the last freshet, the river rose
over forty feet and it would have done immense damage had it not
been that all the towns are located upon these bluffs.

> *Bishop Whipple's Southern Diary,* 1843–44

The capitol was gone; but still the immigrants came. Drawn by the rich
Black Belt soil, they settled in the Alabama and Cahaba valleys, cleared
the land, planted cotton, built houses (some of them "big houses"),
created counties so they could govern, and put the region on a course it
would follow to mid-century and beyond. During this era Alabama
River planters set the social tone as well as the economic direction of
the state, and even without the political clout of the state capitol,
regional politicians remained a force to be reckoned with. The legislature might meet on another river's banks, but this was the age of the
Alabama.

As might be expected, Cahawba had a period of decline, though it
was never as "lonely and deserted" as a resident later reminisced. Some
buildings were left vacant for a while, but the state house was eventually
turned over to the county, which used it as the courthouse until 1834,
when a new one was built. A few people left the former capital and
moved up the Cahaba to Centerville, closer to the new seat of government, but many remained. In 1827 they incorporated the Cahaba

Navigation Company and began making plans to improve the river. Any reports of Cahawba's death were certainly premature.[1]

Downstream Claiborne continued to enjoy the advantages of its location, and one of its citizens remembered how "all was bustle and full of life" in the village on the bluff. Upriver boosters imported a young Pennsylvania journalist to edit Selma's first newspaper and to trumpet that town's advantages and accomplishments. Montgomery's progress was slowed by a malaria epidemic in the summer of 1826 that killed some 20 percent of the population, but the dead were soon replaced: the stream of immigrants seemed endless. Though Andrew Dexter's goats still grazed on the hill overlooking the town, by 1828 Montgomery had over a thousand inhabitants and could boast of hotels, shops, a number of taverns, and a few churches to serve citizens and visitors alike. All along the river economic conditions improved, and by the end of the 1820s prosperity, like the steamboat that brought it, seemed just around the bend.[2]

The key to this flourishing economy was the plantation system born amid the surge of immigration that pushed the population of the state from 127,901 in 1820 to 309,527 by the end of the decade. On to the river they came—over rutted, muddy roads filled with so many people that "but for the very decided style of cussing and swearing," one traveler said he might have mistaken them for the Biblical Exodus. In the ranks were those who had no choice but to come. For slaves, it was a difficult, often brutal emigration. Usually taken from their homes after harvest, they made the forced march during the winter, so they could be at their destination in time to clear land and put in the spring crop. In the winter of 1834–35 Englishman George Featherstonhaugh saw "at least 1000 negro slaves" on their way west, "tramping through the waxy ground on foot . . . wet with fording the streams . . . [and] shivering with cold." Harriet Martineau, another English visitor, saw them, too, and when she asked them where they were going, they called back, "Into Yellibama."[3]

With the coming of the steamboat, the state's population concentrated along its navigable streams, so it followed that urban development in antebellum Alabama was consistent with the growth of river towns. Paradoxically, response to the steamboat often worked against efforts to turn villages into inland ports. As more boats plied the river, more planters built their own landings, where their cotton and cotton from the neighborhood was loaded for market. At the height of the steamboat era there were more than two hundred landings between Wetumpka and the Alabama-Tombigbee cutoff. Counting on these for most of its cargo, in 1824 the steamboat *Columbus* left Montgomery with some three hundred bales of cotton; it had twenty-five hundred when it reached Mobile.[4]

Plantation landings served other functions as well. They were wood yards, where boats bought their fat pine fuel; they were way stations where river travelers waited for the next docking; and they were social centers where residents gathered to catch up on news and gossip. Some passengers complained of the leisurely pace these stops imposed, but to little avail, for as it would always be in the South, there were things that took precedence over haste and efficiency. And besides, river travel was still better then going by land; so travelers accepted the fact that if one wanted to enjoy the conveniences and comforts of the steamboat, one had to tolerate the inconveniences as well.[5]

If the landings provided any entertainment for delayed passengers, it was that unintentional by-product of the way the baled cotton was loaded—a process one veteran traveler claimed to "never weary in beholding." Where the bluff was steep planters built "a slide formed of planks reaching from the warehouse above to the water beneath." Once the steamboat was moored, slaves at the top put a bale on the slide and launched it on its journey down to the deck. "Left to find its own way to the bottom," the four-to-five-hundred-pound missile gathered speed until it arrived with a force "that would send it across the deck [and] far into the river," had it not been "deadened by bales" already there. Once it stopped, workers on board pulled the bale aside to make a place for the next one coming down—moving quickly, or they would be crushed. All of this loading was accomplished, according to one observer, while the laborers were "laughing, yelling, or giving to each other confused directions, [and making] the forest ring to the water's edge."[6]

River plantations and farms grew with the population, though few of either actually overlooked the stream. One curious traveler inquired as to the reason and was told "that the fever-and-ague prevails upon the banks of the river, so that the beautiful sites on the bluffs are neglected, and the planters build back, in what are called the 'piney woods,' where they find pure air and good water." But the planter was moved by other considerations as well. Planters wanted to be at the center of their estates, where it was easier to direct their operations. Since most plantations were on only one side of the river, to be at that central location it was necessary to build away from the stream. When Philip Henry Gosse, a young Englishman recruited to tutor the children of Dallas County planters, stepped off the steamboat at King's Landing in May of 1838, he was surprised to learn that the home of the gentleman who had hired him was ten miles away. The longer he lived in the region, the more common he found this situation to be.[7]

Steamboat *Mary* at Prairie Bluff (1866).
A thriving community in the 1830s, Prairie Bluff's decline was well
underway when this picture was made.
(Courtesy of W. S. Hoole Special Collections Library, The University of Alabama,
Tuscaloosa.)

What travelers did see were "the negroes' cabins . . . erected near the
shore, where they can have access to abundance of water . . . and can
be near their work." Close to those "wretched huts" Philip Gosse saw
"in the fields of some large estates . . . for the first time, negro-slaves
performing the labours of agriculture." This sight disturbed the young
foreigner, and the more he saw, the more convinced he became that the
institution of slavery was "a huge deadly serpent . . . [and] that, some
day or other, it will burst the weight that binds it, and take a fearful
retribution." Other visitors were equally critical of the system (Harriet
Martineau wrote that "a walk through a lunatic asylum is far less painful
than a visit to the slave quarters of an estate"), but most Alabama
planters seemed unconcerned. Their position was simple: "Slaves are
indispensable in Alabama, while present condition endures"; land,
without slave labor, was "a mere waste."[8]

And yet, for those who could look at the land and not be repulsed by
the system that brought it into production, it must have been a
magnificent sight. Tyrone Power, the Irish comedian who came
through in the 1830s, described the "cotton-grounds" along the river as

"rich beyond conception," with fields a mile square that could be profitably picked twice a year, if the labor was available. Power was also impressed by the "fresh clearings" he saw, land made ready for the next season, as planters and farmers prepared for an even more bountiful harvest. In this preparation one finds the Alabama River planter's greatest interest; for according to observers on the scene, these men were, above all else, "money-getters." Harriet Martineau recognized this greed and blamed it for the "false and hollow" principles on which the plantation system rested and for a society where "education is less thought of, and sooner ended, than in almost any part of the world." But Mrs. Martineau was criticizing planters and their families for not having the society they never intended to have in the first place. At this stage Alabama's planters and farmers had other goals, and a remarkable number were achieving them. As Martineau was forced to admit, the Alabama River region was "certainly the place to become rich in."[9]

The river was the planters' agent in these money-getting schemes. They shipped their cotton on it and in return received goods and provisions they could not obtain locally. Once or twice a year they took to the boat themselves, traveled to Mobile, and transacted business in person. There they dealt with a "factor," the middleman who brokered their crop and often advanced them money on what they expected to produce the next year. The process anticipated the crop lien system that would be so prevalent in the second half of the century. But where later the farmer and tenant were bound to the merchant or planter who furnished seed, fertilizer, and land in return for a lien on the next year's yield, in this earlier time the planter received the capital to make a crop (or buy more land and labor) from a Mobile factor whose source of funds might well be a bank or merchant in the northeast. Thus Alabama River plantations became part of the larger, capitalistic world, a world with which their way of life seemed to have little in common.[10]

The question of whether the Alabama River planter was a capitalist or not can be debated best in other forums. For our purposes, and indeed for his, the planter was simply doing what other aggressive businessmen were doing—trying to make money. That he did it with cotton and slaves, rather than machines and free labor, simply revealed a means, which did not alter the end. Successful planters were as innovative as any progressive manager; they sought the newest and best gins, mills, and presses; they patronized the fastest and largest steamboats; and they read agricultural journals to keep abreast of the latest ideas on how to get the most from the soil and from those who toiled upon it. They could be as tight a trader as any Yankee and were, according to one resident, willing to "skin a flea for lucre of the hide and tallow."[11]

Yet for all these capitalistic notions, plantation practices retarded commercial activity along the river. At his core the planter was an individualist, self-absorbed and inclined to go it alone rather than combine with others to promote a local economy. As a consequence, during the antebellum era most river towns were not good places for ambitious merchants. Some might succeed in Montgomery, Selma, and other market centers along the stream, but on the whole planters bought the goods and supplies they needed from the men in Mobile and New Orleans who handled their cotton for them. This practice, as much as anything else, kept the towns along the Alabama small and, in some cases, struggling. It also kept many small farmers, who were more dependent on the local market, struggling as well.[12]

Still, to see the extent to which the Alabama shaped the lives of those along its banks, one had to visit the river towns. Four of these—Montgomery, Selma, Cahawba, and Claiborne—are mentioned so often that it would be easy to believe they were the only ones of any consequence. But that assumption would overlook other important centers that rose, prospered, and then declined, a process that happened more frequently than one might expect. Landings, with roads to feed them, brought farmers and planters with their cotton. Traveling peddlers, on foot, on horse, or in wagons, arrived, saw this ready market, and set up shop. A tavern was opened, then another, and soon storefronts appeared advertising dry goods, groceries, and notions. Real estate companies, which may have been there from the start, subdivided fields and woods and sold lots. As the town grew, factors came upriver from Mobile to contract for the crop before it reached competitors on the coast. At the same time a range of professional men made their appearance. Most prominent among these were lawyers who, according to satirist Joseph G. Baldwin, knew "a legal Utopia" when they saw one and were exhilarated by the prospect of the "fussing, quarreling, murdering, [and] violation of contracts" that was synonymous with life on the frontier. Thus a town was born.[13]

One of these market centers was Prairie Bluff, high above the Alabama in Wilcox County. Roads entering from the northeast and the southwest brought cotton there from inland planters, so a long slide was soon constructed to carry the bales down to the water. Already a voting place when the steamboat arrived, it quickly became a mail distribution point for much of the region, and by the 1830s (before Cahawba's revival was complete) it was second only to Claiborne on the route between Mobile and Montgomery. A former resident remembered some twenty stores "carrying large stocks of goods," along with "2 wagon factories, 1 gin factory and several black smith and shoemaker shops, several tailoring establishments and a large confectionary store"—an array that could supply almost every need. Opportunities for mischief and mayhem were found at the "many barrooms, billiard tables and ten pin alleys in operation" and at the local racetrack. "Some half-dozen practicing physicians and several lawyer[s]" opened offices there and stood ready to serve the needs of citizens who frequented those establishments. Given the nature of society in Prairie Bluff during these early days, it is hardly surprising that "there was no regular church building in the town."[14]

Prairie Bluff was born of a booster's dream of profit. Two real estate syndicates created the town, divided it between themselves, then subdivided their portions and offered lots for sale. "Speculation in real estate" was recalled as "the order of the day," and a good deal of money was made and lost while the firms operated. But the real estate boom did not last, and as the economy slackened, Prairie Bluff's weak foundation began to show. Philip Henry Gosse's observation about towns and townsmen in the Black Belt serves well to explain what followed. Because each citizen was a speculator at heart, Gosse maintained that a villager "always expects to sell his 'improvements' and 'move' to some other region; hence his residence has always a temporary character." The result was that the "rude and make-shift" settlement quickly showed the effects of economic stagnation, and its appearance may have made conditions seem worse than they actually were. As the town appeared less and less prosperous, fewer and fewer new arrivals bought land and settled. Once the deterioration began, it was hard to reverse.[15]

Other circumstances contributed to Prairie Bluff's decline. A series of malarial epidemics in the late 1830s further reduced the population, and though the town did not experience yellow fever outbreaks like other river towns, what it did endure caused some survivors to move farther inland to the rising town of Camden, which was planned and built to serve as the center for Wilcox County government. Cahawba's rejuvenation in the 1840s drew trade away from Prairie Bluff, and as steamboat competition increased, captains sought out cargo at plantation landings, rather than wait for planters to bring their crops to market. Soon only cotton from the immediate area was brought to the bluff, and that was not enough to keep the town going. Stores closed, residents left, and finally, in June of 1845, Dale Lodge, seat of the county's most prominent Masons, moved to Camden. The lodge's departure told everyone who did not know already how low Prairie Bluff had sunk. The community held on through the Civil War, but postbellum changes spelled its end. By the 1880s the site was all but deserted.[16]

During the flush times of the antebellum era, however, upward seemed the only direction river towns could go. Claiborne's prosperity began at the water's edge, where a warehouse stood near the ferry. More buildings stood on the bluff—some "shed-like" and "a hundreds yards long," others "many stories high"—and during the picking season cotton from Monroe and surrounding counties filled them to capacity. At its height Claiborne's "annual sales of goods were estimated to be from one and a half to two million dollars," and old-timers remembered bales "so scattered along the side-walk that much trouble was experienced in passing about the town." Considering this commerce, it is hardly surprising that Baltimore lawyer John H. B. Latrobe, who visited while returning home from New Orleans in December of 1834, found that citizens of Claiborne were "all cotton worshippers . . . [who] talked of nothing else, thought of nothing else and no doubt dreamt of nothing but long & short staple, and twenty cents per pound."[17]

Travelers disembarking at Claiborne were overwhelmed by the bluff, which rose some three hundred feet from the water's edge. To reach the top they had to climb a wooden staircase of some 365 steps while their baggage was hauled up on "a kind of train" that ran on tracks fixed to the cotton slide beside the stairs. The train was secured by a cable and pulled to the top by a wheel driven by several mules; passengers made their way to the summit on foot and usually arrived out of breath. At the top, looking west, they were treated to a view of the river, the broad level of bottom land on the other side, and the line of hills that enclosed the valley, behind which the sun set spectacularly. Turning around, visitors found the village, with stores, houses, and clean, unpaved streets, "straight and wide," and lined with what residents called "flowering ash." Though by now Claiborne's population was less than five hundred, locals still described it as "a considerable place"; and in a region so thinly settled, it was.[18]

In Claiborne frontier and civilization observed an uneasy truce. On one hand, according to local planter Thomas Gaillard, were citizens who exhibited the "virtue of character" expected of true gentlefolks, while on the other were those who claimed that status yet manifested traits he found "exceedingly apalling and odious." In an 1837 letter to his brother in South Carolina, Gaillard observed how "Pistols, Dirks, and Bowie knives are the every day accompaniments of our gentry here, and faith! they are not very dilatory in the use of them." Faced with such conditions, and aware that effort at "restraining vice and subduing violence [were] but feebly felt in the community," Gaillard made it a rule to avoid Claiborne, "unless business requires my presence there, or I go for the purpose of attending divine Services." Some had other reasons for not visiting the town. In 1836, Georgian Richard Wylly

Steamboat *Magnolia* at Claiborne (1855).
This was the longest loading facility on the river. The picture, from
Vallou's Pictorial Drawing-Room Companion (1855) shows the covered
cotton slide, with the 365-step staircase alongside.
(Courtesy of W. S. Hoole Special Collections Library, The University of Alabama,
Tuscaloosa.)

Habersham, in Alabama on business, considered a trip to Claiborne and then decided against it. A physician he had met told him that earlier that year an epidemic had struck, and "there was only one person in the whole town well enough to tend the sick." Despite its elevation, Claiborne was not immune to the "fever-and-auger" of the river, a fact that played no small part in its future.[19]

Upriver, Cahawba, as county seat of Dallas County, continued to be a site of some importance, though here too the frontier was close at hand. Englishman Thomas Hamilton visited the courthouse in 1831 and in that hall of justice discovered "his honor the judge, not better dressed and apparently somewhat filthier in habits, than a English ploughman," presiding over a trial where the appearance of one of the lawyers "seemed to indicate a combination of the trade of blacksmith with that of barrister." The man being tried was accused of practicing medicine without a license, a minor offense in a setting that was, according to a modern researcher, "more like 'Gunsmoke' than *Gone with the Wind.*"[20]

Hamilton found the town to be "a very poor collection of very poor houses," some fifty in number, and for the next decade things did not improve very much. In 1838, Philip Henry Gosse visited Cahawba and observed that despite its former importance it was "now much decayed, and has a very desolate appearance." The business district consisted of "a few 'stores,' a lawyer's office or two, and two or three tradesmen's shops." There was also "the usual proportion of rum-shops or 'groceries,'" but judging from "the number of customers in the verandahs," he concluded that they had been able to avoid "the general decay." To Gosse, these establishments "appeared to constitute the business of the 'city,'" and "finding no temptation to linger," he "quickly" left Cahawba.[21]

Hamilton and Gosse were Englishmen. Unfamiliar with the raw frontier that was Alabama, they expected more from what the locals called towns and cities. Richard Wylly Habersham saw things differently. His home was in north Georgia, a setting that had much in common with the Cahawba region and one that gave him a greater appreciation for what he found. Though he complained of poor accommodations and had little to say about the town itself, he enjoyed a meeting of the Cahawba Polemic Society and was impressed with the "apparently well educated gentlemanly young men" who were there. While in the town he also "attended a concert given by a company of Strollers either from the New Orleans or Mobile Orchestra." These embellishments of civilization may not have impressed Gosse and Hamilton, but to Habersham they suggested that improvements for the better were indeed possible.[22]

Changes were coming. By the 1840s Black Belt land in the Cahaba Valley was producing cotton, and when winter rains swelled the river, bales of the staple were shipped downstream on flatboats. There was other traffic as well, for the *Cahaba River Packett* was only one of a number of steamboats that navigated the stream in the wet season. As this commerce increased, Cahawba's role as an economic and social center increased as well. Larger warehouses were built, existing buildings repaired, and new ones erected; a church was raised; and a number of impressive private residences were constructed by planters and businessmen who made the city their home. By the end of the decade the town's population had swelled to some three thousand people, making it one of the largest in the state. With commercial connections that tied them not only to Mobile and Montgomery but to New York City as well, Cahawba residents found economic and social outlets that made them some of the most cosmopolitan of Alabama's decidedly unsophisticated population. Gosse and Hamilton would have been surprised—Habersham, less so, if at all.[23]

Cahawba's rival was Selma, a settlement that Habersham estimated in 1836 was nearly three times the size of the former capital. But size was not everything, for although at that time Cahawba left much to be desired, Habersham declared that things were "even worse" upriver at the larger town. Still, Selma grew rapidly until the late 1830s, when the *Cahawba Democrat* announced, with some satisfaction, that "the Selma bubble has burst at last." The Panic of 1837 had reached Alabama; cotton prices began to fall, land sales slackened, and those who had bought on credit (and in Selma there were many) found themselves with neither property nor money. This was followed by what local chronicler John Hardy called "the terribly sickly seasons of 1840 and 1841," and these epidemics, "together with the great monetary crash," were more than the city could stand. "Commerce of the place," according to Hardy, "languished," and "instead of a population coming to the town, many of its substantial men left . . . to seek another location."[24]

The most unsettling blow may have come when work on the Selma and Tennessee Railroad came to "a complete stop." The railroad was part of a plan to connect the Alabama and Tennessee rivers, and during the flush times before the crash, it "attracted the attention of the shrewd and business men of Selma." The legislature granted a charter, some $300,000 worth of stock was sold, and in 1837 work on the first ten-mile section began. Then "the great financial troubles came upon the country," and the contractors were "compelled to abandon the work." But the significance lay not in the failure but in the attempt. The whole scheme was conceived to enhance river traffic, not to offer an alternative to it. The age of the railroad might have been approaching, but citizens of the Alabama River valley still believed that the locomotive would never replace the steamboat.[25]

Before the crash, Selma boomed, and as it did, according to Hardy, "schools, churches and prayers, were forgotten." A "splendid race track" opened on the east side of town, and a minister complained that "Jockey Clubs were better supported . . . and more appreciated than religion." Citizens gambled at the Alhambra Saloon, brawls were frequent, and in "Bogle's Assembly Rooms" in Samuel Bogle's hotel, dances, parties, shows—"some kind of amusement"—went on every week. The "good citizens" of the city tried to stop this behavior but with mixed results. Reformers did get the town council to pass an ordinance that closed bars on the Sabbath and fined anyone caught drinking on that day of rest; but it was nothing more than a gesture. Everyone knew that only two men in Selma did not visit McKeaggs's saloon on Sunday, so the ordinance was not enforced. It is remarkable that it passed at all, for the Selma government was noticeably ambivalent on such matters. Once, in a fit of piety, they passed an ordinance to keep boats from landing goods on the Lord's Day; six weeks later they repealed it. Keeping the Sabbath holy was fine in theory, but business was business. If a boat arrived, it would be unloaded.[26]

The financial crash seemed to sober Selma citizens, and in its aftermath reformers gained ground. Where earlier a local minister, the Reverend Samuel M. Nelson, had "opened his batteries of eloquence against gambling" to little avail, now "public sentiment commenced changing." It was an uphill battle, for a town council that passed an ordinance prohibiting cock-fighting and then, according to observers, "adjourned to take a drink" was not made up of men who were easily reformed. Nevertheless, the moral tone of the town slowly improved. During the 1840s more churches were being built, attendance at worship services increased, the Ladies' Education Society was chartered, and schools for boys and girls began operation. The middle class of Selma was growing, and as it grew it shaped the town in its own image.[27]

The real success story of this era was Montgomery. At the big bend in the Alabama, just below the forks, it was the place where most immigrants from the east first came in contact with the river and could transfer from land to water, an attractive alternative after weeks on the Federal Road. The location was also an easily accessible port of deposit for local planters, and after picking season the river bank was "strewn with bales of cotton awaiting the means of transport" to Mobile.

During the 1820s the city became an essential stop for almost everyone and everything bound for the southern part of the state, and a steady flow of customers filled its hotels, inns, and taverns and patronized its merchants and artisans. Trade was so brisk and growth so rapid that by 1828 Montgomery was described as "one of the principal towns" in the region, and two years later a visitor erroneously referred to it as "the capital of Alabama."[28]

During the "flush times" of the 1830s, Montgomery confirmed its place as a major market center. By mid-decade her population was nearing three thousand, and "from the great number of stores" it was easy for a visitor to see that this was "a place of extensive inland business." As early as 1834, John H. B. Latrobe predicted that while competitors might try to gain the upper hand, "nothing can interfere with the growth of Montgomery, which will before long be second only to Mobile in the State of Alabama." Time was to prove him right, for despite a national depression in 1837 and occasional epidemics that depleted the population, from the mid-1830s on Montgomery was "a rapidly increasing and thriving town." County seat of one of Alabama's richest counties, it attracted doctors and lawyers to complement the merchant community, and by the end of the decade, according to an early resident, "no city or town [could] boast a better society than Montgomery."[29]

Of course, like any upstart river town, Montgomery had a lot to overcome. Early in the 1830s one visitor complained that he could not find "one tolerable house" in the village and that "the Court-house seemed fast falling into decay." This condition hardly surprised him, however, for it was about what he expected from a citizenry that was, in his estimation, "exclusively of the poor order." This assessment was not entirely fair, but there was some truth to what he said. Though merchants prospered and the city grew, antebellum Montgomery never quite escaped its frontier origins. Horse racing, gambling, drinking, and perhaps fighting remained the main amusements for male citizens, and though the town could boast a library, according to one historian, it was still a community where "as a rule little attention was paid to purely intellectual pursuits." A visitor seeking more genteel diversions would have to go out of his way to find them.[30]

As time passed the town and its people became more "civilized." Brick and lumber replaced logs for common construction, residents raised impressive homes, and public buildings were repaired and refurbished. Rustic inns with "beds . . . full of vermin" were replaced by "spacious, clean, airy, well-conducted, and comfortable" accommodations, and by the 1840s travelers marveled that "at Montgomery we found excellent quarters in the best hotel we had seen since leaving

New York." Two newspapers vied for subscribers; a bookseller opened a shop and prospered; and traveling lecturers spoke to large and appreciative audiences. One of these speakers, the Englishman James Buckingham, returned the courtesy by attending a local church service, where he was treated to "one of the most chastely eloquent and beautiful addresses" he had heard in America—delivered, it should be noted, by a lawyer. Montgomery was coming of age.[31]

Montgomery's growth was a direct result of the rapidly increasing population of the Alabama River region and of the eastern part of the state in general. With the removal of the last remnants of the Creek Nation, the flood of immigration that had poured into the Black Belt was diverted to the rich lands between the Coosa and Tallapoosa. This shift had political repercussions, for residents of east Alabama soon complained of how difficult it was to do state business with the capitol in Tuscaloosa. Now people in the Alabama River valley, who still deeply resented the loss of the seat of government, had allies in their quest to get it back. Soon they joined the representatives from the Coosa region, and in 1845 this coalition secured the legislation needed to give citizens a chance to relocate the capitol once again. By a sectional vote removal was approved. Eight towns vied for the honor, but it was up to the legislature to make the final decision. The only serious contenders were Tuscaloosa, Montgomery, and Wetumpka, the rising town at the falls of the Coosa. Tuscaloosa led early, but after fifteen ballots Wetumpka withdrew, and they chose Montgomery.[32]

Montgomery was equal to the occasion. Local businessmen raised $75,000 to build the capitol, the city deeded the hill where Andrew Dexter's goats had grazed to the state for the site, and by November 1847 the statehouse was complete. Records and furnishings were transferred from Tuscaloosa, and the business of government began. A fire in 1849 destroyed the building, and before the ashes were cool, some were calling for yet another removal. These critics were quickly silenced, however, and a new statehouse was raised on the same site. Completed in 1851, it still stands as a testament to the importance of the Alabama River region and the power of its leaders. Though a less-than-charitable critic would later describe it as "one of the true Athenian Yankeeized structures of this novo-classic land, erected on a site worthy of a better fate and edifice," along the Alabama it was more than a building. It was a visible symbol of victory.[33]

SIX

The Age of the Alabama:
Life on the River

The boatmen were standing impatiently with the gang-board in their
hands, ready to draw it away the moment we stepped into the vessel.
In the next minute the paddles were in motion, and the tide catching
the boat's bow, round she came. Away we dashed, urged by the
current, and the impulse of a high-pressure engine, at such a rate,
that the dripping banks, the plantations, the negro huts, the
hundreds of cotton warehouses, flitted by us with a rapidity which
looked very hazardous, as we steered round some of the sharp bends
of the river, swooping along like the great Roc-bird described in the
Arabian Nights.

Captain BASIL HALL
Travels in North America in the Years 1827–1828

We hear the distant whistle sound—
    The St. Nicholas comes in sight;
With sweet music from her calliope,
    We see her land at night.

Once more we see the lightwood torch
    and hear the deck hands' song,
As they gayly grapple the cotton hooks
    and pull the bales along,

They roll and tumble down the hill
    From the warehouse, old and gray,
That holds ten thousand fleecy bales
    To be sent so far away.

ANNA M. GAYLE FRY
Memories of Old Cahaba (1905)

Tales of steamboats and steamboat travel are filled with the romance
and adventure that Americans still associate with the Old South. On
these "floating palaces," according to popular mythology, Dixie aristocrats found circumstances and comforts like those they left behind on
their great plantations, except that on the river the elements of their
way of life were distilled into a finer, more elegant liquor. Along the
steamboat's promenade deck southern ladies and gentlemen walked and
talked with a style and grace found nowhere else in the hemisphere,
while in the main saloon riverboat gamblers waited for the planter rich
enough, bold enough, and careless enough to make the trip worthwhile. Just as the modern mind continues to equate antebellum
southern society with what is seen in the first few frames of *Gone with*

73

the Wind, it continues to measure these vessels by images left over from the movie *Showboat* and from modern replicas that ply southern rivers.[1]

The myth persists, of course, because whatever its flaws, it is so attractive. But more than that, it persists because to some degree, it is true. For most passengers a journey on an antebellum steamboat *was* an adventure so exotic, so filled with wonder and excitement that the line between reality and romance blurred, and the distinction lost any real meaning. The captains and pilots who guided the great vessel were heroes equal to those in Sir Walter Scott, and the boats themselves became at once the noble steeds that carried these knights on their crusades and the fire-belching dragons that only warriors pure in heart could conquer. Everyone who was part of the scene, from deckhand to passenger, was transformed into something else, something greater than he would have been on land. Little wonder that there are those who thoughtlessly cling to the dream of these "glory days" with the same rose-tinted tenacity as they hold to the illusion of an Old South of lordly gentlemen and lovely ladies set in manorial splendor and served by numerous, happy slaves; and because it is so attractive, it is little wonder that so many others, knowing better, also prefer the myth. But why labor the point? As one of Selma's loveliest ladies told me on a cloudless October day as we sat by the river at Old Cahawba, "if it did not happen that way, it should have."[2]

Still, a certain respect for the facts demands a more realistic assessment. When steamboats first appeared on the Alabama they were hardly "palaces"—floating or otherwise. At their crudest they were little more than steam-driven cotton barges, lightly built and shallow draft, "with stern as naked as the bow" and, according to one passenger, "far from handsome to the eye." In time they became larger and more elaborate, with a number of them listed around two hundred feet in length and over thirty feet wide—small by Mississippi River standards but well designed for the trip from Mobile to Montgomery. Foremost in this fleet were the "packets," which carried not only freight and passengers on a regular schedule but often boasted a U.S. mail contract, which was like a governmental endorsement of their efficiency. Until about mid-century most Alabama steamers were side-wheelers, which at the time were more maneuverable in the narrow channels and sharp bends of the river. The main deck was open, except for the kitchen, the firebox and boilers, and the "high pressure engine." This arrangement left most of the deck free for the cargo and the stacks of fat pine that fed the furnace. On this level were also deckhands, "roustabouts," "stevedores," and second-class or "deck" passengers who slept wherever they could find room among the cotton bales and firewood.[3]

Saloon of the *James T. Staples*.
Although this was a postbellum boat, built in 1908, it is representative
of the famous packets of antebellum times. Visible are the doors
leading to cabins and the curtain used to separate the ladies from the
rest of the travelers.
(Harvey H. Jackson III Collection)

Travelers who expected and could afford better accommodations
found them on the second, or "boiler," deck. The dominant feature on
this level was what one passenger described as "a vast saloon" that ran
down the center of the boat and adjacent to which were sleeping cabins
furnished with bunk beds. The saloon served as a dining room as well as
a common gathering spot where passengers could talk, play cards, or
read. It could also be divided to give the ladies a section apart from the
men if they wished. Doors led from the saloon to the individual cabins,
from which other doors opened onto a gallery that ran around the
outside of the boat, a promenade from which voyagers could watch
the passing scene. This was the level that gave steamboat travel its
reputation for comfort and luxury, but even at its grandest, most on
board understood, as one of them put it, that "the steam-vessels are
more for the conveyance of cotton than of passengers."[4]
So steamboat travel was not for everyone. In 1834 John H. B. Latrobe

booked passage to "save the disagreables of a land journey of two hundred miles," then changed his plans when he learned that because of frequent stops at towns and landings, the trip would take two to three days longer than if he went by stage or horse. But when time was not a factor, and comfort was, the steamboat, no matter what its priorities might be, was the way to go. Capt. and Mrs. Basil Hall, after traveling overland through Georgia and the Indian territory, took to water and were happily "boarded, lodged, and conveyed swiftly along, without effort on our part." Though the Halls "had found steam-boat travelling extremely disagreeable" in the past, after their experiences on the Federal Road, they enjoyed having "no chases after poultry,—no cooking to attend to,—not so much extra company to encumber us,— no fords or crazy bridges to cross,—no four-o'clock risings, or midnight travelling,—no broiling at noon, or freezing at night,—and lastly, but not least, no mosquitoes."[5]

Larger steamboats often had cabins for the ship's officers on a hurricane, or Texas, deck above the passenger level, and atop this was the pilot house, set high so the master of the boat could see the whole river. There was a disadvantage to this elevation, however, for the wheel ropes running to the rudder were "necessarily very long and the labour of steering [was] very great." This made navigation on the narrow river even more difficult and turned docking into a long and complicated process, carried out, according to one passenger, with "a portentous creaking of the rudder, a frequent ringing of the engineer's bell, mingled with loud cries of 'Stop her!' and 'Back her!'"—while the engine sounded "like the hard breathing of some huge mastadon labouring under the asthma." On one occasion a boat trying to tie up missed the landing, was pulled around by the current, and was pushed "into the nearest grove of willows." Passengers at dinner were shocked when "a huge branch burst open a side door, and nearly impaled a French conjurer of celebrity on his way to New Orleans."[6]

Throughout the antebellum period steamboats and steamboat travel on the Alabama changed. As larger, faster, and better-appointed boats appeared, the crude vessels, the inconveniences, and the discomforts of the early decades slipped from memory. This evolution had a similar effect on the image and reputation of steamboat captains and pilots. During pioneer days on the river, most of the men who guided the boats were as unrefined as the vessels themselves. But time worked upon them the same transformation it worked upon the rest of frontier Alabama, and by mid-century steamboat captains, like their boats, had taken on the heroic proportions from which legends are made. The life they led seemed so glamorous and exciting that theirs may well have been the most envied profession in the state. Though the Alabama never had a writer to enshrine its steamboat nobility as Mark Twain did for the Mississippi, enough attention was paid to these men that their names and exploits would not be forgotten. Long after the steamboat had disappeared from the river and the last captain had gone to his reward, there were still admirers who could name the packets and the masters as if they were reading from a directory. These men and the boats they captained left river folk some of their most cherished river recollections.[7]

Steamboats on the Alabama multiplied in direct proportion to the cotton grown along the stream, and at river landings the same scene was played out again and again. Down the slide the bales rushed, sent by "rollodores" to the "stevedores" who stored them on the deck. By the time a vessel from Montgomery reached Claiborne, it frequently carried as many as a thousand bales, and uneasy passengers watched as the river rose "level with her gunwale . . . [and] amidships was flowing over." In the winter of 1840 Eli H. Lide of Carlowville in Dallas County recorded that with the river up some thirty feet, "about forty Steam Boats [were] plying up and down," and the newest of them would "carry three thousand bags cotton." Along the Alabama that crop was king, and the monarch's subjects paid it continual homage. But those who did not live in cotton's realm were less respectful. One visitor was annoyed to find that in the saloon of his vessel "nothing else seemed to be thought or talked of," and by the time his trip was done he "wished the cotton in the country [was] at the bottom of the Alabama."[8]

Passengers on these steamboats were a cross section of Alabamians in general, and their habits of action reflected the frontier environment in which most spent their days. Some more sophisticated travelers (usually European) were taken aback at this. They were not surprised to find that lower deck passengers were "almost exclusively" farmers and reported with some satisfaction that this class of traveler was "exceedingly offensive both in habits and deportment." But they were surprised when they discovered first-class ticket holders who were equally "course in their manners, and in many instances very disgusting." What particularly set the more cultured visitor on edge was the "inordinate love of Tobacco" that seemed universal among this first generation of Alabama planters. The "mania for this weed" produced a smoking, chewing, spitting population whose conduct led an observer to conclude that it was "out of character for a tobacco-eater to be decent." But those not completely repulsed by the conduct of their fellow travelers discovered, as one foreign gentleman did, "a rough but merry set of fellows." Taking them for what they were, this visitor got to know his companions, spent some time talking to them, and by the end of the voyage concluded that "kinder or better disposed men [were] never met."[9]

In the steamboat saloon outsiders came in close contact with the Alabama frontier aristocrat in all his glory. Englishman James Silk Buckingham found his specimen on board the *Medora* in 1839, when he met a cotton planter "about seventy years of age" with one eye and "only three or four teeth left," whose "white locks hanging over his shoulders" contrasted dramatically with his "sunburnt and wrinkled countenance." The man was said "to be worth 100,000 dollars," which Buckingham found amazing since it was obvious to the Englishman that "his apparel certainly would not sell in any town of the United States for five." Nor had wealth done much to refine the planter's attitude and conduct. When the old man learned that Buckingham "drank neither wine, beer, cider, or spirits" and that he "bathed or washed from head to foot once every day, took exercise for health . . . and never used tobacco in any form or shape," the planter observed that such a "singular course of life" had no charm for him. And when Buckingham suggested that he might like to join the Englishman's party for religious services when they docked, the rustic politely refused, adding that "he had never been in any church in all his life, and thought he was too old to begin." Though this planter purchased first-class accommodations, he would hardly have been out of place on the main deck.[10]

The steamboat saloon brought together residents from points throughout the river region and forced them to live in close proximity for days at a time, but it did little to alter their fundamental character. The freedom of action so often associated with frontier Alabamians, that casual attitude toward those whom they considered one with themselves, caused planters to intrude innocently on the privacy of fellow passengers, engage them in conversations on topics in which they had little interest, make free use of any books and papers that might attract their notice, and take up the property of others as if it were their own—much as they might have done when a guest of a neighbor. And though such informalities and familiarity might upset foreign (or even northern) visitors, for Alabamians fresh from the plantation it was nothing more than the way a gentleman should act—even when closely confined with strangers.[11]

This close association between people accustomed to individual space and few restraints occasionally produced tensions on board, especially when situations arose that did not fit easily into the existing code of conduct. The results of these incidents were often small dramas that revealed how complex an outwardly simple social arrangement might be and how southern society accommodated these difficulties when they arose. James Silk Buckingham, whose accounts of his trips on the Alabama may well be the best of the era, recorded one of these. Among the passengers in the ladies' cabin of his vessel, the *Medora*, were "three coloured females" going from Mobile to Montgomery. Whether they were slave or free was not mentioned, and apparently Buckingham did not consider that status particularly significant under the circumstances. What was important was their race. Though "they were not negresses, but mulattoes" their "dark-brown colour and strongly-marked African features" clearly distinguished them from everyone else in the boiler deck saloon. Yet these women "were each dressed much more expensively than either of the white ladies on board," and that attire, along with their general deportment, caused the Englishman to conclude that they were socially superior to the slaves and free blacks he had encountered.[12]

Buckingham was about to observe what another Englishman, Charles Lyell, later noted on his trip along the river—that on "a Southern steamer abundant opportunities are afforded of witnessing the inconveniences arising out of the singular relation subsisting between the negroes, whether free or slave, and the white race." The women were obviously not of the common herd, but they were of a race that was not accepted on an equal footing with whites. They could not be put on the lower deck with other blacks, but at the same time they could not be treated in ways that would suggest that they were accepted by the first-class passengers. So despite their "silks, lace, and feathers," the women "slept on the cabin-floor, as the coloured servants usually do, no berth or bed-place being assigned them," though apparently better accommodations were available. Meanwhile the other passengers went about their business as if the women did not exist.[13]

At first the mulatto women seemed to understand the part they were to play and were willing to play it. In the morning they rose before the other ladies and "occupied a good hour at their toilette" at the same time and apparently with "the white stewardess." Then they rejoined the main party and "remained sitting in the cabin all day, as if they were on a footing of perfect equality with the white passengers." But all the while they seemed to occupy a different world, one which they would not (or could not) leave and upon which whites refused to intrude. As he watched, Buckingham detected nothing to suggest that either side found anything extraordinary in the arrangement or wished to change it—until mealtime.[14]

Meals were a highlight on a steamboat, and because of the number of different groups who were served separately, "the succession of breakfasts, dinners, and suppers . . . appear[ed] endless." Meals also gave observers like Buckingham another look at the often contradictory manners of southerners. On board the *Medora* there was "considerable etiquette . . . manifested in waiting for the ladies, who [were] always placed at the head of the table." Gentlemen stood behind their chairs until all the ladies had taken their seats, no matter how long the delay. But once they were seated, etiquette and formality as the Englishman recognized them quickly disappeared, and the Alabama "gentlemen," with only a "broad blade . . . round point" knife to "convey their food to the mouth," turned full attention to the meal.[15]

Those not familiar with southern cuisine found little to praise where steamboat fare was concerned. The food served to Thomas Hamilton and his party in the early 1830s was "scanty in quantity, and far from laudable on the score of quality," a situation made worse by "dirty and disgusting" plates, utensils, and tablecloths. A decade later Buckingham was pleased when stewards generously "loaded the plates with . . . everything asked for," then disgusted when servants so completely buried "the whole in gravies or sauces, that it require[d] a very strong appetite to conquer the repugnance" of it. But a "very strong appetite" was just what the Alabama gentlemen on board possessed, so they bent to their task and spent the meal "busily occupied in despatching their own portions." To Buckingham it appeared that "every one seems to think it a duty to accept and be thankful for whatever is set before him," and perhaps it was. Undistracted and undistractible, a gentleman might finish the meal "in ten minutes or less" and still "chewing his last mouthful" hurry to "the forepart of the vessel, to light his cigar." What had begun so decorously ended abruptly, and the ladies were left to retire on their own.[16]

Bells announced the meals and who would eat them. On board the *Medora* the captain and first-class passengers were seated when the first signal was rung. At the second bell the pilot, the captain's clerk, and all the other white crew and travelers gathered. Finally, a third bell called the black stewards, slaves, and servants to their meal. It was with this last group that free Negroes ate, and it seemed to follow that the mulatto women would take their meals with them. Apparently they refused, and with their refusal the intricate rules of race and caste that defined relations in the South were put to the test. Buckingham had been in Dixie long enough to know that the women "were not high enough in rank to be seated with the whites." At the same time he knew that these women, and probably many whites, believed that "they were too high to be seated with the blacks and [other] mulattoes," even though the slaves appeared willing to accept them. Faced with this impasse the sides struck a compromise, one that preserved valued distinctions and reinforced the relative positions of everyone involved.

The mulatto women "had to retire to the pantry, where they took their meals standing," as if the act of sitting would also violate the code. How the other passengers reacted to this solution can only be surmised, but Buckingham found that "the contrast of [the mulattoes'] finery in dress and ornament, with the place in which they took their isolated and separate meal, was painfully striking."[17]

Most blacks never made it above the cargo deck, but if first-class passengers took the time to look down at the work being done below and considered the implications of what they saw, they knew beyond any doubt that, like the cotton economy, steamboat commerce ran on and was run by slave labor. Black cooks and stewards prepared and served the meals, cleaned the cabins, and waited on the captain, pilot, and the white crew. Black stokers and the firemen kept the furnaces fed and the boilers hot. That they went about their tasks with little enthusiasm was frequently noted, but there was little reason to be enthusiastic. On Buckingham's boat more than half the crew was black, most of them hired from their masters on shore. They were paid the same sum as white hands, about forty dollars a month, but it was apparent that "these poor creatures were scantily fed by the master of the ship, and badly clothed by their owners, who received all their wages." Calculating that no more than five dollars was spent on a slave per month, James Silk Buckingham understood firsthand the profitability and inequity of slavery.[18]

When the Englishman pointed out to fellow passengers "the difference between a slave and a freeman in matters of labour and reward," they assured him "that of the two, the negroes were better off than the white men." This conviction was "constantly asserted" by white Alabamians who argued that because a slave's needs were provided for and because the worries that occupied the minds of free men never troubled them, "they had no *cares*." Buckingham pondered this, and then asked those doing the asserting "whether *they* would like to be 'released from all cares,' by some master taking from them the profits of their labour, and merely feeding them and clothing them instead?" To this question, the Alabamians "made no reply."[19]

When the boat pulled to a landing, slaves were there to take the cotton from other slaves who had brought it from the plantation. It was an operation of some urgency, for profit demanded that the bales be brought on board quickly, even if it was night. Such loadings were frequent, and when the sky was cloudy or the moon was new, men worked by the "strong torchlight" of "pitch-pine" knots whose "resinous matter" burned so brightly that the glare obscured whoever held them, and the fire seemed to move "from spot to spot, without any visible agent." A drawing of the steamboat *Atlanta* at Prairie Bluff in

1842, included in Buckingham's published account, caught the drama of night loading—the eerie flickering light, cotton moving down the slide, and men ready to spring into action when the bales reached the bottom. Meanwhile, on the boiler deck and outside the pilot house, passengers and crew watched a scene that few places in the world could match.[20]

Black Alabamians contributed to the river economy in many ways. When the crops were laid by and there was surplus labor on a plantation, crews were frequently set to work cutting trees that grew tall and straight in the Alabama's swamps and along the waterline. Though the lumber trade was just getting started in the antebellum era, already certain trees were commanding good prices, and high on this list was the cypress. Loggers preferred to cut cypress when it was in standing water and the base of the trunk was submerged. Slaves arrived by boat, surrounded the selected tree, and made fast to it; then reaching above "the huge and hard butress [at the waterline], they fell[ed] it with comparative ease." The timber was then trimmed and floated to the landing where it was pulled out and sawn into lumber. Later in the century, logs would be bound together in large rafts and floated all the way to Mobile. Not every log made it to the mill. Some, those with a dense grain, sank to the bottom and became what rivermen called "deadheads." Submerged for decades, they took from the water a rich whiskey brown color, and in the next century they would be searched out, brought to the surface, and sold to furniture makers at premium prices.[21]

There were also black ferrymen, which made this occupation one of the most integrated on the Alabama. Ferries had been an important element in the regional transportation network since the first settlers reached the river. Some towns owed their location to a ferry, though in most cases town and ferry seemed to appear at about the same time. Between 1810 and 1865 there were at least nine public ferries on the Alabama and no telling how many private ones that appeared and disappeared with the seasons. The boats were usually flats that were polled across by men who lived nearby and farmed to supplement what they earned or, in the case of slaves, what they were given by their masters. A bateau, or skiff, transported light loads and carried the ferryman across when he was caught on the side opposite his ferry and his fare. Until bridges spanned the Alabama, the ferry and the ferryman provided a critical service to the river region.[22]

As traffic on the Alabama increased, accidents increased as well. Most of these came at low water, when snags projected close to the surface and when bars and shoals were particularly dangerous. Buckingham made his trip in May, which was usually a wet month, but that year there had been a "long-prevailing drought of several weeks . . . [and] the river was lower than it had ever been at this season." "The Alabama," he complained, "was now so shallow that vessels drawing more than six feet could not ascend it," and though his boat was able to make the journey, it "grounded . . . at least twenty times, and backed off again." It was a frustrating experience for the passengers, but happily it gave the Englishman more time to observe and to record his observations.[23]

Low water also meant a narrow channel, so collisions became more frequent as the river dropped. All these factors combined to steadily raise the number of wrecks and sinkings that were reported—and wrecks meant treasure. Most steamboats carried a strongbox where passengers deposited valuables and where receipts for the cargo were stored. When a boat went down its captain and owners tried to recover the safe first, and along the river there were men willing and able to help—most of them bondsmen. Cato, who had once been a slave on a plantation near Pineapple in Wilcox County, remembered stories about his grandfather, "a fine diver [who] used to dive in the Alabama River for things that was wrecked out of boats." Hired by whites, his ancestor used an anchored rope or cable to make his descent easier, and in the murky water he set about "to find things on the bottom of the riverbed." According to Cato, "he used to git a piece of money for doing it," though it is not clear just who kept the payment—the master or Cato's "grandpappy." Most likely the diver's only reward was that among family and friends, in life and after death, he was a legend along the river.[24]

Slaves were also commerce on the Alabama. In Selma in the 1840s "large droves, some hundreds daily, were brought to the town by men . . . whose business it was to trade negroes." John Hardy recalled how "several large buildings were erected . . . especially for the accommodation of negro traders and their property," and how a particular warehouse could hold four to five hundred at one time. On the ground floor of this structure, "a large sitting room was provided for the exhibition of negroes on the market." There planters could inspect and buy, according to Hardy, "blacksmiths, carpenters, bright mullatto girls and women for seamstresses, field hands, [and] women and children of all ages, sizes, and qualities." The largest parcels of slaves were offered for sale in seasons when the demands of picking, ginning, and planting were greatest and prices were best. At one such time in 1835 the crush of human chattel filled facilities to overflowing, and trader James Hall was "fined two dollars for obstructing Franklin street, between Water street and the river bluff, by offering crowds of negroes for sale." But the fine was nothing when compared with the profits to be made. Even during periods of economic uncertainty, slave traders seemed to do well in this region where, in the words of one resident, everyone "either wanted to buy a 'nigger' or 'take a drink.'"[25]

It was Montgomery, however, that held the dubious honor of being the largest slave market on the Alabama. In 1840 nearly half of the town's three thousand residents were black, and almost all of those were slaves. This number increased on slave sale days, when the Montgomery market did its business in a manner unique unto itself. Georgian Richard Habersham reported that when he arrived at the site of the sale, he found "ranges of well dressed negro men and women seated on benches . . . 80 or 100 in all in different parcels." The women, dressed "as the negro women in Georgia usually are for church," simply sat with the men and waited for someone to approach and buy. With the slaves were "two or three sharp, hard featured white men," who kept order and handled the transactions. Habersham witnessed this scene and confided to a friend that "altho born in a slave country, and a slave holder myself, and an advocate of slavery, yet this sight was entirely novel and shocked my feelings"—yet he was at a loss to explain why.[26]

The Montgomery slave market operated in this fashion for another decade; then some residents, mostly "settlers from the North" who had lived there a number of years, became "annoyed at the publicity of this exhibition" and suggested that it "might as well be carried on quietly in a room." The concern, obviously, was for appearances, for with the mounting abolitionist criticism of this commerce in human beings, "out of sight out of mind" was an understandable response. At the same time, none of the critics expressed opposition to slavery itself or to the sale of slaves. If they had any reservations on these points, they kept them to themselves.[27]

In spite of the variety of men and manners on the Alabama, in spite of the many occupations and activities that were part of life on the river, the fact remains that by the middle of the nineteenth century steamboats and their captains were among the most romanticized aspects of the much vaunted "southern way of life." The boats, at least the best of them, were magnificent—large, white with colored trim, the finest of them adorned with the jigsawed decoration that gave rise to the term "steamboat gothic." They were "floating palaces," and the men who commanded them were royalty. But even among kings there was competition, and on the Alabama rival captains tested themselves and their craft in the river's most dangerous and exciting contest—the steamboat race.

Official Alabama frowned on the sport. Passengers were at risk if there was an accident. A collision of racing boats or even vessels not directly involved was a real possibility, and a wrecked boat might block a channel and tie up traffic for weeks. The state legislature expressed its concern in 1841 when it wrote into the criminal code a penalty of two years imprisonment for steamboat racing "by which human life is endangered." As time passed the code was amended and enlarged to include penalties of up to ten years if life was lost—sanctions that applied to pilots and engineers as well as to the captain. But despite these regulations, racing continued, and the public loved it.[28]

On the Alabama, the race best remembered (or at least best recorded, thanks to newspaperman Thomas C. DeLeon) was between the *Senator* and the *Southern Republic*, on the eve of the Civil War. Rising from some unrecorded and perhaps forgotten incident, or maybe from that simple frontiersman's conviction that no one was better than he, the pilots and their boats became rivals, each watching for the opportunity to best the other. Then one evening, at a spot where the river was "pretty wide and the channel deep and clear," they got their chance. The *Senator* approached quickly from the rear, and almost before the *Southern Republic* was aware of the challenge, the race was on. In an instant, with "both engines roaring and snorting like angry hippopotami; both vessels rocking and straining til they seem[ed] to paw their way through the churned water," each boat sought to best the other. The passengers, whom the law was so gallantly passed to protect, were caught up in the excitement. Among those on board, DeLeon watched as they came out to see: first "the unemployed deckhands, then a stray gentleman or two, and finally ladies and children, till the rail [was] full and every eye [was] anxiously straining to the opposite boat." No one wanted to miss the show.[29]

Then the pilot of the *Southern Republic* miscalculated a turn, and his opponent gained the advantage. With fires so hot that "the shores behind her glow[ed] from their reflection," the *Senator* steamed by her rival, showing as she passed the open furnace door and the "negro stokers . . . like distorted imps of some pictured inferno," heaving into the box "huge logs of resinous pine, already heated by contact till they burn[ed] like pitch." The furnace door closed; the lower deck went black, and the *Senator* raced ahead with only the sparks from her stacks to mark her in the night.

All was quiet on the *Southern Republic* as they watched the *Senator*'s wake. Then the pilot, in a rough whisper that carried through the silence, took the oath: "Damnation! but I'll overstep her yit, or—bust!"

Then it was excitement again. Even the "colonel," who at the start of the race had come on deck "in a shooting jacket and glengary cap" to smoke his cabana with the ease of a man who had seen it all before, was taken by the moment and declared himself willing to "burn the last ham in the locker to overtake her." A gentleman on board offered to "stand the wine" if the pilot "let her out," but his gesture, though appreciated, was unnecessary.

Everything was put to the effort. Stokers plied "their fires with the fattest logs, and even a few barrels of rosin were slyly slipped in"; as she gathered speed "the trees on the bank seem[ed] to fly back past"; "with every glass on board jingling in its frame; every joint and timber trembling, as though with a congestive chill," the *Southern Republic* pushed on.

She caught her rival at "a straight, narrow reach," and as she passed the pilot sang out "Good-bye, Sen'tor! I'll send yer a tug!"

The deck erupted in celebration. "Cheer after cheer" was raised, and the calliope played "Old Gray Horse, come out of the Wilderness." Behind them the enemy faded from view. Everyone agreed that "there is no excitement that can approach boat-racing on a southern river."

Back in the wheelhouse the pilot and his gentlemen admirers made good use of the wine that was his reward, and the colonel (somewhat in his cups) passed judgment on the event as only a southern colonel could: "Egad!" he exclaimed. "I'd miss my dinner for a week for this! Gentlemen, a toast! Here's to the old boat! God bless her ——— ——— soul!"

It was a fitting tribute to an event and to an era.

SEVEN

The Orline St. John

It was delightful for me to stand on the bluff and see the grand old
steamers of fifty years ago, sailing on the broad Alabama, or in the
still hours of the night, hearing the puffing up to the landing, like
some huge monster of the ocean. Little did I dream that a steamboat
on the water would ever bring me to such sorrow.

ANGELINE ELIZABETH EILAND CAMMACK
August 18, 1884

William Harris was deadheading when he saw the hog-chains. It was
the summer of 1954; a drought had been hanging on for weeks, and the
Alabama was low, real low, so it was a good time to hunt for sunken
logs. Curious, Harris moved his boat over to where the metal stuck out
of the water and confirmed what he had found. Hog-chains are not
chains at all but "stay rods" that were used to stabilize the hull of
steamboats that once plied the river. As he moved closer Harris could
see that the rods were attached to the frame of what was once a boat, its
bow (or what appeared to be the bow) resting just out of the water
against the bank. William Harris had found a wreck.[1]

Harris was a river man. Although he owned a store at nearby 'Possum Bend in Wilcox County and was an artist of some note, the
Alabama River was, in his words, "my heart throb." During his forty-
four years, he had never been far from the stream. Master of many
trades, he was a boat builder, a fisherman, a lumberman, and a dead-
header. And like most people who loved the river, he was something of
a historian. All his life he had heard stories of steamboat disasters and
had wondered what might be found if a wreck was located. Now it
looked as if he had one.[2]

Leaving the site just long enough to go home, get a swimsuit, and
recruit a couple of friends—Buford and Gilbert Hollinger—Harris
returned and began diving that same day. The process was simple; as he
put it, "we'd just hold our damn breath and go down"—but it quickly
brought results. Working around pieces of the ship's timber that stuck
out from the water, they determined the outline of the hull and concentrated their efforts there. Soon the divers began to find things in the
mud and silt, and as they brought to the surface pieces of twisted metal,
nails, buttons, bits of copper, and scraps of leather and cloth, their
excitement grew. Then one of them came up with a piece of broken
dinnerware, with something written on it. As they washed away the
muck, the bright blue words came clear: "*Orline St. John* Tim Meaher."[3]

* * *

By 1850 Tim Meaher had been on steamboats for fifteen of his forty years and was one of the most respected captains on the river. He was also one of the most successful. Beginning his career as a mate, he worked his way through the ranks, honed his skills, and saved his money. Finally, in 1846 he quit working for others, purchased the *William Bradford*, and began working for himself. Although competition on the river was fierce, Meaher prospered, and by 1847 he had accumulated the capital to have a boat constructed to his personal specifications. Built in New Albany, Indiana, she was a sidewheeler, 215 feet long, with a 33-foot beam. The local newspaper praised her as "the most thorough steamboat that ever graced the western waters." Her thirty-eight cabins and saloon contained "furniture of the richest and most fashionable styles . . . with bedsteads, handsomely curtained"; her carpets were of a "beauty, style and quality" that could not be surpassed; and her designer thought to include a "nursery immediately under the Ladies cabin." Of particular note was the heating system, which abandoned the use of stoves in passenger quarters in favor of hot air blown into the cabins "through a long sheet iron flue" from a furnace in the front of the boat, so there was "less danger of accident by fire." She was quite a vessel, even by Mississippi and Ohio river standards, and when she was launched her proud owner was ready with a name. Among his neighbors in Mobile was the St. John family. They had a beautiful daughter named Orline, to whom Meaher was attracted. He named the boat *Orline St. John*.[4]

On the first of March, 1850, the *Orline St. John* prepared for the upriver trip to Montgomery, a voyage that would depend heavily on passenger revenue, freight, and what merchant goods the stores of Claiborne, Cahawba, Selma, and Montgomery needed to replenish winter-depleted stocks. But the run promised to be profitable, for with some fifty to seventy passengers, including a number of women and children, the first-class cabins were filled, and the lower deck was crowded. When everyone was on board—passengers and crew—the total may have exceeded 120. Completing the cargo were crates of dry goods, boxes of hardware, travelers' trunks, and the "entire collection" of a French artist, Monsieur Annrien, who was painting a diorama of the main cities on the route between New Orleans and New York. Having already completed a painting of Mobile, Annrien had gone ahead to Montgomery to paint that city and to arrange an exhibit of the canvases when they arrived.[5]

Among the passengers on the *Orline St. John* was Joseph Addison Cammack of Perry County. Originally from Indiana, he had come to Alabama as a young man, married Angeline Eiland, a girl from one of the pioneer families in the region, and settled in the Cahaba valley as a sawmill operator, artisan, merchant, and planter—professions that placed his family high in frontier society. But by the 1840s a combination of national depression and personal ambition convinced him that the time was right to move to greener pastures. His son had relocated earlier and owned a plantation on Biloxi Bay in southern Mississippi, so Cammack was naturally attracted to that region. In 1849 he visited there and liked what he saw. He bought land, built a house, and then announced that "he was going after old Mistress, [for] it was getting time she was there." Shortly he left for Mobile, where he would catch a steamer for home. Because Mobile was a busy port, many vessels awaited him, but Cammack knew how to select the best. As a young man on the Cahaba, he had "built a boat expressly for that stream," and now, in his middle age, he was a veteran river traveler. Joseph Cammack booked passage on the *Orline St. John.*[6]

On board with Cammack was George F. Lindsay, a Pennsylvania-born and educated lawyer who had come South in the 1830s. Arriving in the middle of the state's "flush times," he found central Alabama a land of opportunity and made the most of it. A man of "generous impulses" whom friends described as "true-hearted," "noble," and "chivalric," he was welcomed in the region and soon joined the office of one of Lowndes County's leading attorneys. In 1840 he married the daughter of a prominent Wilcox County family and secured his place in Black Belt society. But his talents could not be confined to rural Alabama. That same year he moved to Mobile, where he soon became one of the city's most respected jurists. Now he was on his way to Selma, "to attend to some matters connected with his wife's estate" and to see his many friends.[7]

At least seven women and maybe as many children were on board the *Orline.* Among these was Mrs. John Hall of Georgia, who was traveling with Miss Laura Hall of St. Louis, "a beautiful young girl in her teens," who was apparently Mrs. Hall's niece. In St. Louis they had been "placed in the care of a young man" who had business in Mobile. When they arrived at the Alabama port, the gentleman assured them that if they would stay with him in the city an extra day while he attended to his affairs, he would "see them safely landed at Selma" where Mrs. Hall's daughter waited. Mobile was pleasant in March, and the young man was a delightful companion, so they tarried. After all, what difference would a day make?[8]

There were others. Mrs. McCain and her young son were on their way to South Carolina. Mrs. Vaughan and her daughter were returning from a visit with friends in Mobile. Preston Noland and Edward Maul were traveling home from the goldfields of California, their sacks of gold dust safely stored in the boat's strongbox. With this treasure was $250,000 in government gold that was in the charge of Purser Price of the U.S. Navy. Also on board were F. H. Brooks, a Mobile bookseller; Dr. John Daniel Caldwell, a physician and one of the founders of Camden; a wealthy South Carolinian, Colonel J. W. Preston; a printer, Thomas Stephens; and Thomas Carson and his young son, bound for their home in Dallas County. These men, women, and children, along with every other passenger on the boat, put their lives and their fortunes in the hands of Capt. Tim Meaher, his brother and first mate, Burns Meaher, and the crew of the *Orline St. John*.[9]

The river was running high from spring rains when the boat moved away from the dock and steamed into the channel. Along most of the route the stream was out of its banks, and instead of a shoreline all passengers could see were the branches of trees, dipping into the current. Moving against the swift flow called for more steam, and the stacks of fat pine that fed the boilers went down fast. With the river up, stops at makeshift woodyard landings were difficult; so when the *Orline* could get to shore the captain loaded as much fuel as the deck would hold—stacking it right up to the mouth of the furnace that would consume it.[10]

Captain Meaher knew that if he reached Montgomery by Wednesday, March 6, his passengers and freight could meet the train scheduled to depart that day, so he "had been pushing the boat" since they left Mobile. Three days into the journey it appeared that he would make it. Early on the afternoon of March 5, the *Orline St. John* docked at Bridgeport, on the river north of Camden, where it took on "an unusually large quantity of wood—rich, light, wood." Then the pilot turned her bow back into the current, and the captain went up to his cabin to take a nap before they reached the next stop. By now "a very strong wind [was] blowing," and combined with the current, it made progress upriver even more difficult. Trying to get all the steam they could, firemen stoked the furnaces to their limits, and as the heat grew the "pitch pine" stacked nearby began to bleed resin. Soon seasoned travelers noticed that the upper decks of the boat were becoming "excessively hot." The *Orline St. John* was a floating tinderbox.[11]

Just before five in the evening about three miles above Bridgeport, sparks from the furnace blew into the stack of resin-soaked logs, and they burst into flames. Believing they could control the blaze, firemen did not immediately raise the alarm, but the fire advanced quickly and soon spread across the midsection of the boat. Fire was a steamboatman's nightmare, and every pilot knew what to do if one broke out—run the boat ashore so passengers could escape across the bow. But this strategy would not work for the *Orline St. John*. Flames had engulfed the forward staircase, cutting off most passengers from the front of the vessel. Their only hope was the lifeboat, a small yawl tied to the stern.[12]

Unaware of conditions below, the pilot, Benjamin Pearce, did as he had been taught and made every effort to reach land. But with the water high, overhanging trees blocked his way, and he had to continue upstream to find an opening. A century later William Harris still could see the charred trees that traced the path, five hundred feet long, where the burning boat skidded along the shore. Finally, Pearce found a large canebrake, but by then the wheel ropes were almost burned through, and he was losing control of the rudder. Immediately, the pilot ordered "the engineer to stop one engine and give all steam to the other." That threw the boat into a hard turn, and *Orline St. John* "rushed across the river with such force as to break down three large trees on the river bank." There it stuck fast.[13]

The first mate secured the bow, while "the engineer, remaining at his post, turned loose the hot water cocks, let off steam, and kept the engine at work, pumping in cold water, so to prevent an explosion." He stayed on the job "until his clothes were literally burned off," and then he rushed to the front and with the fortunate few who were forward, leaped to safety. According to later reports, although under three minutes had elapsed since the alarm was raised, the midsection of the boat was aflame, and the pilot had lost all control of the vessel. With her bow stuck on shore the stern of the *Orline St. John*, where most of the passengers had crowded, swung out into the river, where the current ran "with as great rapidity as in any portion of its course." Immediately, those trapped in the rear rushed for the lifeboat, but it was not there. Later some survivors claimed that frightened crewmen took the yawl and left everyone else to their fate; others reported that deckhands launched the yawl only to discover it had no oars, and they drifted away before they could help with the rescue. What actually happened mattered little to those still on board. Either way, that avenue of escape was gone.[14]

All the women and children had been in the rear when the fire broke out, so they were among those trapped. Far from land, in the deepest and swiftest part of the river, the ladies dressed in the layered and hooped skirts that were the fashion had little hope of reaching shore even if they could swim. The flames continued to spread, and soon the boat was a "sheet of fire, and there was great danger of the cabins falling on them." Panic was everywhere. Survivors recounted how one woman climbed to the wheel house, hoping to escape the heat and smoke, and from there tried to leap to safety. She failed, some obstruction caught her dress, and she hung there until "flames released her," and she fell into the river and drowned. In another instance, a "mother placed her child on a matress" and tried to float to shore, but despite the efforts of the first mate, "she and the object of her final struggles were soon buried beneath the waters." And in the confusion a deck passenger was first "seen on her knees enveloped in flames" and then seen "to cast herself from the burning wreck" into the river and disappear. Meanwhile, the air was filled with "crys for help" which, according to one survivor, "can never be erased from my memory."[15]

Similar fates awaited the rest of the women and children. The gentleman in whose care Mrs. Hall and her companion had been placed found his charges huddled at the stern with the others. Surveying the situation, he told them that he could not save both but offered to get one to shore. Neither "would desert the other and they died together while the young man swam to safety." Thomas Carson took his son and tried to make it to the bank, but the current was strong, and the chilling March water sapped his strength. Although he was "encouraged in his failing exertions by the heroic boy," both were drowned. Joseph Addison Cammack was also at the rear of the boat. Unable to help the remaining women, he and a friend decided that taking to the water was their only hope. Before he jumped, Cammack hesitated, murmured "what an awful scene," and stepped back for his saddlebags. No sooner had he turned than a box thrown from above by a deck hand "crushed his head." He fell into the Alabama and was gone.[16]

With every minute that passed the casualties mounted. Like so many others, F. H. Brooks tried to swim but drowned. Mrs. Vaughan simply went into her stateroom, closed the door, and died in the fire and smoke. As for Judge Lindsay, one witness claimed "that he leaped from the boat into the water and was drowned in his efforts to save a lady," while another told of how "he was seen in the after part of the boat, enveloped in smoke, as the flames approached, with a young girl by his side." The *Alabama Planter*, in publishing the reports, suggested that perhaps "both of these accounts are true and only represent different periods of the catastrophe." That may well have been the case, but conflicting stories also reflect the chaos and confusion of the moment. Some years later the judge's son, George F. Lindsay, Jr., wrote that his family had been told that his father was actually forward when the fire broke out, so when the *Orline* ran ashore, he easily made it to safety. Then the judge "remembered there were several young ladies aboard the boat, without escorts." Disregarding his own safety, "he immediately jumped into the swollen Alabama" and being "a skillful swimmer" made it to the stern of the vessel. Just then "a heavy trunk was thrown overboard"; it struck him on the head and "rendered him unconscious." Like Cammack, he sank.[17]

Some were more fortunate and made it to safety. A number of men (nine according to one report) leaped overboard and "floated down to Bridgeport on boards and barrels." Four of them were brought ashore at the landing, but the others were swept on downstream. Rescuers went after them, and eventually all were saved, "the last after the shades of night had gathered over them, and exhausted[,] numbed, and cramped, they had given up all hope." The current was so swift that another man floated several miles before he could land, while one survivor, according to local tradition, rode "a chicken-coop down the river about thirty miles to safety. Downstream from the stricken boat, men struggled in "death agonies, to reach the shore." Some made it to safety; many did not.[18]

News of the disaster spread quickly, and that night a "telegraphic dispatch" from Cahawba told towns along the river how "the fine steamer *Orline St. John* was burned"; that it was "a total loss"; and that the casualty toll was "fearful." Other reports soon followed. Newspapers seized on every scrap of information, copied from each other and expanded each account; yet, even without these editorial embellishments the extent of the catastrophe was clear. The boat "was consumed entirely to the water's edge," and everything on board was lost "except a trunk belonging to Col. Preston, which his servant threw over the bow into the cane-brake." As for the passengers, within a few days the number of dead had risen past thirty, and back on the scene they were still counting.[19]

Citizens of Wilcox County, on whose shore the *Orline* had burned, responded quickly to the disaster. They formed a committee, and patrols watched and dragged the river "in daylight and at night with torches." Ladies of Camden and vicinity prepared food for these volunteers and made "grave-clothes for the dead." There was much to be done. Wilcox judge Fleetwood Foster, only a boy of seven or eight at the time, remembered that the tragedy was his "first acquaintance with death" and that "for many days thereafter the swollen corpses were borne through our little town." Among these was F. H. Brooks, whose body could be identified only by the papers he carried. Among his effects they also found his watch. It had stopped at "17½ minutes past 5."[20]

Survivors were taken to nearby houses where Dr. Caldwell, although himself "severely injured by the fire," ministered to the sufferers as best he could. Meanwhile local residents, "unaccustomed to such scenes, stopped all work to render aid to the afflicted." Steadily, the death toll mounted. By March 25 at least thirty-nine bodies had been recovered, and other passengers were still missing. Captain Meaher and his brother were among those who escaped, but at least thirteen members of the crew were lost, including the second mate. The remaining twenty-six dead were passengers, including every woman and child on board.[21]

Several days after the disaster and some fifty miles downstream, Judge Lindsay's body was taken from the river by the steamboat *Beacon*. The only mark on the body was "a wound in the head," and although his features had been altered by the time spent in the water, he "was identified very readily by papers found in the clothes." Since the *Beacon* was on her downstream voyage, some friends of the judge who were on the *Mary Clifton* heading upriver took charge of the remains. The body was carried to Wilcox County, where he had met and married his wife, and in Camden he was laid to rest. Judge Foster recalled the scene—how they stood by the grave, "eyes fixed on the coffin" and "thoughts busy with the events of the past few days." Then, just as the minister pronounced "the solemn 'dust to dust and ashes to ashes,'" the distant whistle of a boat signaled its arrival at Bridgeport. Instantly, "tears came to all eyes" as the mourners turned in the direction of the sound.[22]

Back in Perry County, Angeline Elizabeth Cammack waited for her husband, unaware of the fate of the *Orline St. John*. A neighbor, who heard the report first but could not bring himself to tell her, passed the word along to Cammack's nephew. The young man rode to his uncle's house but found when he arrived that he too could not break the news. Although Mrs. Cammack knew something troubled him "by his looks," he kept it from her until the next day. Then, he finally collected himself and told her that "his uncle was lost." Angeline Cammack "caught hold of him, almost frantic, and asked what he had done to be killed." The Alabama frontier was a violent place, and death could come in many ways, but at that moment, she remembered, "the boat never crossed my mind." Then he told her.[23]

Meanwhile, survivors along the river took stock of what had been lost and what had been saved. Passengers like the California gold seekers, who had "all the rewards of a life of toil" taken from them, and others who were "deprived even of necessary clothing" felt lucky to be alive and "proceeded with thankfulness to their families." In the days that followed passengers praised the "almost unparalleled kindness and deep sympathy manifested by the people in the vicinity of the wreck," and some of the rescued published a notice in the *Alabama Planter* commending the "devoted courage and energy" of Tim Meaher, his brother, and the pilot. It was a tragic accident; no one was at fault, and everyone seemed sure that the captain of the boat would not be denied the "sympathy of the public in this his terrible misfortune."[24]

Also singled out for praise was "the noble conduct of Abram, a slave . . . who, at infinite peril and labor, rescued nine persons floating in the river several miles below the wreck." "Such an act of heroism," correspondents observed, "has rarely been witnessed, and should place this man . . . beside those who have received the highest testimonials for the voluntary preservation of human life." And then there was "that model of the American gentleman, Colonel Preston," who not only survived the wreck, but in the weeks that followed opened his "princely purse to the destitute sufferers" and took care of their needs. Some who helped received more than thanks. When the officers of the steamer *Emperor* were praised for "their liberality in offering [the rescued] a free passage and distributing clothing," fifteen signers "recommended this fine and admirably conducted vessel to the traveling public"—an endorsement that was worth much in the competitive world of Alabama steamboats.[25]

The *Orline St. John* was insured for $16,000, a sum that helped Captain Meaher recover and prosper during the next decade. He and his brother raised the capital to open a shipbuilding firm in Mobile, and before he quit steamboating in 1870 he had an interest in or owned outright at least six more Alabama "floating palaces." On the eve of the Civil War he was master of and shareholder in one of the grandest boats afloat—the *Southern Republic*, built by the Meaher Brothers Company—and may have been the unnamed captain who raced that vessel against the *Senator*. After his retirement, Captain Meaher became something of a legend along the river. In 1890, Isaac Grant, editor of the *Clarke County Democrat*, sought him out and asked him to reminisce about his career. Though over eighty years old, he still clearly recalled the names of the boats he had owned and commanded, including the *Orline St. John*. But despite his keen memory, he made no mention of the wreck.[26]

Meaher's post-*Orline* success may have been simply a testament to his skill as a businessman, but rumors persisted that there was more to his recovery than met the eye. Though it was later reported that Purser Price had only $15,000 in gold, not the $250,000 published earlier, that cache, plus the money and gold dust that other passengers had carried, made the *Orline St. John* a rich salvage. In the summer, when the waters began to recede, word got out that someone (possibly Meaher) had brought divers from the Caribbean who searched the wreck and took the treasure, but no one came forth to confirm the story.[27]

Upriver in Montgomery, Monsieur Annrien, upon hearing of the loss of his paintings, was inspired to replace them with "a diorama of the burning ship." Working quickly, he produced "a grand scene," which included fire created by "transparency lights" placed "behind the canvas with the room darkened," the "appearance" of the boat collapsing, and "people jumping into the water." As a final, dramatic touch, an associate described how the lights gradually were extinguished behind the canvas; the flames expired, and darkness covered the scene. Well received in Montgomery, the artist took his exhibit to Selma and then to Marion. From there he planned three more stops before he returned to Montgomery.[28]

It is unlikely Mrs. Cammack went to see the diorama when Annrein was in Perry County. The memory was too fresh, and besides, she had begun to sell her husband's land and to prepare to move. This transaction occupied her through the summer, and by fall everything was done. Then her party began what she remembered as its "lonely and cheerless drive" to Mississippi—a widow, her five children and their black nurse, heading west "in the cool October winds."[29]

When Harris identified the wreck, he tried to find out all he could about the *Orline St. John* and its cargo. His research soon led him to newspaper accounts of California gold dust, of what Purser Price had brought on board, and of the "strongbox." Now he really got excited.[30]

Friends and neighbors got excited too, and when the divers "found a quarter or two" in the wreckage, "the news spread like wildfire." Soon the newspapers were writing about the "Wilcox Gold Hunters" and the "treasure" that lay at the bottom of the Alabama. Curious sightseers descended on the scene, coming upriver (it seemed to Harris) "in everything from horse troughs to damn might near zinc tubs." As the crowd grew the divers became concerned for the future of their find.[31]

To secure the site, Harris sought legal help and by the end of 1956 obtained salvage rights to the wreck. All the while the divers continued. After hooking up a "centrifugal pump" to blow away the mud and silt, they began to work the whole length of the boat and in the process probably blew as much out of the hull as they exposed within it. Still, they brought up an impressive array of artifacts—dishes, razors, knives, forks, needles, thimbles, buttons, shoes, bolts of cloth, barrels, kegs, thousands of nails, and a lump of molten metal that appeared to be lead. They also found items that personalized the tragedy: "a miniature locket" with a "blue and pink enameled design" that was surely worn by one of the women who perished and a "dainty baby dress" that had survived the fire and almost a century underwater but fell to pieces when it dried.[32]

What they did not find was gold. Although the newspaper reported them bringing up "lumps of coins which have been melted together by intense heat [and] other monies in perfect condition with their milled edges showing no signs of wear," these hardly constituted a treasure. They did find pieces of what apparently was a strongbox, but if it once held gold, no trace of it remained. Perhaps the river claimed it; perhaps the rumors of divers brought in by Captain Meaher were true. Still, Harris and his friends kept at it. Working in the late summer and early fall, when the river was low and the weather still warm, they mined the wreck again and again, and soon Harris had such a collection of artifacts on display at his store that he was considering opening a museum.[33]

Then everything came to an end. By 1969 a Corps of Engineers dam was under construction at Miller's Ferry, about twenty miles below the site of the wreck. Efforts to raise money for one last, large salvage operation failed, and Harris had to give in. Slowly the Alabama backed up, leaving the hull and all that remained within it under forty feet of water. Once again, the *Orline St. John* was at rest.[34]

EIGHT

Alabama's Last Frontier: The Coosa and the Tallapoosa

I have been to the Creek nation again . . . and have selected a place
there, or places for us all, which I think comes as near suiting in all,
as I can get. I will give you a description of its advantages &
disadvantages viz. *Health* undoubted, Good Water & a plenty of it,
Good range, Good fishing, land that will produce from 6[oo] to
1000 lbs seed cotton per acre, and from 15 to 30 Bushels corn per
acre, All this lies within 10 to 12 miles of Steam Boat navigation.

JOEL SPIGENER to WILLIAM K. OLIVER
Autauga County, August 18, 1833

As the Coosa rushed over the steps of the "staircase," dashed against
metamorphic reefs, and poured into whirling pools, it created a roar
that was heard for miles. Here was the final leap from uplands to
lowlands, and here was the final test of the boatman's skill as he
guided his load of iron or lumber or cotton into steamboat waters.
Just below lay the entrepot of Wetumpka, at the Coosa-Tallapoosa
junction, where dealers and agents were ready to take over rafts and
freight from the up-countrymen for shipment down the Alabama.
The up-countrymen made their return overland, and often had to
become footmen as they hit the trail homeward. They have handed
down stories of covering as much as ninety miles in two days.

H. C. NIXON
Lower Piedmont Country, 1946

In 1814 the Treaty of Fort Jackson gave the Creeks most of the land
between the Coosa River and the Georgia line. When compared to
what the tribe once held, it was not much; but the land was good, and
within it, especially between the rivers, the Indians seemed safe from
covetous whites. The Coosa marked a well-defined boundary that
squatters could not claim to cross by accident, and its rapids made
getting goods to market difficult, which discouraged white settlement
along the western bank, across from the Creek reserve. To the south the
rich Black Belt beckoned immigrants, so it seemed reasonable that with
good land and better navigation to be had elsewhere, the Indians would
be left alone.[1]

But if the Treaty of Fort Jackson was designed to give the Creeks a
sanctuary between the rivers, the plan contained a fatal flaw. Land deep
in "the Fork," where the Coosa and Tallapoosa joined to form the
Alabama, was not included in the "nation." It became part of Montgomery County and was soon opened for settlement. This parcel gave

whites a foothold across the streams, where there was no geographic barrier to separate them from tribal holdings. Immigrants quickly moved into the rich bottoms and "table lands," and on that prime real estate "a wealthier class of farmers" rose to prominence. At first these settlers were few, and since their interests seemed connected to the river culture emerging downstream, the Creeks believed, or at least hoped, that their land was safe. They should have known better.[2]

Other forces were also at work to break down the Indians' isolation. For some time whites had been interested in opening a water route from Tennessee to Montgomery and then to the Gulf, a route that would take commerce down the Coosa, the Creek nation's western boundary. As the population north and south of the Creek lands grew, communication and trade between the two regions became a greater concern. The solution selected by residents of East Tennessee was to carry their goods down the Tennessee River to its juncture with the Hiwassee, then up that stream to a point only some twelve miles from the headwaters of the Coosa. The portage from stream to stream was relatively easy, and once done it was a clear float until the fall line. The shoals and ledges that followed could be navigated at high water, as could the last great rapid, the "Devil's Staircase," just above the river's juncture with the Tallapoosa. It would not be a simple trip, but it could be done, and there were those ready to do it.[3]

It is difficult to say just when this commerce began, but in 1818, some settlers in the East Tennessee region made the trip with flatboats. The run must have been profitable, for trade increased rapidly. Soon boat houses were built at landings at either end of the portage, and local entrepreneurs made a good living hauling vessels from one stream to the other. Whiskey was the main commodity, and in 1821 an estimated 12,000 gallons were carried across. By then keelboats, some over fifty feet long, were making the trip, and "flour, cyder, green and dried fruit," and other produce were being listed as part of the cargo. Though roads were still the major means of transportation in the region, the river was becoming an attractive alternative to many.[4]

Along the way, boatmen were free to trade with whites who had begun to settle on the west side of the river but not with tribes on the east. Efforts to enforce restrictions on commerce with the Indians, however, seemed to do more to enrage whites than protect the natives. In 1825, James and Samuel Reid of McMinn County, Tennessee, set out for the Coosa. They never made it. A Cherokee nation official arrested them on the portage and, according to their affidavit, "violently took six hundred and fifty-three gallons of whiskey, and seventy-three gallons of peach brandy," along with twenty barrels of flour—an accounting that suggests the magnitude of the trade and makes it clear what sold best in

Alabama. The Reids continued with what they were allowed to keep, but with whiskey selling for up to a dollar a gallon and flour bringing twelve dollars at Cahawba, their loss was considerable.[5]

The post–War of 1812 interest in internal improvements and the subsequent "canal boom" meant that it was only a matter of time before someone would propose a water link between the Coosa and Tennessee. When the idea came up, both states agreed that it was a good one, and in 1823 the Alabama legislature went so far as to charter the Coosa Navigation Company. Little came of it, for the next year Secretary of War John C. Calhoun's report on the transportation needs of the United States concluded that a Muscle Shoals canal on the Tennessee River was more important and should receive federal support; but national priorities were only part of the problem, as anyone who lived below the fall line clearly knew.[6]

For a Coosa-Hiwassee canal to benefit the lower Alabama region, commerce would need to flow both ways—over or around the falls on the lower Coosa. Floating over these rapids at high water, though always dangerous, was simple when compared to getting back upstream. An 1820 survey on the navigability of this stretch of water clarified the situation. "To be able to ascend the river," according to the report, "it will be necessary to insert ring bolts in the rocks at suitable distances, to which the boatmen may attach stout ropes." Then, "aided by a windlass" they would be able to work their way through the rocks. The report also suggested a special boat for the journey, "a batteau built with a tray-head . . . [and] with splash boards temporarily fixed on their gunwales which would prevent water dashing over the sides." Though the author was certain that "these boats could at all times navigate the river and be easily managed," their construction suggests just how dangerous the rapids were and how difficult navigation would be. This difficulty, combined with the cost of building the boats and preparing the river route, dissuaded even the most energetic advocates of the project, and though the plan died a lingering death, it died nonetheless.[7]

Boatmen on the river and settlers on the west bank coveted the land set aside for the Creeks, but farther south, in the region in and near "the Fork," contact with whites was taking its greatest toll on the Indians. There, according to Lafayette's secretary, Levasseur, "persons whom the love of gain had assembled from all parts of the globe" set about "to turn to their own profit the simplicity and above all the new wants of the unfortunate natives." The Frenchman was appalled by the way the Creeks were treated in a village near the Tallapoosa, and he left the scene thinking "poor Indians! You are pillaged, beaten, poisoned or excited by intoxicating liquors, and then you are termed savaged." All along the Indian frontier conditions were much the same, for the region had become a haven for fugitives from the law, whiskey traders, and "avaricious wretches" of every description.[8]

Some citizens of Alabama were determined to end this situation— not by removing the lawless but by removing the Indians. An insatiable desire for land, plus a philosophical (and pragmatic) allegiance to the theory of state rights, gave Alabamians reason and rationale for selecting this solution; and since it was popular in other states, the pressure on Washington to adopt it as well was impossible to resist. In 1832 the Creeks signed the Treaty of Cusseta and ceded all their land east of the Mississippi, except individual holdings, which would be theirs if they occupied them for five years. The government agreed to remove intruders from the nation and protect the Indians who remained, but the promise could not, or would not, be kept. Whites began moving in almost immediately; Alabama's Gov. John Gayle defended the squatters, and the Indians' fate was sealed.[9]

"Everything as we advance into the Creek country," wrote an English visitor in 1835, "announced the total dissolution of order." The decline of the tribe was rapid and complete. Drunkenness was epidemic; warriors were reduced to beggars; women and children went naked and hungry; thieves, renegades, and land speculators preyed on them; and finally that ancient curse, smallpox, returned to decimate their ranks. Some of the Indians' resistance to white encroachments raised rumors that a new Creek War was imminent. Troops were sent, suspects were captured and collected, and in July of 1836, 489 Indians, manacled and chained, were loaded onto steamboats and taken down the Alabama. By the time the removal ended in 1838, some 4,000 Indians were sent from Montgomery to Mobile and from there taken west. Not all of them made it. The Alabama River was the Creek's Trail of Tears.[10]

For every white man who crossed the Coosa and Tallapoosa to exploit the Indians, there were scores who came for land and for the opportunity that went with it. Though not oblivious to the Indians' plight, these immigrants paid only incidental attention to what individual Creeks owned or did. The Treaty of Cusseta put vast tracts under federal jurisdiction, and its disposition was their main concern. They represent the last great migration into the Alabama River region, and their arrival set in motion the events that brought the land between the Coosa and Tallapoosa into the affairs of the state of Alabama.[11]

My own ancestors, the Spigeners and the Olivers, were fairly typical of this group. They had come to the Orangeburg District of South Carolina in the 1750s, received land from the royal government, and settled down to the life of frontier farmers. At least one of them served on the Whig side in the Revolution, but (according to family tradition) some were Loyalists, a stance that kept them at odds with their neighbors long after the war was over. In time the families grew, their acres multiplied, and they became slaveholders—middling planters of the sort common to that region. This way of life survived the War of 1812 well enough, but in the aftermath stories of rich Alabama land and declining prospects in Carolina proved enough to inspire some of them to join the westward movement. About 1817 a large contingent from the Orangeburg District—Spigeners, Whetstones, Zeiglers, Stoudenmires, and others—arrived in Autauga County and settled along the river. There they farmed the rich bottom land, floated goods downstream to market, witnessed the arrival of the age of the steamboat, and generally prospered. They also kept watch on what was happening in and to the Indian nation.[12]

These settlers sent glowing reports of the Alabama region to relatives in Carolina, and even before the Treaty of Cusseta was signed, relocating west was an increasingly attractive idea. News of the settlement with the Creeks was enough for Joel Spigener. Thirty-five years old, married with three children, a younger son in a large family, he was ready for new prospects. In 1833, Spigener traveled the Federal Road to Montgomery, crossed the river there, and moved in with his uncle, whose house would serve as his home and headquarters while he searched for the piece of land on which he would make his fortune. But he was not looking for himself alone. Joel Spigener was the advance man, the scout, for the rest of the family, which waited in South Carolina while he found land for them all.[13]

In the summer of 1833, shortly after he arrived in Alabama, Spigener began writing back to William K. Oliver who, as a result of the system of unions that often bound frontier families together, was Joel's stepbrother and brother-in-law. Spigener's responsibility was to find the land and make the purchase; Oliver would bring the family out. Although only Spigener's letters have survived, and not in the best of condition, the correspondence between the men reveals just how carefully planned migration into Alabama was for many. These were not families who had failed in the east and were moving west to make a new start. They had done well enough back in Carolina, as records of their efforts to sell their Orangeburg land and collect debts owed to them clearly reveal. Alabama was opportunity, not escape, and they were ready and able to take the risk.[14]

The venture was not without hazards, and as Spigener observed when his mare died and spring planting was threatened, "missfortuns never come Single"; but despite such problems, he continued to urge family and friends back east to make the trip. His letters were filled with praise for a country "whose soil and production are superior to Carolina," a region blessed with "many beautiful millseats, and the best springs my eyes ever beheld." His only complaints were that things were moving too slowly and that he might be "compelled to play squat" on the land he wanted until the government put it on the market. But finally the restrictions were lifted, and Spigener entered the nation with the other land-hungry settlers who had been waiting with him. He made his choice quickly, perhaps knowing all along which lot he wanted, then proudly wrote Oliver of the land he had claimed for them. The "*Health*" of the tract was "undoubted"; it had "Good Water & a plenty of it, Good range, Good fishing"; and most important, the soil "would produce from 6[oo] to 1000 lbs seed cotton per acre, and from 15 to 30 Bushels corn per acre." Then, for the final touch, Spigener observed that "all this lies within 10 to 12 miles of Steam Boat navigation." Any disadvantages were insignificant when compared to the benefits.[15]

Others, however, wanted the same land, so the competition was keen, and Spigener did not get every tract he desired. Still, he was able to secure a "small plantation . . . containing 200 acres . . . in the fork of Coosa & Tallapoosa, Convenient to Market." It was healthy and fertile and had "plenty of neighbors, [and a] School and Church house near." Here they found a "friendly[,] religious kind of people," and Joel's sister, who had accompanied him, reported back after joining the local Methodist church that, "I believe I have enjoyed more religion this year than I ever did." Spigener's purchases were among the first deeds recorded in Coosa County and were only the beginning. Between 1834 and 1836 he bought nearly a thousand acres from the government. All the while he continued to urge those back in Carolina to settle their affairs and come west. In the end he was successful. By 1836 his mother and at least four other family members had settled in the region. All their Orangeburg District property was sold, except "one half acre for the Grave Yard." Alabama was home now.[16]

Even before settlers like the Spigeners crossed the Coosa, the east side of the river, below the rapids known as the Devil's Staircase, had become the seat of what would be that region's first true river town. This was the head of steamboat navigation, where the Coosa slowed and spread wide and where traders and flatboatmen had for decades gathered their goods for the trip down the Alabama. Buildings had appeared there as early as 1830, and by 1833 the location boasted a boarding house, a blacksmith shop, a mill, and a post office named, appropriately enough, "Falls of Coosa." A year later the designation was changed to Wetumpka, which an English traveler was told meant "the falling stream." With the roar of the staircase ringing in his ears, he had no reason to dispute the story or wonder why they chose the name.[17]

Private dwellings were concentrated on the west shore, while on the east side, the jumping-off place for squatters and speculators heading into the nation, the usual collection of taverns, hotels, stores, and bars served the needs and desires of visitor and resident alike. Closer to the river "Chicken Row" clung to the bank, a haven for the most disreputable of the community and an instructive example for preachers needing to remind their flocks of the wages of sin. The same year the town was incorporated, 1834, a charter was given to the Wetumpka Bridge Company, which went to work and spanned the stream in less than a year. Now more settlers, including the Spigeners and their kin, came, paid the toll, and crossed to take up land. By 1836 the population of the town had swelled to twelve hundred, and there seemed no end in sight for the boom that brought them.[18]

Those who stayed near the river found the Coosa's bounty little changed from the days when the Creeks were uncontested masters of the region. Schools of fish still came up to the shoals to spawn in the shallow water, and like the Indians before them, white residents set traps and nets in the narrows. Treating the river as an inexhaustible resource, they took more fish than they could use, and "not infrequently quantities would be furnished to Montgomery and other points." One visitor recalled meeting "several persons coming up from the river with many fine large fish, called buffaloes, of which it was said upwards of 500 were caught, at a single haul, by a sein, or net, opposite the wharf at which we lay." Locals would not have given that catch a second look. Around 1850 a fisherman named Joe Skinner reported that he took over 2,300 from his traps in one day. No one thought to comment on how many made it to market and the table and how many were left to spoil.[19]

During these flush times Wetumpka became a critical connecting point. There commerce brought downstream through the shoals and rapids was collected with that coming overland by wagon, then repackaged and loaded for the trip on the Alabama. Goods from as far away as Tennessee and Georgia were brought to this inland port, where steamboats from Mobile waited. Though only two years a town, Wetumpka, some believed, might in time surpass even Montgomery in population and trade. One of these was businessman and manufacturer Daniel Pratt, who in 1835 was attracted to the water power potential of the region and wanted to buy property upstream on both sides of the river as the location for a gin factory. In these flush times, though, he found land prices too high, and when residents met and decided not to lower them, Pratt took his plans elsewhere. His was a decision citizens of Wetumpka would come to regret.[20]

At the time, however, leaders of the community had other things to think about besides Daniel Pratt. The railroad bug bit them hard, and in early 1836 the Wetumpka and Coosa Railroad Company was chartered to build a line up the west side of the river, around the Coosa shoals. Some saw this as only the first step of a project that would cross the river above the fall line, extend into Talladega and Benton (later Calhoun) counties, and from there send branches north to the Tennessee River and east to Georgia. Once completed, Wetumpka would be the hub of a railroad network linking the interior of the southeast to the Alabama River and beyond. Who needed Pratt?[21]

Grading on the project started almost immediately, and in just over a year "a very good road bed" was laid some twelve miles along the stream. Then came the crash of 1837. Land prices collapsed, cotton tumbled, the local bank failed, and the railroad was abandoned. Wetumpka's dreams of being what an early historian called "the great central emporium of Alabama" ended amid panic and financial disaster. Before the town could recover nature dealt it an additional blow. In 1839 the region was struck by a drought that lasted over two months. The river dropped so low that boats were unable to get upstream, so the crops that did not wither in the field were stranded without access to market. Freight could not be brought up to the stricken city, and local newspapers were reduced to printing issues on half-sheets. The river that was Wetumpka's outlet to the greater world now held the city prisoner.[22]

Finally, in the spring of 1840, the rains came, and came with a vengeance. The land, cleared of trees and planted in cotton, could not hold the water. It ran in red clay rivulets into creeks and branches, which in turn fed the river. When the Coosa was driven from its banks, the press reported "a great interruption of travel" from the high waters. The next spring came the "Harrison freshet," named for the president whose inauguration (and demise) coincided with the disaster. Even greater than the flood of '40, it inundated all the eastern part of the town and did great damage to the commercial district. Still it was not over. Three years later, in the spring of 1844, the rivers rose again, this time to even greater heights, and the bridge that united the town was swept away.[23]

A lesser town might have given up, but not Wetumpka. Despite these natural disasters and a serious fire in 1845, the town struggled back. A new bridge was ordered, and though the bid went to the firm belonging to one John Godwin, the man behind the design and

Wetumpka Bridge, Alabama, painted by A. E. (?) Thompson.
The bridge was constructed in 1844 under the direction of African-
American builder Horace King, who was a slave at the time. King
was freed in 1846. Note the last rocks in the Staircase rapids just
below the bridge.

(M. and M. Karolik Collection, Courtesy Museum of Fine Arts, Boston)

construction of the project was Horace King, a slave belonging to
Godwin. "The best practicing Bridge Builder in the South," according
to Tuscaloosa construction and transportation giant Robert Jemison,
Jr., King erected a six-hundred-foot covered bridge, with more than
two hundred feet of land bridge approach. Built on wooden piers held
firm by a truss design, it was a wonder of the age and a tribute to the
skill and resourcefulness of its architect.[24]

A new bridge, however impressive, was not enough. Battered by fire,
flood, drought, and depression, Wetumpka was not ready when its
greatest opportunity arrived. In 1840 the town had been a third larger
than Mongomery, and her future seemed bright, but by the middle of
the decade, her neighbor to the south had gained the upper hand.
When legislators from the Alabama-Coosa-Tallapoosa valley united to
bring the capitol back to the center of the state, Wetumpka's bid for it
fell short. The town would never have such a chance again. As the head

of steamboat navigation it continued to be important in the economic scheme of things, but many boats went no farther upriver than Montgomery, which became the major distribution point for inland commerce. The completion of the Montgomery and West Point Railroad in 1853 linking the Alabama River with planters to the east confirmed the capital's economic importance. Later stories were told of how, as Montgomery rose, buildings in Wetumpka were torn down to supply bricks for the city. The story may be apocryphal, but like so many other river tales, if it is not true, it should be.[25]

The year before Wetumpka's unsuccessful bid for the capitol, the Upper Coosa's first steamboat was launched at the head of the rapids. From there it set out on the first of many trips it and others would make to Rome, Georgia. Built in Cincinnati, the sidewheeler was sent down the Mississippi to New Orleans, then along the Gulf Coast to Mobile, and finally upriver to the foot of the Devil's Staircase. At that point it was dismantled, loaded on ox wagons, and carried overland to be reassembled. Appropriately named the *Coosa*, its voyage initiated the steamboat era on that section of river and set in motion the forces that would end forever Wetumpka's dreams of being the entrepot for upper Coosa commerce. Now settlers above the shoals looked north and east for their economic outlets.[26]

The men who brought the steamboat to the upper Coosa reckoned the return on their investment would be great. After the Creek War, settlers had cleared farms and small plantations on the west side of the river, just outside the limits of the nation, and as this frontier population grew and prospered, it had goods to sell and money with which to buy. Like their counterparts to the south, these settlers watched eagerly for an opportunity to take up Indian land on the other side of the Coosa, and when their chance came they were ready. With the removal of the Creeks the stream of immigrants began, and when the Cherokees were expelled from the northern part of the valley, the stream became a flood. As the whole region opened for white settlers, immigrants from other parts of Alabama were joined by those from Georgia, Tennessee, the Carolinas, and Virginia. Many who claimed tracts in the region were much like the Spigeners—families of moderate means and limited resources who cleared the land, built plantation-plain houses, and began to grow cotton. Compared to Black Belt nabobs they seemed a little crude, a little closer to the frontier and its values, but in their context they were planters, and their less affluent farmer neighbors, who were the majority in the region, looked to them for leadership.[27]

Where they were led was to the Coosa, which with the steamboat was becoming as important to local commerce as the Alabama had become further south. And as had happened on the other river, commerce on the Coosa gave rise to river towns. The first of these, other than Rome, was Greensport. One hundred and forty miles upriver from Wetumpka, at the head of the Coosa shoals where flatboatmen had for decades assembled vessels and cargo for the trip through the rapids, the town grew up at the spot that, in 1832, Jacob Green had begun operating a ferry. Here the steamboat *Coosa* was launched, and in the years that followed, it became the southernmost port of departure for traffic upriver. Though the village was small, business there was brisk, as Green's fine house attested, and within a decade over thirty steamboats were making regular, scheduled trips between the Alabama and Georgia ports. Since the upper Coosa was shallower than the Alabama, boats were smaller and traffic even more seasonal, but during high-water months the river was a busy place. Where the Alabama seemed to have a landing at every plantation, the Coosa had only twelve in the 105 river miles between Greensport and the state line, and at those spots the regional economy concentrated. In time one of these, Double Springs, would become the Coosa's principal river town—Gadsden.[28]

The upper Coosa seemed to lend itself to a more leisurely traffic than the Alabama. Its many bends and few straight stretches made racing less frequent, and the shorter distance took away much of the pressure of timetables. This configuration allowed for more pleasure trips by river residents who could, as one lady frequently did, board the boat at one landing, spend several hours with friends as the vessel made its way around the river's great sweeping curve, then disembark on the other side of the bend to walk the mile or so back home. Excursions from Rome became a major social event on the antebellum Coosa, as boats festooned with colored lanterns provided a festive setting for the entertainment of local gentry. Leaving at dusk, the floating ballroom made its way south, stopping to pick up additions to the party along the way. When they reached Greensport the following day, usually a "happy throng" of friends and family waited to join the fun. A few days later they would relight the lanterns and return home.[29]

The critical event that tied the upper Coosa valley to Rome, and from there to the eastern seaboard, was the completion of the railroad line between Chattanooga and Atlanta in 1851. Now goods that reached Georgia by water could be transferred to trains bound for Savannah and Charleston. With this, the steamboat boom began in earnest, and in what remained of the antebellum period, life on and along the Coosa was not that different from life on and along the Alabama. In both valleys cotton was king, and activities were scheduled to conform to the demands of planting and picking. But from early on a significant part of the Coosa commerce was also logs and lumber. Many of the boats were specially rigged so they could tow large log rafts to sawmills that sprang up along the stream, and some were redesigned with square bows so they could push barges loaded with lumber, an alteration that often doubled their carrying capacity. Until well into the twentieth century, the logging industry kept Coosa River steamboats running.[30]

The Coosa's sister stream, the Tallapoosa, enjoyed no steamboat era above her rapids. Too small, shallow, and narrow and blocked near the end by falls even greater than the Devil's Staircase, her upriver trade was relegated to flatboats between landings, where goods could be transported to wagons for the trek overland to the Coosa or, in a later time, to a railroad. Farmers, most of whom counted their acres in three figures and their slaves (if they had them) on one hand, populated most of the Tallapoosa Valley. In this region Alabama experienced its first gold rush in 1835, and prospectors poured into Cleburne County to make their fortunes. This hastened the Indians' departure, but though the mines ultimately employed hundreds of workers, most did not stay when the vein played out. A second rush, in 1842, gave rise to the town of Goldville in Tallapoosa County, but the ore stream was not large, and the pits soon flooded. The effort did train miners for the California Gold Rush of '49, so in the end it was not wasted. Still, no one seems to have gotten rich from Tallapoosa gold.[31]

The Tallapoosa's fame lay in the future, for its waters would bring industry, not agriculture or mining, to the region. In 1798 Benjamin Hawkins stood at Tallassee Falls and thought them an excellent mill site. Less than half a century later others saw the same potential, and in 1841 the Tallassee Falls Manufacturing Company was chartered "at the great falls" of the river. Nothing was built until 1844, when Thomas M. Barnett and William M. Marks, according to the detailed deed, obtained permission "to erect a dam on the Tallapoosa River from the west side to the island above the falls and construct a race or canal-way" to produce the power needed "for cleaning, spinning and weaving cotton and bleaching and dyeing the same." A short time later the *Niles' National Register* learned of the project and announced to readers throughout the United States that the Marks and Bennett Company was about "to begin an extensive spinning and weaving establishment at the Tallapoosa Falls in the neighborhood of Tallassee." Though interest ran high, it was still nearly two years before the first cotton mill in Tallassee, the second cotton mill in the state, began operation. Once the wheels were turning, the whole region was impressed and excited. The Alabama River System was entering the industrial age, and the Tallapoosa River supplied its power.[32]

NINE

The Alabama in Transition

> We to day, inaugurate the Cahaba Railroad. . . . In this act, we add
> another tributary to the beautiful Alabama, flowing at our feet. It
> may not extend Westward to the Pacific, or to the Atlantic on the
> East, but if it only reaches the confines of Dallas County, it will
> carry with it, that far, the honorable praise of its founders and
> builders, mingled with the blessings of public convenience and
> utility, of social progress and happiness.
>
> JOHN TYLER MORGAN
> Cahawba, Alabama, 1858

The Alabama's last antebellum decade seemed to flow smoothly from
those decades that preceded it. Change was evident, but it came slowly,
and there was little in it that might be called drama. More Black Belt
land came into production, and the demand for slaves increased
along with the price planters paid to obtain them. With more cotton to
be sent to markets, slides at landings like Claiborne were busy every
season. Pressed to control costs without losing efficiency, warehouse
owners and steamboat captains began to replace slave stevedores with
Irishmen, who proved a dependable and, most important perhaps, an
inexpensive source of labor. Slaves still helped with the loading, but
they were usually put at the top of the bluff. There, in relative safety,
they set the bales on the track and sent them speeding on their way to
the deck below, where the Irishmen waited. When asked why this
division of labor, Frederick Law Olmsted was told that "the niggers are
worth too much to be risked here; if the paddies are knocked
overboard, or get their backs broke, nobody loses anything." Nobody,
of course, except the Irishmen.[1]

The one aspect of the evolving river culture where change was most
evident was the size and design of the steamboats, for if there was ever
an era of "floating palaces" on the antebellum Alabama, this was it.
New boats, bigger than ever before, carried bales by the thousands and
transported passengers in a style only hinted at earlier. In 1856 the *St.
Nicholas* arrived on the river and immediately set the standard for those
boats that followed in her wake. An effusive article in the *Montgomery
Daily Messenger* described her cabin as "one of the most splendid ever
put upon any boat here or in the west." Those who could afford first-
class accommodations were ushered through doors decorated with
"celebrated natural and historical scenes," into a saloon where "the
painting, gilding, composition work, and molding are in the best of

110

style." There they could sit on "furniture . . . of costly rosewood" in the company of the cream of Alabama society. "For richness, comfort and elegance," the newspaper concluded, the *St. Nicholas* "surpasses anything we have yet seen."[2]

When viewed from the shore, boats like the *St. Nicholas* made "a grand appearance in a river so narrow as the Alabama." But their very size and elegance made observers more aware of the fact that for every "palace" that plied the stream, there were scores of smaller steamers moving up and down, from landing to landing, much as they had done since the 1820s. These "clean and well-ordered boat[s]," some quite large themselves, served passengers well enough, but their primary concern was freight. Any traveler "accustomed to the punctuality of northern steamers" was in for a rude awakening, since frequent stops for cotton made the trip "exceedingly tedious" for anyone in a hurry. Still, there were the usual diversions on board, if passengers liked to discuss crops, or drink, or try their hands at a game of chance. Although the Mississippi riverboat gambler is far better documented, on the Alabama "professional sharpers" were ready and willing to lighten the purse of anyone foolish enough to sit at their tables or join them in their cabins.[3]

By the 1850s, all along the Alabama the "flush times" seemed to be returning. Montgomery, as the seat of government, had become "a prosperous town, with very pleasant suburbs, and a remarkably enterprising population." That same spirit was evident farther upstream where other enterprising citizens, wanting the region to think of Wetumpka as the head of navigation, built the *Coosa Belle*, which called that town its home. Meanwhile, downriver Selma, Cahawba, and Claiborne survived a yellow fever epidemic early in the decade, recovered, and continued to grow at a steady pace. Schools, churches, civic and fraternal societies, and other symbols of stability multiplied in river towns, while in the plantation districts grander houses were built to shelter a way of life more refined, more chivalric, than that enjoyed by the previous generation. As the frontier retreated before the forces of civilization, what was later remembered as the Old South briefly held sway, but those living then knew how close they remained to their rustic roots. Meanwhile, cotton went downstream, and the boats returned "loaded heavily with all the good things of life." Little wonder one journalist was bold to say: "Oh, we shall have a great time as long as the Alabama chooses to smile upon us."[4]

Just who would be favored with that smile and what effect it would have was not entirely clear. Earlier the Black Belt had been the land of opportunity, but lands farther west, as far as Texas, had begun to attract the ambitious. Now the river became a route out of, or at least through, the region. A new wave of Georgia and South Carolina emigrants entered the state by the old Federal Road, which led them to Montgomery and the Alabama. There they boarded steamers, and as they traveled downstream they were joined by local adventurers, many of them the children of established families, who were heading west for greener pastures. In Dallas County, 54 percent of the sons of planters (those owning twenty or more slaves) joined this migration during the last antebellum decade, and the first leg of the journey for many was the Alabama River.[5]

Even as the Old South of plantations, cotton, and steamboats was in its glory, a New South of mills, railroads, factories, and businessmen was making its appearance. This transformation came as the result of a reassessment of what Alabama rivers had to offer. Up till then, the streams and their tributaries were called on to provide, in the proper season, unobstructed channels for commerce between Wetumpka and Mobile, Greensport and Rome, Centerville and Cahawba. Now a different breed of river men began to consider opportunities at the fall line. Where those who came before them saw rocks, shoals, and rapids as obstacles to be overcome, these men saw falling water and the natural power it generated. They wanted to build dams to harness this force, construct mill runs and races to direct it, bring in wheels to convert water into energy, and raise factories to house the machines this energy would drive. They wanted to bring the industrial revolution to the Alabama.

The first significant attempt to transform the fall line into an industrial center came on the Cahaba, near Centerville. In 1837 the Tuscaloosa Manufacturing Company built a three-story factory to house a cotton yarn and wool carding operation that employed, according to reports, "about twenty hands . . . —all white—some males, some females— some large, and some small." After four years operating at a loss, the business was taken over by Daniel Scott, one of the founders, who named the site for himself and set about to make the company a going concern. He used his first profits to buy a family of slaves, a strategy that gave him a labor force and an accruing investment. Then Scott slowly and steadily built up the enterprise until he managed a work force of over a hundred, black and white. Some three-fourths of them were women, and many of both sexes were his personal chattel.[6]

In the late 1850s the South's most respected commercial journal, *DeBow's Review*, described Scottsville as a village "devoted exclusively to manufactures." The impressed correspondent told his readers how Scott's company "owns 3000 acres of land and all the buildings on the place, which consists of the factory, a large hotel, the store, blacksmith, carpenter, wheelwright and boot and shoe shops, a saw mill, grist mills, a large flouring mill, a church and a large number of cottages." Paternal, even patriarchal, Scott and his stockholders allowed no liquor in the village and made it a policy "not [to] sell an inch of its land to anyone." With stock that had "long been over par, and its dividends this year [1858] . . . at least twelve per cent," Scottsville was considered a model of "enterprise, governed by steadiness, perseverance and skill."⁷

Industrial sites on other rivers were also attracting attention. Since the days of William Bartram and Benjamin Hawkins, visitors had been enthralled by the "beautiful and Romantic" Tallassee Falls, a labyrinth of jutting rocks and cascading water that blocked upstream navigation on the Tallapoosa. In the early 1850s a writer for the *Montgomery Advertiser and State Gazette* described the scene, where "fairy islands" split the river so that "each division, as if daring the other to the dreadful conflict, rush[ed] furiously on its mad career, leaping from shelf to shelf with deafening roar." "Gliding away with increased velocity . . . dashing now from side to side, 'midst foam and spray," the stream went "whirling through the broad cliffs and broken passages to the deep chasms below; then boiling and surging along the rocky ramparts, the confused waters [were] again united." Together as one, the streams "spread out, broad, deep and placid, as if to compose themselves before they proceed on their journey to the ocean."⁸

Even as he was writing, the falls and their "wild, enchanting scenery" were being altered so man could exploit their "extraordinary facilities." The "extensive spinning and weaving establishment" that the *Niles' National Register* heralded in 1844 opened at Tallassee two years later, and in the decade that followed the company and the town grew steadily. Taking advantage of a location "especially designed by nature for a large manufacturing city," the company built a dam and mill race "of rock, laid in hydraulic cement" that channeled the water that turned the wheels. Such was the "immense power and certainty of [the] stream" that promoters boasted how only "a portion" of its energy could drive 50,000 spindles, five times the current capacity of the enterprise. "Unsurpassed for health, and of close proximity to a rich planting country," observers on the scene did not hesitate to declare that at Tallassee, "nature seems to have been lavish with advantages which stand inviting man to improve." The taming of the Tallapoosa had begun.⁹

Despite these natural advantages, it was not Tallassee that set the pattern for Alabama industrial projects. That honor belonged to a site on Autauga Creek, some four miles from the river, a site selected by transplanted New Englander Daniel Pratt. A native of Temple, New Hampshire, who had lived over a decade in Georgia before coming to

Alabama in 1833, Pratt brought with him manufacturing skill and experience rare in the Cotton State. His efforts to start an operation on the Coosa were soon frustrated by his inability to buy suitable land near Wetumpka and by the high rents charged by owners of mill sites. So Pratt moved his fledgling operation west, some fourteen miles downriver from Montgomery, where he found the land and the "bold, clear stream" he needed. There, Prattville was born.[10]

Pratt had lived in the South long enough to know that many in the region equated manual labor with slave labor, and since they believed it "degrading . . . to be seen following the plow, or with a jack-plane saw, trowel, hammer, or any other mechanical tool in their hands," he understood that it might be difficult to recruit them as industrial workers. Indeed, the whole idea of an industrial city ran counter to the southern notion that towns should be natural extensions of the agricultural community. To combat these prejudices, Pratt advanced the notion of a manufacturing village that would complement the southern plantation system and offer "the laboring class an opportunity of not only making an independent living, but to train up workmen who could give dignity to labor." By stressing thrift, sobriety, and hard work, while paying a better-than-living wage to those who successfully adopted these virtues, Pratt believed he could create a community where each worker possessed "a neat, substantial dwelling, the front yard adorned with shrubbery and flowers, a good vegetable garden, a pleasant wife and cheerful children." It would be a New England village peopled with New England workers, in the heart of the Alabama River valley.[11]

What Pratt accomplished was nothing short of remarkable. By the early 1850s his town boasted an industrial complex that included the gin factory, textile mill, foundry, brick planing mill, and a door, sash, and blind factory. In addition, this "loveliest village of the plain," as Cahawba's *Dallas Gazette* called it, contained "three churches, two school houses, four stores, a carriage shop, two smith shops, and about thirty-five dwelling houses." Such a collection of buildings was enough to make Prattville unique among Alabama towns, but what the village did not have made the settlement stand out all the more. There were no saloons in Prattville. "Intemperance," according to one visitor, "has been strictly guarded against." The "sale of ardent spirits" in the town was forbidden, and the Alabama legislature, endorsing the effort, "prohibited the retailing of it within two miles of the place." After cataloging Pratt's efforts and accomplishments on behalf of those who labored in his factories, the Cahawba editor asked his readers, "who has done more? . . . Who the hundredth part more?"[12]

Not everything went as well as Pratt had hoped it would. Mill hands, according to Shadrach Mims, the company's agent, were "brought up from the piney woods, [and] many of them with no sort of training to any kind of labor." They made frequent "mistakes and blunders [that] were . . . fatal to success." Efforts to improve morals, especially when it came to drinking, were frequently resisted, and at least one visitor, after inspecting the town and its people, warned Pratt that "Demon Alcohol has access to your village." Convinced that "no worker about machinery is worth a pinch of salt if he has liquor in his stomach," Pratt doubled his efforts and by 1860 could describe Prattville as a town "universally free of the vices of loafing and dissipation," a town peopled by an "industrious, intelligent and refined" citizenry. But this glowing report seems to have been deceptive, for when asked why Pratt employed slaves as well as whites in his operation, Mims explained that workers from the neighborhood had failed to become the sober, diligent, moral labor force their employer hoped they would be, so he had no choice but to seek others to do the job. That slaves, either by force or inclination, exhibited the virtues he sought says much about labor in the antebellum South.[13]

Despite these troubles, Daniel Pratt became one of the most respected industrialists in Alabama, and his efforts to expand his operations and gain markets for his manufactures took on a special significance. At the outset he, like most of his contemporaries, saw the Alabama River as the transportation artery for Prattville products, and by 1851 he had built a plank road from the town to the stream and there had begun constructing a wharf and warehouse that *DeBow's Review* assured readers "will compare with the best." Before long, however, Pratt became convinced that he could gain better access to market through an expanded railroad system that would connect his operation with commercial centers farther inland. In 1853 he hosted a railroad convention, where he pushed planters and businessmen to seek state aid for a line from Montgomery through Prattville that would extend west to Jackson, Mississippi, and another that would go north to link up with a line being built from Selma toward the Tennessee River. Rivers were still important in this scheme, but less so than with similar projects in the past. Daniel Pratt saw the future, a future in which the Alabama River System would play an ever-diminishing role.[14]

A large cotton factory built at nearby Autaugaville was further evidence of the industrial growth of the Alabama River valley, while up the Coosa and Cahaba, newly opened iron works contributed to the growing interest in a diversified economy for the region. Fueled by increased tension between slave and free states, efforts that promoted economic independence attracted attention from politicians and the press. Coupled with this was the growing recognition that if diversity was where the future lay, a state transportation system based primarily on rivers was woefully inadequate. Although industrial operations at Tallassee and Wetumpka had navigable waterways nearby, most mills and factories in the Alabama-Coosa-Tallapoosa-Cahaba valleys were on smaller streams, and what they produced had to be carried overland before it could be shipped by water. In this traffic, rivers often became barriers before they became roads, so bridges were needed at key crossings. Fall-line towns were the first to span the streams, and by the 1850s the Cahaba at Centerville, the Coosa at Wetumpka, and the Tallapoosa at Tallassee all had bridges. The Cahaba was soon bridged again, nearer its mouth, to accommodate the increased traffic between the former capital and Selma, traffic that preferred paying a toll to cross the river to buying passage on a steamboat.[15]

It would be wrong to believe the rise of industrial villages marked an immediate, significant shift away from agriculture in the river region, but it did help Alabamians come to the conclusion that economic diversity consisted of more than planting a crop other than cotton. And when seen within the context of a growing recognition among state leaders that an agricultural Alabama was doomed to serve the manufacturing North as a colony serves the mother country, the call for diversity stands as evidence of how the two sections of the nation were drifting apart. "Let us, as Southerners," the *Clarke County Democrat* editorialized in 1856, "encourage and support . . . the enterprise and industry of our section. . . . By doing so," the editor argued, "we generally get a better article, and, besides, have the consolation of the reflection that our money is in the pocket of one friendly to us and to our institutions." It was a call for economic self-sufficiency as well as economic progress and reflected the thought of the nationalist more than that of the businessman.[16]

As one would expect, Montgomery, capital of the state, was at the center of the movement for diversity and self-sufficiency. There Noah B. Cloud, founder of the Alabama State Agricultural Society and editor of the *American Cotton Planter*, did what he did best—he organized fairs to promote state products and encourage the economy he believed would free the region from dependence on others. Throughout the South business and agricultural leaders praised his efforts, and by the time the Civil War put an end to such gatherings, the Alabama State Fairgrounds were acknowledged to be among the best in Dixie. For most folks, however, the fair was more than an "interesting, elevating, inspiring exhibition." It was, as one visitor described it:

—a social reunion—a great popular holiday. . . . It was a scene to be daguerreotyped on the heart of humanity—to be "set in a historical frame work" full of suggestions to a thoughtful patriot. There we were, old and young—politicians, merchants, lawyers, doctors, farmers—men, women and children—priest, editors and people—rich and poor—city bred and "sun burnt sicklemen," pedagogue and pedlar—buoyant, impulsive, generous youth and bright, innocent, radiant, fresh blown, blushing beauty;—Age . . . was there in gravity and awful counsels. There, too, were widow and widower, with wink and wile—the young old bachelor and the old young maid. There we were, all, and all delighted.

By 1859 a veteran fair goer knew what to expect and put the scene more succinctly: "There will be a crowd of articles exhibited, . . . there will also be a crowd of legislators, politicians, candidates, rich people, visitors from all parts of the world, editors, fortune-hunters, pleasure-seekers, loafers, pickpockets, black-legs, and," he added with obvious delight, "pretty women."[17]

In the midst of this "Babel of confusion" were men like Cloud and Pratt, working tirelessly to bring economic independence and prosperity to the state. Ideas on just how to accomplish this goal were as varied as exhibits at the fair, but on one point these boosters seemed to agree: If Alabama was to improve its economic prospects, it had to have railroads.

While there was a general consensus that railroads were a good thing, not everyone agreed on how many projects should be undertaken and where the rails should run. The failure to coordinate interests increased competition between various groups and fragmented the rail system when it was actually built. An example of this came at the end of the 1840s, when Montgomery boosters, already involved in building a railroad linking their city to West Point, Georgia, and the Chattahoochee River, decided that a railroad convention held at Shelby Springs in the summer of 1849, was "of too small consequence to deserve their notice" and sent no representatives. The meeting had been called to settle the question of the southern terminus of a railroad linking the Tennessee River to the Alabama, and "Montgomery was the favorite of the people north of the Coosa." When no delegates from the capital appeared, men from Talladega and other Coosa Valley counties "took such umbrage" at being ignored that they "cast off their allegiance to Montgomery and side[d] with Selma," whose delegates were there, lobbying hard for the prize.[18]

To Montgomery's ultimate chagrin, the legislature supported the project, and by 1851 enough track was laid to enable a locomotive, named the *Alabama,* to carry some of Selma's fair ladies on a trial run. By 1853 the line had reached Montevallo, where it turned east toward the Coosa. A year later it had been extended to the river, and by the end of the decade it was across and all the way to Talladega. Now some of the cotton from the piedmont that had been carried by steamboat up the Coosa to railroad connections at Rome, Georgia, was carried south by rail to the Alabama River at Selma. Montgomery's chance to be the hub of an Alabama railroad system, an Alabama Atlanta, was lost.[19]

At that moment, however, it is unlikely that many people outside the capital city (with the possible exception of Daniel Pratt) were disturbed by the fact that Selma, not Montgomery, was the southern terminus for the railroad. In the minds of antebellum Alabamians, King Cotton traveled by water. Railroads were simply a more convenient way to get the crop to the rivers. Whether the landing was at Selma, Montgomery, Cahawba, or Gadsden was an issue only if the element of convenience was lost. Railroads that were built in the decade before the Civil War were laid out with this fact in mind, and whenever politicians advocated increased state aid to these lines, as Gov. Henry Watkins Collier did in his 1851 address to the legislature, they were careful also to voice their support for clearing rivers and improving navigation. To advocate one system of transportation over another ran the risk of alienating power segments of the community, something few politicians were willing to do. So the governor called for state support for both rail and river projects, encouraged the legislature to create the office of state engineer to survey the streams, and left both sides with what seemed at least to be half a loaf.[20]

In actual practice, it was little or no loaf at all. By 1860 Alabama had only 743 miles of rails, and as noted, most lines were laid to link plantation districts to the rivers. Where water transportation was easy and dependable, between Selma and Montgomery for example, no rail line was built, despite efforts by men as important as Daniel Pratt. As for improving the river system, it was a matter of undertaking major projects, such as locks through the Coosa shoals and rapids, or doing little more than pulling snags and keeping channels clear from Wetumpka south and Greensport north. Given the lack of capital in Alabama, the decision was an easy one—pull the snags. The crux of it all was this: Alabama's rivers were just too good. The state needed a cheap means of moving its staple to market, and there it was, flowing free and freely, its rises and falls coordinated by nature to serve cotton commerce. The situation was one that Alabama industries, what few there were, had little choice but to accept.[21]

So it was that while some saw the railroad as the means by which

Alabama would be transported into an industrial and manufacturing age, others saw the rails as evidence of the vitality of the economic system whose principal crop the trains carried to the rivers, just as wagons had once done. It followed then that celebrations opening new lines were more than social ceremonies of self-congratulation and a chance to praise the spirit of enterprise that made it all possible. These gatherings provided an opportunity for speakers and listeners to reflect on the past even as they gloried in the future. Over and again these programs testified to a merging of tradition and progress that more radical reformers faulted for holding the region back and conservative Alabamians praised for keeping progress in perspective.

One such ceremony was the "Railroad jubilee" held on Thursday, August 12, 1858, to dedicate the locomotive that would carry people and products on a line planned between Cahawba and the Black Belt cotton centers of Marion and Greensboro. During the 1850s the former capital's revival continued. Its commerce increased; its population, white and black, slave and free, grew to nearly five thousand; and new buildings, including the grand hotel Saltmarsh Hall, replaced many of the dilapidated shops and dependencies. As the decade drew to a close, the local newspaper saw the railroad as confirmation that "energetic men of wealth" in the town "were not willing to fold [their] arms in quiet content, until other enterprizes had cut off entirely the local trade that naturally belonged to [them]." Now it seemed that Cahawba "may yet be the great inland town of Alabama."[22]

The crowd was large ("really more than was thought would honor our town with their presence," according to the *Dallas Gazette*), and it filled the cotton warehouse where the ceremony was to be held. One wall had been torn away so spectators could see "the engine, decorated with flags and flowers," on the rails outside. In front of the locomotive, over the cow catcher, organizers built the speakers' platform, and at one in the afternoon they assembled: Christopher C. Pegues, the master of ceremonies; Gen. Porter King of Marion; Dr. F. A. Bates, the president of the railroad; and the featured speaker, Dallas County attorney, aspiring politician, and future United States senator, John Tyler Morgan.[23]

Morgan was well up to the occasion. He opened with a tribute to the railroad, and pointing to the engine proclaimed it "the child of the 19th century," an invention that has "fully established its claim to our pride and affections." This machine, he noted, was a monument to "Science and Enterprize," which modern Alabamians now raised on the ruins of two earlier endeavors—a mound and palisade that ancient Indians "skillfully placed, so as to command this splendid sweep of the Alabama river," and the state's first capitol, "kindly fallen down" so "not a stone now remains to tell where it once stood." Symbolically, Morgan noted, the capitol's "remaining dust" and the Indians' "curious pottery, their crude implements of warfare, and their bones," had been heaped "together in the embankment for the Railroad"—to "mingle in a singular tribute to the superiority of their successors in the dominion of this soil."

In closing, Morgan reminded his listeners of how great works, "works of usefullness and public benefaction stand against all changes of time and circumstance." This railroad, he believed, would be one of these. And then, almost as a benediction, he put the whole enterprise in its proper context. "In this act," his voice must have soared above the crowd at that point, "we add another tributary to the beautiful Alabama, flowing at our feet." That brought everything together. Here was progress built on achievements of the past, yet altering, only slightly, the traditional rhythm of life along the rivers. The railroad, this "new project for good and the happiness to our race," was an improved means to the same glorious end. It was just one more stream, one more thoroughfare, carrying commerce to the Alabama. Morgan knew it, and so did the crowd.

His duty done, the speaker declared that the engine "must bear a final test, and if it shall withstand the glance of woman's eye, it shall then be worthy of a name, and that name, when spoken by woman, shall be a token of all success—a talismatic work, in which Cahaba shall be greatly blessed in after times." Mrs. Pegues arose and apparently kept a straight face as the speaker heaped upon her some of his most excessive prose— "while little children strew their flowers along Labor's toilsome path- way" surely drew a guffaw (or at least a snicker) from those on the back rows who came only for the dinner afterwards. Then she took from Morgan "this flagon of pure wine—pressed from the vintage of our Southern soil," and with a mighty swing—surely made mightier by the time she spent waiting for the speaker to get to the point—the lady broke the bottle on the engine. Then she blessed the machine—"our first born, our pride and hope"—with the name "CAHABA."

Now came the good part. The engine's bell rang, and "with her flags flying, [she] moved in gallant style, on her way to the end of the track"—a short distance that could be covered "in a few minutes." Then the president of the road made a few remarks, thankfully brief it seems, and the ladies were invited to make the journey. This continued the rest of the day, back and forth, until "all who desired it, had ridden on the Marion & Cahaba Railroad." Meanwhile, the dinner (barbecue, natu- rally) was laid out, and the press noted with pride that though there was "a large crowd, the utmost order prevailed, and there was none of the scrambling and scuffing that generally occurs" at such an event.[24]

All went well until, "just at the close of the dinner, a thunderstorm came up, which hastened the departure of those from the country." Meanwhile town folks and friends moved inside their homes and stores to continue the party as the rain washed the "vintage of our Southern soil" from the locomotive and down the hill into the mighty Alabama.

TEN

The Rivers at War

When de war started 'mos' all I know 'bout it was all de white mens
go to Montgomery an' jine e army. My brudder, he 'bout fifteen year
ole, so he go 'long wid de ration wagon to Montgomery 'mos' ebry
week. One day he come back from Montgomery an' he say, "Hell
done broke loose in Gawgy." He coundn't tell us much 'bout what
done happen, but de slaves dey get all 'cited 'caze dey didn' know
what to 'spect. Purty soon we fin' out dat some of de big mens call a
meetin' at de capitol on Goat Hill in Montgomery. Day 'selected
Mista Jeff Davis president an' done busted de Nunited States wide
open.

WALTER CALLOWAY
Montgomery County, 1937

Here the flag was presented to the Cahaba Rifles, Dallas County's
bravest and most gallant sons, on the eve of their departure for the
scene of conflict, in an address eloquent with patriotism by Miss
Anna M. Vasser; and here in the name of that company Capt.
Christopher C. Pegues accepted the banner and swore to bear it on
to "victory or to death." Right royally was that oath fulfilled.

ANNA M. GAYLE FRY
Memories of Old Cahaba, 1905

Of all the nights of my experience, this is the most like the horrors
of war—a captured city burning at night, a victorious army
advancing, and a demoralized one retreating.

E. N. GILPIN, U.S.A.
After the Battle of Selma
April 2, 1865

If secession caught anyone in the region by surprise, they probably
were not really paying attention. By January 1861 anti-Yankee sentiment
along Alabama rivers had grown to the point that reconciliation was no
longer an alternative for most representatives sent to the convention in
Montgomery. Although there were a few who felt that "the immediate
secession of Alabama [was] a leap in the dark," they could not stem the
tide. As Walter Calloway, a slave on a Black Belt plantation near the
river, neatly summed it up, "de big mens . . . at de capitol on Goat
Hill . . . busted de Nunited States wide open."[1]

Most of them saw it coming. As 1860 approached, even talk of
agricultural diversity and manufacturing kept returning to the question
of how such measures would be the "right step towards independence . . . on the part of the south, and the proper mode to place our
section in the commanding position it ought to occupy." But as much

as they wanted to rid themselves of Yankee "domination," progress was too great a price to pay. Despite the efforts of men like Pratt and Cloud, by 1860 there were only two more cotton mills operating in the state than there had been in 1850, while production of the raw material the mills consumed had more than doubled. So much for diversity. Now, having rejected the economic revolution that would free them from the hated Yankee, Alabamians chose a political revolution instead.[2]

Of course, what actually brought state leaders to this point was less an attempt to secure economic prosperity—they were hardly going broke sending Alabama cotton to New England—and more an effort to rid themselves of critics who seemed determined to subvert the region's peculiar institution—slavery. They had tried to counter this by asserting that slavery was a "positive good" and that conditions under which bondsmen lived were far better than those "reported in the New York papers where thousands of women and children gathered together to seek bread where there was no bread." This argument had little effect on northerners and less on slaves, and one suspects most southerners knew it. Even as they praised the institution's benefits, slaveholders tightened already tight restrictions and ordered the "arrest of any suspicious persons who might be found . . . tampering with the negroes." When these efforts were not enough to block emancipationists and their "abolition emissaries," they took the South out of the union.[3]

On January 7, 1861, Alabama's "big mens" gathered in that "Athenian yankeeized" capitol in Montgomery. Four days later, they voted for secession. Then the ceremonies of congratulation began. "Amid the most deafening cheers" the doors of the legislative chamber were thrown open, and with "the galleries . . . crowded with ladies and gentlemen . . . [,] the noble-hearted, pure and patriotic women of Montgomery" presented the assembly a banner "to wave over the Capitol of our new Republic." It was accepted amid "peal after peal of applause," while outside "bells were ringing—cannons [were] firing [, and] a steam boat [was] whistling." For the Reverend W. H. Mitchell, it was "one of the most stirring-enthusiastic & thrilling scenes [he had] ever witnessed." Most of those attending probably agreed.[4]

In the months that followed, all along the rivers "gallant young men" rallied to the Confederacy. Downstream, citizens collected money to buy brass buttons and horses for the Claiborne Guards and sent them off to fight in Mississippi. Selma raised five companies, whose membership reflected both the diversity of the growing town and its dedication to the cause. John Hardy, who saw them organized, remembered well the socially prominent "Magnolia Cadets," in whose ranks were "the first young men of the place," the "Selma Blues" made up of "the more sober, settled men of the city," and the "'Phoenix Reds' composed almost entirely of working men." Before the year was out the Queen City of the Black Belt had sent over six hundred soldiers into the army.[5]

At the former capital, in a ceremony reenacted in towns and villages throughout the state, "Dallas County's bravest and most gallant sons" met and formed the Cahaba Rifles. Scions of many a Black Belt family enlisted, including John Tyler Morgan, though he claimed his only military talent was playing the fife. In April, just before they departed "for the scene of conflict," their commander, Capt. Christopher C. Pegues, accepted a company banner from a local belle and swore to bear it to "victory or to death." "Right royally," remembered Anna Gayle Fry, "was that oath fulfilled." Pegues proved an able officer, became a colonel, and might have been a general and later a governor or a senator had he not fallen leading his men at Gaines's Mill, in the summer of '62.[6]

That war was still ahead for them, still ahead for the "wealthy, cultured, young gentlemen [who] voluntarily turn[ed] their backs upon the luxuries and endearments of affluent homes," still ahead for the "working men" who left jobs and families to join the cause, and still ahead for "the more sober, settled men" who probably should have known better but joined anyway.

It also lay ahead for the hundreds of farm boys from a region of farm boys, whose families counted their acres in tens, not thousands, who owned no slaves, and who had never seen a Yankee until they shot at one. They enlisted (and were later conscripted) without ceremony. No flags were consecrated for them, no bands played, no belles gave them flowers and kisses.

It also lay ahead for men like "Massa Cal" from Lower Peachtree in Wilcox County, who understood the slogging horror of war and went anyway. When he made his decision, "Massa Cal" summoned his slave Cato, who through one of those unions that could be neither acknowledged nor ignored was also his kinsman, and told him (according to Cato):

"You's always been a 'sponsible man, and I leave you to look after the women and the place. If I don't come back, I want you always to stay by Missy Angela!"

"Fore God, I will, Massa Cal," Cato replied.

"Then I can go away peaceable," the planter said, and he left.

Had "Massa Cal" and the others stayed at their homes on the Alabama, the Coosa, the Tallapoosa, and the Cahaba, it would have been years before the war came to them, if it came at all. So they went to the war, and many, so very many, never returned.[7]

* * *

Montgomery became the capital of the Confederacy in February; Jefferson Davis soon arrived, took the oath of office, and settled into a "modest villa" nearby. Meanwhile the new constitution was ratified by the seceding states, and the slaveholders' experiment at union was underway. What had begun with much pomp and ceremony now settled into debate and deliberation. Bored at listening to men who were either "legislators or conspirators" (he could not decide) and disappointed at a city that reminded him of "a small Russian town in the interior," British journalist William Russell longed for a new assignment. It finally came in early May, and he "bade good-by to Montgomery without regret."[8]

Waiting for Russell at the river were the "castle-like hulk of the *Southern Republic*" and its captain, Tim Meaher. The two men hit it off immediately, and during the voyage Meaher "favored [him] with some wonderful yarns," which the Englishman hoped the captain "was not foolish enough to think I believed." More stories might have been told later in the year, but this was planting, not picking, season, so there was no cotton waiting at the landings and little reason to stop or tarry. At dusk Captain Meaher guided the *Southern Republic* into the channel, caught the current that spring rains had turned "the color of chocolate and milk," and headed downstream. They made Selma before midnight.[9]

In many ways, this voyage was typical of the hundreds that preceded it, and the Englishman's comments on the "high banks and bluffs" and "sudden bends and rapid curves," might have been made by any number of earlier travelers. At Selma the "lights in the windows, and the lofty hotels above [them], put [Russell] in mind of the old town of Edinburgh, seen from Prince's Street"; but he missed Cahawba, which they passed before dawn, and the rest of the trip was a steady succession of wood yards, landings, empty cotton sheds, and abandoned slides. Below Claiborne, Meaher guided his boat through twists and turns of swamps and "cutoffs"; then he left the Alabama behind when it joined the Tombigbee, and on May 11, the captain brought the *Southern Republic* safely into "the quay of Mobile." The trip took less than two days.[10]

Yet the "wild strains of 'Dixie'" that "the Calliope shriek[ed] . . . incessantly" reminded Russell that this was not a typical voyage. It was a trip through a land of people under siege, a people so brave, so defiant, that they were ready to "burn every bale of cotton, and fire every house, and lay waste every field and homestead, before they will yield to the Yankees." Yet these same people felt so unsure of the foundation on which their Confederacy was built that, "as if uttering some sacred refrain to the universal hymn of the South," they sang the praises of their peculiar institution to anyone who would listen—even to each other. In this the "gallant Captain Meaher [was] quite eloquent," and using Bully, a "stout, fat, nearly naked" slave boy as his example, he declared: "Yes sir, they're the happiest people on the face of the airth!" Meaher seemed convinced; Russell had his doubts; no one knows what Bully thought.[11]

On May 21, the capitol of the Southern Union was moved from Montgomery to Richmond. Now the Confederacy would be defended in the east, and as the blockade tightened, the route through Alabama was essential to the movement of men and material to the front. This presented a problem. Alabama rivers oriented the state on a north-south axis, and railroads were built with that orientation in mind. There were no tracks linking Selma to Montgomery, for up until then, none were needed. Goods brought by rail from Mississippi had to be unloaded at Selma, reloaded on riverboats for the trip to Montgomery, and then transferred to the train for the trip to Atlanta and beyond. This transfer so slowed the process that by the middle of the war it was estimated that there were "countless thousands of bushels of grain west of the Alabama River," rotting in the field while Lee's troops went without.[12]

Where the Confederacy may have been ill served by these conditions, Selma was not. As terminus for the Alabama and Mississippi Railroad, coming from the west, *and* for the Alabama and Tennessee Rivers Railroad, which ran north through the coal and iron fields of Bibb and Shelby counties, the city on the bluff soon became a distribution point from which raw materials were sent throughout the Confederacy. Though it never relinquished this role, before long the city took on another function that was far more important to the war effort. In less than two years, Selma would become the state's most important industrial center.[13]

When New Orleans fell in April of 1862, General Josiah Gorgas, chief of ordnance, decided to move the Confederate arsenal from Mount Vernon on the Mobile River to a safer site farther inland. He selected Selma. That decision started an industrial boom, and in time the town boasted of a naval yard and a naval ordnance works, along with foundries, mills, and factories that employed as many as ten thousand laborers, more than the entire white population of Dallas County when the war began. Together these made Selma a manufacturing center second only to Tredegar Iron Works in Richmond. Labor came from a variety of sources, including women and children who rolled cartridges, slaves who did the heaviest work, and skilled white workers whose value to the cause was reflected in their exemption from military service. During the last two years of the conflict this industrial complex produced nearly half the cannon and two-thirds of the ammunition used by Confederate Armies, along with guns, swords, bayonets, and other types of other military hardware. Atlanta, with its rail connections, may have been a greater prize for union planners, but to the soldier in blue, who had to dodge rebel shot and shell, Selma was no less important.[14]

Like so much of the South, Selma's factories suffered from a variety of shortages, and when these occurred they simply had to make do. A lack of rails needed to finish lines that fed the city was partially alleviated by tearing up the rails of the bankrupt Marion & Cahaba road, which spelled an end to Cahawba's hopes of becoming an inland market center. However, the most unique solution to a shortage problem came from one John Harrolson, the local agent of the Nitre and Mining Bureau, who was responsible for gunpowder manufacturing at the arsenal. In the fall of 1863, finding himself short of an essential raw material, he put the following announcement in the *Selma Sentinel*:

> The Ladies of Selma are respectfully requested to preserve all their chamber lye collected about their premises, for the purposes of making "Nitre." Wagons, with barrels, will be sent around for it by the subscriber.

Thomas B. Wetmore, a friend of Harrolson, was inspired by the notice, and soon this poem was being circulated through the town.

> John Harrolson! John Harrolson!
> You are a funny creature;
> You've given this cruel war
> A new and curious feature.
> You'd have us think, while every man
> Is bound to be a fighter,
> The women, (bless the pretty dears,)
> Should be put to making nitre.
>
> John Harrolson! John Harrolson!
> How could you get the notion
> To send your barrels 'round the town
> To gather up the lotion.
> We think the girls do work enough,
> In making love and kissing;
> But now you'll put the pretty dears
> To patriotic pissing.

John Harrolson! John Harrolson!
　　Could you not invent a meter,
　　Or some less immodest mode
　　Of making our salt-petre?
The thing, it is so queer, you know—
　　Gunpowder like and cranky—
　　That when a lady lifts her shift
　　She shoots a bloody Yankee!

John Harrolson! John Harrolson!
　　Whate're was your intention,
　　You've made another contraband
　　Of things we hate to mention,
What good will all our fighting do
　　If Yanks search Venus' mountains,
　　And confiscate and carry off
　　These Southern nitre fountains![15]

Not to be undone Harrolson responded, and though his verse lacked the skill and satire of Wetmore's, he was able to play on the name of his fellow poet, as his final stanza shows:

Women, yes they'll stoop to conquer,
　　And keep their virtue pure;
　　It is no harm to kill a beast
　　With chamber lye I'm sure.
But powder we are bound to have,
　　And this they've sworn before;
　　And if the needful thing is scarce,
　　They'll "press" it and "Wet more"![16]

Such an exchange could not be confined to a local audience, and soon soldiers on both sides, in almost every theater of the war, were familiar with the verses. It even got as far north as Boston, were it is said that a local widow penned her own response.

John Harrolson! John Harrolson!
　　We read in song and story.
　　That women in all these years,
　　Have sprinkled fields of glory;
But never was it told before
　　That how midst scenes of slaughter
　　Your southern beauties dried their tears
　　And went to making water.

No wonder, John, your boys were brave;
Who would not be a fighter
If everytime he shot his gun
He used his sweetheart's nitre?
And, vice versa what could make
A Yankee soldier sadder,
Than dodging bullets fired from
A pretty woman's bladder.

They say there was a subtle smell
That lingered in the powder;
And as the smoke grew thicker,
And the din of battle louder
That there was found in this compound
This serious objection
The soldiers could not sniff it in
without a stiff e[rection].[17]

There is no record of the success of Harrolson's advertisement, but the arsenal continued to turn out bullets.

Meanwhile, up the Coosa in St. Clair County, coal was being mined for the Confederacy. But getting it to Selma faced the same problem that had always plagued downstream commerce: how to make it through the shoals and rapids. The railroad was available, but that mode meant loading the coal on flatboats, floating it to the trestle, then transferring it to the waiting cars—a slow and expensive process. To overcome this, the Confederate government undertook the first serious effort to make the Coosa navigable. Some of the most dangerous rocks were removed, and "boat shoots," only a little wider than the boats themselves, were blasted, cut, and dredged through the rapids. It was tight maneuvering, and vessels frequently missed the channel and were caught, but if the river was running well and there were no accidents, a good flatboatman could make it to Selma in about five days. There the boats were broken up for their lumber, and the captain and crew caught the train back home. When they arrived they usually found other flatboats loaded and waiting. Farther up the river other industrial sites were developed to help the war effort. In Cherokee County the Cornwall Furnace produced pig iron, which was transported to the Coosa, where it was loaded on steamboats and carried to Rome or on flatboats for the trip to Selma.[18]

In the late spring of 1863, war finally came to the river region. Union colonel Abel D. Streight with over fourteen hundred infantrymen, many mounted on mules, invaded with orders to destroy arsenals at Rome and Dalton and cut rail lines leading from Chattanooga to Atlanta. Though the mules gave him trouble, as any self-respecting mule would, Streight's biggest problem was a unit of Confederate cavalry less than one-third his force's size, commanded by Gen. Nathan Bedford Forrest. In late April and early May the two forces fought a running battle through North Alabama as Federals headed toward the Coosa River and Confederates tried to cut them off. Steadily the fighting moved toward the river village of Gadsden, and there one of Alabama's most revered heroines appeared on the scene—a young girl named Emma Sansom. Streight crossed rain-swollen Black Creek near the Sansom home, burned the bridge behind him, and headed for the town. Forrest, hot on his heels, was blocked until Emma risked her life to show him a ford where his troops could cross. Impressed by her courage, Forrest asked for a lock of her hair as a keepsake; then he and his men rode after the enemy.[19]

Streight's forces burned the Coosa River ferry and a few buildings in the Gadsden vicinity, but with Forrest coming up fast he headed on up the Coosa toward Rome. Now the running battle began again, and though Streight was an able commander, the constant harassment took its toll on his men. Upriver from Cedar Bluff the Confederates finally caught the "mule brigade," exhausted from a night of wandering on woodhaulers' roads that seemed to run in all directions. Surrounding the Federals, Forrest's men made enough noise to convince Streight that he was badly outnumbered, and after a brief skirmish he surrendered. The Coosa Valley was free of Yankees. According to tradition, a grateful Alabama legislature set aside a section of public land for Emma, and in time the city of Gadsden raised a statue in her honor. The Federal prisoners were taken to Rome, and Nathan Bedford Forrest went on to fight another day.[20]

There were other Yankees who came to the Alabama River region that year, but they came as prisoners, not invaders. They were collected at Cahawba and housed in a warehouse left unfinished when the railroad was dismantled and commerce declined. At first they were only waiting for shipment to Andersonville, but as the Georgia facility filled to overflowing, the Alabama stockade was made a permanent prison. Unofficially known as Castle Morgan, it would house more people in the one-third of an acre compound than were found in the whole town, and at times it became so crowded that men barely had room to lie down to sleep. There human dramas were enacted on a daily basis, with heroes and villains enough to go around. One Confederate officer seemed to take delight in tormenting prisoners, while another received nothing but praise from the captives under his charge. Local ladies shared books with the confined and cared for sick and wounded as if they were their own. When the war ended, it was said that prisoners who emerged from Castle Morgan were among the healthiest released from Southern stockades, a remarkable record considering the conditions of their confinement. Most, however, were just happy to have survived.[21]

By 1864, it was obvious that the war was going against the Confederacy. Thus far most of Alabama had been spared the destruction of battle, but just to the northeast, a Union army under Gen. William Tecumseh Sherman was massing at Chattanooga for the push south. Though Sherman's objective was Atlanta, Rome with its industries lay on his right flank, and if that tempting prize was taken, the upper Coosa would lie open to invasion. In early May the Federal army began its march, and all along the Coosa, residents watched and waited to see what Sherman had in store for them.[22]

On the scene at Rome was Cummins Lay, captain of the steamboat *Alphfretta*. Lay was a true son of the Coosa. Born in Cherokee County, Alabama, near the banks of the river in the house his father, John Lay, built soon after his arrival from Virginia, Cummins had grown up with the stream as his companion, and it was only natural that when he was able he began working with his father convoying flatboats downstream to Greensport and Wetumpka. From flatboat to steamboat was an easy transition, and by the eve of the Civil War, he was an accomplished pilot and captain. During the early years of the conflict, he took the *Alphfretta* back and forth between Greensport and Rome, carrying soldiers, prisoners, supplies, and pig iron from the Cornwall Furnace. In 1863, when it appeared that Streight's mule brigade might make it to Rome, he helped get the steamships out of the city, lest they fall into Yankee hands. When the news arrived that Sherman was on the march, he knew that he might have to do the same thing once again.[23]

The Union army was not far into Georgia when Sherman sent a column under Gen. J. B. McPherson to capture Rome. Moving swiftly, the Yankees were soon on the outskirts of the town, and on May 17, they began shelling the factories and the riverfront. Accounts differ as to what took place next. According to one report, under Lay's orders the *Alphfretta* and another boat, the *Laura Moore*, raised steam and, stacked with bales of cotton to protect them, ran the Federal guns and escaped—the *Alphfretta* with Lay at the wheel leading the way. Lay's son, John, told a different story. He remembered his father relating that both boats were trapped at the wharf when McPherson took the town. Lay waited until dark, extinguished the fires under the boilers of the

Laura Moore, then cut her loose to drift silently down the river. She was away before the artillery could be used to stop her, and the small arms fire she took was deadened by the cotton stacked on her deck. Once the craft was safe, the boilers were fired again, and the *Laura Moore* steamed down to Greensport.[24]

If the escape (no matter how it happened) was not dramatic enough, what followed would make Cummins Lay a hero among Coosa captains and a legend on the river. About the time he reached Greensport a late spring rainstorm had hit the valley, and the river was out of its banks. Fearing that the Yankees might not be content with Rome and would follow the Coosa into Alabama, he decided to take advantage of the high water and pilot his boat farther south, where it would be safe. He moved downstream, gliding "'high wide and handsome' over inundated cotton and corn fields" as if the shoals and rapids had never existed. At Wilsonville, midway between Greensport and Wetumpka, he moored the *Alphfretta* (which one account has making the trip as well) and decided to do what no other pilot had done—take a steamboat from Rome to Wetumpka.[25]

Stripping the *Laura Moore* to make her as light as possible, Lay took her into the most dangerous stretch of rapids on the river. Following boat shoots when he could see them, using his river sense when he could not, Cummins Lay guided the *Laura Moore* around rocks, through channels, and finally over the Devil's Staircase, whose roar must have drowned out every sound made on board by either engines or men. Then the vessel and crew rested in the pool at Wetumpka before continuing downstream. Whether Lay took his boat on to Mobile, as one tale is told, or whether she was turned over to the Confederate government at Montgomery where she stayed for the rest of the war, the result is the same. The *Laura Moore* with Capt. Cummins Lay at the wheel is the only steamboat ever to run the whole length of the Coosa, and as one historian of the region noted, the feat "will doubtless stand as the most daring exploit ever attempted on any river in Alabama."[26]

Captain Lay did well not to tarry at Greensport, for in less than a month a Union army was there, on the banks of the Coosa, at the same ford Gen. Andrew Jackson had used when he came down against the Creeks in 1813. In early June of 1864 General Sherman ordered Gen. Lovell H. Rousseau, with a force of some three thousand, to move south from Decatur to a point near Opelika, where he could cut the Montgomery & West Point Railroad and deprive Atlanta of needed supplies. Leaving quickly, Rousseau's raiders reached the river on June 13, and the next day, at Ten Islands, routed a small enemy force. Then they began crossing. It was, according to one report, "a beautiful sight," with "the long array of horsemen winding between the green islands and taking a serpentine course across the ford—their arms flashing back the rays of the burning sun, and guidons gaily fluttering along the column." To the writer it was a scene "recalling the days of romance, and contrasting strongly with the stern hardships and vivid realities of the every-day life on the duty march."[27]

Maybe it was such a scene for the Yankees, but not many people on the other side recalled "days of romance" when they saw that "long array of horsemen." Southerners feared the worst, and in some cases those fears were realized. Though the objective was farther south, Rousseau's men took the time to burn an "extensive iron furnace" they found near the river. Then they moved down to Talladega where they captured large quantities of sugar, salt, flour, and bacon that the Confederacy could ill afford to lose. They took what they could use, spoiled the rest, destroyed two gun factories and a railroad complex, then rode away. Meanwhile, word had reached Montgomery that the capital was Rousseau's goal. "Instantly," according to the *Montgomery Daily Mail*, "the bells were rung and the citizens turned out in large force." But while "arrangements were [being] made for arming the whole male population," the Union column swung east. In a few days it was across the Tallapoosa and moving toward the objective. It easily overcame what resistance it met, and by the end of the month, according to one of Rousseau's men, "the work for which the expedition was sent out was now thoroughly accomplished." Thirty miles of track were destroyed, along with depots, rolling stock, and large quantities of precious rations. More than that, the raid "struck terror into the heart of rebeldom." The Union soldiers soon left the state, but the memory of what they did, and how easily they did it, remained.[28]

Rousseau's men joined their comrades outside Atlanta and waited to see what their raid had accomplished. In under six weeks they had their answer. On September 1, Confederate forces withdrew from the city, and soon General Sherman was making plans to march to Savannah and the sea. Now the war closed in on Alabama as Federal armies (there seemed no end to them) pounded away at rebel remnants in Tennessee, Georgia, and Mississippi. The Gulf coast, including the mouth of Mobile Bay, was blockaded tightly. By early 1865 the state was an island surrounded by a sea of Union blue.[29]

As spring approached Maj. Gen. James Harrison Wilson with three divisions of Federal cavalry, over thirteen thousand seasoned veterans, waited at Gravelly Spring on the Tennessee River, hoping the weather would clear so he could move south. The plan was to take and destroy supplies and industrial facilities at Tuscaloosa, Elyton, and Montevallo, and if all went well, they might make it as far as Montgomery. But the real prize was Selma, which by 1865 was the most important industrial center left in the Confederacy. Between Wilson's army and the town was a Confederate force under Gen. Nathan Bedford Forrest, who was having to round up deserters and absentees to fill his ranks. Troop strength in the state was so low that Gov. Thomas H. Watts had called on sixteen- and seventeen-year-old boys to enlist. Meanwhile, reports had reached the city that "large numbers of [Union] vessels loaded with troops . . . [were] in the outer bay of Mobile." If Mobile fell, there was nothing left to stop an upriver invasion except a battery of cannon at Choctaw Bluff—and that was a weak reed on which to lean. Selma was vulnerable, and everyone seemed to know it.[30]

On March 22, 1865, the Federal army crossed the Tennessee. Though usually called "Wilson's raid," the movement was hardly the quick, efficient "attack and withdraw" campaign that the term "raid" implies. During the next two weeks Union columns moved steadily south along parallel roads, deep into Confederate territory. Raiders were sent out from the main body, but they were auxiliary elements of the larger scheme. Anyone who saw Wilson's divisions knew his was no raid—it was an invasion.[31]

Union forces were four days into the march before Forrest learned they were coming. Racing to head them off, his horsemen engaged the Federal cavalry in a series of skirmishes, some on the scale of battles, that slowed the Union advance but did not stop it. Tuscaloosa, Elyton, and Montevallo all were taken as Wilson dealt blow after blow to Southern hopes that they might be able to continue the war even if Richmond fell. Forrest's force, less than a third the size of Wilson's, was inexperienced, poorly supplied, and scattered. To make matters worse, the Union commander knew it, for his men had captured some of Forrest's dispatches. Though one Confederate veteran later speculated that if Forrest had been able to assemble his ragtag force, "the cavalry battle of the ages" would have been fought, it is unlikely that would have done more than delay the enemy. Wilson's army was just too strong. The Confederate commander did all he could, and in some cases more than might have been expected, but he was unable to halt the blue tide. Relentlessly Wilson's divisions moved down the Alabama and Tennessee Rivers Railroad and into the Black Belt, rich with forage and fodder. Then, on April 1, they paused at Plantersville, nineteen miles north of Selma. They had been on the march only eleven days.[32]

Selma was heavily fortified with earthworks, stockades, and parapets, but there were not enough troops to man the defenses. With the enemy so close, city fathers met in a council of war with Gen. Richard Taylor, Confederate commander for Alabama and Mississippi, to decide on a course of action. Taylor rejected all thoughts of surrender. Instead he told Selma's leaders that war material they could easily move should be sent west by rail or east on the Alabama and that the rest should be thrown into the river. Then he promised the group that Selma would be defended at all costs. When counting those costs, Taylor did not include himself. The next day, after meeting briefly with Forrest, General Taylor took the only remaining locomotive and, it was said, "left the city as fast as a steam engine could carry him."[33]

Wilson's troops were already on the march. At six in the morning they rode out of camp and headed south; at about two on a beautiful April Sunday afternoon they reached the city's defenses. Forrest had issued an order that every male in Selma would go "into the works or into the river," so by noon some four thousand citizens, "not more than two thousand of them reliable" according to John Hardy, stood ready to meet "the flower of the Federal armies." With detailed knowledge of the breastworks, given him by an Englishman who had helped build them, Wilson moved his men into position. Once there, they were told to make coffee, remain calm, and wait for orders to attack.[34]

The Battle of Selma began about sundown. The Confederate line held briefly, then gave way. A second stand was made at a partially completed inner defensive line, but this hardly slowed the advance or the retreat. Though it was not the "disgraceful stampede" a Georgia newspaper called it, it was a rout, as inexperienced conscripts and volunteers threw away their weapons and withdrew or surrendered to the first Union soldier they saw. Regular troops, what few there were, fought better and sustained heavy losses in the process, but their stand had no effect on the outcome. In the confusion Forrest escaped; by dark the Battle of Selma was over.[35]

Union troops moved into the city and began rounding up soldiers and citizens who were trying to flee. A few got away by swimming the Alabama, but the river was running high, and others drowned in the effort. When the prisoners were assembled and counted, they totaled about twenty-seven hundred; no one could determine the number of dead and wounded. Union losses were light—forty-six killed, three hundred wounded. The captured were confined in the stockade previously occupied by Union prisoners, where they were generally treated well, even to the point of allowing Confederate officers to share the Union officers' mess. Some Southern soldiers probably enjoyed the best food they had eaten in the past year. Complaints were few, though Lt. Col. Frank Montgomery of the First Mississippi remembered how a Yankee band playing Dixie kept him awake and depressed.[36]

What followed has become so much a part of legend and lore that, despite admirable efforts on the part of scholars to set the record right, citizens of Selma still argue that what the Yankees did to Atlanta can hardly compare to the fate of their city. If the "Queen city of the Black Belt" had been blessed with a Henry Grady or Margaret Mitchell, Selma, not Atlanta, would be remembered as the "martyred city of the South." Support for Selma's side, at its most exaggerated, can be found in a speech made to a New York audience by former governor Lewis Parsons, titled appropriately enough "The Sacking of Selma." Tales of drunken soldiers looting homes and stores, brutalizing women and old men, and eventually setting the torch to the town were made believable to generations of Selmians who expected nothing less from an army they were told had been recruited when "prison and penitentiary doors had been opened to swell the columns of the invading hosts." Even as the years passed and reason began to temper emotion, there were those who believed (and still believe) that though it may not have been as bad as all that, it was bad nevertheless.[37]

Some of it is true. Selma officials had tried to destroy supplies of whiskey, but defeat came too quickly, and when Union troops entered the city they found the spirits. The result was predictable. One Union sergeant came across men "making very free" at a liquor store (a southerner would say "looting") and was asked to join them. "No soldier," he remembered, "needs a second invitation of that nature at the end of a campaign." So there were drunken soldiers, just as the stories tell. And there was looting and robbing; but Wilson moved quickly to post guards and protect people and property. As for the fire, retreating Confederates torched some thirty-five thousand bales of cotton and a number of warehouses in the commercial district. This fire spread to other buildings but did not consume the entire city, as Selma's antebellum architecture testifies today. Still, many businesses along downtown streets were lost, and as far away as Cahawba, refugees could see the red glow in the sky. In Selma, the bitterness would last long after the fires burned out.[38]

The next day the cleanup began, and the Alabama River became a great, handy dump. Dead horses that littered the town were thrown in on top of the cannon and munitions tossed down the bluff by retreating Confederates. Then Union soldiers dismantled what they could not use, and it went into the Alabama as well. Piles were so high that they were visible above the water, and almost a century later, during the Second World War, some of the metal was brought up and used as scrap. Today divers still find artifacts that can be traced to the battle. Like the people of Selma, the Alabama River would long feel the effects of that day in April.[39]

Union soldiers did their work well. The arsenal's twenty-four-building complex that had produced everything from ammunition to knapsacks was destroyed; the naval foundry where the gunboats *Tennessee*, *Selma*, *Morgan*, and *Gaines* were built and armed was razed; and a score of other installations, public and private, were torn up or burned down. This catalog of destruction reveals just how important Selma was in the South's effort to supply itself and how much the Alabama valley lost when the city fell. As the news spread up and down the river, it seemed to confirm that Alabama's resistance was almost over. Though some in the state believed Wilson would soon withdraw to the north, it was more a statement of hope than conviction. "Yankees at Selma," shouted the headlines of the *Clarke County Journal*. Where would they be next?[40]

Next would be Montgomery. Sherman had marched three hundred miles to convince Georgia that "resistance was in vain." Wilson would need only fifty miles to accomplish the same thing in Alabama. A pontoon bridge nearly nine hundred feet long was built across the flooded river, and on April 9 the Union army began moving. The crossing took all night, but their way was illuminated by the flickering light of buildings burning on the bluff. Then the Federal army turned east and headed for the former capital of the Confederacy and the capital of Alabama.[41]

There was no one in their way. Black Belt swamps were far more troublesome than Confederate forces as the Union column pushed steadily on. It was spring, and though the roads were a quagmire, the Cherokee rose was in bloom, and it seemed to the soldiers that "the very air was new and delightfully sweet." The heart of the Alabama River plantation district was all but deserted. When they arrived at Lowndesboro just after midnight, "no living creature appeared in the town, not a light was seen, not a sound was heard except the subdued rattle of arms in the column." According to one observer, "It was a dream world, through which the war-worn soldiers marched silently in the deep shadows of the oaks."[42]

Now they were more like tourists than an invading army. Wilson issued and enforced strict orders against looting, so Union soldiers simply looked and marveled at what they saw. And when they could, they talked to residents—often to black Alabamians who until recently had been slaves. When they asked one freedman what had happened to his former owner, he replied that "old massa headed down to Big Swamp, crying all done gone, Selma gone, Richmond gone too." Selma they knew about, but Richmond? The Union soldiers assumed that reference was just another example of the southern flair for the dramatic overstatement. But "old massa" was right. Before they reached their destination they learned that the day Selma fell, Jefferson Davis fled the Confederate capital. Richmond was, indeed, "gone too."[43]

There was only Montgomery, whose significance now was largely symbolic. Still fearing, nonetheless, that the symbol might inspire diehards to make a last stand for the Confederacy's first capital, Wilson took Montgomery seriously. But in the capital, diehards were few. Selma's fall and the Union army's rapid approach demoralized the town. Montgomery's commanding general Daniel Adams had promised to mount a "full defense" of the city, but there was little enthusiasm for it, and the citizens were probably relieved when he later received orders to abandon the capital when the enemy arrived in force. When that moment came, Confederates began burning the over eighty thousand bales of cotton stored in the town. Anything else that might be of use to the Federals was also destroyed or looted by residents anxious to fill larders depleted by wartime shortages. Bushels of corn were torched, and the street outside the commissary was "ankle deep" in syrup poured out by retreating Confederates. Fires spread; for a while it looked as if the city might be consumed, but the wind shifted, and it was spared. News of what had happened spread rapidly, further demoralizing Southern supporters. Ironically, it also left some of those who had every reason to rejoice at the outcome with a sense of personal loss and sadness. Walter Calloway "warn't up dar," but he "heern tell dey burn up piles an' piles of cotton an' lots of steamboats at Montgomery an' lef' de ole town jes 'bout ruint"—just about.[44]

Now reason—or resignation—won the day. At three on the morning of April 12, Montgomery mayor W. L. Coleman and a party of prominent citizens rode out to Union lines under a flag of truce. There, to the delight of Wilson and his men, they surrendered the city. The general immediately posted guards at key streets and buildings, and when everything was secured the entire force, with the band playing and their commander at the head, rode four abreast into the capital. On they came, an onlooker recorded, "host upon host of blue coats . . . fine looking men—handsomely dressed . . . brass buttons, brilliant epaulets, sabres drawn and clashing, . . . mak[ing] their entrance at full gallop." Anyone who compared these soldiers to the ragged Confederates who burned the cotton and retreated east understood why Wilson had won and why for Montgomery, as for the Confederacy, surrender was the only real option.[45]

Four years to the day after the South fired on Fort Sumter, the first capital of the Southern union was occupied by Union troops. But if citizens felt traumatized by defeat, it hardly showed; and why should it?

for surrender was everywhere. Though some felt "humiliated" and wondered if "the good Lord will allow us long to be so downtrodden by such people" as the Yankees, soon they learned that even Robert E. Lee had given up the fight, proof enough that there was no disgrace in what they had done. Many in the city became, according to the *Montgomery Advertiser*, "Union Men of the 11th hour," and the ladies of the town were so friendly that victorious soldiers were disappointed when they learned that they would stay only a few days. The Montgomery Arsenal, including a niter work, foundry, and some shops was destroyed, along with the railroad station, a locomotive, and the rolling stock. Three steamboats discovered upriver loaded with food were brought back to the city and burned, "making a brilliant bonfire for the multitude which lined the shore." But these were spoils of war, and their destruction was accepted as such. Personal property was protected, soldiers were generally well behaved, and though it was not the outcome residents would have wished, stories coming to them from Selma suggested that things could have been a lot worse.[46]

By April 14, Wilson had learned that Mobile had fallen and that his troops would not be needed in the south. Columbus, Georgia, with its arsenal and factories was the obvious target now, and the next day he and his army were gone. The war on the Alabama was finished, and Alabama had lost.[47]

Downstream, Union soldiers held at Cahawba got the news. They had lived through cold, heat, floods, shortages, and every other hardship prisoners on either side endured. They had seen the best and the worst that war could make of men, and now they were going home. One of the captives, Jesse Hawes, remembered vessels arriving to carry them away—some to Selma where they would catch the railroad, others downriver to Mobile. The prisoners assembled on the bluff above the river, where they were officially paroled. "This performance over," Hawes later wrote, "the command, 'Right face' was given," and free at last, he and his companions were "marched down to the landing and put on board an old steamboat." When everyone was loaded the vessel "pushed out and started up stream, to the great delight of all." At other camps, North and South, more prisoners were released. On distant battlefields soldiers in tattered gray stacked their weapons, furled their flags, and turned South. Across the lines Union veterans were mustered out. The war was over.[48]

ELEVEN

*The War Comes to an End;
the Coosa Comes of Age*

Atter we was freed, Ol' Marster come out in de yard an' got in de
middle ob all ob us, an' tole us dat de ones dat wants to stay wid
him, to stan' on one side, an' de odders to stan' on de odder side. So
mah paw got on de side wid dose who wanted to leave, an' us lef'
Ol' Marster an' paddled down de river, in a paddlin' boat to Belle's
Landing.

GEORGE TAYLOR
Gosport, Alabama

Gadsden is still the Queen City of the Coosa, the finest stream in all
the South. It is the only place of any consequence in mineral
Alabama where there is an abundance of the raw material for iron
and steel production in close proximity to an inexhaustible supply of
water. This is our seal of greatness, affixed by the creator of the
universe, and protects us in our destinies. Keep your faith in
Gadsden, no matter whether the winds blow good or ill, the clouds
of doubt will but emphasize the sun of final triumph.

Gadsden Times
January 25, 1867

The soldiers came home, those who could. During the war nearly two
hundred of Dallas County's finest served in the Cahaba Rifles and
fought for the cause at Malvern Hill, Antietam, Chancellorsville,
Gettysburg, and Cold Harbor. By 1865 a third lay buried on or near
those fields, felled by battle or disease. Some seventy others returned
wounded or disabled, and the rest just returned. The story was much
the same all along the rivers; from Cedar Bluff to Claiborne the war
took a fearful toll. Even the survivors were casualties. "The young mens
in grey uniforms" that the former slave Cato remembered "used to pass
so gay and singing" grew old in four years. Later generations would
fight the war again in myth and symbol, but the veterans wanted no
more of it.[1]

"Massa Cal" returned to his Lower Peachtree plantation "all wore
out and ragged." He called his hands together in the front yard and told
them, "you are today as free as I am. You are free to do as you like,
'cause the damned Yankees done 'creed you are." He promised that any
who wished could stay and "work and eat to the end of his days, as long
as this old place will raise peas and goobers," but those who wanted to
leave were free to do so. It was a common scene, played out to a
common conclusion. Some stayed, just as Cato did with Massa Cal; but

140

others took freedom to be more than that, and they "lef' Ol' Marster an' paddled down de river, in a paddlin' boat."[2]

Most white southerners seemed to accept emancipation as a logical outcome of the war, and there was more resignation than anger at the loss of their property and the end of the peculiar institution. What whites did not accept was the end of the racial code that had defined master and retainer, superior and inferior. Anna M. Gayle Fry made this resistance clear in her account of her father's postwar efforts to enlist his former slaves to help bring in the harvest at his plantation near Cahawba. Mr. Gayle went to Selma, where he found his old servant Patty. In the past, according to Mrs. Fry, she was "the one of all others who expressed the greatest devotion to her 'young master.'" But "freedom had worked a marvelous change" on Patty, for when Mr. Gayle called to her "she turned, saw who it was, and flounced off, exclaiming: 'Lord a massie, Chile, I ain't got time to fool with you now.'" Gayle was stunned. It was "the first time in his life a negro had ever refused to come at his bidding," and that refusal, compounded by the "offhanded manner" in which he was answered, "was too much to be borne." Mr. Gayle returned to Cahawba, "gave his crop to the Confederate Soldiers," and made "no further overtures" to his former bondsmen.[3]

Amid the social and political disorder, the physical destruction, and the economic dislocation that made the postwar era one of the most turbulent in American history, Alabama's rivers continued to flow as they always had. With most of the state's railroads in ruins, rivers were needed more than ever, and rivermen saw their opportunity and seized it. Though some steamboats had been sunk or burned, there were boats enough to begin serving plantations in the region. One of these was Tim Meaher's *Southern Republic*, which had been sent up the Tombigbee to safety when Union forces moved on Mobile. After the war Meaher tactfully dropped "Southern" from the name, and the rechristened *Republic* began running a regular schedule between Mobile and Montgomery. Meaher continued on the river until 1870, quitting (he later recalled) "when the colored citizens demanded cabin passage." For Captain Meaher, as for Mr. Gayle, social revolution, not economic distress, was "too much to be borne."[4]

Not everyone had the resources of Meaher and Gayle to sustain them. In early 1866, it was estimated that some fifty-three thousand of the nearly three hundred thousand white Alabamians were destitute. Many of these lived on farms and small plantations in counties drained by the upper reaches of the Coosa, Tallapoosa, and Cahaba, where conditions were especially bad. Things were somewhat better for Black Belt whites, though planters in the region complained bitterly of the level to which they had sunk. Necessity soon forced former slaves to return to the land as sharecroppers and tenants, and former masters regained much of the power emancipation had taken from them. In the process, black Alabamians learned what it meant to be landless in the land of cotton and came to realize that while slaveholders had lost the war, freedmen lost the peace.[5]

Despite these hardships, signs of recovery soon appeared along the rivers. Cotton slides were busy once more, and former slaves, their value depreciated by freedom, labored both on the bluff and on the dangerous decks below. In Selma "the hammer, the saw and the trowel were again heard," and "new and large stocks of goods were opened almost every day." It was not long, according to local chronicler John Hardy, before the "artizan was again ready for business; the doctor ready to cure the sick; and the lawyer ready for his fee." Recovery was even more evident in Montgomery where money raised by Radical Republican taxes sparked a building boom that proved an "economic tonic" for the city. A new city hall, a municipal waterworks, and public schools were built by the Republican regime, to remind future generations that corruption and debt were not the only legacies of carpetbagger government. These were hardly flush times, but for many the recovery was real. Cotton prices were up, and the riverfronts at Montgomery and Selma, the wharfs at plantation landings, were strewn with bales waiting to be carried south. Brokers were busy, steamboats were loaded to capacity, and the mighty Alabama rolled on down to Mobile and the Bay. Citizens of the river region seemed determined to put the war behind them and build a New South from the ashes of the old.[6]

Meanwhile at the foot of Wetumpka's falls, Captain Cummins Lay waited aboard the recently refitted *Laura Moore*, hoping for water high enough to carry his boat over the rapids to the flat water of the upper Coosa. In the spring of '66 the rains came. The river rose, and when it crested the *Laura Moore* steamed out into the channel. Fighting the current and dodging debris, Lay made it to Greensport and from there had an easy run on into Georgia. Having etched his name in river records as the only man to take a steamboat down from Rome to Mobile, Cummins Lay now held the distinction of being the only captain to make the return trip. Records are usually broken; this one still stands.[7]

Along the way the *Laura Moore* passed Gadsden, a thriving village of some four hundred citizens, poised on the heights above the Coosa. A road cut in the bluff ran from the town to the river, connecting warehouses to the wharf and ferry. Though Gadsden was small, already there was talk of its rising to challenge Rome as the commercial capital

Coosa Shoals
(Courtesy Alabama Power Company Archives)

of the upper Coosa. The postwar recovery was well underway when Lay steamed by, and in the next few years cotton production in the area increased faster than anywhere in the state. With men like Captain Lay to put the boats on the river and carry the commerce, market centers were sure to thrive. Gadsden's city fathers predicted a glorious future for the valley and saw no reason why they should not lead the way.[8]

Since there were few in the state who wanted Rome and Georgia to benefit from northeast Alabama's bounty, Gadsden found allies ready to help her in her quest. With the political climate in Montgomery favoring internal improvement projects, a coalition of legislators from along the Alabama-Coosa corridor took the initiative, and in 1867 they pushed a bill through the legislature authorizing a survey from the state line to Wetumpka to determine "whether or not said river can be made navigable for steamboats, or other boats, and what would be the advantages to the State of Alabama." After decades of talk and speculation, it seemed that Alabama might finally do something to realize the potential of the Coosa River.[9]

The project and its $3,000 budget were handed over to Maj. Thomas Pearsall who shortly set out for Rome, where he hoped to enlist the help of a Colonel Pendleton, who had made an unofficial survey in 1858. Arriving on June 2, he found no colonel, but the absence did not really matter, for when Pearsall got a copy of Pendleton's report, he discovered that his survey was made "without *Compass - Level -* or *Transit*" and was of no use whatsoever. While trying to track down Pendleton, Pearsall explained his purpose to local leaders who claimed to be "quite interested in the survey and opening the 'Lower Coosa,' but beyond mere expression of their earnest hope" that the project would benefit the region, "they were silent." The only help the Alabama expedition got from Georgians was free passage from Rome to Gadsden, "granted unsolicited" by the owner of the steamship *Undine*.[10]

Arriving at Gadsden on June 5, Pearsall and his party tarried long enough to purchase tents, supplies, and two boats built by local craftsmen; then they set out downstream. They took only one day to cover the thirty miles to Greensport, where they began what the major called the *"Survey proper."* From that point they went around Embry Bend, through Broken Arrow Shoals, then over rapids and between islands, until they reached the railroad bridge that crossed from Shelby to Talladega County. The date was June 28. In just over three weeks they had traveled over two hundred miles on what Pearsall described as "one of the most beautiful rivers I have ever seen," a stream that, when "taken in connection with the country through which it threads its way, . . . presents almost every attraction that *land* & *water* combined can impart."[11]

As for the stream's navigability, to that point in the survey, Pearsall had found little to impede the project. The river from Rome to Greensport was so free from obstacles that he "did not deem it essential to devote much time to determine the exact location" of the few "hidden rocks" along the course, and from Greensport to the bridge he found nothing that could not be easily overcome. As they rested "in camp" before beginning the last phase of the journey, an optimistic major wrote Gov. Robert M. Patton that though he expected "more *falls* to the mile and more *wild water*" on the rest of the route to Wetumpka, he did not "anticipate any serious difficulty." If anyone had told the major what lay ahead, he apparently had not listened.[12]

Below the bridge, as the land sloped down and the stream gathered speed, the Coosa began to fall away. They had names now, those places where the water was the wildest, names that helped rivermen remember them—the Narrows, Devil's Race, Butting Ram Shoals, Hell's Gap, Peckerwood Shoals, the Nigger, Closet and Moccasin reefs, and of course, the Devil's Staircase. In its last sixty miles, the river dropped over 275 feet before reaching Wetumpka and the eddy water below the town. For anyone hoping to tame the Coosa, this stretch was the greatest challenge.[13]

His last few weeks on the Coosa's white water tempered Pearsall's earlier optimism, and the report he prepared in the months that followed left no doubt that the project would be more ambitious than anything previously undertaken by the state. To "render the river navigable for steamboats of 200 tons burthen" from Greensport to a point fourteen miles above Wetumpka, Major Pearsall recommended no fewer than eighteen dams, each 10 feet high, and eighteen locks, 210 feet long and 25 feet wide. The last segment of the stream, which contained the Staircase and its roaring cauldron, would demand seven more dams and locks, unless it was found practical to dig a canal around the falls. Either way, Pearsall estimated that the effort would require "a sum not much less than $2,500,000," which he believed was a reasonable investment, for when the river was opened, the Coosa Valley, a country "of surpassing beauty, rich in soil, abounding in minerals, and other valuable commodities, such as coal, iron, marble, and timber," would send its commerce south for the benefit of Alabama instead of north for the benefit of Georgia.[14]

But the investment was beyond the means of a state in such disarray that when Pearsall tried to submit his report to the legislature in January of 1868, he found that federal authority had been reimposed to reconstruct Alabama's irreconcilables and that "there [was not] any such body now in session at the capitol." Things soon went from bad to worse. Plans delayed by the chaos of Radical Reconstruction were all but abandoned in 1873, when the nation sank into a deep depression. Businesses failed, land values plummeted, state revenue fell far short of expectations, and resources to support an undertaking the size of the Coosa navigation project were simply unavailable. With railroads prominent among the businesses going under, trade on the river remained brisk, but prewar patterns were unchanged. As far as commerce was concerned, the Coosa and the Alabama were two rivers that flowed in different directions.[15]

If the state had anything to do with it, the rivers could continue to flow that way. In 1875, while the nation was still struggling with the depression, conservative Democrats who had recently returned to power presented Alabamians with a new constitution. Convinced that public works undertaken by the Radical Republicans did little more than loot the treasury and reward supporters, these Democratic guardians of the common good added a clause to the constitution prohibiting state or local aid for internal improvements of any kind—including the locks and dams needed to make the Coosa and the Alabama one river. Filled with righteous indignation, these "Redeemers," for whom "states' rights" was an uncontested creed, created conditions that forced Alabama time and again to appear a supplicant at the federal altar.[16]

Residents along the upper Coosa could not wait for the matter to be decided in Montgomery or Washington. Though as Alabamians they might have preferred to send their goods downriver to Wetumpka, they had products to get to market, and Rome with its rail connections was their only real option. The result was a thriving river trade that, despite its advantages for Georgia, started Gadsden on its way to becoming the "Queen City of the Coosa." Incorporated in 1871, the town survived the Panic of '73 and at mid-decade boasted some nineteen businesses, annual receipts of over a million dollars, and a population of more than two thousand. Six steamboats made regular trips between Greensport and Rome during that decade, and Gadsden was midway on the route. Most of these were smaller, more plebeian vessels than the prewar "palaces" of the Alabama, and the cargo they carried reflected the region they served. The steamer *Undine* once reached port with "357 bales of cotton, 40,000 shingles, 625 pelts, 50 cowhides, 50 baskets of poultry, 200 bushels of corn, and 250 bags of wheat." It was as if the agricultural economy of northeast Alabama had been made small and packed aboard.[17]

With the Coosa critical to Gadsden's economy, shipbuilding became one of the town's earliest industries and one in which residents took special pride. The Gadsden Steamboat Company, founded in the winter of 1879–80 by a group that included veteran river man James M. Elliott and local entrepreneur R. B. Kyle, launched the first locally made vessel, the *City of Gadsden*, that following August. It was a festive occasion, and citizens lined the banks to cheer as "the props were knocked up and away went the monster, sliding into the river . . . with the speed of lightning." Promoters were pleased all the more because the boat was "entirely a Gadsden enterprise" and would therefore "run in the interests of Gadsden"—"independent of all railroads and every combination" that might be less sensitive to local needs. Lest this "pro-Gadsden" attitude frighten other customers, the local newspaper assured its readers that "all persons who patronize the boat will be fairly and equally dealt with," for with "God's highway," the mighty Coosa, available without charge or restriction, the *City of Gadsden*'s "freight rates will be the cheapest." No other "corporation or locality" could offer so much, so it followed that what was good for Gadsden was good for its neighbors.[18]

Other boats were launched at Gadsden over the years, and as they joined Rome-built steamers, the river grew crowded, and competition between captains was fierce. Of all the vessels on the Coosa, the one that clearly stood with Alabama's best was the magnificent *Magnolia*, commanded by Elliott, whose family is as famous in river lore as that of Cummins Lay. The *Magnolia* was such a dominant force on the Coosa that a group of rival river men built their own boat, the *Sidney P. Smith*, to challenge Elliott's craft. Their contest reached its most bitter when the *Magnolia* arrived one day at Greensport to pick up a load of cotton only to find that the shipment had been taken by the *Sidney P.* Outraged, Elliott gave chase. He caught the culprit at an upriver wood yard, boarded her, lashed the boats together, and took the cargo. The *Sidney P*'s captain, not to be undone, sent word ahead to Gadsden, and when the *Magnolia* arrived its captain and crew were arrested and charged with piracy. The dispute was finally settled and charges dropped, but the incident reveals how commerce was conducted on the Coosa and how seriously those involved took the informal arrangements on which their livelihood depended. The frontier may have given way to civilization in some quarters, but on the river, its code of honor and sense of justice still held sway.[19]

The Coosa carried a lot of cotton, but that was not the region's only commodity. In this era a thriving lumber industry developed along the stream, and Hokes Bluff, just upriver from Gadsden, became one of many logging centers. Trees were cut and hauled there to the "log roll," where they were pushed down the bluff and into the river. Then they were lashed together with hickory boughs and saplings and floated as rafts down to the sawmills clustered at the railroad bridge at Gadsden. Guided, and sometimes pulled, by tugboats built for the task and by steamers when it was not picking season, the rafts filled the river almost from bank to bank. The thought of rounding a bend to meet this floating juggernaut must have been a steamboat man's nightmare, and the fact that no accounts of collisions have come down to us is testimony to the skill of pilots and crew.

In time other mills appeared along the Coosa. Some were little more than "peckerwood" operations, but other locations, like Riverside, about twenty miles below Greensport, grew to become "rip-roaring sawmill towns." The largest sawing operations were usually found at the end of a long stretch of flat water, so the river could bring logs from miles upstream. Because they preferred to be close to a railroad, which could take the lumber to market, major mills usually had spur lines built to them. But no matter how large or how small, sawmills were an important alternate occupation for river region farmers.[20]

Wood cut at Hokes Bluff and other yards was used for more than lumber. For years local residents had known, or at least suspected, that riches lay beneath the soil, and even the casual visitor was "astonishe[d] . . . that the superb material resources of the state should remain undeveloped." In the 1870s that situation began to change. Wartime iron mining and smelting operations were revived and expanded, new ones were begun, and by the end of the decade forests were going down to feed the furnaces of the Gadsden Iron Company and other foundries. The railroad's arrival in Etowah County coincided with this industrial expansion, and in 1877 the first bridge to span the upper Coosa opened at Gadsden, built by the mineral division of the Louisville and Nashville Railroad. Despite this flurry of activity, the river region would not become the iron and steel center of the state. That honor would go to the town of Birmingham, rising at that moment near the headwaters of the Cahaba. This failure was not entirely for lack of trying, as the infant industries of Gadsden testified. But for the time, at least, the Coosa Valley was a land of farmers, and there was more to that way of life than a means of making a living. Seasonal work in a sawmill, something to supplement what the earth provided, was one thing. Yearly labor in the mill or the mine was something else entirely. Conditions on the farm were hard, but not that hard. Such a move would have to wait for more desperate times.[21]

With the state constitutionally prohibited from using its resources to improve river navigation and develop the Coosa Valley, some citizens hoped that private corporations would step into the breach. But men and concerns that had the money to make such investments seemed bent on using their resources to build railroads. Edward R. King, who visited the region in the 1870s, concluded that "Alabama [was] indulging in an 'overcrop' of railways" and chided investors for ignoring "the abundance of her superb water-courses" that stood ready to take goods to market. But in the minds of postwar capitalists, railroads were the sure route to prosperity, and nothing could convince them otherwise. The locomotive was the symbol of the future, and while Alabama industrialists waited for the future to arrive in all its glory, they embraced the symbol for comfort and reassurance. Besides, during the decade of the '70s, everything suggested that the government, the distrusted federal government, would take care of the rivers.[22]

It seems a bit surprising that in this age of rail and steam, Washington would expend so much legislative energy on America's waterways, but between the end of the war and the turn of the century, act after act to improve inland navigation was passed by Congress and signed into law. Alabama's rivers were mentioned in most of these, with the Coosa receiving special attention. Apparently not satisfied with

Major Pearsall's earlier conclusions, Congress, under the River and Harbor Act of 1870, authorized another survey. This time there was a human cost to add to the outlay, for an accident at Devil's Race claimed one of the party. Despite high water and the loss of a comrade, the survey team pushed ahead and finished by the summer of 1872. Their report was essentially the same as Pearsall's. The river was found "exceptionally favorable . . . for improvement" with stable banks and a good flow. Between Rome and Greensport there were some thirteen shoals that might be troublesome in the dry season but that could be made passable by excavations or with "wing or spur dams" that would "confine a greater volume of the water into the channel, and thus deepen it." Since some work had already begun on upriver improvements, it was estimated that if Congress moved promptly to provide the funds, that part of the stream could be made navigable year round by 1878.[23]

Below Greensport was another matter entirely. For this stretch the surveyors recommended building a "slack water navigation" system consisting of low-lift dams and locks to get boats over most rapids and two short canals to move commerce around the major falls. Other sections of the river could be cleared by "the removal from the channel ways of dangerous and inconvenient rocks." The plan was similar to that used to improve the Ohio River, and it reflected the belief widely held by engineers at that time that high dams were neither safe nor practical. Considering that steamboats and barges drew little water, low-lift dams seemed more than sufficient to do the job. Someone estimated that all of this work could be accomplished for the sum of $2,340,746.75—a figure impressive if for no other reason than the certainty of the cents.[24]

Now the question was no longer what the project would cost, but whether Congress would fund it. The answer was not long in coming. That same year, Washington adopted a plan for thirty-one low-lift dams and locks on the Coosa. Then came the Panic of 1873, and the government, like the economy, slowed to almost a standstill. Local interest in the undertaking remained high, however, and in 1875 a convention of regional leaders meeting at Rome pressed for congressional support. Washington responded and in the River and Harbor Act of 1876 reaffirmed its commitment to build the Coosa dams and clear a four-foot channel from Rome to Wetumpka. Then it underscored that commitment with an appropriation of the princely sum of $30,000— roughly 1 percent of the money needed.[25]

But before becoming too critical of Congress, remember that the nation was still in the grips of the panic, so any grant was significant. Besides, the Rome convention's first priority was clearing the river between Rome and Greensport, the stretch where the most could be accomplished at the least expense. Work began the next year and moved along well enough to convince Congress to add another $75,000 to the River and Harbor Bill of 1878. With these two appropriations, conditions around the "troublesome bars and shoals" in the upper section were improved, and by 1880, steamboatmen could count on a three-foot channel year round. Now the Coosa between Greensport and Rome became even more crowded, as northeast Alabama commerce made its way upriver to Georgia markets. The situation was not one in which state leaders could take much satisfaction, but residents of the valley scarcely complained.[26]

In those optimistic days when the first Corps of Engineers survey was being completed and hopes ran high that the river would indeed be opened, Congress once again began considering the age-old question of how to link the Coosa to the Tennessee. In 1871, a potential route was surveyed, and the report concluded that a canal from Guntersville to Gadsden, a distance of some fifty miles, was feasible. It proposed a ditch 56 feet wide at the bottom, 70 feet wide at top-water, and at least 5 feet deep. There would be towpaths on either side, and the locks would be 120 feet long and 30 feet wide between the gates. The whole project would cost just over $9.5 million. Then the Panic of 1873 claimed another casualty. Despite efforts by Alabama congressmen, nothing was done beyond the survey. A hundred years later the Tennessee finally would be connected to a river in Alabama, but not to the Coosa.[27]

By 1879, as the grip of the depression weakened, the federal government authorized improvements on a ten-mile stretch of the river from Greensport downstream to the East Tennessee, Virginia & Georgia Railroad bridge. Planners in Washington may have decided to end this next phase at that point, simply because it was a reasonable distance given the money available, but the fact that they carried the venture far enough to link with a railroad suggests the important shift in priorities taking place all along the river corridor. Where once railroads were built to carry commerce to the rivers, now the rivers were being improved to bring goods to the railroads. A contest between transportation routes and systems was being waged, a struggle which would alter market centers and redefine population patterns throughout the region. When it was done and victory declared, Alabama would be a very different state indeed.[28]

The project began well enough. During the next decade three "cut stone masonry locks," each with an exterior capacity of 40 by 175 feet,

Steamboat *Hill City* on the Coosa River, probably Lock #1
(Courtesy Scarboro Photography, Gadsden, Alabama)

were finished and opened for navigation. Lock #1 was .68 miles below Greensport, #2 was at the 3.86 mile marker, and Lock #3 was constructed about a mile and a half farther downstream. They made the river navigable through the first serious rapids and shoals. Then came a stretch of flat water some twenty miles long, through which a channel was easily dredged. Then there was another series of rifts and ledges, where a fourth lock and dam were planned. By the late 1880s construction on the last of these improvements was underway, and it seemed finally that the navigation of the Coosa, from Rome to Wetumpka, would become reality.[29]

But there were many in the state who believed that more could and should be done, and in March of 1887, men of this mind, representing nine counties in Alabama and seven in Georgia, met in Montgomery to discuss how best to advance the interests of all concerned. With the usual overblown rhetoric that observers had come to expect when "wise, prudent and dispassionate" southerners gathered in convention, "every question touching this splendid project" was covered. When they were finished the delegates affirmed their intention to press Congress to open the river and with it the "vast mineral wealth" that lay in the region. Already, according to John H. Disque of Etowah County, iron in Gadsden was manufactured "cheaper than anywhere else in the world," and if such local commodities could be moved economically and efficiently to market, Alabama would become "the richest, thriftiest and most populous state in the union." Why would anyone object to such a project?[30]

No one, at least no one at the convention, did object, but between the hype and hyperbole there were indications that at least some of those present were beginning to understand the ideological implications of what they were proposing, and they were a bit uncomfortable with the precedent being set. Aware that neither Georgia nor Alabama was able financially or (in the case of Alabama) constitutionally to underwrite the effort, and uneasy with the idea of a private corporation carrying out the project, delegates turned to the federal government for aid. Sensing the uneasiness this request created among conservatives, some felt it necessary to remind the audience (and themselves) that such a course was compatible with the beliefs of the greatest of all states'-rightists, John C. Calhoun, who held it appropriate for Congress to sponsor internal improvements of a national character—which they all believed the Coosa River project was. Knowing it was easier to break with the past if one had history's blessing, they raised Calhoun's endorsement from the grave, and with it they were ready to face the future.[31]

There were those in the hall who were willing to go even further and to blame history for the fact that such a convention had to be called in the first place. After a few delegates complained that the South had never received its fair share of federal appropriations, Col. W. P. Chilton of Montgomery rose to remind the audience that before the war "it was the policy of the Democratic party not to ask or advocate appropriations for internal improvements" and that development in Dixie suffered. But states' rights and the Democratic party were not entirely to blame. With remarkable candor Chilton also observed that earlier "the struggle of the South to keep hostile legislation off of slave property and to prevent aggressions upon Southern rights" had so preoccupied congressmen that other needs were left unattended. Now, he concluded, "that issue is gone and our representatives have turned their attention to the long neglected water ways of the South." Put another way, the Civil War had freed Dixie to develop its resources.[32]

Although letters endorsing the project arrived from Alabama senators John T. Morgan and James L. Pugh, along with a number of other national figures, speakers at the meeting urged those present not to be complacent. Success would come only if they returned home to organize committees, print pamphlets, and "burn this matter into the hearts and minds of the people," who in turn would press congressmen to do more than correspond with the convention. Delegates at Montgomery were charged to become delegates at home, for as former governor Thomas H. Watts told them, "the people, the whole people of Alabama have never taken proper interest in the great enterprise, and united their energies to bring it properly before Congress." But now things were different. The leaders of the state were behind the effort, and if asked, the people would surely join the cause. "When," Watts asked his audience, "has such a body as this ever met for the purpose of asking Congress to do anything to help us?" "Never in history as far back as my memory runs," was his answer. Governor Watts was born in 1819, the year Alabama entered the union. His memory ran back a long way.[33]

So the convention sent a memorial to Congress, pleading its case and asking for continued support and more funds. Congress, in a response that was becoming routine, called for a study and at the end of 1889 received yet another report confirming what everyone already knew. But this time things were different. Convention delegates had done their work well, and not long after the report arrived, Congress appropriated $300,000 for work on the Coosa. Half of the grant was designated for improvements downstream from Greensport, and the rest, in a significant deviation from previous planning, was to be used to start work on the river at Wetumpka. The legislation was the most important thus far, and it raised expectations all along the valley.[34]

Local leaders realized that if one convention could move Congress to act, a permanent organization working for river improvements might press the case even more successfully. This reasoning led third-generation river man William Patrick Lay, son of Capt. Cummins Lay, to bring together a group of Gadsden businessmen in 1890 to form the Coosa-Alabama River Improvement Association. The name is significant, for it not only announced to the public that they intended to make the two rivers into one, but it also acknowledged that to do so, they would need the help of citizens all along its course—from Rome to Mobile. Interest was high, construction was underway, and everything seemed to be falling into place.[35]

Through the 1890s work continued on the project. The three sets of locks and dams below Greensport were completed and put into operation. Construction began at Lock #4, and plans were made for the next phase at the Lock #5 site. "Dipper dredges" kept the channel clear along the route, and traffic was brisk. Downstream at Wetumpka another lock was built, but without the rest of the system in place, there was little for it to do. Meanwhile more surveys were made, more reports were filed, and more hopes were raised. Then, in 1905, the board of engineers that oversaw the project concluded that the cost of creating a navigation channel along the lower Coosa was not worth the return. It recommended that Lock #4 should not be completed and that no work should be done below it. In the board's opinion, improvement of the Coosa and Alabama should be limited to snag removal, dredging, and whatever else could be done for no more than $25,000 a year. Despite the stunning blow to regional ambitions, the association and its supporters did not give up. Rallying their resources, they lobbied hard to have the lock and dam at #4 completed and put into operation and a fixed dam, without a lock, erected at #5. But with few places below Greensport to go, and less and less to carry there, commerce on the Coosa continued to decline. In time, all the lockmaster posts were combined into one, and that person was never very busy. The association kept the dream alive, but more and more river men were coming to accept it for what it was—a dream.[36]

Few were more disappointed when the low-lift project was abandoned than the river interests in Wetumpka. Between the forks and the falls, competition between river and rail heated up quickly after the war, and the Coosa's supporters seemed to get the worst of it. High on their list of complaints was the railroad bridge across the Alabama between Wetumpka and Montgomery that had "rendered navigation so hazardous as to amount to a practical blockade of the river." That obstacle made the railroads an even more attractive alternative and depressed river travel to the point that by spring of 1872, the *Mist* was the only steamboat running all the way to the falls of the Coosa.[37]

Despair turned to optimism in 1876, when the River and Harbor Act not only authorized improving the river for navigation but allocated money to begin. Though the appropriation was small and designated to improve navigation to Rome, it raised hopes, and when it was followed with money to improve the river below Greensport, the Wetumpka press waxed eloquent speculating on what the future held. "With the Coosa opened to steam boat navigation," the editor observed, "floating down the riches from mine, quarry, forest, and farm to our door, . . . our Wetumpka might become the Pittsburgh of the Lower South." But work on the project moved slowly, and little impact was felt below the fall line. Wetumpka was far down the river, and conquering the Devil's Staircase seemed low on the congressional list of priorities.[38]

Hopes in Wetumpka soared once more when, in 1890, Congress specifically allocated $150,000 to begin construction at the southern end of the Coosa rapids. Work on a "detailed survey" began in December, but winter rains and high water delayed completion until the next summer. Meanwhile plans for the lock were drawn, submitted, and approved, and in September of 1891, work began. William Clark Edwards, a young man from Elmore County, signed on with the engineers and supervised much of the construction, beginning a career as a river man that would last, off and on, for four decades. But those years would not be spent at the falls of the Coosa. The stone and concrete walls were built when an 1897 progress report recommended that gates and operating machinery not be installed "until there is some prospect of the lock being required for navigation." That day never came. Edwards stayed on until 1900, working on other projects in the area, then left for another assignment. The lock, however, remained; and there it sits today, just below the bridge, a monument to the effort and a reminder of what might have been.[39]

Meanwhile, Wetumpka languished. Even before the lock was abandoned, the town's population was slipping, and now nothing could halt the decline. In 1875, Wetumpka had been a thriving city of 3,000. In 1899, the population stood at 619. Instead of a major inland port at the midpoint of a river that ran for nearly 650 miles from Georgia to Mobile Bay, Wetumpka settled down to become a village cut off from Alabama's mineral belt by a run of rapids 100 miles long. There would be no Pittsburgh of the Lower South at the falls of the Coosa.[40]

So it was that Wetumpka never challenged Gadsden's right to be called the Queen City of the Coosa. Ideally located to serve the river region as both a market and a social center, Gadsden by 1890 had a population of almost 22,000. Electric lights had been installed three years earlier, a new water works had been started up the year before that, and the Gadsden Ice Company was open and supplying the needs of the city and surrounding area. There were hotels, dry goods stores, real estate offices, and groceries; and there was George Washington Cureton's Coosa River Bar, where men in town from the farms spent time "playing pool, listening to the music of a break-down fiddle, telling yarns, and occasionally imbibing the liquid merchandise of the establishment" while they waited for the steamboat that would carry them home. When the whistle sounded they had only fifteen minutes to gather what they had bought, grab a "jug full of Cureton's merchandise," and make a mad dash for the river. The return trip they spent in a chair on the upper deck, keeping company and communing, no doubt, with Cureton's best.[41]

Had the clientele at Cureton's taken the time to wander around Gadsden they would have found a rising industrial center. Cotton was still king in the valley, and there were gins nearby with presses that could reduce a five-hundred-pound bale to half its original size, so more could be packed on steamers for the trip upriver to Rome. But no longer did the gins, the presses, or even boats loaded with the white staple fill residents with dreams of greatness. The Gadsden Iron Foundry, that harbinger of the city's industrial future, had been joined by other manufacturing concerns, among them the Elliott Car Works, established by the steamboating family to build rolling stock for railroads in the region. The Elliotts knew the river would not reign much longer. Soon cars built locally would be loaded with products made or grown locally, then coupled to engines and drawn away from the stream or across it on the L & N bridge. Rivermen like the Elliotts and the Lays watched interest in Coosa commerce slowly, steadily decline. What did it matter if the stream was not opened to Wetumpka; why wait for locks and dams when the rails were standing ready? The twentieth century was at hand, and Gadsden, like the rest of the Coosa Valley, was being pulled toward it by a locomotive.[42]

TWELVE

End of the Golden Age

Steamboat coming round the bend,
Good-bye my lover, good-bye.
She's loaded down with railroad men,
Good-bye my lover, good-bye.
"Papa's song"
"Those were days to be remembered,
days of riverboats,"
ROBERT W. KINCEY,
Birmingham News, August 3, 1958

Our rivers will never float such boats again. The faster age of railroads
has driven them from our waters forever.

Clarke County Democrat
October 24, 1889

When the veterans came home in '65, they heard roustabouts and
deckhands singing the same old song:

See that boat go round the bend,
Loaded down with steamboat men,
Good-bye, my lover,
G-o-o-d - b-y-e.[1]

In those uncertain times, the words must have given folks in the
Alabama valley a sense of security. If they could count on nothing else,
they knew the land would still grow cotton, which the river would
carry to market. So there would always be steamboats, "loaded down
with steamboat men."

For a while at least they were right. River commerce recovered so
rapidly that to many along the Alabama the war soon seemed little
more than an unpleasant interlude in a golden age that stretched back
to the time the *Harriet* first steamed from Mobile to Montgomery and
whose end was nowhere in sight. Though in the second half of the
nineteenth century, state and federal agencies paid more attention to
improving the Coosa than the Alabama, they did so only because
there was more to improve. The same acts that funded Coosa projects
also allocated funds to the Alabama, which got less only because it
needed less.

Like a faithful beast of burden, the Alabama River stood ready and
willing to serve. Still ideally suited for the task, it ran fullest in the
winter and spring, when commerce was heaviest. During the other
months, river men could usually depend on a flow sufficient to float

boats fully loaded, though low water narrowed the channel danger-
ously, and a grounding could block the whole river. One retired pilot
remembered seeing fourteen vessels tied up at Yellow Jacket Bar while
the crew of a stranded steamer worked to get her free. That drought
may have been the same one during which a captain trying to maneuver
his vessel through exposed sandbars and mudflats saw a man on shore
filling his bucket from the stream and threatened him with bodily harm
if he did not put the water back. At times like those, even a shallow-
draft steamboat needed all the river she could get.[2]

What Congress proposed for the Alabama was an 1872 "plan of improvement" that called for "scouring out" passages through the worst
shoals by means of "jetties and dykes to confine the low water flow to a
narrower channel." In the mid-1880s, eight of the most critical spots
were cleared in this way, and although appropriations were never sufficient to do the work as river men believed it should be done, a deeper
path free of "dangerous snags and overhanging timber" meant safer
navigation, more regular schedules, larger loads, and less time to make
the trip. Between 1879 and 1899 the federal government spent nearly
$400,000 on channel improvements, and as a result steamers on the
Alabama could "run by night, as well as by day, at all stages of water,"
and run they did.[3]

Even the Cahaba attracted attention from government engineers
during the postwar era. Hoping for cheaper access to the Cahaba coal
fields and the rising city of Birmingham, Congress authorized surveys
of the river in 1874 and again in 1880, and from these efforts came the
estimate that the locks and dams required to open the river from Centerville north to Shades Creek would cost $382,000. This sum was more
than the government was willing to spend, so the focus shifted south of
Centerville, where improvements were more easily (and cheaply) made.
Citizens of Centerville had never given up dreams of becoming a major
inland port and even supported a small shipyard, which in 1883 launched
the *Duke*, a locally built paddlewheeler. No doubt encouraged by this
sort of activity, between 1882 and 1892 the government spent $45,000 to
remove snags and overhangs and cut through the gravel and soft rock to
open a channel that would be three feet deep in low water. But the most
important commerce, the ore and the iron, was above the Centerville
falls, where the railroads ran and the river could not compete.[4]

Almost as an afterthought, in 1882 the government allocated $5,000
to improve the Tallapoosa from the forks to the foot of Tallassee Reef.
The course, about forty river miles, consisted of long, wide reaches of
navigable water, broken by tight bends and shoals where banks had
caved in. Work on the project never amounted to more than infrequent

snagging, overhang cutting, and a little dredging, but when it was completed in 1889, the river could boast of a "fairly cleared channel" ready for steamboats. Few came, however, and little commercial use was made of the stream, so plans for further work were abandoned. The River and Harbor Act of 1892 appropriated no money for the Tallapoosa River. The factories of Tallassee, recovered from the war and by 1900 over 76,000 spindles strong, found other means of transportation.[5]

Though the Alabama's shoals were nothing like the Coosa's wild water, the larger stream resisted improvement in its own way. Floods occurred frequently, and man's puny efforts seldom withstood the onslaught. Farmers who lived along the stream, many of them former slaves, were particularly hard hit. One freedman, Dellie Lewis, recalled "Alabama River floods, dat swep' ober de lan' an' washed away lots of de food." Survivors were faced with starvation until "de gover'ment sont some supplies of meat, meal an' 'lasses" packed in barrels marked "U.S." When officials were slow to distribute the goods, one of the refugees, "bein' tired of waitin' an' bein' powerful hongry," told his fellow sufferers "dat de U.S., on de barrell meant Us, so us commence' to eat." Lewis remembered with satisfaction how, when agents in charge finally "come to gib us de meat and 'lasses, us be done et it all up."[6]

The flood of April 1886 was especially bad. Upcountry rains filled the Coosa, which rose so high at Gadsden that steamboats could go all the way up Town Creek and tie up at Fourth Street. From there the water roared through Greensport, down the rapids, over the Staircase, and to Wetumpka with such force that it carried away the covered bridge that linked the residential area on the western shore with the business section across the river. Most of the men were at work when the bridge fell, and the only adult male left in the suburbs with the women and children was the Presbyterian minister. During the crisis wives and mothers took charge of their fatherless families and saved what they could from their flooded homes. Days passed before men were able to ferry across to learn if their loved ones had survived nature's fury.[7]

Downstream, Montgomery and Selma felt the river's wrath, and farmland all the way to the cutoff was inundated. In places the Alabama was reported to be three miles wide, and the current was so strong that "landings, if made at all, [were] outside the channel, and attended with considerable danger." One witness remembered how "stock was carried down stream" and people trapped by the rising water "were found clinging to trees and high places, and only made their escape in small rowboats sent to their rescue." Backwater pushed the tide up creeks and branches and "covered the country for miles." Days passed before the water finally receded, sometimes leaving the land richer but always leaving the people poorer. There would be other floods, but they would be measured against the "great overflow of '86."[8]

Maybe just because they were keeping better records or because there were more people around to remember, after the war, floods seemed to come more frequently and hit more fiercely. In '65, '66, '72, '86, '88, and '92, the rains fell, and the rivers rose, fast, for the land could not contain the water as it had before. Hardscrabble farmers and debt-ridden planters had clear-cut any land that would grow cotton, and fields ran down to the creeks and out to the edge of the river bluffs. Consequently, in the spring, before the crop was up, the bare earth soaked in what rain it could and rejected the rest. The runoff, heavy with the soil it was supposed to nurture, flowed into the river, and the river, after taking what water it could, turned the rest back on the land.[9]

River men saw the results. Days when the stream flowed dark and green were fewer now, and as the silt that colored the water settled out, it clogged the channel and hindered navigation. Pilots had to be all the more alert for shifting sandbars and mud banks, which appeared and disappeared with each freshet; and dredges, when they finally arrived, fought an ongoing battle against this new enemy. But more was involved than a threat to commerce. What they could not see was the beginning of an ecological alteration that continues to threaten the river today. As the land wore down, farmers turned to fertilizers to replenish the soil. These supplements washed away as well, and in the streams they began to work changes on vegetation that would not be realized for decades. At the time, what was there to notice? Schools of fish still came upriver to the Wetumpka shoals to spawn, sturgeon were frequently caught in the Cahaba, and catfish thrived no matter what happened to the river. There was no time for concern—not yet.[10]

Despite all Alabamians were doing to them, the Alabama, Coosa, Tallapoosa, and Cahaba seemed to endure, eternal, unchanging as the land, and like the land, there solely for the people and their use. And the people used them—to transport themselves and their goods, to carry off their waste, to supply their tables, and to keep themselves entertained. Alabamians enjoyed their rivers. They fished the waters, hunted the banks, swam, boated, and reveled in the variety the streams offered them. "Tub races" were popular on the Coosa, where contestants sat in large wooden washtubs, their legs dangling in the water, and with a paddle tried both to propel and to steer their craft. The rules decreed that each vessel was fair game, so occupants spent as much time trying to capsize opponents as they did trying to get to the finish line. Victory was as much the result of survival as boatmanship. A more sedate but no less popular spectacle was the Selma "regatta" sponsored at the turn of the century by the "YMCA boys" of the city and conducted, the newspaper boasted, in a "business like manner." "The stream of life," one observer noted, has found "a fitting type in the Alabama river." He could have written the same about any of the waterways in the system. That Alabamians loved their rivers was no secret.[11]

There still remained something mysterious about the streams, as if the Indians had been right and the waters hid sinister spirits, which should be approached only with care. Those who were not wary often fell victim, for there were concealed step-offs and cold undercurrents waiting to trap them. Parents warned their children; old men urged caution on the young; everyone knew the danger. But warnings were never enough. Every summer, the saying went, "the old Alabama river receives her toll." Then people endured the sad search, the dragging and the waiting. Finally, if nothing was found, bales of fodder were cast on the water to float to hidden eddys and be pulled down to the body below. The ritual was repeated each season, wherever the rivers flowed.[12]

Pleasant memories, however, usually won out. The boats were always grand, the captains noble, and the trips to Mobile "to do the season's shopping or attend a play or circus" described as nothing less than adventures. Who is to say it was not so? Even the few "professional travelers" who took to the river after the war praised the conduct of the vessels and confirmed that on the better boats, at least, the good life was still available for those who could afford it. In the mid-1870s, a correspondent for the *Morning Star and Catholic Messenger* booked passage on the "elegant little *Mary*," commanded by its "Catholic Captain," the young John Quill. Though the traveler was accustomed "to the grand style and princely fare of our Mississippi steamers, [he] found nothing to regret in the accommodations of the cabin or in the arrangements of the table on board." Alabama's best was as good as any afloat.[13]

What he did find on the *Mary* that he claimed was missing on the Mississippi "was the gentlemanly tone and manners of all the officers of the boat," and he was pleased that "during all the busy and exciting labor of cotton loading there was not heard a single oath, nor so much as one rude word to shock a lady's ear." Not wanting his Catholic readers to miss the point, the writer credited this conduct to the "example of its young commander," who "exercis[ed his] silent influence in a way most creditable to himself and to that religion so dear to his true Irish heart." Although the writer could not discover if the *Mary* was christened "in honor of Our Blessed lady," since the name "seemed suggestive of all that is pure and noble," he departed with the wish that the designation would "bring good luck to all connected with it."[14]

Steamboat *City of Gadsden* (c. 1900).
Although large packet steamers, the so-called floating palaces, are the
riverboats modern Americans know best, vessels like the *City of
Gadsden* were common on the river as well. They carried few
passengers and mostly local, short-run cargo.
(Courtesy Scarboro Photography, Gadsden, Alabama)

Of course there were other steamers, like the *Lula D*. "Not one of
those high-living boats," according to A. G. Moseley, the nephew of its
owner, she was a working craft whose master was "of the pioneer type,"
a man not inclined to waste time or money on that "grand style and
princely fare" that attracted discerning passengers. Moseley remembered how his uncle was "not fastidious about his eating," and it was
rumored that "he assigned his poorest deck hand to the cooking task," a
job made no easier by the fact that "in those pre-ice-using days, the beef
bought at landing stops soon became too strong and the eggs were that
way" from the start. So unappealing was the food on the boat that
crewmen once scraped the sides of empty molasses barrels and "got
from them a bountiful supply of sugar" to add flavor to "the saucer
sized biscuit that our chef produced." There were many *Lula D*.s on the
Alabama, and they were a far cry from the "elegant little *Mary*."[15]

Issam Morgan, a former slave, may have been one of the deckhands who scraped the sides of the barrel. Still a boy when the war ended, Morgan stayed on the plantation until he was twenty-one and might have stayed longer had his "Massa" not come one day and simply told him, "Isaam, you is a grown man now. You is got to boss your own business. . . . I can't keep you no longer." "Massa" wished him "good luck," assured him that he would "make somebody a good worker," and sent him on his way. With that Morgan joined the ranks of landless freedmen who had to make do in a world over which they had little control. Isaam Morgan headed for the river. In the years that followed, he recalled how he "worked diff'ent jobs, sich as: loader, roustabout on different steamboats an' [in harvest season] cotton picker." Interviewed by the WPA in the 1930s, he remembered the vessels, and "one of de ole songs sang on de boats":

> De John T. Moore
> De Lula D.
> An' all dem boats is mine.
> If you can't ship on de Lula D.
> You ain't no man o' mine.[16]

The golden age of steamboats continued through the Civil War and late into the nineteenth century. Up on the Coosa, some thirty-nine boats plied the stream, stopping at landings that sprang up to serve them, carrying passengers and freight from embarkation to destination. Coosa steamers and the men who ran them were cut from much the same cloth as their counterparts on the Alabama, and the deckhands and roustabouts who loaded and unloaded took the songs all laborers sang and shaped them to fit their river:

> Some folks say dis boat can't run,
> But I done seen what she done done.
> Left outa Rome just 'fore light,
> Gets inter Gadsden long 'fore night.[17]

Meanwhile, a whole new generation of steamboats plied the Alabama. They appeared in many shapes and sizes and performed many tasks, but of them all, the packet continued to catch the popular imagination. Just as before the war, packets had to meet three essential criteria: They had to be large enough to carry freight, sufficiently well appointed to attract passengers, and dependable enough to follow a posted timetable. Not surprisingly, with this combination of size, speed, elegance, and a regular schedule, some packets became so famous that they seemed to take on a life of their own. There were the *John T. Moore*, "said to be the finest boat that ever traveled the Alabama river"; the *James Battle*, which could stop at every landing between Bridgeport and Montgomery and still cover the 175 miles in fourteen hours; and of course the *Mary*, the "most popular passenger boat" on the river. Experienced travelers knew which vessel to book and when to book her, for the boat with small, warm cabins was best in winter, while large, cool cabins were preferred when the weather was hot. Even after they considered climate, in the late nineteenth century passengers seeking first-class accommodations had a number of packets from which to select, and competition was such that one traveler recalled a trip on which he "had a stateroom and four good meals, all of which cost a sum total of $2.65." Between visits to the table, those with cabins on the better boats often enjoyed "boiled oysters and steamboat toasted bread crusts" that were "passed during the forenoon and in mid-afternoon [so that] the passengers might interestingly while away the time." These people were transported in comfort and style that no railroad could match.[18]

The fact remains that steamboats and steamboat men were a varied lot, and any effort to generalize always begs the exception. If a traveler on the *Mary* could brag that during the entire trip he did not hear "one rude word to shock a lady's ear," a woman on another boat, hearing that comment, might wonder if the *Mary's* passenger was really listening. During her voyage, that lady was kept awake by a "profane mate" whose only concession to the fairer sex was that he cursed at night, when the women were supposed to be asleep. On some boats the captains superstitiously refused to carry corpses, while others believed gray horses and preachers brought bad luck. However, John Quill gave free passage to ministers and must have felt safe to do so, given the "gentlemanly tone and manners" of the *Mary's* officers and crew. Preachers, however, especially those with temperance leanings, would have been nothing but trouble on most steamers; for after the war, bars remained a standard feature, and according to one observer, "an intoxicated man on board was no uncommon sight." It was no place for a man of the cloth.[19]

Then, in the 1880s, shore-bound folks (and perhaps a few river men like Quill) concluded that the conduct of certain Alabama citizens was a disgrace and that it was the duty of people like themselves not only to set the example but also to take on the whole armor of the Lord and smite the serpent of sin whenever it raised its ugly head. Reform ran unbridled across the land, and demon rum fell early under its assault. Prohibition became law, and guardians of the public good set out to impose their values on less-than-willing consumers. In towns and villages the impact was immediate, as politicians and preachers rallied to the cause. But the river and river men just kept rolling along. As soon as most travelers boarded steamboats, they seemed to leave the law and their inhibitions behind. James Morrison Campbell witnessed this change, and in a 1946 interview with the Mobile *Press Register*, he told of how "men gambled away time . . . right out in the open while whiskey and beer, oysters and other delicacies were served from the steamboat's storeroom." On the river, the law was what the captain said it was.[20]

Prohibition did take its toll. On both the Coosa and the Alabama, public pressure closed some steamboat bars, and gambling was slowly reduced to "a friendly game of very high stakes in the privacy of the cabins." Not all captains gave in, but those who did (or did not) could be identified by the excursion trade they attracted. This was an important source of revenue for some boats. An organization would reserve the vessel, hire a string band, pack food and drink if the steamer could not supply it, and set off. Dancing was enjoyed in the saloon, while courting couples walked around the upper deck, watched by the ever-present chaperon. There were also instances when an all-male group commissioned a boat for what amounted to a floating stag party. One of these was witnessed by a lad of twelve who hid on board. He later recalled the "laughter, the ribald shouts, songs, and speeches" that grew louder as the day progressed, and he thought it wise that the captain had "strung ropes all around the lower deck" to keep his increasingly unsteady passengers from falling overboard. When the "wild and jolly trip" came to an end, the stowaway remembered what "fun [it was] to see the drunks hauled up the muddy river banks." If a church made the charter, however, the band and dancing, the "ribald shouts, songs, and speeches," and naturally the drinking were dispensed with. Almost everything else, including the food, the courting couples and, of course, the chaperons, was much the same. Each summer for many years the Centre Methodist Sunday School booked the *Dixie* for a day trip on the Coosa to the spring at Davis's Landing at Pollard's Bend. There members enjoyed "unforgetable picnics"—all very proper and, naturally, quite dry.[21]

On the Coosa some river men, aware that prohibition did little to slake the thirst of the region's drinkers, refused to accept the law's limitations, and soon "blind tigers" began to appear on the river. Often converted steamboats, these floating bars and dance halls became legendary on the stream. They would tie up near bridges or ferry crossings to maximize their contact with the public, then open their doors to the thirsty. If authorities tried to close them down, they simply cast off the lines and moved to another location. Some felt safer anchoring midstream, where the arm of the law could not (or would not) reach, but what was best for the proprietor was not always best for his customer. After an evening at the tiger, many found it harder to row back than it had been to row out. Accidents on the return trip were frequent, and the occasional drowning provided an instructive example of the wages of sin for Sunday's sermon. Some tigers stayed so long in the same place that they became landmarks for travelers and a problem for local residents. Not wanting to cause undue distress, the owners of establishments located where two ferry roads converged responded to complaints and "guards were hired to escort women and children through that place" when customers became too rowdy. Prohibition might have been the law of the land, but accommodating the public was the rule of the river.[22]

On the Alabama, just below Claiborne, some river residents thought they had found another way to quench their thirst. Over fifty years before, in 1825, the steamboat *Henderson* had sunk about a mile from the ferry. On board was a cargo of "fine whiskey, brandy and wines." The wreck was not deep, for a few years later, when a drought exposed the bow of the boat, Thomas Gaillard, a member of one of the area's most prominent families, saw the hull and was "impelled by the spirit of laudable enterprise" to try to rescue the contents. He failed, but in 1883, a drought that the *Wilcox Home Rule* described as "nature's silent protest against prohibition" exposed the boat once again. Believing that the "casks containing these precious fluids . . . may have withstood the action of the water during the half century that has passed over them" and convinced that "those spirits are still emphatically good," the editor encouraged a new effort to free the treasure. But if another attempt was made, it, too, failed. The *Henderson* and its cargo would have to wait for another time and other men.[23]

Although some river folk remembered the era as one of excitement and adventure, for others it was a time of constant struggle and frequent failure. Farmers along the streams suffered during the Panic of 1873; for them recovery came slowly, if at all. The blame for this failure, in part at least, was credited to "exorbitant tariff of freight and passage charged by the Alabama River steamers," a cost that dissidents, inspired by the anti-monopoly rhetoric of groups like the Farmers Alliance, believed was caused by "combinations" of owners and captains that drove out competition. In the summer of 1879, outraged citizens of Wilcox County held a meeting "to consider the propriety of purchasing a steamboat and putting it on the river in time for the fall trade," so people would have an alternative means of transportation. Though the *Camden News* reported that the people "are in earnest and mean what they say," no boat appeared, and not until 1883 did a competing steamer finally enter the fray.[24]

That fall the "independent" *Peninah* began running between Mobile and Montgomery and "cut rates so that the other boats were forced to do the same." The *Peninah* was not an alliance boat, and neither did its owners appear to have the needs of river region farmers high among their concern. The new steamer was reportedly launched "in retaliation for a like invasion by an Alabama boat into the Mississippi" a few years earlier, so any relief it gave to common folk along the river was only incidental. Still, opponents of monopolies were encouraged when the *Peninah* appeared and were bitterly disappointed when "the venture turned out an unprofitable one and made nothing." This time was not the only one when competing boats tried to drive others from the river. In 1891, a letter in the *Monroe Journal* charged that Capt. John Quill's recent decision to slash rates on the *Nettie Quill* was "not [done] for the good of the people" but rather "to cut out the *Tensie Moore*." Two weeks later Quill replied that he was only responding to rate cuts by the competing steamer and the move was nothing more than a business decision. Many remained convinced that no matter what Quill said, he was trying either to "run the *Tensie Moore* off or force her into his combination." Was her failure his goal? Was he successful? We do not know. We know only that the two boats stayed on the river and that the profits kept coming in.[25]

Indeed, there were profits to be made. It was estimated that in 1890, some $10 million in freight was carried on the Alabama. That year three large stern-wheeler packets made weekly trips from Mobile to Montgomery, "touching all intermediate landings" on the way. Scores of smaller boats made frequent, if irregular, trips and contributed significantly to commerce on the stream. Forest products were now an important part of this trade, and at some landings barrels of resin or turpentine came down the slides that once carried cotton to the deck. Up on the Coosa, these were Gadsden's boom years; while on the Alabama, Montgomery's population rose from 16,700 in 1880 to 22,000 a decade later. Although the major railroad lines that ran to the city contributed much to this growth, Montgomery's economy still depended heavily on what came and went on the river. Consequently, to the casual observer the "cradle of the Confederacy" looked more like the Old South than the New.[26]

Selma also grew apace, so to accommodate her expansion and the trade she was attracting, the city built the first bridge (except for railroad trestles) to span the Alabama. Opened as a toll bridge in 1885, the iron structure rested on five stone piers, with a wagon way and footpaths for traffic on the road and a draw that could be opened for steamboats on the river. Its $50,000 cost came entirely from public subscription, and when it was dedicated, schools and businesses closed for "Bridge Day." There was a grand procession through the "decorated and illuminated" town, and "all that oratory, poetry, and fireworks could do was done to make the day memorable." *Harper's Weekly* praised the structure as "an achievement of the new spirit of material development that is making such notable changes in the Southern States" and suggested that the old ferryboats that "had done their slow and humble services for a hundred years" should be retired. Soon they were, and another feature of river life became history.[27]

Even for towns, the post–Civil War recovery along the Alabama was anything but uniform. The floods of '65 and '66 hit Cahawba particularly hard, and as the second freshet receded, Dallas County citizens went to the polls to decide whether the county seat would remain at the old state capital or move upriver. Mrs. Fry's melodramatic couplets summed up the results:

> By the power of vote, and a small local faction,
> Our town now lost its greatest attraction;
> All the "Records of Dallas," so aged and gray,
> Were carried to Selma, just ten miles away.

But Cahawba's "greatest attraction" had become, for many, her *only* attraction, and removal simply confirmed the fact. Sensing this loss, the Selma *Daily Messenger* invited Cahawba residents to relocate as well. Some did, but the population had already declined to the point that there were not many to leave. The once-proud capital was on its way to becoming the ghost town of legend and lore.[28]

River towns below Cahawba fared little better. Antebellum landing communities like Bridgeport and Prairie Bluff entered the postwar era as little more than convenient wood yards and cotton slides, while Claiborne, which many thought would become the river city of the lower Alabama, watched its population drift eastward to the healthier heights at Purdue Hill. Cycles of yellow fever took their toll, and like Cahawba, Claiborne slowly faded away. In 1884 the Masonic lodge where Lafayette was entertained was moved by ox cart to the higher location, and by the end of the century a few buildings, the slide and staircase down to the river, a town well, and the graveyard were all that remained to remind residents of the glory years. From Selma to Mobile, the Alabama was a river without towns, an avenue through, not to, one of the richest regions of the state.[29]

Closer inspection suggests that floods and fevers were not entirely to blame for the decline of these locations. Once their access to the river had made them important regional market centers, but as the railroad rose to offer alternative transportation, they lost that function. This shift in economic activity, already begun before the war, continued through the economic ups and downs of the Reconstruction era and into the 1880s and 1890s. By then the readjustment was all but over. There was a new river now, one made of steel rails, and commerce flowed to its ports—Greenville, Monroeville, Evergreen. Slowly folks along the real stream began to realize that the river was no longer enough. Selma and Montgomery prospered, and Gadsden rose, because they were also rail centers, and their citizens prided themselves in this traffic. Meanwhile, the river seemed to be taken for granted. John Hardy's 1879 history of Selma included a chapter on railroads and manufactures but no chapter on the Alabama. The whistle of the locomotive, not the shrill of the steamboat, signaled success in the New South.[30]

So it was that despite the golden age it seemed to be enjoying, the steamboat's day was over. Folks should have seen it coming, for there were warnings. In 1888, near Yancey's Bend on the Coosa, the steamer *John J. Seay* burned and sank. Its cargo was not cotton, but rather "heavy timbers for building a bridge . . . for the Rome and Decatur Railroad." The flow of commerce was turning, and the river was becoming servant to the rails. Now they sang a different song:

> Steamboat coming round the bend,
> Good-bye my lover, good-bye.
> She's loaded down with railroad men,
> Good-bye my lover, good-bye.

In 1890, the United States canceled all mail contracts with river boats on the Coosa and turned that symbol of governmental endorsement (and regular source of income) over to the railroads. Meanwhile, as if to ridicule government efforts to improve the Cahaba, railroads built bridges across the stream ten and twenty-two miles above its confluence with the Alabama. Officials in Washington and in Centerville seemed to accept that act as the final blow. No efforts were made to have draws put in the bridges, no more funds were allocated to improve the stream, and steamboat commerce on the Cahaba became a thing of the past. Old rivermen spoke of how "the railroads [had] invaded our territory," and the analogy rings true. There was a war, and the river was losing.[31]

The rivermen did not give up without a fight. New boats were launched, old ones were refitted and renamed, and cotton still made its seasonal journey down to Mobile and up to Rome. Despite objections from the L & N Railroad, Montgomery built a new city wharf and warehouse and then added insult to injury by constructing an underpass beneath the tracks so traffic could move more easily to the Ala-

bama. The railroad retaliated by moving some thirty employees from
Montgomery to Louisville and cutting back operations in the state
capital. Up on the Coosa, valley leaders continued to push for government help to improve the river, and in the fall of 1899 they met in
convention once again. Sen. John Tyler Morgan, among the "prominent parties" who attended, promised "to do all in his power to secure
favorable action" from Congress. This support may have kept the
project going for a few more years, but that was all. As other means of
transportation became more readily available, fewer and fewer people
cared about opening the Coosa.[32]

The loss of passenger trade, however, truly signaled that the end was
near. Steamboats could still carry great cargoes of cotton more economically than railroads ever could, but income from passengers and
their baggage was necessary if the boats were to break even in the slack
months between planting and harvest. The saloons and cabins had
always been filled with factors and brokers, who seemed to conduct as
much business afloat as they did on land. The railroad changed all this
activity. Now the commercial traveler could leave and arrive on the
appointed hour, where the best packet could seldom offer more certainty than a morning, afternoon, evening, or night docking or departure. In the hustle and bustle of the New South, that pace simply was
not good enough. C. K. Foot, a Mobile cotton merchant, explained the
situation neatly in a turn-of-the-century letter to his friend and client,
E. M. Portis of Suggsville:

> We want to ride in a railroad car, to and fro at our pleasure,
> without paying tribute to a warehouse keeper, and to remain upon
> the cold wet bleak banks, thereof, for several days and nights. . . .
> by that time you are so glad to get a steamer, something to eat,
> bed, etc., you are willing to pay two prices to get to Mobile, and
> repeat that dose in getting home again. Ere the ides of March, you
> will step upon the train, dry shod, go to Mobile, transact your
> business and return home again at less expense than the time you
> have lost laying at the river banks for a steamboat. Your home is of
> four fold value to you, and yours, by the railroad.[33]

The decline was slow but relentlessly steady. Packets like the *Nettie
Quill, John Quill, Tensie Moore,* and *City of Mobile* continued to make
trips to Montgomery and back. Snagboats did their work, and channels
were dredged, but each year activity was less than the year before. River
travel grew increasingly unpredictable, as a bridal party learned early in
this century when the boat it chartered grounded on a sandbar below
Claiborne. Sympathetic citizens rowed out to bring "dainties" to the
"'happy couple' and their guests," but they were no substitute for a safe

Steamboat *Helen Burke* at Selma in 1930,
two years before she sank in the Mobile River. This last of the
Alabama River packets had been reduced to a towboat. She and the
barges with her were said to be carrying over 4,000 bales of cotton.
(Courtesy of W. S. Hoole Special Collections Library, The University of Alabama,
Tuscaloosa.)

docking and a threshold to carry the bride across. There would not be
many more pleasure cruises. Steamboats were caught in a vicious circle.
As railroads drained away business passengers, captains could not afford to refurbish worn cabins and saloons, and the shabbiness drove
the more sophisticated travelers away. By the 1920s only two packets
were operating out of Mobile, and they were mere shadows of their
former glory. In 1932, the last of these, the *Helen Burke*, was tied up to
the bank about fourteen miles above the city on the bay. Because
she was "old and practically condemned," no one saw any reason to repair the leaks in her hull, and that summer she settled slowly to the
bottom.[34]

Things were similar up on the Coosa. Competition from the railroads locked steamboats into the same hopeless cycle, and by the late
1930s only a few steamers were left on the river. One of these was the
sternwheeler *Leota*. Built in Gadsden in 1888, she was purchased by the
government in 1892 to serve as a dredge boat. Later she passed through

a series of owners, one of whom shortened her stacks so she could get under bridges and tried to run excursions between Rome and Gadsden. Even this modification was not enough, so the *Leota* was pulled up to the bank at Gadsden, where she was used as a tea room, a social club, and then a USO canteen during World War II. Finally the *Leota* became the home of local author Mary Elizabeth Counselman. Occasionally Gadsden residents would take their children down to the water to see the last Coosa steamboat, but her planks were so warped and rotted that no one expected her to put out into the river again. Finally, on Mother's Day in 1945, the seams gave way, and she sank.[35]

In the end, however, steamboats were victims of economic changes that went far beyond a matter of alternate transportation. On the Alabama, what railroad competition did not accomplish the boll weevil finished off. In the 1920s that invader decimated crop after crop, and it seemed that with each failure, a steamboat left the river. By the 1930s, what little Alabama River cotton trade remained was carried on by more efficient steam and motor tows, utilitarian crafts that made no effort to return the river to the romantic days of the packet. New Deal regulations further limited cotton production, but by then cattle had replaced row crops in much of the Black Belt, and beef rode the rails.[36]

Because the boll weevil did less damage in the Coosa Valley, cotton production actually increased in some areas, but a growing textile industry in the region bought up the bales and carried them to the mills by train. Meanwhile, mining and manufacturing became increasingly important to the local economy, and these employment alternatives made the difficult decision to quit farms for towns and factories a little easier for depression-wracked families. Changes on the river itself were in no small part responsible for this shift, for as hydroelectric dams shaped and reshaped the streams, new industries with their railroad retainers appeared across the land. Trains went where rivers did not run, carrying products to market centers that no stream served. Fewer and fewer Coosa valley citizens thought of transportation when they thought of the Coosa now. Instead of flowing rivers with steamboats riding on them, they saw huge dams, large lakes, and powerful generators that put electric lights in their homes and drove the machines in the factories where they worked. The river was entering a new age and carrying valley folk along with it.[37]

THIRTEEN

Putting "Loafing Streams" to Work

To gather the streams from waste and to draw from them energy,
labor without brains, and so to save mankind from toil that it can be
spared, is to supply what, next to intellect, is the very foundation of all
our achievements and welfare.

> OLIVER WENDELL HOLMES
> *Mount Vernon-Woodberry Cotton Duck Company*
> v. *Alabama Interstate Power Company* (1916)

Electric power in 1911 was man multiplied, and because of that, electric
power could be man glorified, lifted from poverty and from
acceptance of poverty to undreamed of standards of living and of
human welfare.

> THOMAS W. MARTIN
> *The Story of Electricity in Alabama,* 1952

I think the whole country ought to be run
> By *e-lec-tri-ci-ty!*

> WOODY GUTHRIE
> "Talking Columbia," 1941

Before the Civil War, the symbol of progress for towns along the
Coosa-Alabama waterway was the steamboat: The more vessels serving
a community, the more important that community was. After the war
railroads slowly but steadily claimed the field, and the river became less
important as a gauge for measuring advancing Alabama. Then as the
nineteenth century drew to a close, a new means of assessing progress
appeared, and with the flip of a switch the rivers once again became the
focus of regional attention. A community might have a railroad, but its
significance diminished if the locomotive pulled into a station dimly lit
by flickering oil or gas lights. Electricity illuminated the way to the
future; towns and people without it were condemned to darkness.

The connection between Alabama rivers and electrical power was not
forged immediately. At the turn of the century the Coosa–Alabama
River Improvement Association's first priority was still navigation, and
its members continued to press the federal government to finish the
locks and dams already on the drawing board and survey the rest of the
system. Their success was mixed. Though they convinced Congress to
include over $400,000 in the River and Harbor Act of 1910 for the
completion of Lock #4 and the building of the dam at site #5, the
government was not interested in carrying the project any further. To
many in Washington, and indeed in other parts of Alabama and the
South, funding a Rome-to-Mobile waterway was just another example
of "pork barrel politics"—a waste of taxpayers' money. But along the

river, folks considered it sound legislation, and they continued to hope for the day when their stream would be one of the great inland waterways of America.[1]

That day remained a long way off. Except at those sites where locks and dams had been built, the Coosa still flowed free, and life in it, on it, and along it, seemed to have changed very little. Steamboats still made occasional runs above Dam #5, carrying cotton and other commodities up to Gadsden and Rome. Meanwhile, fishermen worked pools behind natural shoals and ancient Indian weirs as they had for decades, and their catch sold well at local markets and supplemented many a farm family's diet. But there were other creatures in the water, more easily overlooked but nonetheless important in the natural scheme. During the first decade of the twentieth century, biologist Herbert H. Smith collected thousands of snails and mussels from the Coosa and left for modern Alabamians a glimpse of a river so rich that a scientist could gather 150 specimens in "a space not twenty yards long." Unfortunately, his interest in mollusks was so consuming that Smith left only hints about the condition of the stream in which his subjects lived; but from these casual observations, we can still get some idea of the Coosa running wild.[2]

Herbert Smith saw firsthand the great rapids of the Coosa—the Devil's Staircase, Hell's Gap, Devil's Race, the Narrows—but he spent little time there. The less dramatic sections of the stream were the most fruitful fields for the scientist, so he became intimate with locations where shoals and reefs were "intersected with small water-channels" and where there were "numerous back-water pools . . . crowded with small species." At these spots he collected specimens while "cling[ing] to rocks with one hand [and] fishing for stones with the other," and more than once he "got a dowsing" for his trouble. During much of 1904 Smith scoured the stream from Wetumpka to Cedar Bluff, groped for snails while he sat on rocks, crawled more than once "on hands and knees over a reef a furlong long," marveled at the "quiet and deep" water below Peckerwood Shoals, and took note of the "change in the fauna" that occurred at Weduska, near the site of the proposed, but yet unbuilt, Lock #12. Even in the "improved" section of the stream, Smith found much to collect, for despite decades of dredging and blasting, there were still "reefs of rock extending quite across" the river and "a constant succession of shoals, either along the shores or forming islands" that were home to snails but hazardous to boats. So it was that while Smith's observations reflected the natural richness of the waterway, they also revealed just how little the "improvements" had accomplished. Dreams of easy navigation on the Coosa were far from realized.[3]

* * *

Not everyone's Coosa thoughts were filled with snails and mussels, or even steamboats and barges. William Patrick Lay, scion of river valley pioneers and a leader in the Coosa–Alabama River Improvement Association, was beginning to imagine other uses for the stream. By the late nineteenth century the age of electricity was dawning, and Lay was one of Alabama's pioneers in the field. In 1887 he built the first electric power plant in Gadsden, a steam operation to serve only the town. While it was under construction, so the story goes, he visited Lock #2, where he supposedly "bemused himself" watching water flow through the flume. Looking down at the current, Lay wondered if this wasted energy might turn a dynamo, and if the power it generated could be conveyed from the river to towns and cities far away. He would have to wait for over a decade before advances in electrical technology made feasible the type of long-distance transmission he envisioned, but when that finally happened, he was ready. By 1903, William Patrick Lay was producing hydroelectric power at a plant on Big Wills Creek and selling it in the Attalla vicinity. The venture prospered, leading him to the conclusion that if electricity could be profitably generated on a small stream, more power and more profits could be produced on a river, a river like the Coosa.[4]

Despite his growing interest in hydroelectric power, Lay remained a river man at heart, and like most river men, he believed the future of the region still lay in opening the Coosa to navigation. But by the turn of the century hope for a channel from Rome to Wetumpka was fading. Survey after survey, report after report pointed out that the cost of a score or more low-lift dams and locks was higher than the commerce through them could justify. Lay and his friends in the association argued otherwise, but privately even the most enthusiastic supporters of the project had to admit that their cause was failing. Without something to revitalize the plan and reanimate its advocates, the future for Coosa navigation looked bleak. Lay provided that something. Abandoning the multi-dam proposal on which river improvement enthusiasts had rested their case, he began advocating bigger dams, some as high as two hundred feet, which would create large, slackwater lakes stretching from dam to dam, all the way back to locks below Greensport. Falls and rapids would be inundated, and boats could ride a permanent flood, where his father and the *Laura Moore* had to make do with a temporary one. High-lift locks would move commerce from level to level, and the Coosa would be open to all.[5]

Government engineers would have none of the scheme. In 1889, at Johnstown, Pennsylvania, a high dam broke, and over twenty-three hundred people died. The disaster cast a pall over high dam projects,

Lock #2, Coosa River (c. 1900).
While watching water flow through this flume, William Patrick Lay is
said to have come up with the idea that grew into the Alabama Power
Company.
(Courtesy Scarboro Photography, Gadsden, Alabama)

and there was an understandable reluctance to endorse such plans. So
Lay waited them out, and before long improved engineering, better
technology, and above all a growing demand for hydroelectric power
gave high dam proponents a better position from which to advocate
their cause. Once again, Lay saw his opportunity, and he seized it. The
plan was simple. Build high dams on the Coosa to create a safe, effective route for regional commerce. Then install turbines in the complex
to generate electricity that would light the region and supply the factories with power to make the goods that the river would carry. It was a
neat, complete equation, and one that progressive Alabamians happily
endorsed.[6]

There were still problems, however. Federal law prohibited dams on
navigable streams without congressional approval, so Lay and his asso-
ciates had to convince congressmen that their hydroelectric plans not
only would produce much needed power, but also would ultimately

improve navigation. At the same time, there remained a number of legislators who continued to believe that large dams were unsafe, a fear that forced the Alabama developers, according to one account, to present their proposal while "shrewdly concealing the fact that [they] contemplated erecting a high dam." But the Coosa coalition was up to the task. Organized under the name the Alabama Power Company, they presented their proposal and lobbied hard. In March 1907, Congress passed legislation allowing them to build a dam "of such height" as the chief of engineers and the secretary of war approved. All they lacked was the actual permit to begin construction; but when they made application, the size of the dam could no longer be hidden. Officials listened skeptically as Lay assured them of the soundness and safety of the proposal, but many remained unconvinced that the new, and in some cases untried, technology would remove the danger. Then William Patrick Lay played what proved to be his trump card. "If the dam is experimental," he argued, "private capital is supplying the money for the experiment, and even though the dam does wash out, it will be nothing out of the pocket of the government." The fact that a washout would not endanger any major population centers helped make the decision easier, and so the government, freed from both expense and responsibility, allowed the Alabama Power Company to proceed.[7]

Now Lay and his newly created company set out to raise the money for a dam on the Coosa at the Lock #12 site below Weduska Shoals. This funding was the hard part. The company was founded with only $5,000 in capital, which was soon exhausted, and Alabama investors proved few. Lay looked for regional funds, but there were none to be had. Then he swallowed his southern pride and turned to bankers in New York and other financial centers, but no one would support him. "I journeyed North, East, South and West," he later wrote, "presenting my plans to anyone who would give me the opportunity—but with no success." Then, just as every avenue seemed exhausted, he met James Mitchell.[8]

Mitchell was not a river man; he was not even an Alabamian. Born in Canada in 1866, he moved to Massachusetts with his family while in his teens, attended local schools, then went to work with a Boston electrical firm. After trying his hand at a number of jobs, he ultimately became involved with electric railways, worked in the United States and Brazil, and in time developed connections that led him to London and into investment banking. A trip to Japan to assess the possibilities for hydroelectric development guided him into that field, so when he returned to the United States in 1911, he began looking into sites for dams and power stations. Georgia and the Savannah River first attracted him, but the size of the stream and the area that would be dammed and flooded required technology not available at the time, so he turned west to Alabama. That fall James Mitchell, already recognized as "one of the most experienced men in the world of electric power development," found what he was seeking at Cherokee Bluffs, on the Tallapoosa River about ten miles above Tallassee.[9]

The Tallapoosa was not an undeveloped river. Tallassee's antebellum industries survived the Civil War and continued to prosper until the Panic of 1873 forced many of the mills into receivership. New owners and better economic conditions brought renewed prosperity to the town and its people. Coosa-Tallapoosa Valley farmers grew the cotton, and wagons and locomotives brought it to the mills, where river-powered machines turned out the finished products. Workers accustomed to long, hard hours on the farm accepted the factory's six-day week as uncomplainingly as they accepted their paychecks, and when the mills closed at four-thirty on Saturday afternoon, "the town was gay," residents remembered. Weekly square dances entertained locals, and when customers from the town's two saloons joined the party, the combination was often combustible. But the town also had three churches, so the repentant from the night before had plenty of places to seek forgiveness on Sunday. By the end of the nineteenth century, Tallassee was a typical mill town, with all the good and the bad that term suggests.[10]

While exploring the river above Tallassee, Mitchell could not have helped noticing a dam and power station already in place. Running from shore to shore, over twelve hundred feet long and twenty feet high, it was owned and operated by the Montgomery Light & Water Power Company, and since 1902 it had generated electricity for lights at the state capital, while Tallassee's mills were still driven by water power. Here was an opportunity waiting to be seized. At Tallassee and Cherokee Bluffs nature had provided sites where electrical power could be generated for mills and towns throughout the region. Needed was someone who could organize such a project and raise the capital to carry it through. James Mitchell had little doubt that he was the man to do it.[11]

Mitchell learned that Cherokee Bluffs was owned by the Birmingham, Montgomery and Gulf Power Company. That information took him to Montgomery, and in November of 1911 he appeared in the law office of Thomas W. Martin. Martin was a member of the Cherokee Bluffs development group and legal representative for a number of other investors who held options on dam sites in the area. If Mitchell wanted his plan to get the widest possible circulation among the people who counted, Martin was the man to see. If one takes Martin's word, and there is no reason not to, he and Mitchell had an almost immediate meeting of the minds and soon became, in effect, partners. But their collaboration would go well beyond the development of Cherokee Bluffs. Shortly after that first meeting they were talking of a statewide power system that would serve much of Alabama, for Mitchell was convinced that only a project on such a scale would attract the capital he hoped to raise. To make that dream a reality, they needed more than the Tallapoosa River.[12]

With this goal, Martin and Mitchell turned naturally to the region's other hydroelectric developer, William Patrick Lay. Before selecting the Lock #12 site Lay had "tramped up and down the river," evaluated other sites, and obtained the rights to some of them. Considering what he owned, and what he knew, Lay's involvement in the scheme was essential. The Coosa River man listened to Martin and Mitchell with interest, for the act of Congress that allowed his company to build the dam also set a limit on the time in which it was to be finished. That deadline was approaching, and here was a means of meeting it. So Lay enthusiastically joined them, and together (according to Martin) they "explored the rivers of the state, travelling by horse and buggy, with much foot-work at the scenes." They saw a number of sites, but none better than the one at Lock #12, which Lay was probably pushing as hard as he could. Not only did that location have the natural advantages they sought, but it was on the Coosa. The involvement of two rivers broadened the scope of the venture and gave Mitchell what he needed to sell the plan to investors. So they were ready—Mitchell with his financial contacts; Martin with his legal expertise; and Lay with his vast knowledge of the river and its people. They were a rare combination of talent, and that was just what the project needed.[13]

Thus a confident James Mitchell sailed for England in December of 1911, leaving Martin and Lay to work out the details. The planning did not take long, for on March 1, 1912, the Coosa River group's holdings were transferred to the Alabama Traction, Light and Power Company, Ltd., which had been set up to finance the purchase and development of the properties they planned to accumulate. These were frantic months. In England Mitchell sought investors, while in Alabama Martin and Lay tried to sort out a situation in which some fifteen corporations held dam sites, water rights, and land at the best locations on the rivers. The success of these men was remarkable. During the first six months of 1912, Martin and Lay moved the project far enough along to assure potential investors that they would have adequate legal protection, and

James Mitchell was able to convince these financiers that the profits they would reap were well worth any risk they might take. By the summer of 1912, Mitchell had attracted enough capital to start, and the Alabama Power Company, a new company with an old name, was ready to begin operations.[14]

Although Lay was anxious to begin construction on the Lock #12 site, the company decided the natural advantages of the Tallapoosa location were such that it should be developed first. Even that site was not without its problems. Downstream from Cherokee Bluffs were two dams: the Montgomery Light & Water Power Company's complex and a smaller, older operation run by the Mount Vernon–Woodberry Cotton Duck Company. Meanwhile, upstream from the site, in the area to be flooded, Benjamin Russell's Industries Light & Power Company was building a dam to supply electricity to his mills in Alexander City. Martin, as general counsel of Alabama Power, opened negotiations with the parties involved. Industries Light & Power was easy. Some years later Martin recalled how "Broadminded Russell recognized the greater public benefit from the complete development of the power of the stream," and as a result a "satisfactory agreement was reached" that turned his site over to Alabama Power. Russell, "broadminded" though he might have been, was concerned with more than "the greater public benefit." According to Judge C. J. Coley, who knew Benjamin Russell well, the "satisfactory arrangement" included cash up front, electricity for his mills, and electricity for Alexander City. When the city paid its bill, the money went into the account of Industries Light & Power, and "Mr. Russell would transfer it out wherever he wanted to." It was a deal "satisfactory" enough to broaden anyone's mind.[15]

Downstream was another matter. The Montgomery company accepted Alabama Power's contention that the project at Cherokee Bluffs would increase the volume of water available to them and make the flow more consistent, so an agreement was easily reached. But the other company resisted. Mount Vernon's concern was that a high dam would decrease the Tallapoosa's volume, and its manager argued that since "the river does not now afford sufficient power to operate the mills constantly," the company's production would suffer. Martin responded that there would be far more water than Mount Vernon needed; citing a 1907 Alabama statute that expanded the law of eminent domain to allow power companies to acquire by condemnation the right to water in excess of what other companies might need or use, he turned to the courts for relief. Mount Vernon countered that the Alabama law deprived the company of its property without due process of law, and with that contention the issue was drawn.[16]

The complex case finally reached the United States Supreme Court in

1916, where it was decided in favor of the Alabama Power Company and the state. Writing for the court, Justice Oliver Wendell Holmes handed down a ringing endorsement of what the company intended to do with and to Alabama's rivers, an endorsement that must have been music to Martin's ears: "To gather the streams from waste and to draw from them energy, labor without brains, and so to save mankind from toil that can be spared, is to supply what, next to intellect, is the very foundation of all our achievements and all our welfare." The significance of the victory would be realized again and again. "Few cases in the annals of water power," Martin reflected later, "transcend the importance of this litigation, either to issues involved or as to influence on future legislation." The way was clear, and Alabama Power Company was already on the move.[17]

Martin, Mitchell, and Lay had not stood idly by while the Mount Vernon case wound its way through the court. With the Cherokee Bluffs project delayed, Alabama Power turned to the Lock #12 site on the Coosa. Using the capital Mitchell had raised, Martin secured options to sites along the river and purchased land that would soon be underwater. Some of it was worn out, eroded land that the owners let go easily; some of it was timber, which the company cut, sold when there was a market, and burned when there was not; but some of it was still farmed as it had been since the Indians were driven out, and though the owners left their land with little comment, they must have left reluctantly. He also purchased several local utilities, and in 1912 work on the project began. After decades of government inertia on its river projects, the speed with which the dam and power station went up must have seemed like a miracle to valley folks. And as the dam and the water rose, so did the expectations along the stream. They had heard how electricity would bring industries and jobs, free them from crop liens and tenant farming, and make life better for them and their children. They had heard, and they believed.[18]

By early 1914 the turbines at the Lock #12 dam were generating power, and electricity was humming across transmission lines to sites as far away as Birmingham. But electricity did not come quickly to farms and rural homesteads in the Coosa Valley. What they got, that summer of 1914, were mosquitoes. As the reservoir slowly filled, local residents claimed they noticed a dramatic increase in the pests. Putting two and two together they came up with $3 million, the sum for which a group of them sued Alabama Power, on the grounds that the lake forming behind the Lock #12 dam was a breeding ground for the malaria-carrying insects. The company, with the war in Europe threatening its English capital, now faced a lawsuit that if lost might force it into bankruptcy. Martin knew what was necessary. He did his research, took his depositions, laid out his case, then called on Dr. William Crawford Gorgas.[19]

Martin might have saved himself that legal preparation, for as he later recalled, "Gorgas was enough." Surgeon general of the army and the nation's leading authority on malaria, William C. Gorgas's word on the subject carried great weight in scientific circles worldwide. More important, it carried great weight in Alabama, for Gorgas was a native son and one of whom the state was justly proud. So Martin went to Washington and convinced the surgeon general to investigate the charges against the company and testify in court as to what he found. Gorgas returned to Alabama, inspected the lake, and then went before the jury. Knowing the "twelve good men and true" were not scientists, the doctor explained "in language all could understand" that the breeding place of the mosquito was not the lake, which was too far away, but actually the area just adjacent to the homes of the plaintiffs. If, he pointed out, residents paid attention to standing water in their neighborhood, the problem could be solved. The jury, swayed by his logic and awed by his presence, found in the company's favor, and the remaining "mosquito suits" were dismissed.[20]

The dam at Lock #12 marked a turning point in the decades-old effort to make the Coosa navigable. In 1915, the year after the turbines were turned on, yet another survey of the Coosa River was authorized under that year's River and Harbor Act, a study undertaken specifically to determine if current plans should be modified or if they should be dropped altogether. The evaluation was carried out, a report was made, and finally in 1920 the chief of engineers recommended to the secretary of war that "the whole existing project should be abandoned due to lack of commercial use." The government agreed. Over the years that followed money was allocated to maintain existing locks at a minimum level, but with fewer and fewer boats to pass through, the quality of service mattered less and less. As for residents of the river valley, the decline in Coosa commerce affected them little, if at all. Although the government required that the utility company construct its dams so that navigation locks eventually might be added, there was little pressure on the federal government to allocate the money to build them. If Captain Lay had been in charge, he might have pushed Washington harder, but as Alabama Power grew, Lay's role in it diminished. Martin and Mitchell were in control now, and under their direction the importance of the river as a transportation corridor was supplanted by its importance as a source of hydroelectric energy. Apparently that suited most people just fine.[21]

* * *

By the 1920s, with the Coosa dam in operation and the Mount Vernon company case settled, Alabama Power was ready to begin work at Cherokee Bluffs. By then Tallassee residents were understandably wary of a dam project above the town, especially one as large as what Alabama Power was proposing. Floods had always been the curse of river folk, and opponents of high dams still argued that the tall structures and their large reservoirs would only make matters worse. In December 1919, nature added weight to their argument. After several days of heavy rain the Montgomery Light & Water Power Company dam above Tallassee broke, and a wave of water swept down the river taking out all in its path. The bridge that linked one side of town to the other was washed away; mills were flooded and looms carried downstream; the railroad that ran along the river was damaged, and when the water receded both of its trestles were gone. A writer in the *Tallassee Briefs*, published by a local mill, summed up the feelings of most citizens: "We hope if the Montgomery Light & Power Company ever build[s] another dam they will make it 14 times as thick as the one that washed away."[22]

So it was with a cautious eye that Tallasseeans watched workmen arrive at Cherokee Bluffs in the summer of 1923 to begin that long-delayed project. Concern soon combined with awe when they saw the magnitude of the operation. Over sixty square miles of land had to be acquired from its owners; trees had to be cut and houses torn down or removed; grave by grave, twelve cemeteries had to be dug up and transferred, but only after the not-always-easily-obtained permission was granted by the next of kin; and finally the grade and bridge of the Central of Georgia Railway had to be raised. But the biggest task was the dam. Construction required enough workmen to populate a small town, which is exactly what appeared at Cherokee Bluffs. Alabama Power crews erected housing for the workers and their families, along with a mess hall that could feed 480 people at once. They built barber shops, bath houses, an ice house, and of course a company store. Soon there were churches and schools to look after souls, enrich minds, and serve as theaters for weekly movies. There were also dance halls and pool halls for those whose recreational needs went beyond preachings and films. And as the "good folks" of the community would tell you, wherever you find dancing and pool, you find liquor. Prohibition was the law, but while the dam was under construction the camp foreman, who served as chief of police and was a deputy sheriff of both Elmore and Tallapoosa counties, averaged arresting a bootlegger a month. But for each one who went to jail, another came to take his place. When the men at Cherokee Bluffs worked, they worked hard; they played the same way.[23]

In just over two years the job was done. Situated in a natural amphitheater, the dam's 2,000 feet of solid concrete stretched from county to county and towered 168 feet above both. Behind it was a forty-thousand-acre lake with over seven hundred miles of shoreline. The Cherokee Bluffs dam stopped the Tallapoosa River, then told it when and where to run. The company laid the cornerstone in November 1925. At the ceremony Thomas Martin, now president of Alabama Power, expounded the corporate philosophy that would be repeated time and again. "The continued progress of our State," he insisted that day, "consists in lifting the burdens of drudgery from the shoulders of man to the tireless shoulders of the dynamo. Every loafing stream is loafing at the public expense and every added kilowatt of power means less work for someone, more freedom and a richer chance for life." It also meant, they all knew, considerable profit for investors in the Alabama Power Company.[24]

Over 3,000 people attended the ceremony and waited patiently through the speeches until the barbecue was served. Most were local folks, and many among them were closely tied to the land being covered by the lake. Some of it may have belonged to them, or to their family, or to a friend. They had visited the now-flooded home sites, worshiped in the churches, and carried their dead to the cemeteries. For them, a way of life was disappearing beneath the water, and though these people left little to tell us how they felt, Benjamin Russell, one of the speakers, sensed their uneasiness and tried to address it. "I am not unmindful of the fact," he told his audience, "that upon Tallapoosa soil, back of this giant dam, will rest the larger part of this enormous body of water necessary to be impounded to make this enterprise capable of serving this and other sections in time of water distress. This means the loss to Tallapoosa County of large acreage from cultivation and yield but I firmly believe that under the changed conditions, attentiveness on our part will make for better advantages and more opportunities for Tallapoosa County than hitherfore existed." Perhaps so. But the land and what it sustained were gone. The money residents received might buy another farm, or a house in town near the mill, or an automobile; they could buy something else, but life would never be the same.[25]

If the '20s roared for any organization in the South, they roared for the Alabama Power Company. Even before the dam on the Tallapoosa was completed, the company had obtained a license to build a second dam on the Coosa, at Duncan's Riffle, about fourteen miles downstream from the Lock #12 project. Below the Narrows and Devil's Race but above Hell's Gap, located in an area that was "barely accessible" to the outside world, it was one of the wildest sections of the river and of

Mitchell Dam under construction at the site of what would have been Lock #18
(Courtesy Alabama Power Company Archives)

Alabama. Roads had to be cleared and graded, men and equipment brought in, and the whole enterprise planned as if it were an expedition into the unknown—which in a way it was. A group photograph, taken that bright December day in 1921 when construction formally began, shows company leaders and engineers standing above a rock-filled river looking across at a wooded hillside. Two years later there was a dam at the site and behind it a lake. Alabama Power had added another link to the chain that would tame the Coosa.[26]

James Mitchell, the man most responsible for the plan Alabama Power was pursuing, did not live to see the turbines turn at Duncan's Riffle. Mitchell died in 1920, and to recognize his contribution to the company, it gave the dam his name. Still, his vision had kept the company on track during these boom years. As soon as the Cherokee Bluffs project was completed, workmen and equipment moved over to the Coosa, above Wetumpka, and in the fall of 1926 they began building the dam that would sit astride the Devil's Staircase and flood the upper portion of the river's most famous rapid. Dedicated a year later, with a barbecue that attracted 5,000 this time, Jordan Dam was generating power by January 1, 1929. Meanwhile, over on the Tallapoosa, a new dam built at the old Montgomery Light & Water Power Company site had begun operation in the summer o f 1928. That same year work began on the Thurlow Dam, which was superimposed on the old Mount Vernon–Woodberry structure, and by 1930 its turbines were humming with the rest. In less than two decades the Alabama Power Company had built six dams and changed the Coosa and Tallapoosa rivers forever.[27]

On a cold winter day in November of 1929, with the Goodyear blimp circling overhead and the smell of barbecue in the air, prominent men in their heavy coats and hats stood with curious (or hungry) local citizens at the Lock #12 site to hear it renamed Lay Dam for the man who had founded the Alabama Power Company and nursed it through its early years. The name was a fitting tribute to one of Alabama's great river families and to its most famous member. The talk that day was of electricity and the changes it was bringing, but surely there were those in the crowd who dreamed old dreams of steamboats and barges and hoped someday their dreams would be realized. Behind the dam, the lake stretched upstream, just as its namesake envisioned it would, pushing slack water over rocks, rapids, and some three hundred islands, until it almost reached the channel below Dam #5. Downstream it was only a short distance to the slack water from the Mitchell Dam, and below Mitchell Dam was Lake Jordan. If upriver improvements were completed and locks were added as planned, the Coosa would be navigable from Rome to Wetumpka—almost. Ten miles remained, but they were critical miles. From the foot of Jordan Dam to the pool below the town, half the Staircase lay exposed, a skeleton now, with rocky bones protruding from the stream, but as much a hazard to river traffic as ever. True, the level of the stream could be controlled, but no matter at what height the water flowed, between the dam and the town the Coosa was unnavigable. Looking upstream from Jordan, one could sense how close an Alabama-Coosa waterway was to completion; looking downstream, one could see how much farther they had to go.[28]

Many of those present at the Lay Dam dedication in 1929 had attended another gathering that past June to discuss, once again, the question of Coosa-Alabama navigation. Gov. Bibb Graves, whose administration had completed the $10 million Alabama State Docks in Mobile "to facilitate and stimulate water borne commerce," called the meeting. According to the *Montgomery Advertiser* over 150 business, industrial, and commercial leaders assembled in the capital. William Patrick Lay attended as head of the Coosa–Alabama River Improvement Association, along with Alabama Congressman John McDuffie who was on the House Rivers and Harbors committee, and William R. Dawes, president of the Mississippi Valley Association. Dams were built or abuilding; lakes were full or filling. If the Coosa was ever to be opened, this seemed the time.[29]

Though the *Advertiser* noted that the meeting was "marked by a courageous and enthusiastic attitude . . . toward the project," the representatives had their task cut out for them. The work already done by the Alabama Power Company, along with the industrial growth of Gadsden and Rome, was cited as evidence that the cost of the venture could be kept well within the range justified by the expected commerce on the stream, but undocumented estimates were not enough for the government. Lt. Col. Mark Brooke, representing the Army Corps of Engineers, assured them that a survey authorized two years earlier would be carried out—a safe prediction with Representative McDuffie there—but it would be up to the "industrial leaders of Alabama" to help them "arrive at the probable tonnage that will come from a nine foot channel" from Rome to Mobile, the figure on which the final disposition of the project would rest. That put the burden of proof right on the shoulders of Alabama advocates, and although they claimed to take it up willingly, it was a heavy weight to bear. Even William R. Dawes, whose Mississippi Valley Association was the model which Alabamians hoped to follow, seemed at a loss to tell the audience just how they might convince skeptics that an Alabama-Coosa waterway was the key to future development in the region. "I am asked many times," he noted in his remarks to the assembly, "'why go back to a slow movement of merchandise in this age of speed?' My answer is just this. . . . the airplanes flash across the sky, the automobiles dart hither and yon across the country, the railroads with their passenger and freight trains rush and roar from one ocean to the other, from the Canadian border to the Gulf, but gentlemen, 'Ole Man Ribber just keeps a rollin' along.'"[30]

Dawes's assurance fell far short of what his audience needed, for whatever enthusiasm the delegates took with them from the meeting that summer of 1929 diminished in the fall and was all but gone by winter. That was the year of the Wall Street crash, and though much of agricultural Alabama had been in a state of depression for some time, now the relatively prosperous manufacturing sector declined as well. Though some industrialists did gather statistics in an effort to justify appropriations for a Coosa-Alabama project and the influential magazine *National Waterways* endorsed the idea as one that, if completed, would create "the third greatest navigable waterway system in the United States," neither the money nor the spirit was there to support the effort. During the next few years mills closed, factories sat idle, farms lay fallow, and "roll along" was about all the rivers did. So no one was surprised when the report from yet another river survey completed in 1935 concluded once again that "on the basis of the volume of commerce that might use the waterway," there was still no economic justification for the improvement of the Coosa and Alabama rivers.[31]

Another reason for the lack of congressional interest in the Coosa-Alabama project was that during most of the decade Alabama Power and the federal government were adversaries in court, a condition that made cooperation on the Coosa unlikely at best. In May 1933, Congress created the Tennessee Valley Authority to develop the Tennessee River system for navigation, flood control, and national defense. In addition, TVA would also generate and sell electrical power. Alabama Power, which had interests in the Tennessee Valley, protested that this law forced them into competition with the government in a market where the government held an unfair advantage. The company filed suit challenging the act, and litigation dragged on for years before TVA was finally upheld. Not until 1939 did Alabama Power and TVA end the dispute with what Martin remembered as an "informal understanding that TVA would confine its operation to . . . North Alabama," leaving those parts of the state served by the Coosa-Tallapoosa dams to the private utility. In the future the agreement worked well for both sides, but the confrontation that it settled absorbed energy and resources that might have been used to improve the streams.[32]

The inclusion of flood control as a justification for river development by the TVA was seen by some as a smoke screen to hide the government's real purpose, to generate and sell electricity, but for river residents, floods were a yearly threat, and anything that could be done to control them was of critical concern. The increasing frequency and severity of floods were well documented, and though most were still measured against the great flood of 1886, later freshets came close to its record reading of 59.8 feet. In the forty-three years between 1886 and 1929, the Montgomery area experienced fifty-nine floods that crested at 35 feet or more, and nearly half of these went over the 45-foot mark. Every spring the rivers rose, and even when they did not reach flood stage, the rise alone was enough to remind the region just how powerful, and how unpredictable, nature was.[33]

In spring 1929, as final arrangements were being made for the Coosa-Alabama navigation convention, the rains came as they always did, and the rivers rose as they always had. This time the rains kept falling, and the rivers kept rising, and by the second week in March most of the streams were out of their banks. South Alabama was hardest hit, and the town of Elba was covered by more than fifteen feet of water. All the rivers in the Alabama system rose above flood crest, and low areas from

Wetumpka, 1929 Flood
(Courtesy Alabama Power Company Archives)

Cedar Bluff to the cutoff, from Centerville to Cahawba, were inundated. Accurately assessing the loss of life and property is difficult,
record keeping being what it was, but it might have been worse if not
for radio warnings sent out by the Department of Agriculture over the
Auburn station WAPI, which urged threatened residents to evacuate.
Damage might also have been worse along the Coosa-Alabama corridor
had not engineers at Martin and Jordan Dams lowered the gates to
control the flow. The effort succeeded for only a short while, because
upstream rains soon forced them to release the water. Even this brief
respite from the rising tide was significant, for it confirmed in the
minds of many that flood control was a legitimate reason for future
dams. This added the last element to the river improvement coalition,
and for the rest of the century a combination of hydroelectric interests,
flood control advocates, and Coosa-Alabama navigation supporters
worked to harness the streams.[34]

The alliance of interests was not without popular support, for by the
end of the decade, largely through Alabama Power's river improvements, much of the state had happily been brought into the twentieth
century. In the region the Power Company served, cities and towns
were lit by electricity; there were radios and refrigerators in homes that
could afford them; industry was more widely disbursed; and farmers
far from rivers had employment alternatives never available before. Hydroelectric dams on the Coosa and Tallapoosa changed the lives of Alabamians, and most would have said for the better. The dams also

changed Alabama. The great falls at Tallassee were gone; Lake Jordan covered Welonee Creek Reef, Hell's Gap, Fish Trap Shoals, and most of the Devil's Staircase; Mitchell Dam sat on Duncan Riffle; and the water behind it rose over shoals named Tuck-a-league and Butting Ram and over the Devil's Race. Meanwhile Lay Lake washed over the Narrows and Weduska and Peckerwood shoals, in whose clear, swift waters Herbert Smith had found "thousands" of specimens. Gone were islands and ferries, named after their people—Johnson, Smith, Knight, Pate, Sauley, House, Gray, Noble, Thompson, Higgins, Adams, and a score of others—a roll call of the region's pioneers lost beneath the waves. The "loafing streams" had been put to work, and this loss was the price Alabama paid.[35]

FOURTEEN

Hard Times, Better Times

There is nothing exactly like Gee's Bend anywhere else in the United States. There are similar bends, of course. Canton Bend, across the river from Gee's, is almost identical in shape and size, though its bottle neck is wider. But Gee's Bend represents not merely a geographical configuration drawn by the yellow pencil of the river. Gee's Bend represents another civilization. Gee's Bend is an Alabama Africa.

RENWICK C. KENNEDY
Christian Century, 1937

No, sir, I don't want t' get offen this river. Hit's th' only place I could live. I been down hyar 'mong th' coons an' moccasins too long t' ever make a go of hit in town. I wouldn't know how t' act, and I'd git runned over by a damned automobile. Down hyar, a man kin raise all manner of hell; fer they ain't nothing to fight but th' pine trees. But effen I was in town, I guess they'd have me in jail all th' time.

ORRIE ROBINSON
Coosa River near Talladega Springs (1938)

Yuh Know, th' good Lord was int'rusted in fishermen.

BOB CURTIS
Coosa River (1938)

In April 1925 over ten thousand people descended on the once-thriving town of Claiborne to celebrate the centennial of Lafayette's whirlwind visit and to feast on "a massive meal consisting of 5000 pounds of barbeque and brunswick stew." A pageant, directed by local arbiters of taste and involving over two hundred school children and their teachers, "offered impressions of spirits of the different times"— odd tableaux that included "Indians with feathers and paint" along with tributes to "Christianity, Community, Music, Art, Drama, Child Welfare, Forest Reserves, [and] the Red Cross." The expected corps of politicians was present, and "historic figures were re-enacted by dignitaries of the Senate." The United Daughters of the Confederacy played a prominent role as did the American Legion and the Boy Scouts. "A French embassy official" was on hand, and Miss Charles Finklea performed "a solo dance as the 'Golden Butterfly,'" which may have been the highlight of the afternoon . . . until the barbeque was served. After all had eaten, farm folks returned to their homes while the cream of Monroe County society headed inland to Perdue Hill for a ball at the Masonic lodge where Lafayette was entertained in 1825. Only then the Lodge was in Claiborne. Only then there was a Claiborne.[1]

191

* * *

No one talked about restoring Claiborne to its former glory that day, any more than they talked about rebuilding old Cahawba or remounting the Civil War cannon that lay rusting downstream at Choctaw Bluff. In the 1920s, those who thought about history in a public sense seemed to favor romantic ruins over restoration. Still fat from the wartime economic boom, the middle-class elites who dominated social and economic life in the river region wanted progress, and to their way of thinking progress meant something new. Though they occasionally celebrated the past in poem and pageantry, its physical presence was of less importance. If an old building stood in the way of a new one, the old building had to go. The bricks might be recycled; an architectual feature, like the dome from the Cahawba capitol, might be put to use at another location; but in the public mind at least, progress and preservation were incompatible.[2]

Privately, history was another matter. In cities, in towns, and out in the country, prominent families treasured a way of life based on some mental calculus of the Old South—complete with columned mansions and black retainers. They creatively charted family trees through the Civil and Revolutionary wars, all the way back to English or Scottish nobility (preferably through an illegitimate line, for aristocratic bastards offered that rare combination of royalty and rakehell so treasured by New South gentry) and with these in hand joined the DAR and UDC. For them history was deeply personal, and from it they distilled and superdistilled a fine liquor that they served to reinforce the social foundation on which their class rested and to cement the ties that bound them to each other. From these families came the planters, merchants, politicians, mill owners, doctors, lawyers, and bankers who constituted the core of Alabama's socially conservative, economically progressive bourgeois Bourbons. Captured in its essence, this class produced men like the merchant in Selma whose sign reminded customers that "my grandfather did business with your grandfather." To these folks, the past mattered.[3]

But not everyone along the rivers enjoyed the luxury of history. In the Black Belt sharecropping and tenant farming still tied most blacks and many whites to land that belonged to others and left them little opportunity or desire to consider the past they shared. Consigned to the lower end of the social and economic scale, they were too busy trying to cope with the present and too worried about their future to give the past much thought. History was something that happened to someone else. In the 1920s, with cotton prices falling and landowners turning to cattle, the lot of the landless became increasingly hard. To explain just how bad it was and how trapped farmers felt, a story, a parable really, was told of a Wilcox County tenant who took his harvest to the gin only to find that when the processing was done, he owed the operator more than the value of the cotton he had brought in. So the farmer surrendered his crop and promised to fetch back a chicken to pay the remainder of the debt. About a week later he appeared with not one, but two chickens.

"Why did he bring the second?" a listener would ask.

"Because he had another bale to gin," was the reply.

The story was a knee slapper at crossroad stores, especially when the tenant in the tale was black and the audience was white. But the laughter always had a bitter edge to it, for farmers knew that their situation was every bit as absurd as the story's central character, and they also knew that they, too, had little option but to bring another chicken when they brought another bale. History—how they got into this mess—was not important. They just wanted to get out.[4]

Some were escaping. As electricity began to light up the Coosa-Tallapoosa valley, new mills opened, and farm folks jumped at the opportunity to make thread and cloth from the cotton they once had grown. A. B. Moore, whose *History of Alabama* published in 1934 reflected the thinking of his generation of scholars, waxed eloquent on how factories gave "slaves of the hills a chance to come out into the currents of life," and for many, no doubt, this was true. "Industrious, reliable, responsive, practical-minded, and possessed of the power of gratitude," hill folk were (according to Moore) "psychologically fit for the work" and the working conditions. Fiercely independent, they were reluctant to join unions, an attitude the companies encouraged. So they left their farms to work the looms in Wetumpka and Tallassee, to make tires for Goodyear in Gadsden, and to labor in a score of smaller operations throughout the region. They brought with them what little they had of value, including their rural folkways, and became mill people.[5]

Such was life along the rivers in fall 1929, when newspapers announced that the stock market had crashed and hard times were ahead. That came as a surprise to those at the bottom of the heap, who believed hard times were already there; but before long just about everyone discovered things could get worse. In mill towns wages were cut, layoffs came with increasing frequency, and the "stretch-out," the devil's design to make men produce more, faster, for the same (or less) pay, became the order of the day. These devices got some companies through the crisis, but in Selma nothing worked, and two of the city's largest employers, Alabama Textile Mills and Sunset Mills, went bankrupt. Factory folks were not the only ones affected. Even the urban middle and upper classes, who had thrived during the boom years, were hard hit. Stores closed or cut back operations, clerks and bookkeepers were sent home, lawyers found fewer and fewer fees, and the ranks of street peddlers selling apples, ice cream, and candy grew. City revenues fell, and had teachers not agreed to accept part of their pay in warranties instead of cash, Montgomery would have had to close its schools. Signs of decline were everywhere. Fine old homes were allowed to run down; some were chopped up into apartments and boarding houses; others were sold. In Selma the billboard that boosters raised proclaiming their town the "fastest growing city in Alabama" fell over, and residents let it lie there. Meanwhile, upstream the only commerce in Montgomery that did not seem to suffer was the red-light district on Pollard Street near the river—but everyone knew that was just another sign of despair.[6]

Montgomery did not remain long in the depths of the depression. In 1932 a $1 million infusion of federal money to expand Maxwell Air Field started the capital on the road to recovery even before New Deal public works appeared on the scene. Other cities and towns were not so fortunate, and the more rural the region, the harder things seemed to be. Selma's banks survived the crash, but in smaller towns those symbols of stability closed with alarming frequency, and savings accumulated in the good times of the twenties disappeared. Meanwhile cotton prices, which had been declining since the war, hit bottom, and Black Belt planters, still recoiling from the boll weevil, found that even when they made a crop, the price they received hardly covered the cost of production. Now the parable of the man and his chickens became more than a lower-class allegory. The planters adapted, first by raising more cattle and then by turning to the government. New Deal programs that paid them not to plant gave landowners a reliable source of income, but less production meant fewer workers, so sharecroppers and tenants increasingly found themselves without farms. It was the end of an era. Planters, who sat on the local committees that were set up to administer federal programs, oversaw the dismantling of labor arrangements that had existed since the 1870s. Soon pickers and choppers worked for wages in their seasons and worked little if at all the rest of the year. Tenant houses stood vacant, fences sagged and fell, barns and cribs rotted. In the spring, flowers planted once by a sharecropper's wife to add a bit of beauty to an otherwise drab existence still bloomed to outline a walkway or seedbed, but there was no one to gather them. The crop-lien system had been bad, no one could deny, but for many, what replaced it was no better, and maybe it was worse.[7]

It is ironic that in this time of hardship, history came to the rescue of some of those very people who only recently had wanted nothing more than to escape it. All along the rivers, rural residents resurrected the folkways of an earlier era, returned to a pattern of life they had all but abandoned as the modern world invaded the region. Hunting and fishing once again became survival skills, traditional crafts reappeared, and river folk revived a community culture that revolved around crossroad stores, clapboard churches, and branch-head cabins. The return grew not out of any reverence for the past but because necessity demanded it. Yet they preserved in the process a heritage that might otherwise have faded and died. In this reaffirmation of frontier values, characteristics, and habits of action, W. J. Cash found what he called "the mind of the South"—an often unappealing amalgamation of individualism, hedonism, violence, Protestantism, and romanticism that Cash claimed had shaped Southern life as long as there had been a South. Perhaps he was right, though there is evidence to suggest that these ways of thinking and acting were retreating under a modern assault until the depression revived them. Either way, the speed with which the folkways reappeared suggests that the past was nearer the present than New Southerners wanted to admit, and as Cash believed, the link between 1830 and 1930 had never been broken.[8]

While one can argue that in the rural South, white men of property reaped the greatest benefit from New Deal programs, in at least one instance federal assistance did go to those who needed it most—the farm families of Gee's Bend on the Alabama River. How residents of the Bend came to be counted among the state's most distressed is a story that underscores just how complex were the causes and circumstances of poverty in the region. What was done to alleviate their suffering, and what was actually accomplished by the effort, reveals how persistent the forces that perpetuated rural poverty could be and how difficult it was to bring about a permanent solution. Gee's Bend was unique only in the degree and concentration of its problems. All along the rivers there were farmers and farm communities that would have understood the plight of the "Benders" and would have hoped the government might have done as much for them.[9]

Joseph Gee, a planter from North Carolina, settled the Bend before Alabama was a state, carved a plantation from the rich bottoms and fertile hills, and then died in 1824, leaving the property and some forty-seven slaves to his two nephews back east. One of them, Charles Gee, moved to Alabama where he raised cotton and traded slaves until the 1840s; then to settle a debt he and his brother signed the operation over to Mark H. Pettway. In 1846 Pettway, his family, and over a hundred slaves made the trek across the Carolinas, through Georgia, and into the heart of the Alabama Black Belt. There Pettway's slaves cleared more land, planted more cotton, and built their master a "big house," which he named Sandy Hill. Gee's Bend became, according to one student of the region, "a dukedom in the vast Southern cotton empire," and there Pettway lived in splendid isolation. Deep in the heart of a bulb-shaped peninsula, almost entirely surrounded by the river, Mark Pettway was free to do whatever he wished, and he did.[10]

Emancipation changed life in the Bend little, if at all. Former slaves stayed on the land as sharecroppers and tenants, and the Pettways stayed as masters, an arrangement that lasted until 1895, when the owners sold the plantation, some four thousand acres, and left. But there were still Pettways in the Bend, black Pettways, who clung to the name as they clung to the old ways. By 1900 the Pettway property, plus some three thousand adjacent acres, had come under the control of the Van de Graaff family of Tuscaloosa, who ran the plantation as absentee landlords for the next quarter of a century. The tenants hardly noticed the change at all. They raised most of their food, lived in houses of skinned pine logs, ran pigs and a few cattle, and conducted themselves much as frontier farmers had a century before. Though others held title to the land, legal niceties meant little. This was home, and as Renwick C. Kennedy, a Presbyterian minister from Camden, observed, "they love the Bend with an affection that is almost personal."[11]

The result, by the 1920s, was a place unlike any other in the nation— "another civilization" according to Kennedy "an Alabama Africa." Sixty-four black tenant families, 456 people, lived on the Van de Graaff estate, and at least that many rented farms on neighboring plantations. Some were Pettways, though Bender Mattie Clarke Ross recalled that others "was something else but they signed their name 'Pettway.'" They were all one big clan. The only whites among them were a rural letter carrier and his family. The nearest town, Camden, was less than four miles away, but it was on the other side of the river, which they crossed on "an ancient and primitive ferry" that high water rendered useless at least two months of the year. When the river flooded, they could go by land and cross the Miller's Ferry bridge, but the trip was over forty miles, so they seldom went. Closer was the railroad town of Alberta, eighteen miles to the northwest by way of a road that at its best was almost impassable. Little wonder that residents became a people unto themselves, a people whose language, customs, and conduct were so unlike their counterparts in the rest of the county that blacks outside the Bend took to calling them "Africans."[12]

As a rule, Gee's Bend farmers needed yearly loans to put in a crop and cover expenses until it was picked, ginned, and sold. Many of them arranged for this with a merchant in Camden, who advanced what they needed, marketed the cotton when it came in, and took his cut from the profits—usually leaving them enough to pay their rent and survive until spring, when it was time to borrow again. Immediately after the First World War, when a bale was bringing over $150, this system worked fine, and farmers did well, even after expenses were deducted. But toward the end of the 1920s, cotton was down to a nickel a pound, and everyone whose livelihood depended on the fine white fiber was hurting. Hoping that prices would rise, the merchant began holding the Benders' cotton off the market, while still advancing the farmers what they needed to get by. As a result, his books showed an ever-mounting debt with nothing sold to cancel it. Meanwhile the Pettways and their friends, unaware of what was taking place, continued to bring in the cotton, which they assumed was settling their accounts. It was not.[13]

In the summer of 1932 their benefactor died, and the books were opened. The debts were there in black and white, but the cotton had disappeared. "No one," Reverend Kennedy wrote in *The Christian Century*, "has ever known the inside story," but the merchant's "family was utterly ruthless in settling the estate." Kennedy's description of what happened to one tenant tells the story: "White men with pistols on their hips, riding horses, and leading a train of wagons driven by Negroes, came to William's lonely farm deep in the fertile bottoms. They took his corn and potatoes, his chickens, his hogs, his plows and tools and wagon, they cut his sugar cane that was ready for the mill, they loaded his cows and tied his two mules to the rear of the wagon and then passed on to the next family. William's debt was liquidated. He was at last free of that burden." In October and November sixty-eight families, 368 people, were "broken up" or "closed out"—Alabama phrases that described both a physical condition and a psychological state. Men, women, and children "faced the winter with nothing to eat save a handful of peas, a handful of corn and a handful of peanuts the raiders graciously left."[14]

Had the Red Cross and the owner of a nearby plantation not come to their aid, some Benders surely would have starved. Short rations of flour, meal, and meat pulled them through, but just barely. A few men found occasional work clearing land at fifty cents a day, which bought food but left nothing with which to purchase working stock, tools, or seed for the planting season. Van de Graaff and the other plantation owners realized their plight and let them stay on the land rent free but could do little more to help them. So as the weather warmed and the smell of spring came up from the river carrying the promise of a new beginning, families in Gee's Bend found that more had been broken up than their farms and their spirits. The cycle of life, of planting, plowing, chopping, laying by, and picking, had been broken up as well. It was what they had always done, and they wanted to do it again—only now they couldn't.[15]

Few crops were made in 1933, but in the summer of 1934 a federal rural rehabilitation program for cotton tenants got under way. Seed, tools, and animals were sent to the Bend, along with food allowances to help them through the year, and by the spring of 1935 they were ready to plant again. That was a good year; 1936 was even better, and when their crops were picked, ginned, and sold, folks in Gee's Bend were able to pay their debts and have money left over. On the Van de Graaff plantation alone they made some fifteen thousand bushels of corn and six thousand bushels of sweet potatoes. Cribs and larders were full, chickens scratched in the yards, and hogs were fattening in pens or rooting up mast in the bottoms. Life was good, and Benders, who knew how bad times could be, enjoyed it to the fullest.[16]

This newfound prosperity was the result of a combination of good weather, improved prices, and low-interest loans from the government's Resettlement Administration, which did not take the "usual heavy cut" from the profits that advancing agents had taken in the past. Things were about to get even better. In February 1937 the Alabama Rural Rehabilitation Corporation, which operated under the Farm Security Administration, bought the Van de Graaff's plantation and began adding most of the rest of the Bend to its holdings. Gee's Bend had been chosen as the site of a cooperative farming experiment that would be "the darling of the FSA." Officially it was "Gee's Bend Farms, Inc.," but locals simply called it "the project."[17]

The scheme combined many of the ideas floating about in the fertile minds of Washington's social planners. Land would be divided into farms of sixty to one hundred acres, which could be purchased by former tenants through long-term, low-interest loans. The loans would also pay for new homes, built and painted to government specifications, with outbuildings including a state-of-the-art privy. There would be a bored well and hand pump in each yard, so long walks to the spring would be a thing of the past; a fenced area would be set aside for a garden, and the lady of the house would have a cast-iron stove complete with a "precious" (pressure) cooker. But it did not end there. The "project" received loans to build a cotton gin and a cooperative store, plus a gristmill and a canning center. It built a grammar school, a nursery, and a federally subsidized church that doubled as a community center (First Amendment restrictions notwithstanding). A home economist, an agricultural agent, and two physicians made regular visits, and there was a full-time nurse at the government-sponsored health clinic to treat the sick and teach the well. The federal government brought the twentieth century to Gee's Bend.[18]

For all that changed, much remained the same. Agricultural programs in Wilcox County were administered by a local committee of "reputable white farmers" who were sympathetic to the needs of the poor but at the same time were skeptical of programs that raised the status of blacks and set them on the road to independence. Benders, isolated and ignored for so long, were already the most independent blacks in the region, and the project promised to make them even more so. But to the Benders' disappointment (though probably not to their surprise) the county establishment decided that "there were no local people capable of managing the store or keeping the books" and put whites in charge. What followed was the merging of planter paternalism and governmental beneficence, Black Belt traditions and New Deal innovations, to create a system with which the powers in Camden and Washington could live. Soon the cooperative began to look more and more like the plantation commissary, even though profits (or at least most of them) stayed in the community. Left out of the equation were the Benders. Though some residents admitted that, as far as bosses were concerned, "the 'Government' was a fine boss indeed," it was still someone else telling them what to do, and many of them resented it.[19]

How well did the project work? That depends on the perspective. Despite the role they played, whites in the region still considered the project a gross example of Washington meddling in local affairs and cited it as evidence of the New Deal's socialistic designs. More than that, they considered it a waste of money. As they told it, the federal government gave residents a farm, a house, and an ox, only to have them sell the farm, trash the house, eat the ox, and be no better off than they were at the start. They laughed at stories of how simple Benders, failing to understand and appreciate the advantages that now were theirs, even cut holes in window and door screens to let in the fresh air—apparently ignoring the fact that if the stories were true, the fault lay not with river region blacks but with the people who denied them access to the modern world and now were laughing at them.[20]

Local whites were not the only critics. Farm Security Administrators complained that the profits from the cooperative were never high enough to justify what it cost to run it, and folks in the Bend complained that too little from the operation was plowed back into the community. Indeed, the community seemed to get lost in the process. Despite their poverty, or maybe because of the common status it imposed on them all, Benders constituted an organic unit, a living community held together by shared relationships and common commitments. Rather than build on this community, the project sought to transform it, and in the end it wasted one of Gee's Bend's most precious resources. One can only wonder what might have been accomplished if local people and their leaders had been allowed more control over what was taking place. Still, a lot was done. Health care, housing, and education improved markedly; many residents were able to purchase farms, and some of them made a good living, kept up their houses, and set the example for others to follow. Many more were disappointed in what their land produced, and when opportunities outside the Bend beckoned, they left the plow and hit the road.[21]

This exodus was brought on, in part, because Gee's Bend could not overcome its greatest obstacle—history. By the late 1930s, the one family, two mule (or one tractor) cotton farm was a thing of the past, and even the mighty federal government could not bring it back. Profit was the yardstick by which success was measured, and in that category the farms of Gee's Bend came up short. In the years that followed more and more houses went without repairs, barns sagged and fell in, animals and people grew thin and tired, and finally farmers in Gee's Bend did what farmers thoughout the South were doing: Those who could moved on, and those who remained languished. Though the decline did not happen overnight, it happened. Still, one must not forget that for a brief time, before many were drawn away, and before the nation found other priorities and cut funding, the project made life better for some of the river region's poorest citizens. Maybe it was a success after all.[22]

Things were not much better farther north—only different. Farmers in the Cahaba River valley got by much as farmers did down on the Alabama; mill workers had to cope with the same wage cuts and closings; middle-class merchants and professionals watched banks fail and stores go under. Even with New Deal programs, times were hard. Attempts to organize a sharecroppers' union met with some success in Black Belt counties, but in the end a combination of planter power, racial prejudice, and anti-communist hysteria won, and the movement died out. Unions fared better in the mills and factories in the Coosa-Tallapoosa valley. Independent rural folk rejected unions as long as they believed the mills and mill managers had the workers' best interest at heart, but when industrial paternalism collapsed under the weight of the depression, they figured it was time to look after themselves. The struggle was bitter, especially in the Gadsden area, but by the end of the decade, with federal legislation to back them up, unions were there and there to stay.[23]

Though traffic on the Alabama River continued to decline, there were still snags to pull, jetties to repair, and channels to clear, so the United States Department of Engineers' fleet of towboats, quarter-boats, warehouse boats, tenders, and barges continued its work between Montgomery and Mobile. Some cotton was still carried downstream in the winter, but barges loaded with sand and gravel made up more and more of the trade. Finally there was so little to do that the U.S.D.E. fleet stayed at or near the Selma landing long enough for Capt. Clark Edwards to buy a couple of pigs, fatten them up on government garbage, and sell them at the local market. Life on the river was good, but it was not what it used to be.[24]

Edwards was not the only river man with time on his hands. Up on the Coosa, lockkeeper Joseph Moses Sullivan found himself in much the same situation. As Coosa commerce dwindled, fewer employees were needed, and Sullivan, who had built and maintained locks most of his life, became one of the last lock men on the river. "The lockkeeper's job," his grandson remembered, "was just about retirement." "You got a government check and . . . you were kinda looked up to and there was little to do because there was so little traffic on the river." Sullivan filled his idle hours hunting and fishing. He shot quail and duck, which he field dressed and sent to restaurants in Birmingham. Fish were caught in funnel-shaped nets, adapted from Indian fishing baskets, with an opening big enough for a man to walk through. These traps quickly filled with catfish, drum, and buffalo, which he sold in Anniston. It was, according to his grandson, "a real good government job at the time."[25]

There were others on the Coosa whose condition and circumstances were very different from those of Joseph Moses Sullivan. They were what writer Jack Kytle called the "human driftwood" that floated up to "tangle the State's social structure." Kytle, as assistant director of the Alabama branch of the Federal Writer's Project, was attracted to "down and outs," and he found some of his best examples on the Coosa. These were people who turned "to the rivers and a bare existence when the mines, the steel plants, and the textile mills cut down on employment." They were the rejects, unskilled and uninspired laborers who had been the first laid off and who Kytle was sure would not be rehired until things improved "to a point where any able-bodied man or woman, no matter how shiftless and ignorant, may be able to accomplish a job of sorts." Jack Kytle did not expect to see that day any time soon.[26]

The writer had no idea how many were on the river. Hundreds, surely, but it was hard to tell since so many came and went. Some had returned to live on isolated family plots; others settled on power company property for three dollars a year, which they never paid; and others just came in and squatted, as Orrie Robinson did when he "discovered he could obtain more food from the river and the forests than from the poor land" he had been trying to farm. The homes Kytle described were of a kind—"a squat heap of rough pine lumber, thrown together carelessly," with "no window panes, only pine boards on hinges, which fail to keep out either the biting winds of winter or the swarms of flies in summer." Inside there were "straw-mattress bunks," also out of pine, and "a pallet or so piled carelessly upon the floor." There were no chairs, only nail kegs. On the front porch there were "a zinc water bucket, . . . a washpan and a bar of cheap soap." And there were "fish hooks and lines . . . strung from a dozen nails that had been driven into the walls." These shacks could have been the home of any number of black families down in Gee's Bend before the project. They were home to many white families up on the Coosa River in 1938. Such was the equality of poverty.[27]

Despite Kytle's reference to "shiftless and ignorant," many of these folks were neither; it was just that the main thing they worked at, the main thing they knew, was survival. And it followed that if society had rejected them, why should they, in their struggle for a better life, be governed by society's rules? So many of them took to making whiskey—"shine," "shinny," "likker," "corn," or as some with a finer feeling for words call it, "popskull" and "busthead." One of them, Bob Curtis, summed up the attitude neatly: "Shore, I've monkeyed with 'shine. Who wouldn't when hit brung in some cash money?" Next to being a lockkeeper, a successful bootlegger may have been the best job on the river.[28]

Willie Bass and a friend, Son Capp, made moonshine on Hatchet Creek, which ran into the lake just above Mitchell Dam. When a batch was ready they took it upstream to where a truck from Birmingham was waiting. Bass remembered a transaction between honest men—"Me an' Son'd unload th' likker, an' then one of th' men'd stick some bills in one of our han's. It'd be dark, an' we wouldn't count it till we got back to th' river, but we never was beat." At two dollars a gallon, Bass was doing well until the county caught him, and he went before the judge. A black man had just been found guilty of the same crime and sentenced to a year and a day in prison when Willie arrived in the courtroom, and he remembered how "my heart sunk [and] I knowed I's a goner." Getting sent to prison was a poor man's greatest fear, for it was general knowledge that down at Kilby they treated an inmate "wors'n a barefooted nigger boy" and "whooped him fer not sayin' 'Yes-sir' to a guard." But southern justice was done. Bass had not been in trouble before, and he was white, so the judge let him go with the warning that "if you ever come in hyar ag'in it's go'nter be two years in th' pen." "I never was as happy as when I heerd them words," Bass recalled, "an' I ain't never seed nothin' as purty as this ol' river when I sot eyes on it ag'in." That event was the end of his bootlegging. "I made up my min' then that I wasn't never go'nter make no more likker, an' I ain't. It's hard as hell to get enough to eat by jes' fishin' an' piddlin' with that ol' pore land of our'n, but it's better'n bein' in jail."[29]

Outside of whiskey, there were not many options for these river folk. "Jes' sawmillin', cotton millin', an' fishin'," according to Bob Curtis. Lumbering was one of Alabama's most depressed industries, and cotton mills had more workers than they could employ. That left fishing. So they seined carp and bream from sloughs, ran trotlines for blue and yellow cat, and in the spring fished below the locks for bedding drum and buffalo. When the catch was good they ate well, or at least ate plenty, for as any of them would tell you, though a man "can eat a bellyful o' fish . . . he'll git tard as hell eatin' 'em." Then they took the catch to town. Ten cents a pound in Sylacauga was not much, but one big yellow or a mess of "little old squealer cats" could bring in enough for "sowbelly an' bread," "canned stuff an' side meat," "hard-rolled" cigarettes, snuff, or "whiskey and a roaring drunk." Still, fishing seemed to bring out the philosopher in folks. "The Lord keers for his own," Bob Curtis observed. "When hit gits t' whar hit seems we'urns will starve, a catfish gits on one of my lines. . . . Yuh know," he reflected, "th' good Lord was int'rusted in fishermen."[30]

Curtis and Bass both fished Lay Lake, but while Curtis believed the Lord and the lake would provide, Bass was not so sure. He did not like the lake. "I remember back when I was a boy," he told Kytle, "that fishin' was good on this river. . . . But that was 'fore th' dam was built and 'fore th' river was full of mud." Because "fish jes' don't like mud," Bass believed that most of them went upstream, "whar th' bottom is sandy." The few fish left behind were "kept skeered to death" during the week, when the dam gates were opened to generate electricity. That was why, Bass concluded, "most of my good catches is made on Saturday an' Sunday," when the gates were closed and the lake filled. "That sends the fishes closer to th' banks," he reasoned, "an' they got their min's on feedin' ag'in." Everything was the power company's fault.[31]

More than poor fishing bothered Willie Bass. "They was lots of people died when the dam was built," he recalled, and one man he knew "come down with chills so hard that he shuk th' bed posts." Convinced this illness came from the lake, Bass's friend "sued th' power company fer th' biggest figger of money he could think of." It was one of the mosquito suits, which science settled to the satisfaction of Alabama Power but not to the likes of Willie Bass. To his way of thinking, the sick man never had a chance. Though the plaintiff "went to court lookin' like he was already dead, an' he had a chill or two sittin' right up thar . . . the jury didn' pity 'im." Bass was not surprised. "He might a knowed," the riverman reflected, "that they ain't no pore man can win nothin' off'n th' power company. They look at us folks hyar on th' river like we'uns was no better'n a dog. A pore man don' stand no more chanct than a June bug in January."[32]

Though the river had little to offer them, many could not bring themselves to leave, and some who did regretted it and hurried back. Orrie Robinson was not concerned that he "hain't never seen Birmingham" and had no desire to "onless I could watch hit from a good piece off." "Uncle Bud" left but "kep gettin' my mind back hyar on this river," so he returned. Neely, a widow living in abject poverty, never left. "I was borned hyar," she told Kytle, "an' been livin' up an' down hit all my life. It's got to whar I coundn't stan' not hearin' it." Jim Lauderdale, former fisherman, miner, and moonshiner, a man Kytle described as a "river wreck," stood in the shambles of his life and proclaimed, "I ain't never ben happier." But it was an empty joy. They were the fraternity of the defeated, the resigned. As Lauderdale confessed of himself, they were "a-dyin' by the graduals." And when they were gone, not many marked their passing.[33]

A few people found the depression good for business. Down in Montgomery WPA writer Adelaide Rogers met "Uncle" Henry Baysmore, who until recently had spent his life "trying to farm on shares, and trying to please white folks." Baysmore told her how he had "started out fer to be a preacher once" and seemed on the road to success until he found "in de Bible where hit say fur Ministers to keep deyse'f unspotted fum de worl'. Den hit say to visit de widows. Yessum, hit say bofe er dem things." Adelaide Rogers may not have seen the conflict involved, but Baysmore certainly did. "If you is ever been acquainted wid any widows," he explained, "you knows a preacher can't visit 'em an' keep his-se'f unspotted. Hit can't be did." So he made the only decision he could—"I give up de preachin' an' went back to farmin' on shares an' to singin' all day while I hoed out de cotton rows in de fields."[34]

Now, in his seventy-fifth year, Henry Baysmore had found his calling. He was a fortune teller and conjure man, talents which, in those unsettled days, were always in demand. In fact, he told Mrs. Rogers "respectfully but with twinkling eyes, 'I got more white customers what wants to see into de future den cullud ones.'" With times so hard, whites were "anxious to know about money . . . how kin de keep what dey got . . . or get a holt to somebody else's"; and they were concerned over property, "who gwiner inherit dat house dey craves, or is ole Aunt Lucy gwiner up an' leave it to somebody else—after all?" Baysmore did not come cheap. His price was ten dollars, and if they protested he just told them "if you can't 'ford ten dollars, fur a lil supernat'chal infor'mation, de property jus hafta go to somebody else." That usually got them, and "dey'll more 'en likely come back to hand over de cash." So the tables had turned, and "instead of white folks working him, ["Uncle" Henry] works white folks." Adelaide Rogers and Henry Baysmore both found a certain justice in that.[35]

New Deal programs eased the pain of the depression; the war brought it to an end. By 1940 government planners could feel it coming and began laying the foundation for facilities that would become America's military-industrial complex. It did not take them long to see the Alabama-Coosa-Tallapoosa system with its abundant water and hydroelectric resources. The bases came quickly. That year the Southeast Air Corps Training Center was established at Maxwell Field in Montgomery, a facility that would bring millions of dollars into the city. Just outside town, on a site that included a small airport, an abandoned prison, and a pecan grove, work began on Gunter Air Force Base. The two facilities grew so rapidly that auxiliary fields were built at Shorter, Deatsville, Elmore, and Danley, and before the conflict ended over a hundred thousand cadets were trained in the area. Craig Field opened in Selma in 1941 and in time had a military employment of two thousand, plus almost as many civilians. Up the Coosa the Anniston Ordnance Depot and Fort McClellan hired hundreds, indeed thousands to build and expand those facilities. By the time the war actually started, people who wanted a job could get one.[36]

It was a transformation of unprecedented proportion. Near Childersburg, Du Pont Chemical built the largest smokeless powder and explosive plant in Dixie, and what had been a town of five hundred had to find a way to accommodate some fourteen thousand construction workers. But there was always the other side to the boom. Over thirty-two thousand acres of land were taken for the plant complex, and some three hundred family farms disappeared. Yet as with the dams, complaints were few. Meanwhile, textile factories set up round-the-clock shifts; timber companies kept crews in the woods from dawn until dark and saw mills ran night and day; worn-out farms were left to grow up in weeds as owners headed for the towns and cities; King Cotton was finally deposed, and economic diversification became a reality.[37]

For many employment meant military service, and thousands of young men and women from the river region went off to war. This opened jobs to some who would not have had them otherwise— women, who by 1944 were 48 percent of the Du Pont work force, and blacks. It also opened the door to folks like those Kytle found on the Coosa. The Hurts, a clan described by writer Herman Clarence Nixon, were that breed. They were a "household of two double-up families, former sharecroppers," eight of whom held down jobs. Three were farm laborers, so the group had a tenant house and could keep a garden. One was a pipe fitter at Childersburg, over seventy miles away, and the rest went "near and far to industrial work." But rural river ways died hard, and despite an income approaching middle class, the Hurts rejected the values of that segment of society. They were "neither saints nor money savers." In four months they bought, sold, traded, or wrecked some thirteen automobiles; at one point four of them were in jail at the same time, where they stayed until the others pulled together enough bail to get them out. Two of them reported for the draft but were apparently rejected. They were just "good old boys," who worked hard, paid their bills, and, except for those times when they got drunk and started fighting, usually left folks alone. They were the modern personification of W. J. Cash's frontier southerner. Nixon found them "dynamic and cooperative," traits Kytle seldom observed among his contacts. The difference, it seems, was the jobs. The Hurts had them.[38]

Down in the Black Belt, what little was left of the tenant farming system crumbled with the migration from farm to factory, and those planters who had tried to preserve old relationships now complained that most of the workers who had remained on the plantation had finally "taken off for the war industries and the saw mills." But the landlords adjusted quickly. "I miss their labor," one reflected, "but at the same time I am putting more land into pasture" and buying tractors, for "the more machines I use, the less labor I'll need." Wages for those hands who did stay were $1.50 a day, three times what they were before the war, but as the planter noted, "the price of cotton is higher too. We manage alright." Still, he did not believe the boom would last forever and confessed, "I dread the time when those tenants who left come knocking at my door after their city jobs close down." He knew that by then their cabins would be gone and their land would have disappeared into larger fields. If they returned, they would find only seasonal wage employment and no place to live. They had not left very much, but they would come back to even less.[39]

Everyone gave their all for the war effort, even the rivers. A railroad bridge over the Coosa that had collapsed in 1902 was pulled up and turned into nearly a million pounds of scrap. Meanwhile in Selma divers went down and retrieved metal that had been on the river bottom since retreating Confederates and victorious Yankees had used it as a dumping ground during the Civil War. River water, piped into busy factories and growing towns, was discharged with a different color and a different smell, and some folks claimed it made the fish taste funny. But no one seemed too worried—it was progress. Everyone was busy. Most farm families now enjoyed a nonfarm income, derived from either "public works" or "defense works," and with the money they earned they bought "things"—clothes, cars, radios, washing machines, and Frigidaires. "Things" meant they were no longer poor. That so much of what they acquired came as the result of government largess, and that the relationship between the region and the federal government had been transformed to bring this about, was something these folks let the Big Mules of Alabama agriculture and industry worry about. All their lives they had been pulling "hind tit"; it was good to be near the front for a change.[40]

Herman Nixon was not sure all this activity was for the best. Down in the lower piedmont country, between the Coosa and Tallapoosa, he found that though folks had "less time for drinking," there was also "less time for religion," and congregations in rural churches seemed smaller and grayer. New people had moved into the neighborhood, more were coming, and that old southern xenophobia, that fear of strangers, was taking hold. Residents talked less to each other, there was less local gossip, and "frequently a man cannot give the name of a family living a mile away." The spirit of community that sustained so many through the depression seemed to disappear as times got better. Down in Gee's Bend, the migration out changed things. Small farm life and project amenities could not compete with Mobile society and shipyard pay, so the youngest, the brightest, the leaders left, and most did not come back. In 1940, the river region had begun to prepare for war. Late in the summer of 1945, World War II came to an end, and a very different river region heard the news.[41]

FIFTEEN

Reviving the Rivers

Work will start soon on the vast project to harness the Coosa river for flood control, navigation and power production. . . . It means that the Coosa will eventually become the third largest hydro-electric producer in the nation, that the Coosa Valley will be free from the menace of floods, and that the glamorous days of steamboats on the stream will return on a much larger and more important scale. . . . For old timers it is not difficult to vision the celebrations in Rome, Gadsden, Selma, Anniston, Talladega, Wetumpka, Montgomery and Mobile when small warships will be sent here by the government to aid in the glorious realization of a century old dream.

Gadsden Times
April 21, 1946

Many people paid dearly for this symbol of progress [Logan-Martin Dam on the Coosa River, 1964]. . . . The site of Easonville, which was settled in 1821, is now under twenty feet of water. It is a sad thing when a community this old must be uprooted and moved. There were homes in Easonville over a hundred years old. There were three stores, one cotton gin, four dairies, one cemetery, two churches, and one of the best schools in the county. At least two hundred persons were affected by the removal. Citizens whose ancestors established the community stood by while trees estimated to be three to four hundred years old were pushed over and burned.

MATTIE LOU TEAGUE CROW
History of St. Clair County, 1973

World War II did little to slow the decline of river commerce that had been going on since the turn of the century. The military and industrial establishments that rose in the Coosa-Alabama valley moved most of their goods by rail, not water; and the people who worked in the factories and trained on the bases traveled on highways built or improved under New Deal public works programs or on "Big Jim" Folsom's farm-to-market roads. On the Coosa, the last master had retired from the locks that once symbolized a national commitment to opening the river for navigation, and their "cut stone masonry" walls were little more than reference points for local fishermen. Meanwhile wartime traffic on the Alabama was reduced to an infrequent dredge boat clearing the channel so an occasional log raft could float down to a riverside mill or a barge with sand and gravel might make its way to the cement works.[1]

Still, dreams of a major inland waterway running through Alabama refused to die. Early in 1945, with the end of the conflict in sight

Congress began to consider ways to employ returning veterans and keep the nation from slipping into a postwar recession. River improvement advocates were ready. Dusting off a 1941 report that had been shelved when Japan attacked Pearl Harbor, they began to push once again for the multiple-purpose development of the Coosa-Alabama rivers and raised hopes in the region that this might be the next great New Deal project.[2]

No one anticipated the enthusiastic reception the idea would receive. When the 1945 River and Harbor Act cleared Congress, the *Montgomery Advertiser* announced that Alabama had come up "with the biggest single plum" in the bill—$60 million for a "waterway cutting through the heart of the state down the Coosa and Alabama Rivers." The plan was not an attempt to revive the old low-lift system and bring abandoned locks into service. Instead it called for seven new navigation dams and locks, six power dams with locks, and three flights of locks at existing Alabama Power dams. There would also be fifteen dams and reservoirs on tributaries of the Coosa to help with flood control. Where it was necessary the streams would be dredged, and when the project was complete there would be a nine-foot channel running six hundred miles from Mobile to Rome, Georgia. Sen. Lister Hill, one of the waterway's strongest supporters, was hardly understating the case when he called the legislation "an epochal event in the life of Alabama."[3]

On March 3, 1945, President Roosevelt signed the bill, and all along the rivers there was "rejoicing." Only one hurdle remained, but it was a big one. Congress still had to appropriate the money. Now opponents of the measure rallied against it. Railroads charged that inland waterways could never deliver the benefits that advocates claimed; veterans' groups argued that the money should go into their insurance fund; and power company lobbyists worked hard to block funding for a project they believed, according to local residents, was "gonna be another TVA." Under this pressure the bill was rewritten, revised, and amended, and when it finally passed almost a year later, the only dam funded was one at Allatoona, on the Coosa's Etowah tributary in Georgia. Optimists claimed it was a good beginning and that it was only a matter of time before there would be "celebrations in Rome, Gadsden, Selma, Anniston, Talladega, Wetumpka, Montgomery and Mobile . . . [at the] glorious realization of a century old dream"; skeptics were doubtful, and the skeptics were right.[4]

While the fate of Alabama's rivers was debated in Washington and Montgomery, the region began to feel the economic slowdown postwar planners had warned was coming. Defense plants closed, machinery was dismantled and shipped to other sites, military bases reduced operations, and laid-off workers headed for larger cities and greener pastures. Towns with industries that could be adapted to peacetime production fared well enough, but for much of the region the high times were over. The New Deal and its public investment philosophy was history. Faced with a massive national debt, politicians now talked about balanced budgets and spending restraints, not federally funded projects and government jobs. With each session of Congress the chances of a Coosa-Alabama waterway steadily diminished.[5]

As the economy adjusted to these new circumstances, life along the rivers, away from towns and cities, returned to prewar patterns so familiar that it seemed as if the years had made no difference at all—patterns that were precisely why so many had left, and why at least one expatriate, Harold Rozelle, returned. Rozelle had grown up near Lincoln, Alabama, not far from the Coosa. Before the war he had joined the exodus and ended up working as an aeronautical engineer in postwar California's booming aircraft industry. But the job and west coast culture were not what he had hoped, and as his frustration grew he began to long for a simpler life, one free from the pressures of modern society, a life like the one he remembered from his youth. Finally, in 1949, Rozelle had had enough. He and his wife, Pauline, packed up and "just took off"—back to Alabama, back to the Coosa.[6]

Harold Rozelle "didn't want things modern," his brother Ed recalls, so he and Pauline repaired a cabin near the stream where they settled down to live, as Thoreau had done a century before. With his brother's help Harold raised a sunken ferry, put it back in service, and ran it according to whatever schedule he chose. The job fit his ambitions well enough, for with so many New Deal era bridges around, ferries on the Coosa were fast becoming a thing of the past. Some ferries had hung on for a while, like the one that operated where Highway 78 crossed the river. There was a bridge there, but it charged a toll, and since the ferry was cheaper, most area folks took it. One night, though, a car load of local boys, full of themselves and more than their share of Birmingham whiskey, hit the tollbooth head on. Nickles, dimes, and quarters scattered everywhere, and neighborhood children descended on the wreck for their share of the bounty. The booth was never replaced, much to the satisfaction of local folks who had resented it from the start, and soon the ferry went out of business. The end of other ferries was less dramatic, but their passing was just as certain. If Harold Rozelle wanted an occupation that harked back to an earlier, less complicated time, he could not have picked a better one.[7]

Rozelle's ferry served an infrequently traveled dirt road, so he was free to spend his days observing neighbors who seemed to have found that simple way of life he sought. These folks earned a little money farming, or logging, or in some cases bootlegging, and to him that seemed enough. They had gardens, and they had the Coosa. As one of them put it, "we don't worry when we get broke. We just go fishing." And fish they did. They caught fish in traps as the Indians did centuries before; they set out trotlines as their ancestors had; and they pole-fished whenever they got a chance. Some sold their catch to the "store man" in town, while others peddled them live from tubs on street corners and from roadside stands. Rozelle, still a river boy at heart and wanting to be one with them, fished too.[8]

It was a hard life, and most who lived it by chance, not choice, wanted something better. They knew already what Harold Rozelle learned that year on the Coosa: Living simply meant doing without. River residents had their fill of that and wanted something better. Though farmers in the valley still listened patiently to county agricultural agents telling them how to earn a living from infertile fields and farm wives still met with the area home economist to learn how to make the most out of what the land produced, like Rozelle's ferry, they were part of a way of life that would soon be gone. The future belonged to men like the veterans who attended government-sponsored adult education classes at local schools in the evenings to prepare themselves for better jobs and picked up a little "G.I. money" in the process. Families might still live in a tenant shack, but a refrigerator on the front porch, "plugged in and running," announced to the world that they had electricity and the appliances to use it. Even the fishermen, who seemed to Rozelle the personification of that older, purer time, happily abandoned traditional methods and embraced more modern and less legal ones—telephoning and dynamiting—to fill their tubs, stock local stores, and feed the crowd that gathered at weekend fish frys. After its brief postwar revival, the old Coosa culture was disappearing once again.[9]

Harold Rozelle mourned its passing, but he understood why this way of life could not survive. Wartime prosperity gave river folk a glimpse of the future, and they wanted more. The economy may have slowed for the moment, but locals remained convinced that good times would come again, and when that happened, they would be ready. Rozelle did not have to wait. A year of the simple life, and he knew it was time to go back to California, back to the future. He had, Rozelle reflected as he prepared to leave, "drifted on the river long enough."[10]

Down in Gee's Bend things were also changing, but not in the way residents had hoped. The same Congress that failed to fund the Coosa-Alabama waterway abolished the Farm Security Administration and with it the cooperative farming program. Arrangements were made for qualified co-op members to buy their farms with long-term government loans, and many did, but though the purchase gave them a measure of pride and independence, it also tied them to an economic system whose future was doubtful at best and to a social system that offered them little opportunity to advance. Also diminishing their prospects was that Washington's shift in policy meant the end of the cooperative store, the clinic, and all those other federally sponsored programs that had made life better for Benders. The government was no longer the "fine boss" it once had been.[11]

Folks in Gee's Bend faced a future much less promising than did their counterparts up on the Coosa. Down in the Black Belt there were no Goodyear plants or textile mills where residents might work when farms were not enough, no better jobs for which veterans' training programs could prepare them. There were logging, sawmilling, and doing odd chores for the white man, just as there had always been. Anything more than this lay far beyond the Bend, outside the region, and more and more Benders left to find it. Those who remained came to accept the fact that history had caught up with them once again, and the forces at work in their lives were forces over which they had little control. Then in 1949, as if to remind them how powerless they were, the government built a post office deep in the Bend and announced that the community it would serve would be named "Boykin," after a congressman from Mobile who, as best residents could remember, had never set foot among them. It seemed that someone in Washington wanted to wipe Gee's Bend from the map and from memory. The bureaucrats could only do so much. The map was changed, but Benders knew where they lived, and they knew what to call it.[12]

By mid-century government activity on and along the rivers had slowed almost to a standstill. Across the Georgia line the Allatoona Dam on the Etowah was finished, and there was little hope that Washington would do much more. Some folks blamed this neglect on budget deficits left over from the war; others faulted the economy in general; still others thought the money was being spent (or misspent) on foreign policy priorities. On the other hand there were locals who appeared just as happy that the dams were not built, since it had been rumored that under the 1945 plan the whole Coosa valley would have been flooded and that "the water in Lincoln would fill up to the eaves of the depot." There was just so much progress a person could take, and that was too much.[13]

Now there were those on the scene who were willing to step in where the federal government refused to tread. "By the early 1950s," according to Alabama Power Company president Thomas Martin, "it seemed again feasible for the company to complete the development of the Coosa River." There was a new administration in Washington, a Republican one, and in 1953 it announced its intention to encourage development of the nation's waterways through private investment. In October of that year the Coosa-Alabama River Improvement Association requested that the Alabama Power Company consider doing just that, and the company, with speed that suggests it was considering the matter already, sprang into action. On November 12, 1953, Alabama Power filed an application with the Federal Power Commission for a preliminary permit for a multidam project on the Coosa. A new era in Alabama river development had begun.[14]

In the months that followed Alabama Power held "frequent discussions" with the Corps of Engineers, the Federal Power Commission, federal and state health authorities, and representatives from the Fish and Wildlife Service of the Interior Department so that, Martin said, "all viewpoints could be considered." Meanwhile city governments in Selma and Montgomery endorsed the idea and called on Congress "to take necessary action to allow construction." The state's congressional delegation rallied around the plan, and in the spring they announced that legislation to allow Alabama Power to begin developing the Coosa would be introduced shortly. Everything seemed perfect. The company would invest $100 million to build five dams on the river. The project would be completed in no more than ten years, and according to one of its most influential supporters, Congressman Albert Rains from Gadsden, it "does not contemplate the expenditure of one single dollar of federal funds." Conforming "to the plans for the development of the region by the Corps of Engineers," the undertaking would provide new lakes for recreation and home sites and stabilize reservoir levels so "the area will be more inviting to industries needing substantial supplies of water." The electricity produced at these dams would be used to attract manufacturing to Alabama; to guarantee this appeal, a "feature" was added to the legislation specifying which power generated from the Coosa would "never be piped away for use elsewhere." Last, the new dams would "provide a waterway of approximately 255 miles of sufficient depth to permit navigation from Rome to the Wetumpka-Montgomery area when locks are provided by the [federal] government." All of this project would translate into "jobs for thousands of workers" along with "approximately three million dollars per year tax revenues for school purposes." Little wonder Rains and his colleagues called it "the biggest thing we've had in this generation for the development of Alabama."[15]

In late April 1954, legislation authorizing construction was introduced in both houses of Congress. The rest seemed very easy. After being assured that the bill would specify that "the dams must include facilities for flood control and possible future navigation" and that the legislation would not hurt the TVA, doubters fell silent. Everyone apparently understood, as one congressman put it, that "the choice is . . . not between private power and federal power, but between private power and no power at all." Everyone wanted power, so on June 2 the legislation sailed through the House on a voice vote, and on June 15 it cleared the Senate. Less than two weeks later President Eisenhower signed the bill into law.[16]

Even before the legislation was on the books, Alabama Power Company had applied for permission to begin surveying sites, since the bill required that work on the first dam must begin in a year. In July the Federal Power Commission gave its approval, and the company began running "extensive engineering tests," while making plans for site selection and land acquisition. In this regard Martin assured property owners that they "will continue to have use of the lands we buy for growing their crops until the actual time arises for filling the reservoir" and then they would have "full rights to remove fruit trees, shrubs and other plants before the land is flooded." To those who were concerned that the state might be allowing Alabama Power to take without giving, Martin pointed out that the company had not sought state or local tax exemptions for its projects, as other industries had. However, if governments wanted to help the company and help themselves, he told a meeting of civic leaders in Anniston, they could "extend exemptions and other encouragements to other industries which [would] be attracted . . . by the hydro-electric generating plants." "For every dollar we spend," he told his audience, "someone else will spend $5 to $10 to utilize this power." Thus the company could recoup its investment, pay Alabama's low taxes, and turn a tidy profit. It was a good deal for the region and a good deal for the Alabama Power Company.[17]

Now things began to move fast and furiously. The first project was Weiss Dam, in the Centre-Leesburg area, which would impound water almost back to Rome, Georgia; the second would be Logan-Martin, upriver from Childersburg; the third, H. Neely Henry Dam, would be built at old Lock #3, just below Greensport; and the last, the Walter Bouldin Dam, would hold back a reservoir filled with water drawn from Lake Jordan. On April 26, 1958, the ground-breaking ceremony was held for Weiss, with over 10,000 attending—if the number of barbecue plates served is an accurate indicator. Construction began three months later, and by 1962 the plant was fully operational. Logan Martin came on line two years later. It was the last dam built under Tom Martin's supervision. He died in December of 1964, and with his passing Alabama lost a true visionary. The project he set in motion moved on as planned. The Neely Henry Dam was up and running in 1966, and a year later Bouldin Dam was completed. With a display of organizational ability, engineering skill, and political savvy that goes unappreciated to this day, the Alabama Power Company had conquered the mighty Coosa.[18]

Community and business leaders praised the power company for what it had done, and there was no denying that the dams were an economic blessing for the region and its people. Along the river, however, there were those who looked on it as a mixed blessing at best. Where previous dams had been built in rugged, remote areas, there were complaints that these projects destroyed rich agricultural resources—farms with "rows over a mile long" according to one resident. Others mourned the loss of historic towns like Greensport, Binghamtown, and Easonville, with their homes, stores, gins, schools, churches, and cemeteries. Much was relocated; much could not be. Despite the complaints, most people seemed to think they got what the property was worth. Some of them got more, for as the water rose they found themselves owning lakefront lots, whose value would eventually be greater than the land they lost.[19]

It was not as if smooth-talking company men came in and took the land from simple, trusting, uninformed, and unresisting country folks. Locals knew what these outsiders were after and knew they would eventually have to go along. Still, some of them wanted at least to fire a volley before they had to surrender, and one buyer had little choice but to stand there, hat in hand, wavy hair blowing in the breeze, and take it when a farmer told him, "You curley headed son of a bitch, get off my property." Friends and fellow workers agreed that the resident was at least half right, but not everyone was so belligerent. In another case the buyer had been warned that the owner of an important forty acres was a man "you could not trade with," and he dreaded having to make the visit. When he arrived the man seemed strangely agreeable, so he asked the farmer what he wanted for the property, which was mostly swamp and sweetgums, and the farmer told him $4,000. Because it was a far better price than the company man had hoped, he told the landowner to wait and he would be back with the check as soon as he could. Considering the farmer's reputation, the buyer wasted no time, and when he returned the sale was concluded. Proud of himself for having cut such a good deal, the buyer could not resist telling the farmer, "You know, you could have gotten a lot more for your land." "Yeah," the old man replied, "and you could have got it for a hell of a lot less."[20]

The Coosa was dammed. Generators sent electricity to towns and factories in the region, and just as promised, there were new industries and more jobs. Also as promised, flood control plans were implemented, and river valley residents began to rest a little easier when the spring rains came. The only thing missing was the barges carrying

1 Claiborne Lock & Dam (1969)	8 Mitchell Dam (1923)
2 Millers Ferry Lock & Dam (1969)	9 Lay Dam (1914)
3 Robert F. Henry Lock & Dam (1972)	10 R. L. Harris Dam (1983)
4 Jordan Dam (1929)	11 Logan Martin Dam (1964)
5 Thurlow Dam (1930)	12 H. Neely Henry Dam (1966)
6 Yates Dam (1928)	13 Weiss Dam (1962)
7 Martin Dam (1926)	

Dams on the Alabama River System

commerce down the river to the Gulf. Under the agreement worked out between Alabama Power Company and the federal government, these dams, like the ones before them, were built so that locks could be installed by the Corps of Engineers. But there was just not the support for opening the Coosa for navigation that there had been for damming it to produce hydroelectric power, so money for the project remained in Washington. Even a 1958 report indicating that a Coosa-Alabama waterway might pay for itself failed to generate much enthusiasm. The old locks were gone, dynamited and swallowed up by the lakes, and prospects for new ones seemed to grow dimmer as each year passed.[21]

In 1960, a report on America's inland waterways identified "no traffic of consequence on the Coosa-Alabama system . . . although limited quantities of materials move on the lower reaches of the Alabama." That summed it up pretty well. During the 1950s the yearly traffic, mostly outbound timber products and crude petroleum, never exceeded eight hundred thousand tons. Barges carried much of this, though rafted logs were still floated down to sawmills just as they had been for over a century. On the whole the river was a quiet, peaceful, almost lonely place, as a group of teenage boys found out in 1957, when they drifted down from Montgomery to Mobile on a ten-by-twelve-foot raft. It was an adventure worthy of Tom Sawyer or Huckleberry Finn, and newspapers in towns along the stream kept the public informed of their progress. On their trip they saw all sorts of wildlife, including alligators, saw towns and where towns had been, and saw how the river changed as it cut through Black Belt hills and descended into the swamps of coastal plain. What they did not see was commerce. Not until they reached the Mobile River, just above their final destination, did they meet a barge. Except for a few fishermen, the Alabama was theirs.[22]

These boys, honored as "Alabama's Youngest Admirals," may have been one of the last groups to see so much of the river in so natural a state, for even as they were polling their raft along, interest in improving the Alabama was increasing. During the 1950s the ever-active Corps of Engineers had made "surveys and re-surveys of the river," and though early reports were "unfavorable," they kept at it until, in 1958, the Corps announced that it could design a system that would produce "an 8 per cent surplus of benefits over cost." The Association of American Railroads argued that those figures were wrong and that the project would lose money, but with the Corps's report to give the plan legitimacy, support began to grow.[23]

At this point nature stepped in to play a part. Folks all along the valley knew, as "Uncle Bud" Ryland up on the Coosa once observed,

that the "durned river's like a man. Hit's got t' blow off steam sometimes." That is what happened in February and March of 1961. The
weatherman, Mrs. Viola Goode Liddell recalled, said "a cold front had
collided with a warm front from the Gulf," and when that happened,
"one deluge after another descended on Alabama and North Georgia."
The water flowed into the creeks, and the creeks flowed into the rivers
and into the lakes. The Coosa and Tallapoosa rose rapidly, warnings
went out to get animals to high ground, and more rain came. At the
dams, engineers struggled to harness the flow. No one thought much of
electrical power or navigation now. All that mattered was flood control.[24]

Down in Wilcox County folks anxiously listened to the news from
the north, watching the sky and the river. On March 1, the Alabama
reached flood stage at Miller's Ferry, and they prepared for the worst.
Then things began to improve. The weather cleared and turned
warmer, almost spring-like. It was wonderful. On Sunday, March 5,
when residents of Camden went to church to give thanks for their
"special blessings," camellias were blooming. But things were not what
they seemed. Presbyterian services were already underway when a
farmer eased in and beckoned some of the men in the congregation to
come outside. Then he told them that the radio had reported that
upstream there was more water than the Coosa dams could hold, and
they were opening the gates. Word spread quickly. There was not much
time before the tide heading their way would arrive.[25]

What happened in Wilcox County happened all along the river.
People in low-lying areas were the first priority, and from Montgomery
to Mobile every effort was made to get residents to safety. In the Black
Belt, where the civil rights struggles of the 1950s had divided the races
as never before and where the national news had found some of its best
(or worst) examples of racism, residents later spoke with pride of
"white men bringing out Negro children and old folks in their arms,
helping mothers and babies into and out of boats, then returning for a
load of trussed-up hogs and goats, chickens (if they could be caught)
and even squally cats tied up in gunnysacks." It was, Mrs. Liddell
recalled, "an epic to warm the hearts of the most cynical," and one local,
stung by what he thought was unfair treatment by the media, was heard
to remark "what a pity that Huntley and Brinkley couldn't have their
cameras here now."[26]

For twenty-eight days the waters stayed at flood stage, and when they
finally went down river folk emerged to survey the damage. Homes and
businesses were ruined; livestock by the hundreds had drowned; roads
were washed out; and fields were full of sand and river muck. Some
residents tried to look on the bright side and convince farmers they

should be happy for the rich sediment deposited in their fields. Virginus Jones of Wilcox County would have none of it. "Man," he told the smiling optimist, "if I were able, I'd make you eat every damn grain of the beautiful stuff." A few of the older residents argued that earlier floods had been worse, but everyone agreed that this one was bad enough. In time, one of the region's "reference points" would be "the flood of 1961."[27]

Could the disaster have been prevented? If there had been dams on the Alabama to stem the tide and regulate the flow, would things have been better? No one, of course, could say for sure, but studies suggested dams would have helped, and river residents returning to mud-filled houses and ruined fields were ready to give the Corps a chance. The flood might not have changed many minds in Washington, but it changed minds back home, and politicians could count votes. With plans for the first dam nearly completed and others on the drawing board, all the Corps needed was authorization to begin construction. They got it. The state's congressional delegation delivered as promised, and "the good Lord," Representative Rains modestly proclaimed, "smiled on us and the Alabama River system." On April 17, 1963, ground was broken for the Miller's Ferry lock and dam. The development of the Alabama had begun.[28]

With the federal government and the Corps of Engineers in charge, all aspects of the plan—dam, lock, and power plant—were built together and went into operation together. Before the Miller's Ferry complex was finished in 1970, two other Alabama River projects were underway—downstream at Claiborne and above Selma at Jones Bluff. By 1972 all three were completed. Representing a total investment of almost $178 million, the dams promised to provide power for over a hundred thousand homes, supply water for domestic and industrial use, control floods, and "create a sportsman's paradise in south Alabama." They also promised to turn the region into another Tennessee Valley. The Tennessee River, according to the *Montgomery Advertiser*, was "fenced with smokestacks largely because North Alabama has what South Alabama has not—a navigable waterway to serve and reach its markets." Now South Alabama had a nine-foot channel from Mobile to Montgomery. Could the smokestacks be far behind?[29]

The development of the river drew almost universal praise from business and commercial interests as well as from sportsmen for whom the lakes were "stars in the crown of the Alabama." But as was so often the case when it came to changes along the river, not everyone was happy. People who lived close to the waterway saw things in a different light. Down at "Boykin" news of the Miller's Ferry project brought with it reports that the dam would push water over nearly a third of Gee's Bend and that the government would buy back hard-won farms with what was being called "flood money." It was a sad turn of events for many Benders, for the value of their land was in its ownership, not in its price. Even if they could find another farm to buy, their "place" was gone, and that was what mattered the most. Willie Q. Pettway lost some fifty-five of his sixty-six-acre farm, and with it he lost a link to land that had sustained his people for generations. He could not plant cotton and corn where those before him had; there was no place for cows or hogs, no place for a farmer. "All I can do," he later lamented, "is sit here and look at a lake."[30]

Meanwhile, up on the Coosa, work on the Alabama dams and locks revived "the old, old dream of direct water passage from Rome to Mobile" and raised hopes that a "new generation of riverboats" would soon appear. In 1969 the legislature created the Coosa Valley Development Authority and gave it the power to "hold and dispose of funds to develop the Montgomery-Gadsden leg of the waterway." Later that year Alabama voters approved a $10 million bond issue to pay for construction not covered by anticipated federal appropriations. Behind much of this activity was the Coosa-Alabama River Improvement Association, which was now receiving a small appropriation from the state to help it promote the project. What the association wanted, and what the Corps of Engineers was willing, indeed anxious, to carry out, was the construction of the long-planned locks in the Alabama Power Company dams and the dredging of a nine-foot channel in sections of the Coosa not covered by backwater. What the *Montgomery Advertiser* called "the flowering of one of the largest underdeveloped waterways in the United States" seemed finally at hand.[31]

The Corps went to work surveying sites and drawing up plans. As supporters lobbied hard in Congress, reports of increased commercial traffic going through the locks on the Alabama gave strength to their case. Inflationary pressures in the mid-1970s caused Washington to move more cautiously than it might have in better times; but even so, Congress continued to lay out money for the Corps to spend on "design and engineering." As late as 1977, reports indicated that when the project was finished, some $3.60 would be generated for every federal dollar spent—"a positive return on our federal investment" that would make everything worthwhile. Then everything seemed to go wrong. In 1978 a survey of the Logan Martin lock site found "limestone catacombs" near and below the dam, which meant that the lock must be relocated over half a mile to the west and that canals would have to be dredged to it. Problems were also found in the location of the lock site at Mitchell Dam, necessitating the decision to move it some two hun-

Jordan Dam with lock approach channel marked
(Courtesy Alabama Power Company Archives)

dred feet east so barges could have room to maneuver. These changes, plus inflation, turned a 1977 project estimated to cost $490 million into a $1.1 billion project by 1982. A year later that figure was up to $1.3 billion and rising. And that, according to C. R. Carlson of the Improvement Association, was "too much for Congress."[32]

It was too much for just about everyone else as well. Although one congressman from the region argued that the project should be continued so that the $18 million already spent by the Corps would not be wasted, Washington was unwilling to stand accused of pouring good money after bad. By now, earlier reports of the project's economic feasibility had been revised downward as a result of inflation, and chances of the waterway paying for itself seemed remote at best. After reviewing the reports and recommendations, the chairman of the House Appropriations Subcommittee on Energy and Water Development, Alabamian Tom Bevill, concluded that the project should be put "on hold indefinitely." Some protested still, but when it was revealed that the state would have to pledge $30 million to relocate highways and bridges before construction could begin, objections were quietly dropped. In March of 1983, less than a month before work on the waterway was scheduled to begin, Chairman Bevill announced that he had "directed the Corps to undertake an orderly suspension" of the project.[33]

Nothing is ever really over. A year later a new Corps of Engineers report produced figures to show that while it would take nearly a hundred years for a Coosa-Alabama waterway to pay back its cost, the project would indeed save $25 million a year in transportation costs through lower freight rates. If gasoline prices rose, the savings would be greater and the pay-back time reduced. By now the problem was the project itself. Under the Carter administration a distinction had been made between national and regional benefits, with national undertakings getting top priority. The Reagan White House continued with this policy, and the Coosa-Alabama River Improvement Association was hard pressed to show how its project would directly benefit the nation as a whole. A waterway through Alabama might bring industry to an undeveloped area and increase employment in some of the poorest counties in the nation, but it was hard to argue that this project had national significance. In the eyes of the federal government, the Coosa-Alabama was a state river system; it belonged to Alabama.[34]

SIXTEEN

Fencing the River with Smokestacks

Our reasons for coming to Wilcox County were primarily economic.
Trees are the fundamental requirement for the pulp and paper
industry. We're right in the midst of the fastest growing pine. . . .
We have plenty of water and good transportation. Now this means
not only roads to get to you, but railroads to get the product away.

> ANGUS GARDNER
> President of MacMillan-Bloedel
> 1970

They ought to put em in the penitentiary about poisonin the earth
and the air and the waters, killin the fish in the rivers and the water
coasts and all like that. The devil is just loose on earth and the laws
is not hard enough on em.

> NATE SHAW [Ned Cobb]
> *All God's Dangers*, 1973

In October 1964, with the Miller's Ferry lock and dam under construction and other projects on the drawing board, the *Montgomery Advertiser* put out a special issue on "waterways and industrial progress in Alabama." The "largest edition ever published by the Montgomery newspaper," it was an extravaganza of chamber of commerce ballyhoo that highlighted almost every town and city, every mill and factory along the state's river systems. It also brought in a bundle of advertising revenue for the paper. As might have been expected, much of the special issue focused on the development of the Alabama-Coosa inland waterway and the industrial expansion its completion was supposed to bring. The edition was boosterism at its best, and it depicted a future that made Alabamians proud.[1]

Among the rapidly expanding businesses praised by the *Advertiser* was Alabama's timber industry. Demands for forest products continued to be high after the war, and Alabama farmers soon began thinking of trees as a crop. Of course, there had always been a timber industry in the region, and "the buzz of sawmills" was a familiar sound. Now, in addition to lumber, the nation needed, indeed demanded, a variety of cellulose-based products, the most important of which was paper. It followed that some of the first postwar smokestacks to appear along the river were paper mills. The region was ideal—plenty of electrical power, plenty of water for processing and disposal, and plenty of the sort of trees that some claimed could "grow and reproduce themselves faster than in any other part of the North American continent." Pines that might have been considered scrub by a sawmill made fine pulpwood, and farmers in the area cut and replanted as fast as they could. Meanwhile the mills ran around the clock, turning out reams of paper, making payrolls, and filling the air with a foul smell that locals breathed in like perfume. Many are the stories told of how a visitor, after checking his shoes and the baby's diaper, wondered aloud what the odor was, only to have a resident reply simply, "progress."[2]

Despite the expansion of paper manufacturing, in the late 1950s and early 1960s the biggest industry on the river was construction. Dam projects offered jobs to the skilled, the semiskilled, and those with no skills at all, and unemployment in the area where one was built fell dramatically. Construction was always far from population centers, and there were never enough skilled workers locally to meet a project's needs; so new people, "dam people," had to be brought in. This influx had little effect on folks up on the Coosa. They had learned to adjust to outsiders years before, when strangers came there to work on Alabama Power projects and in wartime industries. But down on the Alabama things were different. The Black Belt had never taken well to change or the people who brought it, and this traditional inclination was magnified when the "dam people" began arriving just at the time when local whites were uneasy over the growing strength of the civil rights movement in their region. Who could say, they asked themselves, if there was not among the newcomers that dreaded "outside agitator," there to "stir up" blacks and incite them to confront the carefully constructed caste system that kept them "in their place."[3]

Local whites really did not have much to fear. Most of the "dam people" were white southerners, and their racial attitudes were much the same as those of the long-time residents. When tensions did arise, they resulted instead because many of the workers arriving from larger towns and cities outside the Black Belt had little knowledge or appreciation of local conduct and customs. Mrs. Mary Lowe, who came down from Tuscaloosa when her husband got a job as a welder and pile driver on the Miller's Ferry project, recalled how "local women raised a ruckus" when she and her friends wore "short shorts" in Camden. When the ladies of the town tried to get up a petition to stop this affront to the local sense of fashion and decency, Mrs. Lowe and her friends simply "wore them shorter and shorter and shorter." Apparently not everyone was offended. The city fathers took no action, so the opposition withdrew to their parlors to bemoan the decline of life as they had known it, while Camden went about its business much as it always had.[4]

The Black Belt survived this first onslaught of outsiders, who despite local concerns were never really much of a threat to the status quo. Though Mrs. Liddell did note that a few of them, northern engineers no doubt, were "disapproving of our racial attitudes," she also observed that these same people "refuse[d] to allow a Negro nurse to mind their children," which struck her as both an act of hypocrisy and a breach of good manners. For blacks in Wilcox County however, this duplicity also signaled that those who hoped the new people would bring new attitudes and opportunities would be sadly disappointed. Even construction at Miller's Ferry proved less than blacks hoped, for the good jobs there usually went to whites, who had the advantage of skills and training blacks had been denied. In the end it seems that despite the dam, the most profitable activity for black residents may have been the sale of handmade quilts over at Gee's Bend. Sewn for generations to help keep off the chill of river-bottom winters, these quilts became recognized as important works of folk art, and before the decade was out they were found in many of the nation's important museums and private collections. What money the Freedom Quilting Bee brought home could not sustain the whole community, though. Times may have gotten a little better down in Gee's Bend, but times were still far from good.[5]

Construction work was not permanent work, and as soon as a dam was completed most of the dam people moved on. Some were no doubt happy to leave, for though "they liked us well enough," according to Mrs. Liddell, they never quite fit into the community. Others, however, found that life in rural Alabama had its charms. By the time Miller's Ferry was finished, Mrs. Lowe, whose short shorts had caused such a stir, was talking about how she'd "hate to leave this town" and the "many good folks" she had met. "It's true," she admitted, that "a few people run this county," but that seemed fair to her, since "they've lived here all their lives, and for generations before that their families have been here." A willingness to accept things pretty much as they were was an important qualification for anyone who wanted to live a quiet and happy life in rural Alabama, and despite her earlier rebellion against local conventions, Mrs. Lowe seemed to have come around very nicely.[6]

For those who wanted to stay, the means to do so was at hand. "Even before the dam was finished," Mrs. Liddell recorded with a poetic ease that obscured the dramatic change taking place, "a great papermill, MacMillan-Bloedel, coming from faraway Canada, lighted down beside the river in the middle of our pine forests . . . ," and dam people like the Lowes joined locals seeking employment, first in the mill's construction and then in its operation. MacMillan-Bloedel chose Wilcox County for the same reason other paper mills selected sites along the river— plenty of fast-growing trees, plenty of water, low taxes, and assurances from state and local officials that there would be roads and rails to get the pulpwood to the mill and the paper to the consumer. Apparently what was not a factor in the decision was the Alabama waterway, for though the site they selected was only a short distance from the stream, their biggest concern was not how to use it but how to cross it. Angus Gardner, president of the company, told Gov. George Wallace they would build the mill if the state built a bridge over the river and a system of paved roads into the plant, something Wilcox residents had wanted for years. But MacMillan-Bloedel had the clout local people lacked, and Gardner got what he wanted.[7]

In the years that followed MacMillan-Bloedel transformed the landscape and the economy of Wilcox County. The "wilderness" Gardner found when he first saw the site was cleared away, dirt roads were paved, the mill was built, and people went to work. By the early 1970s the company employed over a thousand, with a yearly payroll of over $8.5 million, and it was spending some $15 million annually on raw material. This led to even more jobs as locals hired on with logging companies or simply got themselves a truck, put together a crew, and started "paperwooding." Stores opened to sell things to people who now had money. The price of land skyrocketed as "land po'" planters found they could lease their holding to the company at rates unheard of in the past. To anyone who had lived long in the region, a revolution seemed to be taking place.[8]

MacMillan-Bloedel did more than change the economy. Against the backdrop of the civil rights struggle and black political gains, it gave people a means to improve the way they lived that did not leave them beholden to planter landlords or local elites. Riding down a newly paved road, Gardner could see "not only white families, but black families with new roofs, new porches, new homes." Had he stopped to talk with them, he would have found a new attitude, a new sense of independence and worth. Although the majority of the mill workers, some 65 percent, were white in the 1970s, there were "several black foremen" and at least one black superintendent. That created problems at first, and some of the white workers let it be known that they "didn't care for it." But when Gardner let them know in return that their choice was to work for a black foreman or lose the job, they accepted the situation and the paycheck.[9]

Company officials were not surprised when racial tensions caused problems in the workplace, but they were taken aback when local leaders warned them that the Black Belt's "work ethic" might not be what they expected. When the mill announced plans to operate "right around the clock, seven days a week," managers were told that "country people—both black and white—like to work at their own time," which did not include nights and weekends. Not surprisingly, those doing the warning believed that the biggest problem would be with blacks and patronizingly told Gardner of how "the tradition of the Negro [was] to spend all Saturday getting into drink and fights [and] then, if he can sober up, [go] to church on Sunday." He did not appear to be a particularly promising employee. It is difficult to say whether these words were an effort to discourage the company from hiring blacks, or whether they were a well-meant warning based on white beliefs about black social life, or whether they were perhaps some combination of both. Whatever the messenger's motives, Gardner soon discovered that night and weekend work did not fit into the schedule of either race. "We had a frightful time," he recalled, with "a turnover of fifteen to twenty percent." But the company held the line, and "if a man showed up drunk or if he didn't show up, we fired him." Before long "the message finally got around that if you wanted a paycheck, you had to be at work in a reasonably sober state," and turnover was "substantially reduced."[10]

Having survived the influx of dam people, citizens of Wilcox and surrounding counties did not seem particularly worried at the prospect of mill management personnel moving in, even though they promised to be permanent additions to the community. Perhaps they should have taken more seriously Gardner's offhanded warning that locals "would be glad to see us come, but after we'd been here a few years, they might not be so glad to have us," but they did not. Soon strange cars with out-of-state and even Canadian tags appeared on the streets of Camden, and there were "flush times" on the housing market. Then the moving vans came and unloaded so many new families that Mrs. Liddell recalled how "the natives were hardpressed to keep tab on them." The easy familiarity that had been part of the region's way of life began to disappear, for "no longer did everyone know everyone else or speak to everyone." At the same time, locals no longer suspected someone "merely because they were strangers." The Black Belt's closed society was opening, just a bit.[11]

Soon older residents began to realize what Angus Gardner meant when he told them "the people we bring in [will be] different than the Southern country people." Newcomers arrived without that respect for traditional sources of authority that defined politics in the region, and they showed little deference to "customs and traditions" that interfered with life as they wanted to live it. No doubt to the relief of local whites, these strangers among them had scant interest in the racial issues of the day, apart from how they affected work at the mill, and they were apparently content to allow the changes already taking place to run their course. However, new folks were upset, or at least perplexed, at the local attitude toward liquor. Most of the recent arrivals liked to take a drink, and apparently they found a lot of their neighbors and coworkers liked to imbibe as well, even though Wilcox was a dry county. Seeing no reason why a law that was being so widely violated should not be changed, these innocents led a drive for a wet-dry referendum. Once the issue was out in the open, the uninitiated learned that in the rural South, "custom and tradition" were not something to trifle with. Local ministers rose to oppose the measure, and Gardner was shocked when he examined a Baptist sponsored anti-liquor petition and found that "ninety per cent" of the men who signed were men "I'd had a drink with." But though he denounced them as "a bunch of hypocrites," the mill president missed the point. In the river region, as in many other places in the South, hypocrisy was a personal matter, and so long as the hypocrite did not interfere with "the way things were done around here," he was pretty much free to go about his business. So the measure was defeated.[12]

The setback was only temporary. Unable to sway traditional forces, mill "wets" allied with other new voters—black and white—who were just coming into the electoral equation, and it was not long before beer and liquor were legal. "We push[ed] them," Gardner said, referring to the folks who usually decided issues in the county, and "when they complain[ed], I reminded them that they were forewarned." Yet when measured against the political changes that were going on in the Black Belt, and when compared to the hopes these changes raised, legalized liquor was really a minor matter. Still, the controversy did reveal how companies like MacMillan-Bloedel affected the areas in which they settled. Some of their employees, imported and otherwise, took an active part in county and community affairs, and eventually they began to "influence their local form of government and politics." Considering the social and political revolution going on at that time, the pressures that these dam people put on the river region were not great. Actually, the new arrivals may well have served as a buffer between rising black political power and entrenched white resistance to change, for it was to the company's advantage to work with both and keep conflict at a minimum. MacMillan-Bloedel and other mills along the Alabama-Coosa corridor came to the river region to make money. Anything else they accomplished in the process was not unimportant, but it was incidental.[13]

Thus industry came to the river region. By the late 1980s there were four paper mills on the Alabama—Union Camp at Prattville, International Paper between Selma and Montgomery, Alabama River Pulp at Claiborne, and MacMillan-Bloedel—and there was one on the Coosa, Kimberly-Clark near Childersburg. Spaced along the rivers, thirty to sixty miles apart, they drew resources and workers from as far north as Gadsden and as far south as the Alabama flowed. Though they scarcely fenced the streams with smokestacks, the mills created jobs where none had been before, helped expand local economies, and gave governments more resources with which to work. As barges with wood chips began to move through locks on the Alabama, the mills kept alive dreams of an inland waterway, but paper mills could not do everything. Though they changed and improved the lives of many Alabamians, they could employ only so many people, leaving the rest of the population little better off than before. For those who benefited, the mills were a blessing, for others, one more possibility just beyond their reach.[14]

Yet, while industry had come, the river region and its people would not be, could not be industrialized. Workers adjusted to the mill's demands and accepted the fact that, as President Gardner said, "you don't just come and go as you please"; but despite the changes forced on them, the rhythm of life never became the rhythm of the factory. Though workers arrived and left according to schedule, when shifts changed they did not make their way to some "dirty and nasty" factory town, the sort of place many locals feared would rise with the mill. Instead they got into their pick-up trucks and as fast as the law allowed (usually faster) headed home to towns and farms where many of their families had lived for generations. For some the trip took an hour or more, and woe be to the unsuspecting motorist who happened to be driving by when they roared out of the gate. In a sense, their commute reflected a regional determination to hold to a way of life that was usually threatened, if not destroyed, by industrialization. But one must understand that the world they sped home to survived because of the mills, not in spite of them. If the forest products industry was to succeed, it had to have forests, so it followed that paper mills promoted and praised rural life and values. Apart from already established towns like Selma, Montgomery, and Gadsden, the urbanization usually associated with industrialization did not occur along the rivers, and folks there liked it that way.[15]

Although most Alabamians living on or near the streams welcomed the dams and the mills, a few remained unconvinced that the benefits outweighed the disadvantages. Not everyone smelled "progress" when the "high odor" came in on the breeze, and there were complaints that the chemicals fouling the air were doing even worse to the rivers. Down in Wilcox County, Pat Nettles remembered that before MacMillan-Bloedel came in, he and his friends "used to catch thousands of fish, pack them in ice, and they were fine eating," but not any more. "Since the paper mill's been here," he complained, "we catch little things that ain't fit to eat." Over at Lower Peachtree John McCoy told the same story. "Time was when we sat by the river and caught fish by the hundreds. Since the factory's come in, it's lucky if you can find one." The company claimed they exaggerated and noted that a Tulane University professor they hired to assess the environmental impact reported that "he had never studied a river before where there was no apparent effect on the fish life after industrialization." But Pat Nettles had a test of his own. Once the river was "pretty and blue," he observed, but "now it's green looking." By his test the company had failed.[16]

MacMillan-Bloedel and the rest of the paper industry were hardly the streams' first polluters. Before the Civil War historian Albert J. Pickett wrote eloquently of how, when the Indians ruled the land, "The Great Spirit had blessed them with a magnificent river, abounding in fish; with delicious and cool fountains, gushing out from the foot of the hills." By 1851, the year his book was published, he reported that "the country is no longer half so beautiful; the waters of Alabama begin to be discolored; the forests have been cut down; steamers have destroyed the finny race." "Now," he continued, "vast fields of cotton, noisy steamers, huge rafts of lumber, towns reared for business, disagreeable corporation laws, harassing courts of justice, mills, factories, and everything else that is calculated to destroy the beauty of a country and to rob man of his quiet and native independence, present themselves to our view." In this case, Pickett was as much the prophet as the chronicler. He seemed to sense that what he saw was only the beginning, and he feared that there would be a day when Alabamians would be called to task for what they were doing to their streams.[17]

That day was a long time coming. Over the next century state leaders and the public at large continued to believe that "the solution to pollution was dilution" and used the rivers as if they were an ever-renewing resource. By the second half of the twentieth century, as a wave of environmental awareness swept the land, this attitude began to change. The Alabama Water and Pollution Control Association was organized to study conditions and make occasional reports on the status of the streams. Its findings were disturbing, and some Alabamians began to share Pat Nettles's concern over what was happening to the rivers. A few of them organized and lobbied the legislature for restrictions on discharge and development along the streams. They made some progress. In 1971, the state passed a water quality law that was, at the time, the toughest in the Southeast; but the state's well-financed and well-coordinated business lobby was able to see that enforcement of the law was put into the hands of industry's allies, so it never accomplished what its supporters intended. Most Alabamians accepted this failure with little or no protest, for despite the work of dedicated environmental activists, the public saw no reason for concern. Although there seemed to be a general consensus that the rivers were not what they once were, or what they might be, citizens appeared unaware of the extent of the environmental changes and of the impact those changes might have on their lives.[18]

Then, in December 1990, the *Alabama Journal* published a series of articles that were subsequently reprinted in a special edition entitled "Alabama's Rivers: An Endangered Resource." It was no exercise in boosterism like that the *Advertiser* had published a quarter of a century earlier. This time a team of reporters and photographers went out to document what had happened and what was happening to the state's rivers and to inform the public, whether the public wanted to know or not. What the reporters found was startling, even to people familiar with the streams. Alabama's rivers, which had been the pride of the state as long as it had been a state, were being killed by the very development that officials had worked so hard to promote. Paper mills, chemical plants, urban waste, dams, agricultural pollution, and silt from mining and construction were all combining to destroy life in the streams, and agencies that were supposed to protect the environment were either unable or unwilling to act. The series was a stinging indictment of the state, the business community, and the unconcerned citizens of Alabama.[19]

That the rivers had been altered came as no surprise to most people, but the extent of the changes and what they portended for the future was unsettling. Even making allowances for the natural tendency of a fisherman to exaggerate the size of yesterday's catch, it had been known for years that the fish population in Alabama's waterways was not what it once had been. *Journal* reporters revealed that at least twenty-three species of fish were endangered or had been eliminated from the streams. Other water creatures had suffered even more. The Coosa River, where Herbert H. Smith had found a wealth of mollusk life at the turn of the century and which, as late as the 1940s, was believed to have "more endemic molluscan genera and species than any other [stream] in North America," had been "so offishly treated" that of the twenty-four fresh-water snails that the American Fisheries Society listed as believed to be extinct, all were from Alabama. "No other state," according to the society, "is suspected of killing off an entire snail species." At least seventy more Alabama snails and mussels were listed as threatened or endangered.[20]

Most of the blame for this annihilation lay with the dams on the Coosa, Tallapoosa, and Alabama, which had turned "miles of reefs . . . and formerly quiet reaches between rapids . . . into silt-accumulating lakes." The dams did more than destroy habitats of aquatic life; they literally exiled some species from the river. In 1930, an Atlantic sturgeon came into the system through Mobile Bay, swam up the Alabama past Selma and Montgomery, took the right fork, and was caught near Tallassee. The fish weighed over four hundred pounds and reportedly contained "a tub of roe." Sturgeons had been caught high on the Alabama and its tributaries for years, but with the dams at Claiborne, Miller's Ferry, and Jones Bluff, their migration ended, and as far as the rivers were concerned, the fish were extinct. Gone too were birds that once fed on life in the swift-flowing streams. The dams had created a whole new ecosystem.[21]

More significant than what the dams prevented from coming upstream was what they stopped from going down. It had earlier been argued not only that dams would provide flood control, power, and recreation, but also that the "downstream flow will be regularized with benefits to pollution abatement." In reality the dams did just the opposite; they hindered the flow of the stream and made it difficult if not impossible for the river to clean itself: Dilution was no longer a solution to pollution. The ten dams on the Coosa, Tallapoosa, and Alabama rivers became "sediment traps," where pollutants harmful to fish and human beings could accumulate. As far as reporters could discover, in Alabama there was not "a single state agency looking into sediment quality." The problem did not end there. When the older dams generated power they pulled water from deep in the lake, where there was less oxygen. As a result the water they sent down stood a good chance of containing more of what the river did not need, pollution, and less of what it did need.[22]

No one was suggesting that the dams be removed. Even environmentalists agreed that was impossible and probably was not even desirable. A flowing river was a different ecosystem, but not necessarily a better one. The challenge, therefore, was to manage the rivers and lakes so that the public health would be protected and the environment would be preserved, without driving industry and jobs from the state. That was a tall order, especially when health practitioners, environmentalists, representatives from the industries, and state officials often disagreed on the extent of the problem and what should be done to solve it. A classic example of this conflict was the debate over dioxin, a toxic chemical and suspected human carcinogen that is a by-product of the bleach kraft process used by two paper mills on the Alabama and the Kimberly-Clark plant on the Coosa. In 1990, in an effort to put strict limits on how much dioxin could be discharged into Alabama rivers, environmentalists and public health officials called on the Alabama Department of Environmental Management (ADEM) to adopt the dioxin standards set by the U.S. Environmental Protection Agency (EPA). Paper industry officials claimed that the limits were unnecessarily high, lobbied hard for their own standards, and hinted broadly that "lawsuits would be forthcoming if the industry recommendation was not adopted." ADEM, which critics claim has been pro-business since its creation in 1982, sided with the paper industry and ruled that the companies could discharge eighty-six times more dioxin than the EPA suggested. Though paper officials disputed the claim, opponents charged that under the industry standard nearly 350 more people would develop cancer in Alabama.[23]

The problem may have been even greater than that estimate suggests, for in most cases, ADEM relied on dioxin test data supplied by the very companies it is supposed to monitor. The result, critics point out, was that polluters set the standards, then told the state if they were meeting them or not—a situation that invited abuse while keeping politicians and the people uninformed about the extent of the danger. Dioxin tests were expensive, and given the disagreement over just what constituted a safe level of that substance, state officials argued that there were better uses for their regulatory resources. As they pointed out, even the EPA had not one but three models to determine how great the danger from dioxin might be. However, when these models were used to produce lists of mills where cancer risks should be a concern, Alabama-Coosa river mills appeared on two lists out of three. In the most sensitive of the categories, the EPA's "hot spot" list, eight of the nation's forty-one worst mills were in the state.[24]

Still, ADEM had a point when it argued that money spent monitoring dioxin might be more usefully spent in other areas, for the paper mills were hardly the only river polluters. In the fall of 1990 Greg Wood and Joe Capps of Fairhope canoed the Coosa-Alabama from near Rome to Mobile Bay. On the trip they passed mines of various sorts, some seventy sewage treatment plants, hundreds of farms and timber operations, and scores of industries, large and small, only five of which made paper. All of these polluted the river in some way, and if the river was to be cleaned up, all of them would eventually have to be monitored by ADEM. The two most obvious problems Wood and Capps reported were discharge pipes, which "you could sometimes smell for two or three miles before you arrived," and "timber cuts up to the banks of the river, which enhance erosion." What they did not see were underwater discharge pipes, which drained directly into the stream, or the dumping that took place up tributaries and flowed into the river. Nor did they get a good look at the most widespread cause of water pollution in the state, the rainwater that washed pesticides and animal wastes from farms and carried oil and other city waste through storm drains and into streams. When the rivers changed color after every downpour, more than silt was being carried south.[25]

The state was not sitting idly by and letting the rivers die. Waste from towns was being treated, and efforts were being made to stop erosion. Industries sensitive to environmental concerns had taken steps to reduce toxic chemical releases and spills, and agreements had been worked out between polluters and ADEM to lower discharges even more. By the end of the 1980s the Kimberly-Clark plant, which had polluted the Coosa for over thirty years, was discharging less pollutants into the water than at any time in its history. Though environmentalists argued that these efforts constituted little more than a good start, the progress being made seemed to have satisfied most Alabama legislators, who thought there was little cause further to restrict industries and municipalities. Efforts to substantially increase penalties for violating the state's Water Pollution Control Act died waiting to be voted on by the Alabama Senate. Even legislation supported by ADEM had trouble getting passed, despite the agency's sympathy to business and industry. Frustrated by this impasse, the department decided to fight fire with fire and received permission to hire "one of Montgomery's more high-powered lobbyists" to carry its cause to the legislature. It was, according to the *Birmingham Post-Herald*, "a sad commentary on the realities of Alabama Politics" when a state agency was forced to conclude that "its best chance of getting the Legislature to approve its legislative requests" was to hire outside help. "Unfortunately," the newspaper concluded, "ADEM is probably right."[26]

The sensitivity of industry to any legislation dealing with pollution, and the strength of its lobby in Montgomery, came clear in the reaction to what has been called the "Fishermen's Right to Know" bill. This legislation required that industries with permits to release waste into the rivers must "post a conspicuous sign near the point of discharge to advise the public of any discharges which contain toxic pollutants." Having had little success reducing toxic dumping, the bill's advocates believed that at the very least people using the rivers and lakes should know what was legally being put into the water, and that knowledge might in turn move the public to call for sterner measures. Supported by environmental and health groups and organizations like Bass Anglers Sportsman Society (B.A.S.S.), with seventy-seven thousand of its half-million members from Alabama, the proposed bill was believed by many to have a chance. They were wrong. Paper mills, chemical companies, and other industrial interests, working through the Business Council of Alabama (BCA), lobbied hard against it. Claiming the law would cost too much, bring "unnecessarily . . . heightened fear among the public," lead to lawsuits, and "do nothing to improve water quality," the BCA lined up its allies. For three consecutive years the act was introduced (1991 through 1993), and each year the opposition kept it from coming to the floor for a vote. The fight continues. Though supporters acknowledge that "there are powerful interests with tremendous amounts of money" who, according to the *Birmingham Post-Herald*, "don't want people to know what is in their rivers," they plan to introduce the act again. "This bill," said one of its drafters, "will be before the Legislature as long as I live."[27]

Still, it is easy to see how industries got and kept the upper hand, for folks along the rivers saw the mills and mines not as polluters but as jobs. The forest industry is the best case in point. In 1990 some 21,000 Alabamians worked for the state's pulp and paper companies and took home a combined payroll of about $825 million. Another 170,000 were employed in related and support industries, most within the mills' sphere of influence. With families and friends they formed a powerful voting block ready to oppose anything that might restrict a mill's operations and reduce its work force. The power of the forest industry went far beyond those who worked directly for it. According to the Alabama Forestry Association, the $8 billion generated yearly by the forest industry was roughly one-fourth of the state's gross economy, and industry spokesmen were not shy in suggesting that what hurts them hurts Alabama. Were this not power enough, the forest industry usually worked in tandem with Alabama's other agricultural interests. United, these groups owned or controlled vast tracts of land (in 1990 the forest industry alone owned 14 percent of Alabama), so it followed that almost every legislative delegation contained at least one member who spoke for their concerns. While most critics of this coalition have focused on how it has kept ad valorem and severance taxes low and deprived the state of much-needed revenue, its efforts to prevent the state from adopting more stringent regulations regarding the rivers have been just as successful.[28]

Yet as the '90s approached, there was a growing awareness that clean rivers had direct economic benefit that must also be calculated into the political equation. Though on one hand the lakes created by power company and Corps of Engineers dams destroyed much of the rivers' ecosystem, it was replaced with a new system that the public used and enjoyed. A 1985 report by the U.S. Fish and Wildlife Service estimated that nearly 1.2 million people visited the lakes annually and spent $536.5 million on recreational or subsistence fishing. Fish that thrived in flowing rivers might be gone, but lake fish such as bass, crappie, and some types of catfish flourished, and sportsmen came from near and far to catch them. Add to this recreational boating, waterfront real estate development, and the host of auxiliary enterprises that sprang up along the lakes, and there emerged an industry to which clean water mattered and which could, if organized, put considerable pressure on the legislature.[29]

This lake lobby was slow to take shape, but by the end of the 1980s events began to suggest that it might not be long in coming. In 1990 homeowners on Lay Lake rose in protest over a brown scum that drifted down like "a nasty rootbeer float," fouling the water around the docks and marinas and driving down property values. Blaming the Kimberly-Clark Coosa Pine paper mill, they called on ADEM to force the company to stop the discharge. The controversy resulted in charges and countercharges, at least two lawsuits, a lot of newspaper coverage, and a heightened political awareness among residents. It did not, however, move ADEM to crack down on the company, nor did it force Kimberly-Clark to admit that it was at fault. The company was already under a 1989 administrative order to reduce pollution in the lake, and as state officials noted, what was coming out of the pipes was legal. "Paper mill discharge is brown, [and] there is no getting around it," an ADEM spokesman was quoted as saying. The water may have been discolored, but according to state law it was not polluted—state law did not deal with matters of aesthetics.[30]

But concern over aesthetics led lake residents to question the whole matter of what was dumped into the water and led to increased efforts to reduce the toxic chemicals discharged by factories. At roughly the same time that Lay Lake property owners began noticing the scum on the water, volunteers from the environmental group Greenpeace posted warnings that fish in the lake contained dioxin and were unsafe to eat. This warning, residents claimed, was the first they had heard of the dioxin danger. Concern spread, and in September of 1990, under pressure from the EPA, the Alabama Department of Public Health posted the river below Kimberly-Clark "advising children, pregnant women and women of reproductive age not to eat the fish and telling others to limit their intake." As pressure grew, ADEM and Kimberly-Clark worked out a schedule under which the company would reduce discharges, "including those that robbed the river of oxygen, produced dioxins and the odd colors." Not long after that residents noticed the disappearance of the brown scum and took it for a good sign.[31]

The fact that pressure on a company increased when pollution was unsightly and eased when the river looked good once again underscored one of the biggest problems environmentalists had in rallying the public to their cause. Despite the industrial, municipal, and agricultural pollution, Alabama rivers—whether lakes or streams—still remained things of beauty for those who visited them. Pat Dozier, who owns a marina in Montgomery, saw this when he led a flotilla of "river rats" on their annual trip down the Alabama to Mobile in the summer of 1990. Traveling in boats of various sizes and descriptions, they saw the river as few ever do and returned home with a renewed appreciation for this unique Alabama resource. They did not return with the sense of urgency felt by environmentalists who have studied the rivers. Although they saw industrial discharges and even stretches where "the river turned an inky black and had taken on a foul odor," so much of the trip was "tree lined riverbanks" that the ugly was all but forgotten. "You read so many articles about pollution," one member of the group remarked, "but the river looks so pretty." Dozier may have summed up their attitude best when he observed that these "river rats" were "environmentalists at the shallowest level—and that is not throwing things over the side of the boat." For them, he added, environmental quality was "more of a topic than it is a passion." The same might be said for most of the people who enjoyed the rivers.[32]

Ironically, one of the places where a passion seemed to exist was in a city seldom associated with a river—Birmingham. In the suburbs of Alabama's largest urban center, the Cahaba River rises and from there flows unimpeded southward, until it joins the Alabama downstream from Selma. The Cahaba is the only major stream in the state without a dam, and that absence alone makes it a unique laboratory for studying the effects power production and flood control projects have had on Alabama's environment. But the Cahaba is important for other reasons. In its course it moves from the mountains, through the piedmont, over the fall line, and into the coastal plain; its character reflects these regional transitions. In each section plant and animal life, some of it unique to the stream, survives to help scientists understand the changes that have taken place in the state's waterways. In the Cahaba, Alabama has many rivers in one.[33]

The Cahaba was also an important laboratory because of its own precarious situation, for along its course ten municipal waste treatment plants, thirty-five surface mining areas, a coal-bed methane company, and nearly seventy other state-licensed operations dumped waste of various sorts into its waters. These plus the ever-expanding Birmingham metropolitan area made the Cahaba one of America's ten most endangered rivers, according to one listing. To protect the stream the Birmingham-based Cahaba River Society was formed, and in alliance with other state and regional conservation organizations, it began working to save a unique environment that contained threatened minnow species and the famous Cahaba lily.[34]

Concerned with ecology as well as aesthetics, the Cahaba River Society monitored sections of the stream to determine changes in water quality and keep an eye on polluters, licensed and otherwise. With its allies, the society lobbied hard for regulations that would protect the stream and its wildlife. In some cases they were successful, for late in 1990 the U.S. Fish and Wildlife Service added the Cahaba shiner to the federal endangered species list. On the state level, however, things did not go so well. In the 1980s efforts to tighten development restrictions and establish a 150-foot-wide management corridor along the stream were defeated, largely because of the opposition of mining and paper interests. Efforts to educate politicians to the situation seemed to be making progress, for in the early 1990s a study sponsored by the cities and counties in the Upper Cahaba watershed recommended higher water quality standards as well as "no-build zones" along the river in that heavily developed region. What the local governments will do with these recommendations is uncertain, but representatives from the society saw them as "a tremendous first step" toward saving the Cahaba.[35]

Society members were also encouraged when, in August of 1993, the Alabama Environmental Management Commission voted to designate all but two segments of the Cahaba as "Outstanding Alabama Waters" (OAW). Still, they had hoped for more. For three-and-a-half years the society had sought "Outstanding National Resource Water" classification for the Cahaba, which would guarantee that its water quality would be "maintained and protected." The designation they got, which was "devised" by the commission as a compromise, only "required full consideration of alternatives" before new pollutants could be discharged and "establish[ed] somewhat tighter minimum standards for new discharges." While admitting this arrangement was "not perfect," the society hailed it as "the most important step forward for the Cahaba taken to date by any government or public agency." The Alabama Department of Environmental Management agreed, claiming that regulations under this classification went "far beyond anything this agency has ever required." However, the *Birmingham Post-Herald* was less enthusiastic and noted editorially that "putting the Cahaba under the toughest regs in a state with generally lax environmental standards is hardly a guarantee of purity." The weakness of the classification was compounded when, according to the paper, "the state, using logic that eludes our comprehension, excluded from the OAW designation the most polluted sections of the Cahaba." While admitting that the designation was "a useful tool" for environmentalists, the *Post-Herald* urged the society to continue the fight for "more stringent protection."[36]

If rivers in the Alabama system were not threatened enough by Alabamians, today there are Georgians to worry about. This problem is not new. In the 1960s water pollution agencies in Alabama asked Georgia to "cease and desist the dumping of sewage and industrial waste

The Alabama River Companies Mill Complex at Claiborne.
One of the newest paper mills on the river, it was recently designated a
"Best Available Technology" (BAT) facility by the Environmental
Protection Agency.
(Photograph by Harvey H. Jackson III)

material" into the Coosa, and in time Georgia complied. EPA regulations minimized this type of controversy between the states during the next two decades, but in the late 1980s Alabama became concerned that a proposed system of regional reservoirs in West Georgia might "siphon off millions of gallons of water from the headwaters of the Coosa and Tallapoosa" to supply the rapidly growing Atlanta metropolitan area. Claiming such a plan would ruin the drinking water of Montgomery and other cities, shut down Alabama industries, and kill off at least one endangered species, an unlikely coalition of politicians, business leaders, environmentalists, and river region residents rose to oppose the proposal. Though the debate continues, one thing has been accomplished. As Alabamians prepared their case, many were shocked to learn that theirs was the only state in the union without a water management plan. Moving with uncharacteristic speed and uncommon unanimity, the legislature acted, and in 1993 Alabama came into line with the rest of the nation. Just what this act will mean for the rivers of the state is yet to be determined; however some environmentalists are already concerned that it was written to benefit business and not nature.[37]

If environmentalists are right, if the state's water is managed as an economic rather than as a "natural" resource, it will be an approach consistent with the way Alabama has always dealt with its rivers. Throughout the state's history, the waterways have been there to use, and citizens have used them. Development has meant simply finding a more effective way to exploit the streams. It is an approach to river management historically favored by business, legislated by government, and accepted with little complaint by Alabamians who have consistently disappointed conservationists with their lack of participation in public policy making. Thus it is unlikely that much will be done to improve Alabama's river environment until government, business, and the public find it in their interest to do so.[38]

That long-awaited day might be approaching. By the end of the 1980s, sections of the Alabama and Coosa were so polluted that their capacity to accept more industrial discharge was all but exhausted. Unless the rivers were cleaned up, existing industries would not be able to expand, and the state would be unable to attract new factories and new jobs. Business, government, and even private citizens could see what the future held, and opposition to tighter restrictions on industrial use of the rivers has begun to weaken. Conservationists can take little comfort in this new attitude, however, for they know what it really means. Pollution will be reduced only to make way for more pollution. Such is the irony of environmental politics in Alabama.[39]

EPILOGUE
"Pissing in the Rain Barrel"

> Seventy years ago, a boy in knee trousers, I tagged along at the heels
> of Coosa River fishermen as they raked the shallow ponds for
> crawfish and seined the branches for minnows to bait their trotlines.
> One cold winter evening I sat in the houseboat of a dear old
> fisherman friend as he instructed me in the art of knitting nets from
> cotton twine. Suddenly, he dropped his needle and stick and,
> looking me squarely in the eye and speaking as if in a warning said:
> "Marve-lin, if ye fool around on this old river much hit'll take a-hold
> of ye, and hit'll never turn a-loose."
>
> MARVIN B. SMALL
> "Canoeing on the Coosa"

In 1933, after some forty years of service in the Corps of Engineers, William Clark Edwards retired from the river. He did not want to quit, but he was sixty-five, and New Deal planners, trying to open more jobs for younger workers, were forcing many veteran government employees to take their pensions and go home. Edwards hated Franklin Roosevelt for the rest of his life. The old man went to live with his daughter's family near Deatsville, in the hills of Elmore County, away from the life he loved. He did not rest easy there, and his son-in-law frequently accused him of sneaking out back before bed and "pissing in the rain barrel" to recapture the sound of his nightly ritual on the river and remember.[1]

Though his method was uniquely his own, in those days Clark Edwards was not the only one calling up memories of the river. His retirement roughly coincided with the end of the steamboat era on the Alabama and Coosa, and as those grand old ladies disappeared from the streams, memorials to their passing inspired reminiscences of life and times along the waterways. Leading the mourners was Peter Brannon of the Alabama Department of Archives and History, who in the 1930s and 1940s often eulogized the end of that golden age in his *Montgomery Advertiser* column, "Through the Years." Saddened that there were Montgomerians "who had never heard a Steamboat whistle," Brannon resurrected stories and revived memories of the rivers as they once had been through tales of steamboat landings, dead towns, brave captains, floating palaces, and burning wrecks. At that critical juncture, when so much was changing, Peter Brannon kept interest alive and in the process helped preserve river lore that might otherwise have been lost.[2]

As the years passed others joined Brannon, and by the end of World War II, there was an informal association of collectors and antiquarians preserving artifacts and accounts recalling a way of life that was fading before their eyes. Up on the Coosa, Will I. Martin's column, "If Memory Serves," appeared in the *Gadsden Times,* and the stories he handed down kept the public mindful of the debt that region owed the river. However, the work of another Gadsdenite, Marvin B. Small, would preserve much of the Coosa's history for future generations. Small knew the river firsthand; from the time he was "a boy in knee trousers," he had been up and down it in everything from steamboats to canoes, and his writing reflected both his knowledge of river ways and his personal experience. Marvin Small became the Coosa's spokesman, and through him many of those people intimately associated with the stream—captains, mates, lock masters, and the like—passed down their stories. An "old fisherman friend" had told him once, "Marve-lin, if ye fool around on this old river much hit'll take a-hold of ye, and hit'll never turn a-loose." The words may have been a warning, but Small saw in them a promise, and to his delight, he discovered his friend was right.[3]

Down on the Alabama, the river had also taken "a-hold" of Monroe-ville's Doy L. McCall and Bert Neville of Selma. Both were avid collectors and energetic local historians, and together they saved hundreds of documents, pictures, and stories. Neville was able to turn his passion for river history into something of a cottage industry. Drawing from his own personal archives and from the collections of Small, McCall, and others, Bert Neville compiled books and pamphlets filled with photographs, maps, bills of lading, lists of landings, and the names of boats and their captains. Preoccupied with facts and details, Neville provided little analysis and was usually content to reprint articles by Small and other writers, rather then pen his own pieces. Still, of all this cadre of river men, Bert Neville was probably the best known, and the wealth of information he assembled and published remains a rich source for anyone studying the history of Alabama and Alabama rivers.[4]

Bert Neville was the self-proclaimed "Master" of "The Club, an organization of his own creation, consisting of men with river steam-boat experience." The group, according to "chairman of the board" Capt. Simon Peter Gray, was "composed of carefully selected 'River Bull Shooters'" and was said to include "some brains, some brass, some bums and some fine powder puffers." Though it claimed no roster and held no formal meetings, it listed among its members river buffs like Neville and McCall, along with a good sprinkling of retired captains like Gray and "Buck" Benson. To be included one had either to have been a steamboatman or to "have been down the river in a small boat or raft," a criterion Neville met with "a five-day, five-man crew, 600-foot long raft trip from Walnut Bluff [on the] Alabama River to Mobile, on a high stage in February, 1921." What was really required to be included, however, was an unqualified love for Alabama's rivers and Bert Neville's blessing, for after all, it was *his* club.[5]

Though they were not on the list, Neville and his friends would have had no objection if Peter Brannon, Marvin Small, Will Martin, or even Clark Edwards had been recommended for membership. And if The Club had included women, and assuming women would have felt it proper to join, storytellers like Viola Goode Liddell of Wilcox County and Mattie Lou Teague Crow of St. Clair would have fit right in and held their own with the best River Bull Shooters in the bunch. These ladies' personal accounts of life along the Alabama and Coosa, when the streams flowed freely and steamboats plied their waters, are some of our richest sources of river region lore, and they remain a match for any handed down by the men.[6]

Here then was a group of local historians and river buffs, who shared a common interest in, indeed a passion for, the streams that flowed in the Alabama system. Beyond that, they also shared a sense of urgency, a conviction that an important part of the past was slipping away and that they might well be the only ones who could save it. That urgency is the factor that made their effort so important and made the results so significant. For Neville, Brannon, McCall, and Small, for Liddell and Crow, and for others of their generation who loved the river, history was personal because they had lived it. Even when they wrote of events long before their time and people long gone from the earth, the stories they told fit neatly into their own individual experiences, and they told them with the enthusiasm and sincerity that recognition always brings. Neville's raft trip in 1921 could have taken place a century earlier; Small's experiences on the Coosa were the experiences of river men before him; and the twice-yearly steamboat trip that Mrs. Liddell's mother took to Selma had been repeated over and again by other women in earlier times. These writers and collectors understood the continuity between past and present that remained strong on the rivers well into the twentieth century. They understood history, because history had happened to them.[7]

Sadly, this generation seemed to sense that despite their efforts, the link between past and present that they were trying to preserve would end with them—and they were right. Their position was unique and could not be duplicated by those who followed them. What happened to Bert Neville's "I've-Been-Down-the-River-Small-Boat-and-Raft-Club" bears out the point. The Club, if indeed it was ever really a club, was created by and composed of old men, growing older, and their

Modern "Riverboat," Selma, Alabama, 1990
(Harvey H. Jackson III Collection)

main activity, for many their only activity, was talking and remembering, "pissing in the rain barrel." By the early 1960s, when an article on the group appeared in the *Montgomery Advertiser*, it was already obvious that new candidates for membership, younger candidates, would never meet the criteria to join. It was not just a trip down the river that made one eligible. The trip had to be special; it had to link the traveler not only to the river but with the past. By the 1960s that connection was difficult, for steamboats and log rafts were gone from the waterways. By the end of the next decade, it would be impossible, for the rivers would be gone as well.

The dams built on the Alabama, Coosa, and Tallapoosa in the 1960s and 1970s completed the transformation of those streams into elongated lakes, leaving only the Cahaba truly to merit the name river. Equally important, the dams drew a line across Alabama river history. Brannon, Small, Neville, and their companions stand astride that line, beckoning later generations to use them as a bridge to go back. It is not an easy journey, for the dams have changed the public's perception of the streams and have made it difficult for modern Alabamians to envision what the waterways once were and what they meant to the regions they served. This book is an attempt to cross that line. If it serves no other purpose than to recall an earlier time when there were rapids, falls, locks, and steamboats, and if it does nothing more than give readers a sense of how the streams shaped the history of Alabama and the lives of Alabamians, then it has accomplished the goals set for it. That is enough to ask.

Notes

PREFACE

1. Tennant McWilliams to Malcolm M. MacDonald, January 11, 1989. Copy in the possession of the author.

INTRODUCTION

1. William Bartram, *Travels*, ed. Francis Harper (1791; reprint, New Haven, Conn., 1958), 258; "The Coosa-Alabama River: A Great Waterway in the Heart of the Industrial South," *National Waterways* 9 (September 1930), in Bert Neville, *Steamboats on the Coosa River in the Rome, Georgia-Gadsden-Greensport, Alabama Trades (1845–1920's)* (Selma, Ala., 1966), 181–82, 186; Marvin B. Small, "Canoeing the Coosa," in Neville, *Steamboats on the Coosa River*, 153; Safford [Saffold] Berney, "Handbook of Alabama," in Neville, *Steamboats on the Coosa River*, 15; and Marvin B. Small, "Steamboats on the Coosa," *Alabama Review* 4 (July 1951): 184.

2. Berney, "Handbook of Alabama," 16–17. There are 286 river miles from Rome to Wetumpka. Although the first shoals of the fall line were found near Greensport, at mile 150, the river continued its curving course for more than 50 miles. At that point, just below Childersburg, it began flowing almost due south to Wetumpka. See map of the COOSA RIVER, GA. AND ALA.; Reported in Accordance with H. Doc. 308/69/1, prepared by the Corps of Engineers, Dec. 31, 1928, in the Alabama Department of Archives and History, Montgomery, Alabama.

3. Berney, "Handbook of Alabama," 15–16; Andrew N. Lytle, *The Long Night* (1936; reprint, Tuscaloosa, 1988), 97.

4. "Benjamin Hawkins' Journal," 19–20; "A sketch of the Creek Country in the years 1798 and 1799," 297, 301; both in C. L. Grant, ed., *Letters, Journals, and Writings of Benjamin Hawkins*, vol. 1, (Savannah, Ga., 1980); Bartram, *Travels*, 251–52; James Silk Buckingham, *The Slave States of America* (London, 1842), 261–62; Down Home Designs, "The First Alabamians: A Directory of Indian Townsites in Alabama, 1540–1832" (Selma, Ala., 1979).

5. Elizabeth Hayes, "State waterways took shape along paths of least resistance," *Alabama Journal*, December 17, 1990; Bartram, *Travels*, 283–84.

6. Charles Lyell, *A Second Visit to the United States of North America* (London, 1849), 2:41–42; Thomas P. Abernethy, *The Formative Period in Alabama, 1815–1828* (1922; reprint, Tuscaloosa, 1965), 30–31; Basil Hall, *Travels in North America in the Years 1827 and 1828* (London, 1829), 3:308–9; Hawkins, "Sketch," in Grant, *Letters of Benjamin Hawkins*, 1:297–98.

7. Hawkins, "Sketch," in Grant, *Letters of Benjamin Hawkins*, 1:297; Hall, *Travels in North America* 3:308–9; Buckingham, *Slave States of America*,

265; Albert C. Koch, *Journey Through a Part of the United States of North America in the years 1844 to 1846,* trans. and ed. Ernest A. Sadler (Carbondale and Edwardville, Ill., 1972), 92–95.

8.   Abernethy, *Formative Period in Alabama,* 96; Charles S. Davis, *The Cotton Kingdom in Alabama* (Montgomery, 1939), 122–23, 159.

9.   Louis Xavier Eyma [Adolphe Ricard], *Les Deux Ameriques: histories moeures et voyages* (Paris, 1853), quoted in Weymouth T. Jordan, *Ante-Bellum Alabama: Town and Country* (1957; reprint, University, Ala., 1987), 16–17. Thomas Hamilton, *Men and Manners in America* (Edinburgh, 1833), 2:366; Buckingham, *Slave States of America,* 261–62.

10. Harriet Martineau, *Society in America* (New York, 1837), 2:226.

11. Hamilton, *Men and Manners in America,* 1:368; Martineau, *Society in America,* 1:220; W. G. Robertson, *Recollections of the Early Settlers of Montgomery County and their Families* (1892; reprint, Montgomery, 1961), 72–73; Fletcher M. Green, ed., *The Lides Go South . . . And West* (Columbia, S.C., 1952), 20; James Stuart, *Three Years in North America* (1833; reprint, New York, 1974), 2:111; Bartram, *Travels,* 252–53; H. S. Halbert and T. H. Ball, *The Creek War of 1813 and 1814* (1895; reprint; University, Ala., 1969), 247; and Charles Hudson et al., "The Tristan de Luna Expedition, 1559–1561," *Southeastern Archaeology* 8 (Summer 1989): 37.

12. Rhoda Coleman Ellison, *Bibb County, Alabama: The First Hundred Years, 1818–1918* (University, Ala., 1984), 5–6.

13. Ellison, *Bibb County,* 3; Philip Henry Gosse, F.R.S., *Letters from Alabama, (U.S.) Chiefly Relating to Natural History* (1859; reprint, Tuscaloosa, Ala., 1993), 102; A. Levasseur, *Lafayette in America in 1824 and 1825; or, Journal of a Voyage to the United States* (Philadelphia, 1829), 2:84; Angeline Elizabeth Cammack, "Memoir, 1810–1884, of Angeline Elizabeth (Eiland) Cammack" (typescript in the Virginia Historical Society, Richmond).

14. Levasseur, *Lafayette in America,* 84–85; Una Pope-Hennessy, ed., *The Aristocratic Journey: Being the Outspoken Letters of Mrs. Basil Hall Written during a Fourteen Months' Sojourn in America, 1827–28* (New York, 1931), 245; Tyrone Power, *Impressions of America, During the Years 1833, 1834, and 1835* (1836; reprint, New York, 1971), 2:156–57; Buckingham, *Slave States of America,* 265–74; Benjamin Hawkins to James McHenry, July 16, 1799, in Grant, *Letters of Benjamin Hawkins,* 1:254; Davis, *Cotton Kingdom,* 8; Lester B. Shippee, ed., *Bishop Whipple's Southern Diary, 1843–44* (New York, 1968), 85; and "The Alabama River from Mobile to Selma," *Montgomery Advertiser,* August 26, 1923. The black substance was probably a type of lignite, or soft coal.

15. The Alabama flows 305.1 miles from the junction of the Coosa and Tallapoosa to its junction with the Tombigbee. See Alabama River Navigation Chart, U.S. Army Engineer District, Mobile, September 1972.

1. THE ALABAMA INVADED

1.   Lucille Griffith, *Alabama: A Documentary History to 1900* (University, Ala., 1972), 8–9, contains eyewitness accounts of the Battle of Mabila.

An early collection of most of the chronicles of the expedition is in Edward Gaylord Bourne, ed., *Narratives of the Career of Hernando de Soto,* 2 vols. (New York, 1904). See also Charles M. Hudson, *The Southeastern Indians* (Knoxville, Tenn., 1976), 113–14; and Jay Higginbotham, "The Battle of Mauvila, Causes and Consequences," *Gulf Coast Historical Review* (Spring 1991), 19–33.

2. Albert James Pickett, *History of Alabama and Incidentally of Georgia and Mississippi, from the Earliest Period* (1851; reprint, Birmingham, Ala., 1962), 36; A. B. Meek, *Romantic Passages in Southwest History* (New York, 1857), 227; Halbert and Ball, *The Creek War,* 326–27. John R. Swanton, *Final Report of the United States De Soto Expedition Commission* (Washington, D.C., 1939) contains the findings of the commission.

3. The case for the reappraisal of the de Soto Commission's findings and the relocation of Mabila is found in Chester B. DePratter, Charles M. Hudson, and Marvin T. Smith, "The Hernando de Soto Expedition: From Chiaha to Mabila," in Reid R. Badger and Lawrence A. Clayton, eds., *Alabama and the Borderlands: From Prehistory to Statehood* (Tuscaloosa, Ala., 1985), 108–27. Support for the Clarke County site of Mabila is in Caleb Curren, "The Route of the de Soto Army through Alabama," De Soto Working Paper #3, University of Alabama, State Museum of Natural History, Tuscaloosa, Alabama, 1987. A third position, which puts Mabila west of the Tombigbee River, is in Alan Blake, "A Proposed Route for the Hernando De Soto Expedition from Tampa Bay to Apalachee Based on Physiography and Geology," De Soto Working Paper #2. For a later discussion of the debate, see Douglas E. Jones, ed., "The Highway Route of the De Soto Trail in Alabama," De Soto Working Paper #8, 1988. An indication of Clarke County's continued interest in the issue is reflected in the publication of Caleb Curren and Keith Little, "Mauvila Research 1986–1990," *Clarke County Historical Society Quarterly* 15 (Spring 1990): 8–13, in which the authors reaffirm that the "best current candidate for the site of the town of Mauvila" is the Armstrong Site near Choctaw Lake in Clarke County. It should be noted, however, that there is an Indian tradition that the battle did not take place at Mabila at all. See Thomas S. Woodward to Albert J. Pickett, August 12, 1858, *Reminiscences of the Creek or Muscogee Indians* (Mobile, Ala., 1965), 67–70. For copies of the maps of some sixteen different de Soto routes, see W. S. Eubanks, Jr., "Coosa Too?" *Soto States Anthropologist* 92 (January and April 1992): 143–58. The work of Eubanks and others in numerous issues of *Soto States Anthropologist* takes issue with various parts of the Hudson-DePratter-Smith route. My decision to use the spelling "Mabila" does not reflect a preference for one side in the debate over another.

4. Charles Hudson, "The Genesis of Georgia's Indians" in Harvey H. Jackson and Phinizy Spalding, eds., *Forty Years of Diversity: Essays on Colonial Georgia* (Athens, Ga., 1984), 31.

5. Richard A. Krause, "Trends and Trajectories in American Archaeology: Some Questions about the Mississippian Period in Southeastern Prehistory," in *Alabama and the Borderlands,* 20–21, 37–38; and Bruce D.

Smith, "Mississippian Patterns of Subsistence and Settlement," in *Alabama and the Borderlands,* 70.

6. Griffith, *Alabama: A Documentary History,* 12–13.

7. Smith, "Mississippian Patterns of Subsistence and Settlement," in *Alabama and the Borderlands,* 69–72; and Hudson, *Southeastern Indians,* 269–70, 311, 365–68.

8. James B. Griffin, "Changing Concepts of the Prehistoric Mississippian Cultures of the Eastern United States," in *Alabama and the Borderlands,* 63, contains a general description of Indian trading patterns.

9. Griffin, "Changing Concepts of the Prehistoric Mississippian Cultures," in *Alabama and the Borderlands,* 63.

10. Griffith, *Alabama: A Documentary History,* 5–6; John R. Swanton, *Early History of the Creek Indians and their Neighbors* (Washington, D.C., 1922), 201–3; DePratter et al., "The Hernando De Soto Expedition," in *Alabama and the Borderlands,* 120. Another good example of how a community has aggressively defended its claim to being on the de Soto route can be seen in the efforts of Childersburg to confirm that it was the location of the Indian town of Coosa, where de Soto is said to have left behind two members of his company. For the Childersburg side of this debate, see J. Morgan Smith, "The Antiquity of Childersburg," in the Talladega County Historical Association *Newsletter* (September 1989), 1–2. Eubanks, "Coosa Too?" contains a bibliography on this topic.

11. Jeffrey P. Brain, "The Archaeology of the Hernando de Soto Expedition," 99–101, and DePratter et al., "The Hernando de Soto Expedition," 108–9, 120–21, both in *Alabama and the Borderlands.* Griffith, *Alabama: A Documentary History,* 6–9, reprints the account of a member of the expedition identified only as the Gentleman of Elvas. This encounter described here is on pages 6 and 7, and it is apparent from it that Tascaluza did not volunteer to accompany de Soto. See also Hudson, *Southeastern Indians,* 112–13, and DePratter et al., "The Hernando de Soto Expedition," in *Alabama and the Borderlands,* 121.

12. Griffith, *Alabama: A Documentary History,* 7–8; DePratter et al., "The Hernando de Soto Expedition," in *Alabama and the Borderlands,* 122–23; and Hudson, "A Spanish-Coosa Alliance in Sixteenth-Century North Georgia," *Georgia Historical Quarterly* 72 (Winter 1988): 601–2.

13. Griffith, *Alabama: A Documentary History,* 8–9, contains a contemporary account of the battle. According to DePratter et al., "The Hernando de Soto Expedition," in *Alabama and the Borderlands,* 123, Mabila was probably on the lower Cahaba River, but as has been noted, not everyone agrees with this location.

14. Griffith, *Alabama: A Documentary History,* 9; Hudson, *Southeastern Indians,* 114.

15. Hudson, *Southeastern Indians,* 4–5; Peter H. Wood, "The impact of smallpox on the native population of the 18th century South," *New York State Journal of Medicine* 87 (January 1987): 31, 35–36. Hudson et al.,

"The Tristan de Luna Expedition," 31–43; see especially 42–43. Charles H. Fairbanks, "From Exploration to Settlement: Spanish Strategies for Colonization," in *Alabama and the Borderlands*, 134–36.

16. "Benjamin Hawkins Journal," 1:23–24, in Grant, *Writings of Benjamin Hawkins*. For the impact of European diseases on tribes closer to the Atlantic, see Hudson, "Genesis of Georgia's Indians," in *Forty Years of Diversity*, 25–45, and James H. Merrell, "The Indians' New World: The Catawba Experience," *William and Mary Quarterly*, 3d ser., 41 (October 1984): 537–65.

17. Of the few sources available to trace the evolution of the river tribes during this era, contemporary maps have a particular value. For the best of these see William P. Cumming, *The Southeast in Early Maps* (Chapel Hill, 1962). Maps in this work show how villages disappeared and new settlement patterns formed. See also Swanton, *Early History of the Creek Indians*, 201–3.

18. Hudson, *Southeastern Indians*, 202–5, 440–41.

19. Verner W. Crane, *The Southern Frontier, 1670–1732* (1956; reprint, New York, 1981) 78–79, 82; Hudson, *Southeastern Indians*, 434–35; Jay Higginbotham, *Old Mobile: Fort Louis de la Louisiane, 1702–1711* (1977; reprint, Tuscaloosa, Ala., 1991), 41–42; Daniel H. Thomas, *Fort Toulouse: The French Outpost at the Alabamas on the Coosa*, with an introduction by Gregory A. Waselkov (Tuscaloosa, Ala., 1989), ix. Waselkov's "Introduction," subtitled "Recent Archaeological and Historical Research," is particularly insightful and represents one of those rare cases where an introduction is as significant as the book it introduces. For this reason it will be cited separately from the main work. See also Wood, "The impact of smallpox," 31.

20. Crane, *Southern Frontier*, 22–23, 39, 46, 111–12; Robert M. Weir, *Colonial South Carolina: A History* (Millwood, N.Y., 1983), 17; and Thomas, *Fort Toulouse*, 2–3, 32–33. The best account of this trade is Kathryn E. Holland Braund, *Deerskins and Duffels: Creek Indian Trade with Anglo-America, 1685–1815* (Lincoln, Nebr., 1993).

21. Griffith, *Alabama: A Documentary History*, 21–22; Waselkov, "Introduction" to *Fort Toulouse*, x; Wilber R. Jacobs, ed., *The Appalachian Indian Frontier: The Edmond Atkin Report and Plan of 1755* (Lincoln, Nebr., 1967), 27, 35. Hudson, *Southeastern Indians*, 440–41; Peter H. Wood, "Circles in the Sand: Perspectives on the Southern Frontier at the Arrival of James Oglethorpe," in Phinizy Spalding and Harvey H. Jackson, eds., *Oglethorpe in Perspective: Georgia's Founder after Two Hundred Years* (Tuscaloosa, Ala., 1989), 12–13.

22. Crane, *Southern Frontier*, 67–70, 72–73, 76–78, 82–83, 88, 95, 97, 99, 101–2, 104–5; Griffith, *Alabama: A Documentary History*, 12–13; and Hudson, *Southeastern Indians*, 441.

23. Crane, *Southern Frontier*, 168–69.

24. Crane, *Southern Frontier*, 183–85; Waselkov, "Introduction" to *Fort Toulouse*, ix–x, and Thomas, *Fort Toulouse*, 4–5, 7–8. The name "Creek" seems to have been used earlier, in the Ocmulgee valley of modern

Georgia. There English traders merged a tribal name, "Ochese," with the stream on which these Indians lived and identified the natives as the "Ochese Creeks." In time this was simply shortened to "Creek." See Hudson, "Genesis of Georgia's Indians," 41–42.

25. Crane, *Southern Frontier*, 255–56; Hudson, *Southeastern Indians*, 439–40; Waselkov, "Introduction" to *Fort Toulouse*, vii, x–xi; and Thomas, *Fort Toulouse*, 4–5, 32–33. This is the site now referred to as Fort Toulouse I. Its precise location was unknown until 1986, and excavations then and since have revealed that the post was altered a number of times and enlarged before it was eventually abandoned. Less than a fourth of the site has survived. The rest has been washed away by the river. See also Thomas, *Fort Toulouse*, 1, 10–11; and Griffith, *Alabama: A Documentary History*, 20–21.

26. Crane, *Southern Frontier*, 256–57; Hudson, *Southeastern Indians*, 439–40; and Waselkov, "Introduction" to *Fort Toulouse*, xxviii, x, and Thomas, *Fort Toulouse*, 12–13.

27. Jacobs, *Appalachian Indian Frontier*, 61; Thomas, *Fort Toulouse*, 13; Crane, *Southern Frontier*, 256–57.

28. Jacobs, *Appalachian Indian Frontier*, 60; Waselkov, "Introduction" to *Fort Toulouse*, xix, xxv–xxvi, and Thomas, *Fort Toulouse*, 26–31.

29. Waselkov, "Introduction" to *Fort Toulouse*, xxv–xxvii; and Thomas, *Fort Toulouse*, 34–38.

30. Waselkov, "Introduction" to *Fort Toulouse*, xi–xiii, xix, and Thomas, *Fort Toulouse*, 22–24, 26–28, 42–45, 52. This second stockade has been designated Fort Toulouse II. Irregularly laid out, the fort featured corner bastions linked by walls or curtains. The total length of the palisade was roughly eight hundred feet. For a full description see Waselkov, "Introduction" to *Fort Toulouse*, xiii–xvi.

31. Thomas, *Fort Toulouse*, 52–61.

32. Ibid., 52–61, 66–67.

33. Ibid., 66–67; Waselkov, "Introduction" to *Fort Toulouse*, xxvii–xxviii.

34. Thomas, *Fort Toulouse*, contains surprisingly few references to river commerce on a large scale.

35. Jacobs, *Appalachian Indian Frontier*, 9–10; Thomas, *Fort Toulouse*, 63–66.

2. ENGLISHMEN, INDIANS, AND AMERICANS

1. An excellent published collection of maps that shows the expansion of geographic knowledge is Cumming, *The Southeast in Early Maps*. For a good account of how maps were used for political and diplomatic purposes, see Louis De Vorsey, Jr., "Oglethorpe and the Earliest Maps of Georgia," *Oglethorpe in Perspective*, 22–43.

2. Jacobs, *Appalachian Indian Frontier*, 73–74. Cumming, *The Southeast in Early Maps*, Plate 55, 59.

3. Griffith, *Alabama: A Documentary History*, 29–30, 36–37; William S. Coker and Thomas D. Watson, *Indian Traders of the Southeastern Spanish Borderlands: Panton, Leslie & Company and John Forbes & Company, 1783–1847* (Pensacola, Fla., 1986), 8.

4. James H. O'Donnell III, *Southern Indians in the American Revolution* (Knoxville, Tenn., 1973), 31–32; Griffith, *Alabama: A Documentary History*, 37.

5. O'Donnell, *Southern Indians in the American Revolution*, 8–9, 15, 28–29, 34–49, 59–66. The best general study of British Indian policy in the South prior to the American Revolution is John R. Alden, *John Stuart and the Southern Colonial Frontier: A Study of Indian Relations, War, Trade, and Land Problems in the Southern Wilderness, 1754–1775* (Ann Arbor, Mich., 1944); Bartram, *Travels*, 280.

6. Bartram, *Travels*, 251–52. Bartram was never a good judge of distance, and the river was probably closer to three hundred feet across than three hundred yards. It was, nevertheless, an impressive sight.

7. Bartram, *Travels*, 251–91; quotation is on 282. See also Robert R. Rea, *Major Robert Farmar of Mobile* (Tuscaloosa, Ala., 1990), 135–36.

8. O'Donnell, *Southern Indians in the American Revolution*, 34–48, 80, 82, 95, 113, 138–39; Griffith, *Alabama: A Documentary History*, 43.

9. O'Donnell, *Southern Indians in the American Revolution*, 130–31, 138–39; Griffith, *Alabama: A Documentary History*, 43–46; Coker and Watson, *Indian Traders of the Southeastern Spanish Borderlands*, 4–7, 53, 55; Louis LeClerc Milfort, *Memoirs; or, A Quick Glance at my Various Travels and my Sojourn in the Creek Nation*, trans. and ed. by Ben C. McCary (Savannah, Ga., 1972), 135. An older study, John Walton Caughey, *McGillivray of the Creeks* (Norman, Okla., 1938) remains valuable.

10. Griffith, *Alabama: A Documentary History*, 46; Coker and Watson, *Indian Traders of the Southeastern Spanish Borderlands*, 1–2, 22, 56, 363–66; O'Donnell, *Southern Indians in the American Revolution*, 135; Bartram, *Travels*, 282.

11. John Pope, *A Tour Through the Southern and Western Territories of the United States of North America; The Spanish Dominions of the River Mississippi, and the Floridas; The Countries of the Creek Nations; and Many Uninhabited Parts* (1971; reprint, Richmond, 1992), 46–47.

12. Pope, *Tour through the Southern and Western Territories*, 47–50; Milfort, *Memoirs*, 29; and Griffith, *Alabama: A Documentary History*, 44–45.

13. Griffith, *Alabama: A Documentary History*, 47; Coker and Watson, *Indian Traders of the Southeastern Spanish Borderlands*, 143.

14. Pope, *Tour Through the Southern and Western Territories*, 48; Coker and Watson, *Indian Traders of the Southeastern Spanish Borderlands*, 177, 363–66, 369.

15. Coker and Watson, *Indian Traders of the Southeastern Spanish Borderlands*, 369.

16. Daniel Coxe, *A Description of the English Province of Carolina, by the Spaniards Call'd Florida, And by the French La Louisiane* (London, 1722), Facsimile Reproduction with Introduction by William S. Coker (Gainesville, Fla., 1976), 25. Although its focus is a later period, Thomas P. Abernethy, *Formative Period in Alabama*, has an excellent description of the region's settlement.

17. Abernethy, *Formative Period in Alabama*, 21.

18. The most recent study of Hawkins's career is Florette Henri, *The South-*

ern Indians and Benjamin Hawkins, 1796–1816 (Norman, Okla., 1986); see 94–97. Also valuable is Merritt B. Pound, *Benjamin Hawkins: Indian Agent* (Athens, Ga., 1951). The most readily available collection of Hawkins Papers is Grant, *Letters of Benjamin Hawkins,* and the introduction is an excellent sketch of the man's career. See also Coker and Watson, *Indian Traders of the Southeastern Spanish Borderlands,* 229; and Benjamin W. Griffith, Jr., *McIntosh and Weatherford, Creek Indian Leaders* (Tuscaloosa, Ala., 1988), 46–47.

19. "Benjamin Hawkins Journal," 23; "Sketch," 291, 294–95; both in Grant, *Letters of Benjamin Hawkins,* vol. 1.

20. "Benjamin Hawkins Journal," 22–23, 25; "Sketch," 297–98, 302; both in Grant, *Letters of Benjamin Hawkins,* vol. 1.

21. "Sketch," 293–94, 299–300, 303, in Grant, *Letters of Benjamin Hawkins,* vol. 1.

22. Ibid., 288, 295–96.

23. Hawkins to James McHenry, July 16, 1799, in Grant, *Letters of Benjamin Hawkins,* 1:254.

24. Hawkins to Edward Price, May 29, 1798, in Grant, *Letters of Benjamin Hawkins,* 1:196. Grant's introduction includes an excellent discussion of Hawkins's goals, and Hawkins's own writings make clear the criteria he used to determine if the Indians were moving in the right direction. See also, Henri, *Southern Indians and Benjamin Hawkins,* 95.

25. Hawkins to James McHenry, January 6, 1797, 62–63; Hawkins to David Henley, June 5, 1789, 197–98, both in Grant, *Letters of Benjamin Hawkins,* vol. 1.

26. Hawkins to Henley, 197–98; Hawkins to John Habersham, December 23, 1798, 228; "Sketch," 301; all in Grant, *Letters of Benjamin Hawkins,* vol. 1.

27. Hawkins to Silas Dinsmoore, June 7, 1798, 199; "Sketch," 292–93n, 301; all in Grant, *Letters of Benjamin Hawkins,* vol. 1; Griffith, *Alabama: A Documentary History,* 190.

28. "Journal of Benjamin Hawkins," in Grant, *Letters of Benjamin Hawkins,* 1:24–25, 29.

29. Henri, *Southern Indians and Benjamin Hawkins,* 145–46; Abernethy, *Formative Period in Alabama,* 17; Halbert and Ball, *The Creek War,* 29–30, 308; George Vernon Irons, "River Ferries in Alabama Before 1861," *Alabama Review* 4 (January 1951): 24; Ellison, *Bibb County,* 63–64; Peter A. Brannon, "Old Claiborne: A Story of the Town at Alabama Heights," *Montgomery Advertiser,* May 7, 1933.

30. Halbert and Ball, *The Creek War,* 34–35; Henri, *Southern Indians and Benjamin Hawkins,* 23; Abernethy, *Formative Period in Alabama,* 17.

31. The best study of the impact of the Federal Road is Henry deLeon Southerland, Jr., and Jerry Elijah Brown, *The Federal Road through Georgia, the Creek Nation, and Alabama, 1806–1836* (Tuscaloosa, Ala., 1989). For the origins of the road, see pp. 1–21. See also Halbert and Ball, *The Creek War,* 35–37; Griffith, *McIntosh and Weatherford,* 64–65, 68–69; Griffith, *Alabama: A Documentary History,* 208.

32. Halbert and Ball, *The Creek War,* 31–32; Griffith, *McIntosh and Weather-ford,* 66.

3. THE WAR FOR THE ALABAMA

1. The Creek War was seen as a watershed event by early Alabama historians, an emphasis that has continued to the present day. These initial accounts, though heavy with romantic illusions, are nonetheless valuable sources for the authors who were either veterans of the struggle or were able to talk with those who took part in it. For the best of these see Pickett, *History of Alabama*; Halbert and Ball, *The Creek War,* and J. F. H. Claiborne, *Life and Times of General Sam Dale, the Mississippi Partisan* (1860; reprint, Spartanburg, S.C., 1976). A recent study that treats the war as part of a greater conflict in the southwest is Frank Lawrence Owsley, Jr., *Struggle for the Gulf Borderlands: The Creek War and the Battle of New Orleans, 1812–1815* (Gainesville, Fla., 1981). The reprint of Halbert and Ball's *The Creek War* was edited by Owsley, and his introduction and notes are a valuable addition to the work.
2. To put the Creek War into its larger context, see Donald R. Hickey, *The War of 1812: A Forgotten Conflict* (Urbana, Ill., 1989).
3. Griffith, *McIntosh and Weatherford,* 65–66, 68; and John W. Cottier and Gregory A. Waselkov, "The First Creek War: Twilight of Annihilation," in Jerry Elijah Brown, ed., *Clearings in the Thicket: An Alabama Humanities Reader* (Macon, Ga., 1985), 26.
4. The designation Red Stick or Red Club has been explained in a number of ways, but the most widely accepted is that the name simply reflects the manner in which the Creeks divided themselves into white clans, whose leaders spoke for peace, and red clans, whose members carried red sticks, the Creek symbol for war. See Griffith, *McIntosh and Weatherford,* 7; Hudson, *Southeastern Indians,* 324; and Cottier and Waselkov, "The First Creek War," 25. Another explanation for this name is found in Owsley, *Struggle for the Gulf Borderlands,* 13–14.

    See also Hawkins to John Armstrong, June 28, 1813, in Grant, *Letters of Benjamin Hawkins,* 2:642–43. Other Hawkins letters of this same period stress the way the Red Sticks were disrupting his efforts among the Creeks. Alexander Cornells to Hawkins, June 22, 1813, quoted in Griffith, *McIntosh and Weatherford,* 80. See also pp. 79–81.
5. Hawkins to Big Warrior, Little Prince, and other Creek chiefs, June 16, 1814, in Grant, *Letters of Benjamin Hawkins,* 2:687; Cottier and Waselkov, "The First Creek War," 24–25; and Griffith, *McIntosh and Weatherford,* 69–78.
6. Owsley, *Struggle for the Gulf Borderlands,* 13, 18–19.
7. Halbert and Ball, *The Creek War,* 103; see pp. 105–17 for the forts built by frantic settlers; James Caller to David Holmes, quoted in Cottier and Waselkov, "The First Creek War," 28–29.
8. Owsley, *Struggle for the Gulf Borderlands,* 21–23; Griffith, *Alabama: A Documentary History,* 61–62.
9. Gen. James Wilkinson to Judge Harry Toulmin, June 25, 1813, quoted in

Halbert and Ball, *The Creek War,* 89; Griffith, *McIntosh and Weatherford,* 89–90.

10. Henri, *Southern Indians and Benjamin Hawkins,* 284; Halbert and Ball, *The Creek War,* 130–42. Most of the studies of the Creek War note the presence of mixed-bloods on both sides and the role they played. See Griffith, *McIntosh and Weatherford,* 2, 90–92; Cottier and Waselkov, "The First Creek War," 28; Halbert and Ball, *The Creek War,* xxiv–xxv, 94–95, for some examples.

11. Halbert and Ball, *The Creek War,* 147–51, is an old but respected account of conditions at Mims and of the massacre. It relied heavily on Pickett, *History of Alabama,* 528–43. A more recent assessment is Griffith, *McIntosh and Weatherford,* 99–111.

12. Charles Weatherford to T. H. Ball, October 17, 1890, in Halbert and Ball, *The Creek War,* 174–75, see also xxiv, 152–53. Griffith, *McIntosh and Weatherford,* 104; and Thomas S. Woodward, *Woodward's Reminiscences of the Creek or Muscogee Indians* (1859; reprint, Tuscaloosa, Ala., 1939), 98.

13. For an analysis of Weatherford and his career, see the early chapters of Griffith, *McIntosh and Weatherford.* See also Weatherford to Ball, October 17, 1890, in Halbert and Ball, *The Creek War,* 173–76 and xxiv n. 26. Charles Weatherford was William Weatherford's grandson. Maj. Joseph P. Kennedy's report is quoted in Pickett, *History of Alabama,* 542.

14. Halbert and Ball, *The Creek War,* xxv, 177–203.

15. Claiborne, *Life and Times of Gen. Sam Dale,* claims to be based on interviews with Dale, and it remains the best source on his life. See also Halbert and Ball, *The Creek War,* xxv–xxvi, 129–30, 235–37.

16. Most of the information on the canoe fight has come through Pickett, *History of Alabama,* 562–66; Claiborne, *Life and Times of Gen. Sam Dale,* 122–27; and Halbert and Ball, *The Creek War,* 231–37. See also Irons, "River Ferries," 24–25; John Spencer Bassett, ed., "Major Howell Tatum's Journal, while acting Topographical Engineer (1814) to General Jackson, Commanding the Seventh Military District," *Smith College Studies in History* 7 (October 1921 to April 1922): 36.

17. Pickett, *History of Alabama,* 562–66; Halbert and Ball, *The Creek War,* 231–36.

18. Halbert and Ball, *The Creek War,* 235–36; Pickett, *History of Alabama,* 566.

19. Claiborne to Governor Holmes, November 21, 1813, quoted in Halbert and Ball, *The Creek War,* 242; Cottier and Waselkov, "The First Creek War," 30–31. The location was also known as Alabama Heights. See "Claiborne," *Monroe County Museum and Historical Society Quarterly* 1, no. 1 (1987): 1 (the entire issue is devoted to the history of Claiborne); and W. Stuart Harris, *Dead Towns of Alabama* (University, Ala., 1977), 38–39, 71–72.

20. Halbert and Ball, *The Creek War,* 269, 271–72; The first phase of Jackson's campaign is covered in Griffith, *McIntosh and Weatherford,* 112–32, and Owsley, *Struggle for the Gulf Borderlands,* 61–71.

21. Halbert and Ball, *The Creek War,* 271–73.

22. Owsley, *Struggle for the Gulf Borderlands,* 47–78, and Griffith, *McIntosh and Weatherford,* 126–32, cover the fighting at the Holy Ground. See also Halbert and Ball, *The Creek War,* xxvi, 244–58.

23. Owsley, *Struggle for the Gulf Borderlands,* 47–78; Griffith, *McIntosh and Weatherford,* 126–32; Halbert and Ball, *The Creek War,* xxv–xxvi, 129–30, 235–37.

24. The leap story is told in most studies of the Creek War. A good assessment of the reports of advocates and detractors is given in Halbert and Ball, *The Creek War,* 253–56. See also Griffith, *McIntosh and Weatherford,* 129–31, and Woodward, *Reminiscences,* 100–101.

25. Owsley, *Struggle for the Gulf Borderlands,* 48–50, and Halbert and Ball, *The Creek War,* 260–62.

26. Alexander McCulloch to Frances F. McCulloch, April 1, 1813, in Thomas W. Cutrer, ed., "'The Tallapoosa Might Truly Be Called the River of Blood': Major Alexander McCulloch and the Battle of Horseshoe Bend, March 27, 1813," *Alabama Review* 43 (January 1990): 38. Owsley, *Struggle for the Gulf Borderlands,* 72–85, and Griffith, *McIntosh and Weatherford,* 113–50, cover the rest of Jackson's campaign and the battle of Horseshoe Bend.

27. These accounts of American atrocities are in Halbert and Ball, *The Creek War,* 276–77.

28. There are a number of accounts of Weatherford's surrender, and though the wording often differs, the general story is the same. See "William Weatherford's Speech to General Andrew Jackson at Tohopeka on the Tallapoosa river when he Surrendered March 28, 1814," in Griffith, *Alabama: A Documentary History,* 116–17; Henri, *Southern Indians and Benjamin Hawkins,* 293–94; Owsley, *Struggle for the Gulf Borderlands,* 83–85; Woodward, *Reminiscences,* 92–93; and Griffith, *McIntosh and Weatherford,* 151–55. See also Charles Weatherford to T. H. Ball, October 17, 1890, in Halbert and Ball, *The Creek War,* 173–74.

29. Claiborne, *Life and Times of Gen. Sam Dale,* 128–29; Griffith, *McIntosh and Weatherford,* 92–94, 252–54.

30. Griffith, *McIntosh and Weatherford,* 252–54; Claiborne, *Life and Times of Gen. Sam Dale,* 128–29; and Halbert and Ball, *The Creek War,* 236–37.

4. SETTLING THE ALABAMA

1. Henri, *Southern Indians and Benjamin Hawkins,* 297–307; Halbert and Ball, *The Creek War,* 279. Whites retained possession of the rich land in the forks of the Coosa and Talapoosa; therefore, until Elmore County was created (1866) Montgomery County extended across the Tallapoosa. See maps of Alabama printed by A. Findley, 1824 and 1829, in the Agee Collection of the Birmingham Public Library.

2. Bassett, "Tatum's Journal," 6–7, 10, 45–47.

3. Abernethy, *Formative Period in Alabama,* 25–26.

4. "Petition of Clabon Harris of Munrow County," in Griffith, *Alabama: A Documentary History,* 65–66; Ellison, *Bibb County,* 12.

5. Griffith, *Alabama: A Documentary History,* 65; Abernethy, *Formative Period in Alabama,* 26, 37–39.

6. John Graham to Thomas Ruffin, quoted in Davis, *Cotton Kingdom,* 15–16.

7. Davis, *Cotton Kingdom,* 8, 19; Abernethy, *Formative Period in Alabama,* 66, 74, 120–21.

8. Abernethy, *Formative Period in Alabama,* 35–36, 178–79; Bassett, "Tatum's Journal," 46.

9. This comparison of the evolution of the Alabama frontier owes much to an essay by Jack P. Greene and J. R. Pole, "Reconstructing British-American Colonial History: An Introduction," in Greene and Pole, eds., *Colonial British America: Essays in the New History of the Early Modern Era* (Baltimore, 1984), 14–16.

10. Weymouth T. Jordan, *Ante-bellum Alabama: Town and Country* (1957; reprint, University, Ala., 1987), 34–35.

11. Griffith, *Alabama: A Documentary History,* 211–12; Abernethy, *Formative Period in Alabama,* 90, 93–94; Davis, *Cotton Kingdom,* 117.

12. Abernethy, *Formative Period in Alabama,* 78–80; Davis, *Cotton Kingdom,* 61–65.

13. Bassett, "Tatum's Journal," written during the dry month of August, gives a good account of the hazards of low water.

14. Griffith, *Alabama: A Documentary History,* 179–80; Abernethy, *Formative Period in Alabama,* 93; Bassett, "Tatum's Journal," 35–36; *Monroe County Quarterly,* 1–3. See also Clanton Ware Williams, *The Early History of Montgomery, and Incidentally of the State of Alabama* (University, Ala., 1979), 19–20; Jordan, *Ante-bellum Alabama,* 63–67, 76; and a clipping from the *Montgomery Advertiser,* December 16, 1906, in the Bert Neville Steamboat Collection, Claiborne Notebook, Alabama Department of Archives and History.

15. John Hardy, *Selma: Her Institutions and Her Men* (1879; reprint, Spartanburg, S.C., 1978), 7–9; Alston Fitts III, *Selma: Queen City of the Blackbelt* (Selma, 1989), 1–2.

16. Hardy, *Selma,* 58–59, 167; Fitts, *Selma,* 2–3, 5–8; and Anson West, *A History of Methodism in Alabama* (1893; reprint, Spartanburg, S.C., 1983), 534–35.

17. Williams, *Early History of Montgomery,* 35; J. Wayne Flynt, *Montgomery: An Illustrated History* (Woodland Hills, Calif., 1980), 3–4; William Warren Rogers, ed., "Andrew Dexter: Founder of Montgomery," *Alabama Historical Quarterly* 33 (Fall 1981): 161–62.

18. W. G. Robertson, *Recollections of the Early Settlers of Montgomery County,* 9–10; Flynt, *Montgomery,* 3, 5; Rogers, "Andrew Dexter," 161, 167–68.

19. Williams, *Early History of Montgomery,* 20; Robertson, *Recollections of the Early Settlers of Montgomery County,* 16, 35; Peter Brannon, "Through the Years," *Montgomery Advertiser,* November 21, 1937. It was in the "forks of the river," that land between the Coosa and Tallapoosa that was retained by whites after the Treaty of Fort Jackson (1814), that some of Montgomery County's early planters settled.

20. Robertson, *Recollections of the Early Settlers of Montgomery County,* 36–37. For an early account of the way the Indians were being treated, see Levasseur, *Lafayette in America,* 2:70–82.

21. William H. Brantley, Jr., *Three Capitals: A Book about the First Three Capitals of Alabama: St. Stephens, Huntsville & Cahawba, 1818–1826* (1947; reprint, University, Ala., 1976), 60–61, 107–8n.

22. Brantley, *Three Capitals,* 45–46, 80–83; Abernethy, *Formative Period in Alabama,* 66.

23. Bassett, "Tatum's Journal," 46; Ellison, *Bibb County,* 13–14; Abernethy, *Formative Period in Alabama,* 31.

24. Cammack, "Memoir," 1–2, 6–7.

25. Williams, *Early History of Montgomery,* 20; Abernethy, *Formative Period in Alabama,* 53–55, 57, 69; Brantley, *Three Capitals,* 61–62, 65. An 1817 map by John Freeman shows the outline of an Indian town whose palisade curves along the line of Arch Street. A copy of the map is in the Old Cahawba Preservation Project Headquarters, Selma, Alabama. I appreciate Linda Derry calling this to my attention. I am also indebted to Julie Lyons of the Old Cahawba Preservation Project for a guided tour of the site and for warning me that Arch Street never developed as Brantley's account indicates.

26. Brantley, *Three Capitals,* 63, 74, 89, 89n. (These latter pages rely on Jabez W. Heustis, M.D., *History of the Bilious Remitting Fever of Alabama as it Appeared in Cahawba and its Vicinity in the Summers and Autumns of 1821 and 1822*); Abernethy, *Formative Period in Alabama,* 152–53; Ellison, *Bibb County,* 21, 23–24, 27–28; Irons, "River Ferries," 25.

27. Ellison, *Bibb County,* 32–39.

28. Ibid., 32–33, 35, 37, 39.

29. Griffith, *Alabama: A Documentary History,* 201–2; Brantley, *Three Capitals,* 89–90; Abernethy, *Formative Period in Alabama,* 95–97. Though there is a consensus on the *Harriet* being the first steamboat to reach Montgomery, at least one other may have gotten some distance up the river. Bert Neville, in an undated letter to the editor in the Neville Steamboat Collection, noted that D. L. McCall of Monroeville had a bill of lading from the *Tensas* from Claiborne to Cahawba, dated 1820.

30. Brantley, *Three Capitals,* 71, 121–22, 170–71n, 172; Griffith, *Alabama: A Documentary History,* 357.

31. Brantley, *Three Capitals,* 147–51.

32. Ibid., 147–51; Levasseur, *Lafayette in America* 2:83–84; Griffith, *Alabama: A Documentary History,* 306.

33. Levasseur, *Lafayette in America,* 2:83–84; Hardy, *Selma,* 159. Some suspect that the steamboat was the *Henderson* and that Levasseur or a translator made an error. Other boats, the *Fanny,* the *Balize,* and the *Charles Carroll of Carrolton* were said to have accompanied LaFayette. See "The 'Henderson': A steamer on an historic journey," in Kathy Painter and Anna Tibodeaux, *Steamboat a Landin'!: A river history of Monroe County's people and their steamboats* (Monroeville, Ala., 1992), 6–7; Hardy, *Selma,* 159.

34. Hardy, *Selma*, 159.
35. Brantley, *Three Capitals*, 152.
36. Levasseur, *Lafayette in America*, 2:84; Brantley, *Three Capitals*, 152–53.
37. Levasseur, *Lafayette in America*, 2:84–85; "The 'Henderson,'" 6–7.
38. Brantley, *Three Capitals*, 154, 167–68, 170–207; Fitts, *Selma*, 14–15.

5. THE AGE OF THE ALABAMA: LIFE ALONG THE RIVER

1. Anna M. Gayle Fry, *Memories of Old Cahaba* (1908; reprint, Huntsville, Ala., 1972), 14; Brantley, *Three Capitals*, 68; Ellison, *Bibb County*, 35, 45.
2. Samuel Forwood to Isaac Grant, December 4, 1888; Grove Hill *Clarke County Democrat*, December 13, 1888; Fitts, *Selma*, 15–16; Flynt, *Montgomery*, 4–5.
3. George W. Featherstonhaugh, *Excursion through the Slave States* (1844; reprint, New York, 1968), 152–53; Martineau, *Society in America*, 1:216–17; Jordan, *Ante-bellum Alabama*, 6–7, 37; Abernethy, *Formative Period in Alabama*, 31–32, 75. For a good discussion of migration into Alabama see Southerland and Brown, *The Federal Road*.
4. Peter Brannon, "Through the Years," *Montgomery Advertiser*, March 15, 1928; Davis, *Cotton Kingdom*, 121–22.
5. Davis, *Cotton Kingdom*, 121–22. "River Landings Alabama River," typescript list in the possession of the author, from the papers of Mrs. Viola Goode Liddell, Camden, Alabama.
6. Power, *Impressions of America*, 2:158–60; Gosse, *Letters from Alabama*, 34–35; and John S. C. Abbott, *South and North; or, Impressions Received During a Trip to Cuba and the South* (1860; reprint, 1969), 122.
7. Gosse, *Letters from Alabama*, 32–33, 35–36, 43; Robertson, *Recollections of the Early Settlers of Montgomery County*, 28; and Abbott, *South and North*, 118–19.
8. Abbott, *South and North*, 119; Gosse, *Letters from Alabama*, 40, 253–54; Martineau, *Society in America*, 1:224.
9. Power, *Impressions of America*, 2:158; Martineau, *Society in America*, 1:221, 229.
10. Abernethy, *Formative Period in Alabama*, 106–7.
11. Abernethy, *Formative Period in Alabama*, 81, 107, 109; Hamilton, *Men and Manners in America*, 364–65.
12. Abernethy, *Formative Period in Alabama*, 88–89, 172; Robertson, *Recollections of the Early Settlers of Montgomery County*, 12; Jordan, *Antebellum Alabama*, viii; Davis, *Cotton Kingdom*, 40–45.
13. Joseph G. Baldwin, *The Flush Times of Alabama and Mississippi*, with an introduction and notes by James H. Justus (1853; reprint, Baton Rouge, La., 1987), 47; Davis, *Cotton Kingdom*, 167; Ellison, *Bibb County*, 53–59.
14. Zo. S. Cook to Editor of *The Wilcox Progressive*, reprinted in Grove Hill *Clarke County Democrat*, November 29, 1888. The *Democrat* reprinted this letter for the local audience since Prairie Bluff was well remembered in the area. See also Harris, *Dead Towns of Alabama*, 98–99.
15. Zo. S. Cook to Editor, November 29, 1888; Gosse, *Letters from Alabama*, 156–57.

16. Zo. S. Cook to Editor, November 29, 1888; Daniel Fate Brooks, "Camden: A Sesquincentennial Legacy" ([Camden], n.d.), 1–2.

17. Samuel Forwood to Isaac Grant, December 4, 1888, in Grove Hill *Clarke County Democrat,* December 13, 1888. Forwood wrote to tell of Claiborne in much the same way that Cook had written about Prairie Bluff. See also John H. B. Latrobe, *Southern Travels: Journal of John H. B. Latrobe, 1834,* edited with an introduction by Samuel Wilson, Jr., F.A.I.A. (New Orleans, 1986), 93; and Charles Lanman, *Adventures in the Wilds of North America,* quoted in Griffith, *Alabama: A Documentary History,* 203.

18. Samuel Forwood to Isaac Grant, March 14, 1889, in Grove Hill *Clarke County Democrat,* March 21, 1889; Koch, *Journey Through a Part of the United States,* 89; Buckingham, *Slave States of America,* 272–73; Hamilton, *Men and Manners in America,* 366; Lanman, *Adventures in the Wilds of North America,* quoted in Griffith, *Alabama: A Documentary History,* 203; Lyell, *A Second Visit,* 1:60–61.

19. Thomas Gaillard to Peter Gaillard, December 14, 1837, in Caroline Gaillard Hurtel, *The River Plantation of Thomas and Marianne Gaillard, 1832–1850* (Mobile, 1959), 135–36; Richard Wylly Habersham to Barnard Elliott Habersham, January 28, 1836, in Donald E. Collins, "A Georgian's View of Alabama in 1836," *Alabama Review* 25 (July 1972): 224–25.

20. Hamilton, *Men and Manners in America,* 366–67; interview with Linda Derry, director of Old Cahawba Preservation Project, published in *Birmingham Post-Herald,* September 3, 1991.

21. Hamilton, *Men and Manners in America,* 366; Gosse, *Letters from Alabama,* 102–3.

22. Richard Wylly Habersham to Barnard Elliott Habersham, January 23, 1836, in Collins, "A Georgian's View of Alabama," 219–20.

23. Unidentified newspaper clipping dated July 11, 1846, Steamboat File, Alabama Department of Archives and History, indicates that the *Cahaba River Packett* will navigate the Cahaba "at the beginning of the ensuing season." Derry interview; Fry, *Memories of Old Cahaba,* 15–17, 51, 125–28.

24. Richard Wylly Habersham to Barnard Elliott Habersham, January 28, 1836, in Collins, "A Georgian's View of Alabama," 224–25; Hardy, *Selma,* 40; *Cahawba Democrat,* March 16, 1839, quoted in Fitts, *Selma,* 18–19.

25. Hardy, *Selma,* 24–26, 41.

26. Ibid., 13, 17, 60; West, *History of Methodism* quoted in Fitts, *Selma,* 16.

27. Fitts, *Selma,* 14–20; Hardy, *Selma,* 14, 66.

28. Power, *Impressions of America,* 2:156; Stuart, *Three Years in North America,* 1:110; Hall, *Travels in North America,* 3:308.

29. Latrobe, *Southern Travels,* 96; Buckingham, *Slave States of America,* 1:260, 481–84; Martineau, *Society in America,* 1:225; Robertson, *Early Settlers of Montgomery County,* 13–14; Featherstonhaugh, *Excursion Through the Slave States,* 145; Abernethy, *Formative Period in Alabama,* 164–65.

30.   Hamilton, *Men and Manners in America*, 367–68; Abernethy, *Formative Period in Alabama*, 164–65.

31.   Hamilton, *Men and Manners in America*, 367; Buckingham, *Slave States of North America*, 1:260, 481–84.

32.   Albert Burton Moore, *History of Alabama* (University, Ala., 1934), 186–87; Flynt, *Montgomery*, 16–19; Malcolm Cook McMillan, "The Selection of Montgomery as Alabama's Capital," *Alabama Review* 1 (April 1948): 80–90.

33.   Moore, *History of Alabama*, 186–87; Flynt, *Montgomery*, 16–19; William Howard Russell, *My Diary, North and South* (Boston, 1863), 167–68.

6. THE AGE OF THE ALABAMA: LIFE ON THE RIVER

1.   Bert Neville, Jr., of Selma, Alabama, was one of the great collectors of Alabama River steamboat information and lore. Many of his books and articles will be cited in subsequent notes. In addition, letters and clippings he collected during his lifetime are now in the Alabama Department of Archives and History in Montgomery. Earlier Wilcox County judge and newspaper editor James Fleetwood Foster collected a number of articles that he wrote around the turn of the century and published them as *Ante-Bellum Floating Palaces of the Alabama River and the "Good Old Times in Dixie"* (Camden, Ala., 1904), which Neville republished in 1960. Neville's interest in steamboats was shared by Peter A. Brannon, whose column, "Through the Years," appeared in the *Montgomery Advertiser* and frequently highlighted stories of the boats and their captains.

2.   For her observations on what can be lost if scholars become preoccupied with demythologizing southern history, and for her guided tours of the Black Belt, I am indebted to my cousin-in-law Kathryn Tucker Windham—she is truly an Alabama treasure.

3.   Robert O. Mellown, "Steamboat Travel in Early Alabama," *Alabama Heritage* (Fall 1986): 2–11, contains an excellent description of the vessels and the people who traveled on them. See also Buckingham, *Slave States of America*, 1:263–64; Griffith, *Alabama: A Documentary History*, 202; and Peter Brannon, "Through the Years," *Montgomery Advertiser*, March 15, 1928. The definition of a packet is contained in a letter from Bert Neville to Mrs. Viola Goode Liddell, February 4, 1965, in the possession of Mrs. Liddell, Camden, Alabama. I appreciate Mrs. Liddell making this available to me.

4.   Rev. G. Lewis, *Impressions of America and the American Churches: from the Journal of Reverend G. Lewis* (Edinburgh, 1845), 162, quoted in Jordan, *Ante-bellum Alabama*, 17; Stuart, *Three Years in North America*, 2:111; and Mellown, "Steamboat Travel in Early Alabama," 4–5.

5.   Stuart, *Three Years in North America*, 2:111; Latrobe, *Southern Travels*, 90; Hall, *Travels in North America*, 3:309; Pope-Hennessy, *Aristocratic Journey*, 244.

6.   Mellown, "Steamboat Travel in Early Alabama," 4; Buckingham, *Slave States of America*, 1:262–63, 269; Richard Wylly Habersham to

Barnard Elliott Habersham, January 23, 1836, in Collins, "A Georgian's View of Alabama," 222; Hall, *Travels in North America,* 3:312–13; Pope-Hennessy, *Aristocratic Journey,* 245; Power, *Impressions of America,* 2:156–57.

7. The best of many examples of the way the memory of these boats and men was preserved is Bert Neville, *Directory of Steam—Some Motor—Towboats and U.S. Engineer Department Vessels on the Mobile-Alabama-Tombigbee-Warrior Rivers (1881–1947)* (Selma, 1964), and *Directory of River Packets in the Mobile-Alabama-Warrior-Tombigbee Trades, 1818–1932* (Selma, 1962).

8. Brannon, "Through the Years," *Montgomery Advertiser,* March 15, 1928; Power, *Impressions of America,* 2:160; Eli H. Lide to Caleb Coker, February 10, 1840 in Greene, *The Lides Go South,* 31; Hall, *Travels in North America,* 3:309–11. See also Gosse, *Letters from Alabama,* 303–4; Buckingham, *Slave States of America,* 1:268–69; and Abernethy, *Formative Period in Alabama,* 96–97.

9. Hamilton, *Men and Manners in America,* 365; Power, *Impressions of America,* 2:157–58; Featherstonhaugh, *Excursion through the Slave States,* 144.

10. Buckingham, *Slave States of America,* 2:270–72.

11. For a good example of how Southerners acted in the confines of a steamboat saloon, see Buckingham, *Slave States of America,* 1:448–49, 469–70.

12. Buckingham, *Slave States of America,* 1:479–80. Buckingham had more than one chance to see life on an Alabama River steamboat, for in 1839 he traveled down the river, and in 1840 he returned upstream to Montgomery.

13. Lyell, *Second Visit,* 2:56–57; Buckingham, *Slave States of America,* 1:279–80.

14. Buckingham, *Slave States of America,* 1:279–80.

15. Lyell, *Second Visit,* 2:56–57; Buckingham, *Slave States of America,* 1:466–68.

16. Hamilton, *Men and Manners in America,* 365–66; Buckingham, *Slave States of America,* 1:466–68.

17. Buckingham, *Slave States of America,* 1:480.

18. Ibid., 264–65.

19. Ibid., 265.

20. Ibid., 472. A copy of the print of the *Atlanta* at Prairie Bluff is in Neville, *Directory of River Packets,* 146.

21. Buckingham, *Slave States of America,* 1:265–67. Interview with William Harris of Possum Bend, Alabama, July 13, 1991. Tape in possession of the author.

22. Irons, "River Ferries," 28, 30; Gosse, *Letters from Alabama,* 102–3.

23. Buckingham, *Slave States of America,* 1:476, 479. For evidence that these problems were not uncommon, see C[harles] Commelin to Julianne P. Commelin, May 25, 1844, in Commelin Papers, Alabama Department of Archives and History.

24. "Cato's Narrative," in E. A. Botkin, ed., *Lay My Burden Down* (Chicago, 1945), 84–85; and Griffith, *Alabama: A Documentary History*, 168.
25. Hardy, *Selma*, 16, 61. The reference to the preoccupation with whiskey and slaves is quoted in Jordan, *Ante-bellum Alabama*, 36.
26. Buckingham, *Slave States of America*, 1:482–83; Richard Wylly Habersham to Barnard Elliott Habersham, January 23, 1836, in Collins, "A Georgian's View of Alabama," 221; Lyell, *Second Visit*, 2:42–43.
27. Lyell, *Second Visit*, 2:42–43.
28. Mellown, "Steamboat Travel in Early Alabama," 8–9; note on the 1841 law in the Steamboat File, Alabama Department of Archives and History.
29. Thomas C. DeLeon, *Four Years in Rebel Capitals* (Mobile, Ala., 1890), 42–48.

7. THE *Orline St. John*

1. At this writing William Harris lives at 'Possum Bend in Wilcox County, Alabama, not far from the Alabama River. His accounts of finding and excavating the wreck were related in two interviews, given July 13 and October 21, 1991. Tapes of these interviews are in possession of the author. In addition, Harris has a collection of material relating to the disaster, including many newspaper clippings, which he made available. I sincerely appreciate the many ways he helped me understand the river and steamboating. See also *Selma Times-Journal*, September 25, 1955.
2. Harris interview, July 13, 1991.
3. Harris interviews, July 13, October 21, 1991; *Selma Times-Journal*, September 25, 1955; *Montgomery Advertiser*, August 7, 1960.
4. "The New Steamer Orline St. John," *New Albany Bulletin*, reprinted in the *Louisville Courier* [?], November 1847. Charles Holliday provided this unidentified clipping. Next to the article is a letter to the *Courier* dated November 23, 1847. Foster, *Ante-Bellum Floating Palaces*, 53n; interview with Capt. Tim Meaher, in Grove Hill *Clarke County Democrat*, June 12, 1890; Harris interview, October 21, 1991. Although Foster has the *Orline St. John* being built in 1849, a waybill in the author's possession shows the boat was on the river as early as March 1848.
5. Edward T. Billings to George Fuller, April 21, 1850, Fuller-Higginson Family Papers, Pocumtuck Valley Memorial Association, Deerfield, Mass. See also *Lloyd's Steamboat Directory and Disasters on the Western Waters* (Cincinnati, Ohio, 1856), 207–9.
6. Cammack, "Memoirs," 1–4.
7. Foster, *Ante-Bellum Floating Palaces*, 54; *Montgomery Daily Advertiser*, March 10, 1850; Mobile *Alabama Planter*, March 11, 1850. Variations exist in the spelling of Lindsay. Foster, *Ante-Bellum Floating Palaces*, 54, uses Lindsey, while the Mobile *Alabama Tribune*, March 9, 1850, uses Lindsay. His gravestone in Camden, placed there by his widow, reads Lindsay.
8. *Selma Times-Journal*, October 2, 1955.
9. The names of and information on these individuals come from a

number of sources. See Mobile *Alabama Tribune,* March 8, 27, 1850; *Montgomery Daily Advertiser,* March 10, 1850; Mobile *Alabama Planter,* March 11, 25, 1850; *Camden Sentinel,* March 25, 30, 1850; *Selma Times Journal,* September 25, 1955; *Lloyd's Steamboat Directory,* 207–9. Variations exist in the spelling of Vaughan. Foster, *Ante-Bellum Floating Palaces,* 51, uses Vaughan, while the Mobile *Alabama Tribune,* March 9, 1850, uses Vaughn. One of the anonymous readers supplied Dr. Caldwell's full name and pointed out that he was the great-great-grandfather of Tennant McWilliams, a fact McWilliams confirmed.

10. Mobile *Alabama Tribune,* March 8, 1850; *Montgomery Daily Advertiser,* March 10, 1850; Mobile *Alabama Planter,* March 11, 1850; *Greensboro Beacon,* March 16, 1850.

11. Mobile *Alabama Tribune,* March 8, 1850; *Montgomery Daily Advertiser,* March 10, 1850; Mobile *Alabama Planter,* March 11, 1850; *Greensboro Beacon,* March 16, 1850; *Mobile Daily Register,* March 8, 1850; *Selma Times Journal,* September 25, 1955. For the way steamboats coordinated their schedules with railroads, see Peter Brannon, "Through the Years," *Montgomery Advertiser,* November 21, 1937.

12. *Montgomery Daily Advertiser,* March 10, 1850; Mobile *Alabama Planter,* March 11, 1850.

13. *Greensboro Beacon,* March 16, 1850; Mobile *Alabama Planter,* March 25, 1850; excerpt from an unidentified newspaper in the possession of William Harris; Harris interview, July 13, 1991.

14. Foster, *Ante-Bellum Floating Palaces,* 51–52; Mobile *Alabama Planter,* March 11, 1850; *Lloyd's Steamboat Directory,* 207–9; excerpt from an unidentified newspaper in possession of William Harris.

15. Foster, *Ante-Bellum Floating Palaces,* 52; *Montgomery Daily Advertiser,* March 10, 1850; Mobile *Alabama Planter,* March 11, 1850; *Greensboro Beacon,* March 16, 1850.

16. Mobile *Alabama Planter,* March 11, 1850; Cammack, "Memoir," 3; *Selma Times-Journal,* October 2, 1955.

17. Mobile *Alabama Tribune,* March 7, 27, 1850; *Montgomery Daily Advertiser,* March 10, 1850; Mobile *Alabama Planter,* March 11, 25, 1850; Foster, *Ante-Bellum Floating Palaces,* 55.

18. *Montgomery Daily Advertiser,* March 10, 1850; Mobile *Alabama Planter,* March 11, 1850; Harris interview, July 13, 1991.

19. *Montgomery Daily Advertiser,* March 10, 1850; Montgomery *Alabama Journal,* March 12, 1850; *Lloyd's Steamboat Directory,* 207–9.

20. Foster, *Ante-Bellum Floating Palaces,* 27–28; Mobile *Alabama Tribune,* March 21, 1850; Mobile *Alabama Planter,* March 25, 1850; undated clipping from the *Montgomery Atlas* [March 10, 1850] in Steamboat File, Alabama Department of Archives and History; *Alabama Baptist Advocate,* April 10, 1850.

21. Mobile *Alabama Tribune,* March 12, 22, 27, 1850; *Greensboro Beacon* March 16, 1850; Mobile *Alabama Planter,* March 11, 25, 1850; Montgomery *Alabama Journal,* March 19, 1850; *Camden Sentinel,* March 30, 1850; *Alabama Baptist Advocate,* April 10, 1850; *Lloyd's Steamboat Directory,*

209; *Selma Times Journal,* September 25, 1955; Linda Derry, ed., Diary of James Cotton, entry for March 5, 1850, typescript in the possession of the Old Cahawba Historical Project, Selma, Alabama.

One of the bodies that apparently was not found was that of Joseph Addison Cammack. He is not mentioned in any of the newspaper accounts, so his death would not have been recorded if his wife had not noted the event in Angeline Elizabeth (Eiland) Cammack's memoir.

22. Mobile *Alabama Tribune,* March 25, 1850; Montgomery *Alabama Journal,* March 26, 1850; Foster, *Ante-Bellum Floating Palaces,* 28. Most of the dead were buried at a common, unmarked grave in the Camden cemetery. At least one victim, Hugh Hughes, was buried at Bridgeport, on the bluff overlooking the river.

23. Cammack, "Memoir," 4.

24. Mobile *Alabama Planter,* March 11, 25, 1850; Foster, *Ante-Bellum Floating Palaces,* 52–53.

25. Mobile *Alabama Planter,* March 11, 25, 1850.

26. Grove Hill *Clarke County Democrat,* June 12, 1890; Foster, *Ante-Bellum Floating Palaces,* 51–53.

27. *Montgomery Daily Advertiser,* March 10, 1850; Mobile *Alabama Planter,* March 11, 1850; Vivian Cannon, "The 'Treasure' of the Orline St. John," *Alabama Sunday Magazine,* June 15, 1969, 3, 13; Harris interview, July 13, 1991. For some of Meaher's other post–*Orline St. John* activities, see Russell, *My Diary, North and South,* 184–89.

28. Billings to Fuller, April 21, 1850.

29. Cammack, "Memoir," 4.

30. *Selma Times-Journal,* September 25, October 2, 1955; *Montgomery Advertiser,* August 7, 1960; Cannon, "The 'Treasure' of the Orline St. John," 13.

31. Harris interview, July 13, October 21, 1991; *Montgomery Advertiser,* September 18, 1955, August 7, 1960.

32. *Selma Times-Journal,* September 25, October 2, 1955; *Montgomery Advertiser,* August 7, 1960; Harris interview, July 13, October 21, 1991.

33. *Montgomery Advertiser,* September 18, 1955; *Selma Times-Journal,* September 25, 1955; Harris interview, October 21, 1991.

34. *Birmingham News,* July 2, 1959; Cannon, "The 'Treasure' of the Orline St. John," 3, 13–14; Harris interview, July 13, October 21, 1991. The ruins of the *Orline St. John* have not been undisturbed, for even at this depth divers sometimes go down to the wreck.

8. ALABAMA'S LAST FRONTIER: THE COOSA AND
THE TALLAPOOSA

1. Abernethy, *Formative Period in Alabama,* 30. See also Chapter 4.

2. Robertson, *Recollections of the Early Settlers of Montgomery County,* 15–16, 36–37. The land in "the Fork" that was set aside for white settlement can be seen in the maps of Alabama printed by A. Findley, 1824 and 1829, in the Agee Collection of the Birmingham Public Library.

3. Mell A. Frazier, *Early History of Steamboats in Alabama* (Alabama Poly-

technic Institute Historical Studies, 3d ser., Auburn, Alabama, 1907), reprinted in Bert Neville, *Steamboats on the Coosa River,* 29–30.

4. Williams, *Early History of Montgomery,* 67; Abernethy, *Formative Period in Alabama,* 94; Mattie Lou Teague Crow, *History of St. Clair County (Alabama)* (Huntsville, Ala., 1973) 107, 141, 179; Small, "Steamboats on the Coosa," 183–85.

5. Donald Davidson, *The Tennessee* (New York, 1946), reprinted in Neville, *Steamboats on the Coosa,* 31; Abernethy, *Formative Period in Alabama,* 98–99; Williams, *Early History of Montgomery,* 67.

6. Griffith, *Alabama: A Documentary History,* 201; Abernethy, *Formative Period in Alabama,* 101–2.

7. Hughes Reynolds, *The Coosa River Valley from De Soto to Hydroelectric Power* (Cynthiana, Ky., 1944), 105–7; Davis, *Cotton Kingdom,* 123–24; unidentified newspaper clipping, Coosa River file, Alabama Room, Anniston Public Library, Anniston, Alabama.

8. Levasseur, *Lafayette in America,* 2:81–83; Abernethy, *Formative Period in Alabama,* 161.

9. Griffith, *Alabama: A Documentary History,* 118–19; Abernethy, *The Formative Period in Alabama,* 148; Hudson, *Southeastern Indians,* 457–60; George E. Brewer, *History of Coosa County, Alabama,* originally printed in *Alabama Historical Quarterly* (Spring and Summer 1942), reprinted by Southern Historical Press (Greenville, S.C., 1990), 16–17.

10. Martineau, *Society in America,* 1:217; Hudson, *Southeastern Indians,* 457, 460–61; Walter Bertram Hitchcock, Jr., "Telling Observations: Early Travelers in East-Central Alabama," in Brown, *Clearings,* 51; Featherstonhaugh, *Excursion Through the Slave States,* 152; Griffith, *Alabama: A Documentary History,* 127–29, 138.

11. Letters from Joel Spigener to William K. Oliver are in the Spigener File, Alabama Department of Archives and History. A family history ("The Spigener Lineage," by John C. Hall) and genealogical material compiled by Harvey H. Jackson, Jr., are also in this file. The spelling of the name Spigener has many variations, including Speigener, Spigner, and Spiegner. The spelling used here is the one used by Joel Spigener. Not all of Joel Spigener's letters are in the file in the Alabama State Archives. Another one is printed in Brewer, *History of Coosa County,* 38, and a fragment of a diary kept by Spigener is mentioned on page 20. Neither of these documents has been found.

12. Hall, "Spigener Lineage," 1–8.

13. Ibid., 5–8.

14. Joel Spigener to William K. Oliver, July 16, 1833, Spigener File, Alabama Department of Archives and History.

15. Joel Spigener to William K. Oliver, June 3, 1833, in Brewer, *History of Coosa County,* 38; and July 16, 1833; August 18, 1833; September 24, 1833; and February 17, 1834, in the Spigener File, Alabama Department of Archives and History.

16. Joel Spigener to William K. Oliver, July 16, 1833; August 18, 1833; September 24, 1833; February 17, 1834; May 19, 1834; October 12, 1834;

Christianah Spigener to Caroline R. Oliver, December 5, 1833; all in the Spigener File, Alabama Department of Archives and History. Hall, "Spigener Lineage," 7, 10–13.

17. Elizabeth Porter, *A History of Wetumpka* (Wetumpka, Ala., 1957), 22, 121; Buckingham, *Slave States of America*, 1:261–62; Brewer, *History of Coosa County*, 60–61.

18. Porter, *History of Wetumpka*, 22–23, 121–23; Brewer, *History of Coosa County*, 63–64.

19. Brewer, *History of Coosa County*, 64; Buckingham, *Slave States of America*, 1:261–62.

20. Brewer, *History of Coosa County*, 60, 65, 67; Porter, *History of Wetumpka*, 30, 45–46; Richard Wylly Habersham to Barnard Elliott Habersham, January 23, 1836, in Collins, "A Georgian's View of Alabama," 220–21.

21. Brewer, *History of Coosa County*, 65.

22. Brewer, *History of Coosa County*, 65, 72; Porter, *History of Wetumpka*, 30.

23. Brewer, *History of Coosa County*, 46, 71; Porter, *History of Wetumpka*, 121.

24. Thomas L. French, Jr., and Edward L. French, "Horace King, Bridge Builder," *Alabama Heritage* (Winter 1989), 34–47; Brewer, *History of Coosa County*, 80; Porter, *History of Wetumpka*, 124.

25. Porter, *History of Wetumpka*, 25–26, 30–31; Davis, *Cotton Kingdom*, 161; Buckingham, *Slave States of America*, 269–70; Brewer, *History of Coosa County*, 65–66, 76–77, 81; clippings from the *Wetumpka Argus*, January 1, January 19, 1842, Steamboat File, Alabama Department of Archives and History. A visual representation of Wetumpka in 1847 can be seen in a painting by A. E. [?] Thompson, "Wetumpka [From] West Side River, [Opposite] Low-Water rock," reprinted in Jessie Poesch, *The Art of the Old South: Painting, Sculpture, Architecture & the Products of Craftsmen, 1580–1860* (New York, 1983), 287.

26. Crow, *History of St. Clair County*, 142; Small, "Steamboats on the Coosa," 184–85.

27. H. Calvin Wingo, "Glimpses of Alabama's Last Frontier through the Architectural Legacy of Calhoun County," paper presented at the annual meeting of the Alabama Historical Association, April 1992. Copy in the possession of this author.

28. Crow, *History of St. Clair County*, 141–43; List of Alabama landings in Neville, *Steamboats on the Coosa*, 21; Will I. Martin, "If Memory Serves," reprinted in Neville, *Steamboats on the Coosa*, 158–59.

29. Crow, *History of St. Clair County*, 142; Small, "Steamboats on the Coosa," 190–92.

30. Davis, *Cotton Kingdom*, 165; H. C. Nixon, *Lower Piedmont Country: The Uplands of the Deep South* (1946; reprint, Tuscaloosa, Ala., 1984), 22–23; Small, "Steamboats on the Coosa," 186.

31. Griffith, *Alabama: A Documentary History*, 197.

32. Virginia Noble Golden, *A History of Tallassee for Tallasseeans* (Tallassee Mills of Mount Vernon–Woodberry Mills, 1949), 16–18; Dwight M. Wilhelm, *A History of the Cotton Textile Industry of Alabama, 1809–1950* (Montgomery, Ala., 1950), 25; Griffith, *Alabama: A Documentary His-*

tory, 191–92; *Niles' National Register,* quoted in Jordan, *Ante-bellum Alabama,* 150.

9. THE ALABAMA IN TRANSITION

1. Frederick Law Olmsted, *A Journey in the Seaboard Slave States, with Remarks on their Economy* (New York, 1856), 550–51, 564–65.
2. *Montgomery Daily Messenger,* November 12, 1856.
3. Olmsted, *Journey in the Seaboard Slave States,* 459, 465; Lyell, *A Second Visit,* 2:46–48; Davis, *Cotton Kingdom,* 123.
4. Olmsted, *Journey in the Seaboard Slave States,* 549; Davis, *Cotton Kingdom,* 163; Griffith, *Alabama: A Documentary History,* 327–328; Porter, *History of Wetumpka,* 47; Fry, *Memories of Old Cahaba,* 17–18; *Montgomery Daily Messenger,* November 10, 1856; Peter Brannon, "River Transportation Played Major Part in State's Early Progress," typescript copy and miscellaneous notes, in Steamboat File, Alabama Department of Archives and History.
5. Olmsted, *Journey in the Seaboard Slave States,* 559–60; Lyell, *A Second Visit,* 2:61–62; Davis, *Cotton Kingdom,* 43–44; Harvey H. Jackson, "Time, Frontier, and the Alabama Black Belt: Searching for W. J. Cash's Planter," *Alabama Review* 44 (October 1991), 265-66.
6. Jordan, *Ante-bellum Alabama,* 148.
7. *DeBow's Review,* December 18, 1858, quoted in Griffith, *Alabama: A Documentary History,* 192–93; Jordan, *Ante-bellum Alabama,* 148–49.
8. *Montgomery Advertiser and State Gazette,* December 29, 1853, as quoted in Jordan, *Ante-bellum Alabama,* 151–52.
9. *Niles' National Register* 66:87 (1844), as quoted in Jordan, *Ante-bellum Alabama,* 150–51.
10. Jordan, *Ante-bellum Alabama,* 153; Randall M. Miller, "Daniel Pratt's Industrial Urbanism: The Cotton Mill Town in Antebellum Alabama," *Alabama Historical Quarterly* 34 (Spring 1972): 10, 21–22; Griffith, *Alabama: A Documentary History,* 193.
11. Miller, "Daniel Pratt's Industrial Urbanism," 10–11, 17.
12. Ibid., 19–20; Jordan, *Ante-bellum Alabama,* 153–54 (quotation from the *Cahaba Dallas Gazette* on page 154); Griffith, *Alabama: A Documentary History,* 196, 257.
13. Shadrach Mims, "History of Prattville," quoted in Miller, "Daniel Pratt's Industrial Urbanism," 18. See also ibid., 24–26.
14. Miller, "Daniel Pratt's Industrial Urbanism," 13 (quote from *DeBow's Review* on page 21); Jordan, *Ante-bellum Alabama,* 152, 155–60.
15. Jordan, *Ante-bellum Alabama,* 142, 147, 149–50; Crow, *History of St. Clair County,* 138, 143; Nixon, *Lower Piedmont Country,* 21–22; Ellison, *Bibb County,* 27; Fry, *Memories of Old Cahaba,* 45; Griffith, *Alabama: A Documentary History,* 197, 199–200.
16. Jordan, *Ante-bellum Alabama,* 140–42, 147; Grove Hill *Clarke County Democrat,* January 31, 1856.
17. Jordan, *Ante-bellum Alabama,* 129, 131, 141-42 (quotes from page 134).
18. Hardy, *Selma,* 108; Moore, *History of Alabama,* 310–12.

19. Hardy, *Selma*, 109; Fitts, *Selma*, 30–32.

20. Governor's message printed in the *Montgomery Advertiser and State Gazette*, November 17, 1851; Porter, *History of Wetumpka*, 48–49; Hardy, *Selma*, 109; Davis, *Cotton Kingdom*, 131; Nixon, *Lower Piedmont Country*, 23; James F. Doster, "Wetumpka's Railroad: Its Construction and Early Traffic," *Alabama Review* (July 1850), 174.

21. Griffith, *Alabama: A Documentary History*, 213–14.

22. "Inauguration of the 'Cahaba,'" *Dallas Gazette*, August 20, 1858. Transcript provided by Linda Derry of the Old Cahawba Historical Project. See also William O. Bryant, *Cahaba Prison and the Sultana Disaster* (Tuscaloosa, Ala., 1990), 29, 64; and Fry, *Memories of Old Cahaba*, 17–18.

23. *Dallas Gazette*, August 20, 1858. The rest of this account comes from this source.

24. The official name was the "Cahaba, Marion, and Greensboro Railroad."

10. THE RIVERS AT WAR

1. Griffith, *Alabama: A Documentary History*, 278–79; "Address to the People of Alabama," quoted in Fitts, *Selma*, 37–38; George P. Rawick, ed., *Alabama and Indian Narratives*, vol. 6 of *The American Slave: A Composite Autobiography* (Westport, Conn., 1941), 52–53.

2. Jordan, *Ante-bellum Alabama*, 143–44; *Montgomery Daily Post*, April 18, 1860, quoted in ibid., 146. Russell, *My Diary, North and South*, 166, 179, 183; Griffith, *Alabama: A Documentary History*, 196.

3. *Dallas Gazette*, December 21, 1858, quoted in Griffith, *Alabama: A Documentary History*, 165; Hardy, *Selma*, 14–16, 74–77; Fry, *Memories of Old Cahaba*, 32.

4. Russell, *My Diary, North and South*, 167–68; W. H. Mitchell to his wife, January 11, 1861, quoted in Griffith, *Alabama: A Documentary History*, 382–83; see also 385–86.

5. *Monroe County Quarterly* 1, no. 1:13; Hardy, *Selma*, 46.

6. Fry, *Memories of Old Cahaba*, 33–35, 105; Fitts, *Selma*, 42; Bryant, *Cahaba Prison*, 81–82.

7. Mary Gay, *Life in Dixie During the War*, quoted in Fitts, *Selma*, 47; Botkin, *Lay My Burden Down*, 87.

8. Russell, *My Diary, North and South*, 164–65, 167, 177; Griffith, *Alabama: A Documentary History*, 383, 387–88.

9. Russell, *My Diary, North and South*, 183–86.

10. Ibid., 186–89.

11. Ibid., 184–89.

12. Bryant, *Cahaba Prison*, 5, 30–31; Griffith, *Alabama: A Documentary History*, 388.

13. James Pickett Jones, *Yankee Blitzkrieg: Wilson's Raid Through Alabama and Georgia* (Athens, 1976), 75–76; Fitts, *Selma*, 50.

14. Jones, *Yankee Blitzkrieg*, 76–79; Fitts, *Selma*, 50–53; Hardy, *Selma*, 46.

15. Heavily censored versions of these verses have appeared in a number of publications. The full poems can be found in William Moss, ed., *Con-*

federate Broadside Poems: An Annotated Descriptive Bibliography (Westport, Conn., 1988), 155; and Walter M. Jackson, *The Story of Selma* (Birmingham, Ala., 1954), 200–201. See also Bryant, *Cahaba Prison*, 17, 19; Fitts, *Selma*, 49–52.

16. Jackson, *Story of Selma*, 200–201.
17. Ibid., 200–201.
18. Crow, *History of St. Clair County*, 66, 120, 179–81; Neville, *Steamboats on the Coosa River*, 164.
19. Nixon, *Lower Piedmont Country*, 28–31; Etowah County Centennial Committee, *A History of Etowah County, Alabama* (Birmingham, Ala., 1968), 52–56.
20. *History of Etowah County*, 57–60; Nixon, *Lower Piedmont Country*, 28–31. At least one scholar has suggested that Miss Sansom never got the land. Chriss H. Doss, "The Myth of Emma Sansom," paper presented at the annual meeting of the Alabama Historical Association, April 1992.
21. Bryant, *Cahaba Prison*, 1–2, 64, 84–85, 116; Griffith, *Alabama: A Documentary History*, 424–25.
22. See Moore, *History of Alabama*, 428–33, for an assessment of Alabama on the eve of Sherman's invasion of Georgia.
23. Small, "Steamboats on the Coosa," 187; Reynolds, *The Coosa River Valley*, 241–43; Crow, *History of St. Clair County*, 141–42.
24. For the various accounts of the escape, see Small, "Steamboats on the Coosa," 187–88; Reynolds, *The Coosa River Valley*, 246–47.
25. Small, "Steamboats on the Coosa," 187–88; Reynolds, *The Coosa River Valley*, 246–47; Crow, *History of St. Clair County*, 143.
26. Small, "Steamboats on the Coosa," 187–88; Reynolds, *The Coosa River Valley*, 246–47; Crow, *History of St. Clair County*, 143.
27. Malcolm C. McMillan, *The Alabama Confederate Reader* (Tuscaloosa, Ala., 1963), 255–71. See especially "Report of Maj. Gen. Lovell H. Rousseau, U.S. Army, of raid from Decatur, Ala., to the West Point and Montgomery Railroad (July 10–22), 1864," 263–71.
28. "Report of Maj. Gen. Rousseau," 263–71.
29. Moore, *History of Alabama*, 434–35; Jones, *Yankee Blitzkrieg*, 1–4; Hardy, *Selma*, 47–48.
30. Moore, *History of Alabama*, 435–37; Jones, *Yankee Blitzkrieg*, 19–20, 22; Gov. Thomas H. Watts announcement quoted in ibid., 49; Fitts, *Selma*, 53; Hardy, *Selma*, 48–49; Griffith, *Alabama: A Documentary History*, 406–7.
31. Jones, *Yankee Blitzkrieg*, 35–39, 50–52, 62–68; Fitts, *Selma*, 55.
32. Jones, *Yankee Blitzkrieg*, 67–74.
33. Hardy, *Selma*, 51; Jones, *Yankee Blitzkrieg*, 75–85; Fitts, *Selma*, 57–59.
34. Hardy, *Selma*, 51; Fitts, *Selma*, 58–59; Jones, *Yankee Blitzkrieg*, 85–90.
35. Jones, *Yankee Blitzkrieg*, 85–90.
36. Ibid., 90–92; Griffith, *Alabama: A Documentary History*, 411.
37. For a careful, scholarly evaluation of the varying points of view concerning the "sack of Selma," see Jones, *Yankee Blitzkrieg*, 92–95. The "Selma" interpretation of these events can be found in Sol H. Tepper,

Battle for Selma (n.d.). Forrest's activities in the battle are discussed in Brian Steel Wills, *A Battle from the Start: The Life of Nathan Bedford Forrest* (New York, 1992), 304–14. See also Lewis Parsons, "The Sacking of Selma," an unpublished and undated speech given in New York City, and E. Ellen Phillips, "Reminiscences of War: An Episode of Wilson's Raid Near Selma, Alabama, April, 1865," both located in the Raids-Wilson file in the Alabama Department of Archives and History. A number of the important documents relating to Wilson's Raid and the fall of Selma and Montgomery can be found in McMillan, *Alabama Confederate Reader,* 404–22.

38. Jones, *Yankee Blitzkrieg,* 92–95.

39. Hardy, *Selma,* 52; Jones, *Yankee Blitzkrieg,* 95; Griffith, *Alabama: A Documentary History,* 407; *Atlanta Constitution,* October 9, 1942.

40. Jones, *Yankee Blitzkrieg,* 76, 78, 95–100; Grove Hill *Clarke County Journal,* April 6, 13, 1865.

41. Jones, *Yankee Blitzkrieg,* 100–101.

42. Ibid., 103–5.

43. Ibid., 105–6.

44. Ibid., 106–11; Rawick, *American Slave,* 6:53.

45. Jones, *Yankee Blitzkrieg,* 111–13; Virginia K. Jones, ed., "The Journal of Sarah G. Follansbee," *Alabama Historical Quarterly* (Fall and Winter, 1965), 232, quoted in ibid., 113.

46. Griffith, *Alabama: A Documentary History,* 412; Jones, *Yankee Blitzkrieg,* 113–17; *Montgomery Advertiser,* April 18, 1865.

47. Jones, *Yankee Blitzkrieg,* 117–19.

48. Bryant, *Cahaba Prison,* 113; Jesse Hawes, *Cahaba: A Story of Captive Boys in Blue* (New York, 1888), 458. Many of these prisoners were killed when the steamboat *Sultana* sank on the Mississippi River, just above Memphis, on April 27, 1865. See Bryant, *Cahaba Prison,* 117–38.

11. THE WAR COMES TO AN END; THE COOSA COMES OF AGE

1. Fry, *Memories of Old Cahaba,* 104–22; Bryant, *Cahaba Prison,* 81–82; Fitts, *Selma,* 45–46, 48–49; Botkin, *Lay My Burden Down,* 87.

2. Botkin, *Lay My Burden Down,* 87–88; Rawick, *American Slave,* 6:373.

3. Fry, *Memories of Old Cahaba,* 63–64.

4. Arthur W. Bergeron, Jr., *Confederate Mobile* (Jackson, Miss., 1991), 190–91; *Clarke County Democrat,* June 2, 1890; *Mobile Register,* September 27, 1903.

5. *History of Etowah County,* 67–68; Jordan, *Ante-bellum Alabama,* 137; Walter L. Fleming, *Civil War and Reconstruction in Alabama* (New York, 1905), 282.

6. Hardy, *Selma,* 53–54; Flynt, *Montgomery,* 44, 53–54.

7. Reynolds, *Coosa River Valley,* 247; *Rome News-Tribune,* August 1, 1971.

8. Small, "Old Steamboat Days," in Neville, *Steamboats on the Coosa River,* 80; *History of Etowah County,* 94; Nixon, *Lower Piedmont Country,* 56.

9. Maj. Thomas Pearsall, *Report of the Survey of the Coosa River, Made*

Under Authority of the State (Montgomery, 1868), 2, 12–13; Reynolds, *Coosa River Valley,* 106–7; *History of Etowah County,* 86. For antebellum efforts to survey the Coosa, see D. Gregory Jeane, *Evaluation of Engineering Cultural Resources: Lock No. 3, Coosa River, Alabama,* prepared for the U.S. Army Corps of Engineers (Mobile, Ala., 1981), 19–22. Pearsall's report was also printed in the *Montgomery Advertiser,* January 1, 1868. There had been at least one earlier professional survey of the river, but it was done for the purpose of building a railroad along the stream, not to open it for navigation. See W. C. Abbott, Railroad Survey Report, 1835, manuscript in the Birmingham Public Library.

10. Pearsall, *Report of the Survey of the Coosa River,* 5–6. Maj. Thomas Pearsall to Gov. Robert M. Patton, June 28, 1867, Patton Executive Correspondence, Alabama Department of Archives and History.

11. Pearsall, *Report of the Survey of the Coosa River,* 5–11; Pearsall to Patton, June 28, 1867.

12. Pearsall, *Report of the Survey of the Coosa River,* 5–6; Pearsall to Patton, June 28, 1867.

13. "Map of Lower Coosa River, Alabama, from Gadsden to Wetumpka" [1907?] and "Topographical Map of the Coosa River from Lock #4 to Wetumpka," 1903, both in the Alabama Department of Archives and History.

14. Pearsall, *Report of the Survey of the Coosa River,* 5–11; Pearsall to Patton, June 28, 1867.

15. *Montgomery Advertiser,* January 1, 1868; Flynt, *Montgomery,* 54–55.

16. For a good example of the reasoning behind this constitutional change, see Moore, *History of Alabama,* 497–503. See also Peter Brannon, "Efforts Made 130 Years Ago to Improve Alabama Rivers," *Montgomery Advertiser,* December 11, 1949.

17. *History of Etowah County,* 86, 88, 225; Small, "Steamboats on the Coosa," 188–89.

18. *Gadsden Times,* August 13, 1880, as quoted in *History of Etowah County,* 87.

19. Small, "Steamboats on the Coosa," 189–90; *History of Etowah County,* 86–87, 90–91; *Rome News-Tribune,* August 1, 1971.

20. *History of Etowah County,* 87, 87n, 225, 285, 312; Crow, *History of St. Clair County,* 135.

21. *History of Etowah County,* 170, 226; Edward King, *The Great South* (Hartford, Conn., 1875), 328, 338.

22. King, *The Great South,* 330.

23. Neville, *Steamboats on the Coosa River,* 16–17; Jeane, *Evaluation of Engineering Cultural Resources,* 22–33.

24. Neville, *Steamboats on the Coosa River,* 17–18; Reynolds, *Coosa River Valley,* 248–49; Jeane, *Evaluation of Engineering Cultural Resources,* 22–33.

25. Neville, *Steamboats on the Coosa River,* 18; *Montgomery Advertiser,* March 16, 1887; *Anniston Star,* January 13, 1983.

26. Neville, *Steamboats on the Coosa River,* 18; Saffold Berney, *Hand-Book of Alabama* (Birmingham, 1892), 509.

27. Berney, *Hand-Book of Alabama*, 510, 530; Neville, *Steamboats on the Coosa River*, 21; King, *The Great South*, 329.

28. Berney, *Hand-Book of Alabama*, 509–10.

29. Berney, *Hand-Book of Alabama*, 510; Neville, *Steamboats on the Coosa River*, 132; Crow, *History of St. Clair County*, 143; Reynolds, *Coosa River Valley*, 248–49.

30. *Montgomery Advertiser*, March 1, 15, 16, 1887; also quoted in *The Coosa-Alabama River Improvement Association: "Over 100 Years of Service to State and Nation,"* (Montgomery, Ala., n.d.).

31. *Montgomery Advertiser*, March 16, 1887.

32. Ibid.

33. Ibid.

34. Berney, *Hand-Book of Alabama*, 510.

35. *The Coosa-Alabama River Improvement Association*, n.p.

36. Jeane, *Evaluation of Engineering Cultural Resources*, 37–40; Crowe, *History of St. Clair County*, 143. During this period a lock was also built on the Georgia section of the Coosa, at Mayo's Bar, just below Rome.

37. Porter, *History of Wetumpka*, 80; *Montgomery Advertiser*, March 14, 1875, as quoted in James F. Doster, "Wetumpka's Railroad," 174.

38. Wetumpka *The People's Banner*, as quoted in Porter, *Wetumpka*, 85.

39. Porter, *History of Wetumpka*, 89; Berney, *Hand-Book of Alabama*, 506–7, 510; Jeane, *Evaluation of Engineering Cultural Resources*, 33, 37; "Unfinished lock still undisturbed," *Montgomery Advertiser-Journal*, Wetumpka 150th Anniversary Edition, September 3, 1984; William Clark Edwards, "Abstract of Official Record of Civilian Employee," War Department, Engineers, Office of Personnel Management, St. Louis, Mo. Interview with Harvey H. Jackson, Jr., Grove Hill, Ala., November 27, 1993.

40. Porter, *History of Wetumpka*, 89.

41. *History of Etowah County*, 91; Reynolds, *Coosa River Valley*, 112–13; Small, "Old Steamboat Days," 82–84.

42. *History of Etowah County*, 91–92, 225–31; Small, "Old Steamboat Days," 82–84, and Martin, "If Memory Serves," 158. J. B. Shropshire, "Steamboat Days on the Old Coosa River," unpublished paper in the Steamboat File, Alabama Department of Archives and History; *Rome News-Tribune*, August 1, 1971.

12. END OF THE GOLDEN AGE

1. Reynolds, *Coosa River Valley*, 245.

2. Berney, *Hand-Book of Alabama*, 507; *Anniston Star*, January 13, 1983; *Methodist Christian Advocate*, March 26, 1957; Letter from J. M. Glenn of Midway, Ala., in "The Passing Throng," *Montgomery Advertiser*, September 5, 1949; unidentified clipping in the Bert Neville File, Alabama Department of Archives and History.

3. Berney, *Hand-Book of Alabama*, 507; *Anniston Star*, January 13, 1983; William Elejius Martin, *Internal Improvements in Alabama* (Baltimore, 1902), 53.

4. Berney, *Hand-Book of Alabama*, 516–17; King, *The Great South*, 329,

335–36; Martin, *Internal Improvements in Alabama*, 52; Neville, *Directory of Steam*, 85.

5. Berney, *Hand-Book of Alabama*, 507, 515; King, *The Great South*, 334–35; Golden, *History of Tallassee*, 38, 40.

6. Rawick, *American Slave*, 6:225.

7. *History of Etowah County*, 170; Porter, *History of Wetumpka*, 90–91, 125.

8. Minnie C. Foster, "Trip on Broad Alabama Fraught with Pleasure and Redolent of History," unidentified newspaper dated February 6, 1915, Steamboat File, Alabama Department of Archives and History; *Montgomery Advertiser*, May 1, 1929.

9. *Montgomery Advertiser*, March 2, 3, 5, 15, 17, 19, 1929; Montgomery *Alabama Journal*, August 28, 1951; *Anniston Star*, January 22, 1958.

10. *Rome News-Tribune*, August 1, 1971; Porter, *History of Wetumpka*, 190; Ellison, *Bibb County*, 3–4; Nixon, *Lower Piedmont Country*, 56–57.

11. Reynolds, *Coosa River Valley*, 109; *Montgomery Advertiser*, May 29, 1901; *Morning Star and Catholic Messenger*, October 15, 1876; Porter, *History of Wetumpka*, 116; and Hardy, *Selma*, 153–54.

12. Montgomery *Alabama Journal*, August 28, 1951. The story of searchers using fodder to find a body was told to me by my father, Harvey H. Jackson, Jr., who grew up on the Coosa. Taped interview, November 27, 1993, in possession of the author.

13. *Morning Star and Catholic Messenger*, May 29, 1901; and Mrs. T. W. Dunn to the Editor, *Montgomery Advertiser*, September 29, 1949.

14. *Morning Star and Catholic Messenger*, May 29, 1901.

15. A. G. Moseley to the Editor, *Montgomery Advertiser*, September 21, 1949.

16. Rawick, *American Slave*, 6:284.

17. Reynolds, *Coosa River Valley*, 112–13; *History of Etowah County*, 91; Small, "Old Steamboat Days," 90, 96.

18. *Montgomery Advertiser*, August 17, September 28, 1875; A. G. Moseley to the Editor, ibid., September 21, 1949; Mrs. S. A. Pearce to the Editor, ibid.; *Mobile Register*, September 23, 1903; Peter Brannon, "Through the Years," *Montgomery Advertiser*, November 21, 1937. The definition of "packet" used here comes from a letter from Bert Neville to Mrs. Viola Goode Liddell, February 4, 1965, copy in the possession of the author.

19. J. M. Glenn to the Editor, *Montgomery Advertiser*, September 5, 1949; J. M. Glenn to Peter Brannon, July 9, 1938, Steamboat File, Alabama Department of Archives and History; and Nan Gray Davis, "Steamboat Days on the Alabama," *Alabama School Journal*, October 1944, 10–11, Steamboat File.

20. James Morrison Campbell, *Mobile Press-Register*, October 13, 1946, quoted in M. Louis Zadnichek II, "Early Paddle-Wheelers Helped Alabama Development," *Mobile Register*, June 23, 1971. Peter Brannon, "Through the Years," *Montgomery Advertiser*, November 21, 1937. See also James Benson Sellers, *The Prohibition Movement in Alabama, 1702–1943* (Chapel Hill, 1943), 67.

21. Reynolds, *Coosa River Valley*, 114, 116–19; Shropshire, "Steamboat Days on the Old Coosa River."

22. *History of Etowah County*, 171; Will I. Martin, "Etowah one of the first to attempt prohibition," *Gadsden Times*, August 5, 1946, reprinted October 4, 1990; and Martin, "If Memory Serves," in Neville, *Steamboats on the Coosa River*, 158.

23. *Monroe Journal*, November 13, 1883, quoting from the *Wilcox Home Rule*, n.d., and cited in the *Monroe Journal*, June 16, 1960. Some contend that the *Henderson* is actually the *Anderson*, the boat that carried Lafayette from Montgomery to Mobile. During the early 1980s the *Henderson* was found by divers who took over a hundred wine bottles off the wreck. Some of them still contained the liquor, though its quality was suspect. Taped interview with Charles Holliday, August 26, 1992, in possession of the author.

24. *Camden News*, June 16, 1879, typescript in Steamboat File, Alabama Department of Archives and History.

25. *Monroe Journal*, December 24, 1883, May 21, June 4, July 16, 1891; Montgomery *Alabama Journal*, August 28, 1951.

26. Flynt, *Montgomery*, 64; *Anniston Star*, January 22, 1958; Berney, *Handbook of Alabama*, 508; *Mobile Register*, May 31, 1953. Between 1878 and 1899, commerce on the Alabama varied between $6 million and $10 million a year. Martin, *Internal Improvements in Alabama*, 53.

27. *Harper's Weekly*, July 25, 1885; program printed for the opening of the Edmund Pettus Bridge, May 25, 1940; Montgomery *Alabama Journal*, August 28, 1951.

28. Fry, *Memories of Old Cahaba*, 68, 95–101; Bryant, *Cahaba Prison*, 29; Grove Hill *Clarke County Democrat*, July 25, 1888; Hardy, *Selma*, 53; Fitts, *Selma*, 66.

29. *Monroe County Museum & Historical Quarterly*, 7, 14; Hardy, *Selma*, 101–2, 154; Grove Hill *Clarke County Democrat*, November 29, December 13, 1888; Foster, "Trip on the Alabama."

30. Flynt, *Montgomery*, 54; Hardy, *Selma*, see p. 168.

31. *History of Etowah County*, 91–92, 170; *Mobile Register*, June 23, 1971; Small, "Canoeing the Coosa," in Neville, *Steamboats on the Coosa River*, 155; Berney, *Hand-Book of Alabama*, 516; Grove Hill *Clarke County Democrat*, June 19, 1890; Martin, *Internal Improvements in Alabama*, 52; Robert W. Kincey, "Those were days to be remembered, days of riverboats," *Birmingham News*, August 3, 1958.

32. Montgomery *Alabama Journal*, August 28, 1951; *Gadsden Times*, September 15, 1899.

33. C. K. Foote to E. M. Portis, from the D. L. (Doy) McCall Collection, quoted in the *Monroe Journal*, December 6, 1956. Doy McCall's collection is still in the possession of his family, though some is on loan to the Monroe County Heritage Museum, Monroeville, Alabama.

34. Capt. Simon Peter Gray to D. L. McCall, October 9, 1956, in Steamboat File, Alabama Department of Archives and History; Foster, "Trip on the Alabama."

35. *History of Etowah County*, 87, 87n; *Rome News-Tribune*, August 1, 1971; Small, "Canoeing the Coosa," in Neville, *Steamboats on the Coosa River*,

150–51. Mrs. Bette Sue McElroy of Gadsden remembered how her father took her down to see the *Leota* for this reason.

36. *Mobile Register,* June 23, 1971. For a vivid account of the impact of the boll weevil on the Black Belt, see Viola Goode Liddell, *With a Southern Accent* (1948; reprint, University, Ala., 1982), 139–47. The picture of the *Helen Burke* is in Neville, *Directory of River Packets,* 221. A listing of the boats that kept up the trade after the packets ceased to run the river is in Neville, *Directory of Steam.* Apparently records of the cargo and tonnage carried on the Alabama during these years were not kept, for efforts to uncover them through the Corps of Engineers have proved unsuccessful.

37. *Alabama Agriculture* (Alabama Department of Agriculture and Industries, Montgomery, Ala., 1930), 32–33; Peter Brannon, "Tallassee," *Montgomery Advertiser,* October 6, 1935.

13. PUTTING "LOAFING STREAMS" TO WORK

1. Jesse Richardson, ed., *Alabama Encyclopedia* (Northport, Ala., 1965), 878–79; Jeane, *Evaluation of Engineering Cultural Resources,* 38–39.

2. Calvin Goodrich, "Certain Operculates of the Coosa River," *Nautilus* (July 1944), 1–2.

3. Ibid., 1–3.

4. John R. Hornady, *Soldiers of Progress and Industry* (New York, 1930), 34–36; Thomas W. Martin, *Forty Years of Alabama Power Company, 1911–1951* (New York, 1952), 13; *History of Etowah County,* 108, 108n; Reynolds, *Coosa River Valley,* 249.

5. Hornady, *Soldiers of Progress,* 37–38; Reynolds, *Coosa River Valley* 249.

6. Hornady, *Soldiers of Progress,* 38–39; Reynolds, *Coosa River Valley,* 247–48.

7. Hornady, *Soldiers of Progress,* 39, 59–60; Thomas W. Martin, *The Story of Electricity in Alabama Since the Turn of the Century, 1900–1952* (Birmingham, 1952), 21–23; Martin, *Forty Years of Alabama Power Company,* 13; William M. Murray, Jr., *Thomas W. Martin: A Biography* (Birmingham, 1978), 28–29; *History of Etowah County,* 108–9.

8. Martin, *Story of Electricity in Alabama,* 23–24, 26–28; Martin, *Forty Years of Alabama Power Company,* 13; Murray, *Thomas W. Martin,* 28–29; *History of Etowah County,* 109.

9. Martin, *Story of Electricity in Alabama,* 25–29; Martin, *Forty Years of Alabama Power Company,* 13–14.

10. Golden, *History of Tallassee,* 29, 34–35; Brannon, "Tallassee," *Montgomery Advertiser,* October 6, 1935.

11. Martin, *Forty Years of Alabama Power Company,* 12–13, 18; Murray, *Thomas W. Martin,* 80; Golden, *History of Tallassee,* 38, 40.

12. Martin, *Story of Electricity in Alabama,* 20; Martin, *Forty Years of Alabama Power Company,* 14–16.

13. Hornady, *Soldiers of Progress,* 43; Martin, *Story of Electricity in Alabama,* 22–24, 28; Martin, *Forty Years of Alabama Power Company,* 15.

14. Martin, *Story of Electricity in Alabama,* 28–31.

15. Ibid., 37. Martin, *Forty Years of Alabama Power Company,* 17–18; Murray, *Thomas W. Martin,* 37. Interview with Judge C. J. Coley, Alexander City, Ala., August 26, 1993. Tape in the possession of the author.

16. Martin, *Story of Electricity in Alabama,* 37–41; Martin, *Forty Years of Alabama Power Company,* 17–18; Murray, *Thomas W. Martin,* 36–37, 46.

17. *Mount Vernon–Woodberry Cotton Duck Company v. Alabama Interstate Power Company,* 240 U.S. 30; Martin, *Forty Years of Alabama Power Company,* 18; Murray, *Thomas W. Martin,* 46–47.

18. Martin, *Story of Electricity in Alabama,* 28–34; Murray, *Thomas W. Martin,* 28–39.

19. Martin, *Forty Years of Alabama Power Company,* 18–20; Martin, *Story of Electricity in Alabama,* 45–47; Murray, *Thomas W. Martin,* 42–43.

20. Martin, *Forty Years of Alabama Power Company,* 18–20; Martin, *Story of Electricity in Alabama,* 45–47; Murray, *Thomas W. Martin,* 42–43.

21. Murray, *Thomas W. Martin,* 170; Richardson, *Alabama Encyclopedia,* 885; Thomas W. Martin, "Coosa River Development—Past and Proposed," *Public Utilities Fortnightly* (1956), 4; Jeane, *Evaluation of Engineering Cultural Resources,* 29, 39–40.

22. Golden, *History of Tallassee,* 64–66.

23. Martin, *Story of Electricity in Alabama,* 64–68; Murray, *Thomas W. Martin,* 73–77; Ben Hyde, "Construction Overview of Martin Dam," paper presented at "The Land and The Lake: Tallapoosa County and Lake Martin," sponsored by the Auburn University Center for the Arts and Humanities, October 14, 1990. Paper in the possession of the author.

24. Martin, *Story of Electricity in Alabama,* 64–68; Murray, *Thomas W. Martin,* 73–77.

25. Martin, *Story of Electricity in Alabama,* 64–68; Murray, *Thomas W. Martin,* 73–77.

26. Murray, *Thomas W. Martin,* 66; see the photograph and caption facing page 64 in Martin, *Story of Electricity in Alabama;* "Map of Lower Coosa River, Ala., from Gadsden to Wetumpka," [n.d.], Alabama Department of Archives and History.

27. Murray, *Thomas W. Martin,* 78–80; Martin, *Forty Years of Alabama Power Company,* 24, 27; Alabama Highway Department map, 1939, shows the location of the dams and the extent of the lakes.

28. Hornady, *Soldiers of Progress,* see photograph facing page 54; Murray, *Thomas W. Martin,* 85–86.

29. "Bibb Graves, Governor of Alabama (1927–1930)," *National Waterways* (September 1930), reprinted in Neville, *Steamboats on the Coosa River,* 179; *Montgomery Advertiser,* May 9, 31, June 1, 1929.

30. *Montgomery Advertiser,* June 1, 1929; "The Coosa-Alabama River," in Neville, *Steamboats on the Coosa River,* 185.

31. *Montgomery Advertiser,* June 1, 1929; "The Coosa-Alabama River," in Neville, *Steamboats on the Coosa River,* 181–86; James E. Larson, *Alabama's Inland Waterways,* (University, Ala., 1960), 32.

32. Murray, *Thomas W. Martin,* 89–90; Martin, *Forty Years of Alabama Power Company,* 38; Martin, *Story of Electricity in Alabama,* 95–111.

33. Murray, *Thomas W. Martin,* 89–90; Martin, *Forty Years of Alabama Power Company,* 38; Martin, *Story of Electricity in Alabama,* 95–111; Atticus Mullin, "The Passing Throng," *Montgomery Advertiser,* May 1, 1929. Not everyone agreed that the floods had become more frequent. See "The Coosa-Alabama River," in Neville, *Steamboats on the Coosa River,* 186.

34. *Montgomery Advertiser,* March 5–29, 1929, gives an almost daily account of the rise and fall of the river. See especially March 15, 19, 23, and 24.

35. *Montgomery Advertiser,* May 1, May 9, June 1, 1929. See "Map of the Lower Coosa River, Ala., from Gadsden to Wetumpka," [n.d.], Alabama Department of Archives and History, for the location of these islands, ferries, and rapids.

14. HARD TIMES, BETTER TIMES

1. *Monroe County Quarterly,* 11–12.

2. Peter Brannon, "Fort Stonewall at Choctaw Bluff," June 13, 1937; Brannon, "Cahawba," July 28, 1940, both in the *Montgomery Advertiser.* See also "The Alabama River from Mobile to Selma," ibid., August 26, 1923.

3. American Guide Series, *Alabama: A Guide to the Deep South* (New York, 1941), 236; Morton Rubin, *Plantation County* (Chapel Hill, 1951), 51. Although Rubin changed the names of people and locations, he was writing about Wilcox County.

4. Rubin, *Plantation County,* 21, 24.

5. Nixon, *Lower Piedmont Country,* 76, 146–47; Moore, *History of Alabama,* 713–18.

6. Fitts, *Selma,* 119–21; Flynt, *Montgomery,* 96–102; Clarence Cason, *90° in the Shade* (1935; reprint, University, Ala., 1983), 148–49.

7. Robin D. G. Kelley, *Hammer and Hoe: Alabama Communists During the Great Depression* (Chapel Hill, 1990), 53–54; Flynt, *Montgomery,* 102.

8. Nixon, *Lower Piedmont Country,* 151; Carl Carmer, *Stars Fell on Alabama* (1934; reprint, University, Ala., 1985), 15; Rubin, *Plantation County,* 51. Cash, *The Mind of the South* (1941; reprint, New York, 1969), 32–60.

9. For a first-hand account of what happened at Gee's Bend, see Renwick C. Kennedy, "Rehabilitation: Alabama Version," *Christian Century* (November 14, 1934), 1455–57; Kennedy, "Roosevelt's Tenants," ibid. (May 8, 1935), 608–10; Kennedy, "Life at Gee's Bend," ibid. (September 1, 1937), 1072–75, and Kennedy, "Life Goes On at Gee's Bend," ibid. (December 14, 1938), 1546–47. See also Kathryn Tucker Windham, "They Call It Gee's Bend," unpublished paper in the Tutwiler Collection of Southern History and Literature of the Birmingham (Ala.) Public Library; John Temple Graves II, "The Big World at Last Reaches Gee's Bend," *New York Times Magazine,* August 22, 1937; Nancy Callahan, *The Freedom Quilting Bee* (Tuscaloosa, 1987), and Wilma Dykeman and James Stokely, *Seeds of Southern Change: The Life of Will Alexander* (1962; reprint, New York, 1976).

10. Callahan, *Freedom Quilting Bee,* 31–34; and Dykeman and Stokely, *Seeds of Southern Change,* 311–14.

11. Callahan, *Freedom Quilting Bee,* 31–35; Kennedy, "Life at Gee's Bend," 1072; Kennedy, "Roosevelt's Tenants," 608; Rubin, *Plantation County,* 66-67.

12. Callahan, *Freedom Quilting Bee,* 34–35, 162–63; Kennedy, "Life at Gee's Bend," 1072–74.

13. Callahan, *Freedom Quilting Bee,* 35–36; Kennedy, "Life at Gee's Bend," 1072–74; Kennedy, "Rehabilitation," 1455–57.

14. Kennedy, "Rehabilitation," 1455–56; Kennedy, "Life at Gee's Bend," 1072–74; Kennedy, "Life Goes On," 1546; Rubin, *Plantation County,* 67; Callahan, *Freedom Quilting Bee,* 36.

15. Kennedy, "Rehabilitation," 1456; Kennedy, "Life at Gee's Bend," 1072–74; Callahan, *Freedom Quilting Bee,* 164; Rubin, *Plantation County,* 67.

16. Kennedy, "Life at Gee's Bend," 1074–75; Callahan, *Freedom Quilting Bee,* 36–37.

17. Kennedy, "Life at Gee's Bend," 1074–75; Callahan, *Freedom Quilting Bee,* 36–37.

18. Callahan, *Freedom Quilting Bee,* 37; Kennedy, "Life Goes On," 1546–47.

19. Rubin, *Plantation County,* 67–70; Kennedy, "Life at Gee's Bend," 1074; Kennedy, "Life Goes On," 1546–47.

20. Rubin, *Plantation County,* 66–68; Kennedy, "Life Goes On," 1546–47. A number of the stories told by Wilcox County residents about how Benders dealt with their new situation were told to me at various times by R. A. Duke of Sandflat, Ala. See also Viola Goode Liddell, *A Place of Springs* (University, Ala., 1979), 142–43.

21. Rubin, *Plantation County,* 66–68; Kennedy, "Life Goes On," 1546–47. A film on Gee's Bend, *From Fields of Promise,* produced by Bruce Kuerten and John DiJulio of Auburn Television, Auburn University, suggests that another reason for the failure of the project was that independent Benders refused to trade where they were told, recalcitrance that undermined the co-operative store and other enterprises.

22. Kennedy, "Life Goes On," 1546–47. Callahan, *Freedom Quilting Bee,* tells of the decline of the Bend community.

23. Kelley, *Hammer and Hoe,* 38, 40–48, 55, 140, 161–62; Nixon, *Lower Piedmont Country,* 76–77, 169–71; Cason, *90° in the Shade,* 31–32.

24. Neville, *Directory of Steam,* has pictures of the U.S.D.E. fleet throughout the book. The story of Clark Edwards was told by my father, Harvey H. Jackson, Jr., November 27, 1993.

25. Interview with Judge William C. Sullivan, November 23, 1992, Talladega, Ala.

26. Jack Kytle, "Bob Curtis: River Drifter," Alabama Writers' Project, Works Progress Administration Materials. Typescript in the Manuscripts Division, Alabama State Department of Archives and History, Montgomery, Alabama. Other Kytle articles are found here unless otherwise indicated.

27. Kytle, "Bob Curtis," "Pattern of Ignorance," "Dead Man of the Coosa River," "River Widow: Portrait of Poverty," "Uncle Bud Ryland, the

Coosa Fisherman"; Kytle, "I'm Allus Hongry," in James Seay Brown, Jr., ed., *Up Before Daylight: Life Histories from the Alabama Writers' Project, 1938–39* (University, Ala., 1982), 122.

28. Kytle, "Bob Curtis," "Pattern of Ignorance," "River Widow," "Jim Lauderdale: River Wreck"; Kytle, "A Dead Convict Don't Cost Nothin," in Brown, *Up Before Daylight*, 106–8, 115.

29. Kytle, "I'm Allus Hongry," 119–20, 123.

30. Kytle, "Bob Curtis," "Uncle Bud Ryland," "River Widow," "Dead Man," "Pattern of Ignorance"; "I'm Allus Hongry," 121–23; Sullivan interview.

31. Kytle, "I'm Allus Hongry," 122–23.

32. Ibid., 126–27.

33. Kytle, "Pattern of Ignorance," "River Widow," "Uncle Bud Ryland," "Dead Man," "Jim Lauderdale"; "Dead Convict," 106.

34. Adelaide Rogers, "Gab'ul, Chime Dat Harp!" WPA Writers' Project. Typescript in Manuscript Division, Alabama State Department of Archives and History.

35. Rogers, "Gab'ul, Chime Dat Harp!"

36. William Warren Rogers et al., *Alabama: The History of a Deep South State* (Tuscaloosa, Ala., 1994), 510–14; *Gadsden Times,* October 4, 1940.

37. Rogers et al., *Alabama,* 511–23; Nixon, *Lower Piedmont Country,* 155–58.

38. Nixon, *Lower Piedmont Country,* 158–59, 162–63.

39. Rubin, *Plantation County,* 30.

40. Nixon, *Lower Piedmont Country,* 152, 157–58; *Anniston Star,* October 16, 1942; *Atlanta Constitution,* October 9, 1942.

41. Nixon, *Lower Piedmont Country,* 157–58, 161–62.

15. REVIVING THE RIVERS

1. Murray, *Thomas W. Martin,* 171; Porter, *History of Wetumpka,* 47. The locks officially closed down about 1930, and after that no boats of any size went below Lock #1. In 1939, a new bridge was opened at Gadsden, to link up to a new highway being built. The bridge featured a "swing span" that could be opened to let steamboats pass. According to local tradition, the span was opened as a demonstration and never opened again. *Gadsden Times,* June 18, 22, 1939. Bette Sue McElroy to Harvey H. Jackson III, June 15, 1993, and William C. Sullivan to Harvey H. Jackson III, June 18, 1993, both in the author's possession.

2. Larson, *Alabama's Inland Waterways,* 32–33.

3. *Montgomery Advertiser,* January 3, 7, February 23, 1945; *Anniston Star,* March 13, 1983.

4. *Montgomery Advertiser,* February 23, March 2, 3, 4, May 29, November 24, 27, December 1, 2, 1945; *Gadsden Times,* April 21, 1946; *Anniston Star,* March 4, 1945; interview with Edward Rozelle of Lincoln, Ala., February 8, 1991.

5. Martin, "Coosa River Development," 4; *Montgomery Advertiser,* June 3, 1953.

6. Rozelle interview. Harold Rozelle turned the story of his year on the

Coosa into a novel, *Drift on the River* (Ramona, Calif., 1988), which his family published after his death. Although the names were changed, family members confirm that the people and events were real. Mrs. Pauline Rozelle to Harvey H. Jackson III, August 2, 1989, in possession of the author.

7. Rozelle interview; Sullivan interview; Irons, "River Ferries," 34–35. By 1950 there were only twenty-two licensed ferries in the state. Eight of these were on the Coosa.

8. Rozelle interview; Nixon, *Lower Piedmont Country,* 233.

9. Rozelle interview; Rozelle, *Drift on the River,* 51, 88, 115–20.

10. Rozelle, *Drift on the River,* 198–204.

11. Callahan, *Freedom Quilting Bee,* 37–39; Rubin, *Plantation County,* 58–62, 65, 69–71.

12. Callahan, *Freedom Quilting Bee,* 38–39.

13. *Montgomery Advertiser,* June 3, 1953; Rozelle interview.

14. Martin, "Coosa River Development," 4; Murray, *Thomas W. Martin,* 171–72.

15. *Montgomery Advertiser,* January 13, 17, April 10, 28, 1854; *Anniston Star,* March 13, 1983; Martin, "Coosa River Development," 4–8; *News Briefs: A Digest Published at Intervals for Its Shareholders by Alabama Power Company* (Birmingham, December, 1955), n.p.

16. *Montgomery Advertiser,* April 28, 29, May 19, 20, June 2, 3, 9, 17, 29, 1954; *Anniston Star,* June 28, 29, 1954; Martin, "Coosa River Development," 4–6.

17. *Montgomery Advertiser,* June 17, 29, 1954; *Anniston Star,* June 18, 1954, April 1, 1984; *News Briefs*; Martin, "Coosa River Development," 6.

18. Murray, *Thomas W. Martin,* 172–76, 252. A chronology of the dam building can be found in *The Coosa-Alabama River Improvement Association.*

19. Crowe, *History of St. Clair County,* 63; Rozelle interview; Sullivan interview.

20. Rozelle interview.

21. *Montgomery Advertiser,* June 17, 1954; Neville, *Steamboats on the Coosa River,* 132; Murray, *Thomas W. Martin,* 174–75; Martin, *Forty Years of Alabama Power Company,* 4–6; *Anniston Star,* April 1, 1984; Larson, *Alabama's Inland Waterways,* 34–35.

22. Larson, *Alabama's Inland Waterways,* 31; *Waterborn Commerce of the United States for the Calendar Year 1953,* Part 2 (U.S. Army Corps of Engineers, 1953), 46; *Waterborn Commerce of the United States for the Calendar Year 1960,* Part 2 (U.S. Army Corps of Engineers, 1960), 38; *Mobile Press Register,* July 24, August 4, 1957. The story of the boys' trip down the river is recounted in James L. (Buddy) Estes, *Alabama's Youngest Admirals* (Shreveport, La., 1991).

23. Larson, *Alabama's Inland Waterways,* 34–35; Buddy Estes to Harvey H. Jackson III, October 26, 1992, in possession of the author.

24. Liddell, *Place of Springs,* 168–69; Kytle, "Uncle Bud Ryland."

25. Liddell, *Place of Springs,* 169–70.

26. Ibid., 168–172.
27. Ibid.
28. *Montgomery Advertiser,* April 18, 1963; *Anniston Star,* March 13, 1983.
29. Larson, *Alabama's Inland Waterways,* 33–34; *Coosa-Alabama River Improvement Association*; *Montgomery Advertiser,* April 18, 19, June 20, 1963; *Anniston Star,* April 17, 1963, March 13, 1983.
30. Callahan, *Freedom Quilting Bee,* 39, 150; *Coosa-Alabama River Improvement Association.*
31. *Coosa-Alabama River Improvement Association*; *Montgomery Advertiser,* March 27, April 18, 1963; *Rome News-Tribune,* August 1, 1971; *Anniston Star,* April 1, 1984.
32. *Anniston Star,* March 8, 13, 1983, April 1, 1984; *Water-Born Commerce of the United States for the Calendar Year 1970,* Part 2 (U.S. Army Corps of Engineers, 1970), 61; *Water-Born Commerce of the United States for the Calendar Year 1980,* Part 2 (U.S. Army Corps of Engineers, 1980), 67.
33. *Anniston Star,* March 8, 24, 1983.
34. Ibid., April 1, 1984.

16. FENCING THE RIVER WITH SMOKESTACKS

1. *Montgomery Advertiser,* August 2, 1964. The special issue was published October 18, 1964.
2. Rubin, *Plantation County,* 75; Rozelle, *Drift on the River,* 22; Reynolds, *Coosa River Valley,* 322. Growing up in South Alabama, close to the paper mill belt, the author frequently heard the term "progress" used to describe the smell.
3. Liddell, *Place of Springs,* 175.
4. Bob Alderman, *Down Home* (New York, 1975), 48. This pictorial commentary on Wilcox County contains interviews as well as photographs of the area.
5. Liddell, *Place of Springs,* 175; Callahan, *Freedom Quilting Bee,* describes how this industry affected the people of Gee's Bend.
6. Liddell, *Place of Springs,* 175; Alderman, *Down Home,* 48.
7. Liddell, *Place of Springs,* 175; Alderman, *Down Home,* 120.
8. Alderman, *Down Home,* 51, 122–23; Liddell, *Place of Springs,* 175.
9. Alderman, *Down Home,* 122–23.
10. Alderman, *Down Home,* 122.
11. Liddell, *Place of Springs,* 175; Alderman, *Down Home,* 122.
12. Alderman, *Down Home,* 123.
13. Ibid. For a good general account of the civil rights movement in the rural Black Belt, see Callahan, *Freedom Quilting Bee.*
14. Robert Anderson and Steve Prince, "Mills pump toxic soup into state's rivers," *Alabama Journal,* December 18, 1990. Grove Hill *Clarke County Democrat,* March 8, November 2, 1990. Despite the fact that there are major paper mills in or near Wilcox, Dallas, and Lowndes counties, in 1990 they were listed among the 100 poorest counties in the nation. See *Birmingham Post-Herald,* February 8, 1993.

15. Alderman, *Down Home,* 123, 157. Grove Hill, *Clarke County Democrat,* March 8, November 2, 1990.

16. Alderman, *Down Home,* 70, 122, 157.

17. Pickett, *History of Alabama,* 311.

18. For a description of the legislation see James C. Cobb, *The Selling of the South: The Southern Crusade for Industrial Development, 1936–1980* (Baton Rouge, La., 1982), 236. See also Steve Prince, "Lawmakers ignore ecology," "Water measures down the drain," "ADEM: lax or faced with unrealistic demands?" "Critics charge ADEM's Pegues favors industry over Alabama's environment," all in *Alabama Journal,* December 20, 1990.

19. The *Alabama Journal* series appeared December 17–21, 1990. The special edition, in which the articles and some editorials were reprinted, was published a few months later.

20. Dan Morse, "Man's dams, pollution threaten river wildlife," *Alabama Journal,* December 17, 1990. Goodrich, "Certain Operculates of the Coosa River," 1.

21. Morse, "Man's dams"; Goodrich, "Certain Operculates of the Coosa River," 1.

22. Larson, *Alabama's Inland Waterways,* 33–34; Elizabeth Hayes, "Logan Martin and other dams possibly rob water, fish of oxygen," *Alabama Journal,* December 19, 1990; Morse, "Man's dams."

23. Robert Anderson and Steve Prince, "Dioxin earns state eight 'hot spots' on an EPA list," "Mills pump toxic soup," "Paper industry, scientists differ on dioxin dangers"; Robert Anderson, "Opponent: Unbleached products healthy alternative," "Proponent: Consumers like chlorine-enhanced goods"; all in the *Alabama Journal,* December 18, 1990. Morse, "Man's dams."

24. Robert Anderson, "Accidental Kimberly-Clark spill plagues Lay Lake"; Anderson and Prince, "Dioxin," and [unsigned editorial], "Uncertain effects," *Alabama Journal,* December 18, 1990.

25. Dan Morse, "State's waterways in peril," *Alabama Journal,* December 17, 1990; Elizabeth Hayes, "Erosion, runoff most widespread pollution," Ibid., December 19, 1990.

26. Prince, "ADEM"; Prince, "Water measures"; Robert Anderson, "Lay Lake residents tired of water looking like 'nasty root-beer float,'" *Alabama Journal,* December 18, 1990; Alderman, *Down Home,* 122; *Montgomery Advertiser,* April 20, 1991; *Birmingham Post-Herald,* January 14, 1993.

27. Interview with Sen. Doug Ghee, Anniston, Ala., January 11, 1993; Senate Bill 219, "Fishermen's Right to Know Act"; "Comments before Senate Committee on Energy and Natural Resources about S.B. 219, made in public hearing, April 8, 1992," typescript in possession of the author. *Birmingham Post-Herald,* May 7, 1993.

28. Anderson and Prince, "Mills pump toxic soup"; J. Wayne Flynt and Keith Ward, "Taxes, Taxes, Taxes: The History of a Problem," *Alabama Heritage* (Spring 1992), 6–21.

29. Anderson and Prince, "Mills pump toxic soup"; Anderson, "Lay Lake residents"; *Anniston Star,* November 5, 1985.

30. Anderson, "Lay Lake residents." No small part of Kimberly-Clark's problem stemmed from the fact that it was the oldest of the Alabama-Coosa paper mills, having begun operation in 1949, when environmental concerns were not so great and far fewer people lived and played on the lake below it.

31. Ibid.; *Anniston Star,* September 25, 1990; *Birmingham News,* September 25, 1990.

32. Brian Ponder, "'Alabama River rats': Boaters experience beauty, flaws of the river," *Alabama Journal,* December 17, 1990; Jordan Gruener, "Residents more upset by water color than pollution," ibid., December 19, 1990.

33. Morse, "State's waterways," "Man's dams"; Bill Reeves, "The Cahaba River," *Alabama Conservation* (July/August 1989), 16–18. For a good introduction to the work of the Cahaba River Society, see vol. 1, October 1989, of *Cahaba,* published by the society. An almost mile-by-mile description of the Cahaba, and many other Alabama rivers, is found in John H. Foshee, *Alabama Canoe Rides and Float Trips* (Tuscaloosa, Ala., 1986).

34. Cahaba River Society *Newsletter,* April, December, 1990; Prince, "Water measures." A good analysis of the threat to the Cahaba and the efforts to save it, including the failure to get it listed as a wild and scenic river, may be found in Charles McNair, "Can the Cahaba Be Saved?" *Alabama Magazine* (July/August 1989), 20–25, 54–55.

35. Cahaba River Society *Newsletter,* December 1990; Prince, "Water measures"; *Birmingham Post-Herald,* January 27, 1993.

36. Cahaba River Society *Newsletter,* [September] 1993; *Birmingham Post-Herald,* August 24, 1993.

37. *Montgomery Advertiser,* January 4, 1964; Morse, "State's waterways"; Katherine Bourma, "Diversion plans create dangers for Alabama Rivers," *Alabama Journal,* December 21, 1990; Bourma, "Georgia team quizzes Alabamians on Water," ibid., August 12, 1993; *Anniston Star,* February 3, 6, 1993. Alabama's water management plan can be found in Act No. 94–44 of the regular session of the Alabama Legislature. Environmentalists were quick to note that the Alabama Office of Water Resources created under the act is a division of the Department of Economic and Community Affairs.

38. Morse, "State's waterways"; Elizabeth Hayes, "Indians, settlers, manufacturers all flocked to rivers," *Alabama Journal,* December 17, 1990; Prince, "Lawmakers," ibid., December 20, 1990.

39. Robert Anderson, "Five sections of state waterways near pollution limit," *Alabama Journal,* December 17, 1990.

EPILOGUE

1. Interview with Harvey H. Jackson, Jr., May 13, 1989, with additional information in a letter from Anne Jackson Bennett to Harvey H.

Jackson III, October 10, 1992. Obituary of William Clark Edwards, *Montgomery Advertiser,* November 5, 1942. Edwards was working as a special officer of the police department assigned to help direct school traffic when he was struck by an automobile and killed.

2. Peter Brannon, "The Burning of the *Orline St. John,*" *Montgomery Advertiser,* November 8, 1936. For a complete listing of Brannon's writings in the *Montgomery Advertiser* and elsewhere, see William Stanley Hoole, *Alabama Bibliography: A Short-Title Catalogue of the Publications of Peter Alexander Brannon, former director of the Alabama Department of Archives and History* (University, Ala., 1984).

3. Small, "Canoeing on the Coosa," in Neville, *Steamboats on the Coosa River,* 147–56. See also Small, "Memories," ibid., 170–73, and "Steamboats on the Coosa," 183–94. In addition to Will I. Martin's columns in the *Gadsden Times* during this period, see also "The Passing Throng," by Atticus Mullin, a column much like that written by Brannon, which also appeared in the *Montgomery Advertiser.* In particular see the November 11, 1949, edition. The Steamboat File in the Alabama Department of Archives and History contains a number of clippings indicating the interest in river history and lore between 1940 and 1970.

4. The best examples of Neville's work, and the ones most frequently used in this study, are *Directory of River Packets, Directory of Steam,* and *Steamboats on the Coosa River.* Other material compiled and collected by him may be found in the Bert Neville File, Alabama Department of Archives and History.

5. C. M. Stanley, "When Steamboat Good Fellows Get Together," *Montgomery Advertiser,* June 18, 1961.

6. Liddell's *With a Southern Accent* and *A Place of Springs* both feature numerous accounts of life on and near the Alabama River. In addition see Mrs. Liddell's article "Early River Days in Wilcox County," *Perpetual Harvest* 5 (Summer 1973). Mattie Lou Teague Crow's *History of St. Clair County* contains many stories of the Coosa River.

7. Stanley, "When Steamboat Good Fellows"; Small, "Steamboats on the Coosa," 183–94; and Liddell, *With a Southern Accent,* 75–76.

Bibliographical Essay

What follows is not intended to be a complete listing of the works used in this study. They are cited in the notes. Instead, it is a general accounting of the most significant sources available for the study of Alabama rivers.

Any study of the history of Alabama should begin with Albert James Pickett's *History of Alabama and Incidentally of Georgia and Mississippi, from the Earliest Period* (1851), which has become a significant historical document as well as a work of scholarship. Albert Burton Moore's *History of Alabama* (1934) is beginning to assume the same importance, and though many of its interpretations are no longer accepted (or acceptable), it reflects the intellectual posture of a generation of Alabamians and therefore helps modern scholars understand the era in which it was written. Recently a new history of Alabama—William Warren Rogers, Robert David Ward, Leah Rawls Atkins, and Wayne Flynt, *Alabama: The History of a Deep South State* (1994)—has appeared to give readers an up-to-date account of the state's development. This promises to be the standard treatment for years to come.

Writing a history of Alabama's waterways required an approach to the subject much like one taken in writing a general history of the state. Secondary sources abound, but most refer to the rivers only in passing, so it was necessary to consult a variety of works in order to tell the story of the streams and the people who lived along them. Charles M. Hudson's *The Southeastern Indians* (1976) is useful for providing a broad context in which to place the Indian cultures of the river region. A good collection of essays on this early period is Reid R. Badger and Lawrence A. Clayton, eds., *Alabama and the Borderlands: From Prehistory to Statehood* (1985). Also important in understanding the river valley Indians and their first contact with whites is John R. Swanton, *Early History of the Creek Indians and their Neighbors* (1922).

The arrival of Europeans into the region has been the subject of much study and debate, most of which has focused on the question of de Soto's route through the southeast. This controversy, which is outlined in the notes to chapter 1, depends on interpretations of chronicles written by men who accompanied the de Soto expedition and on the archaeological evidence that has been found. At present there is little to suggest that a scholarly consensus is emerging. The later arrival of Europeans in the Coosa-Tallapoosa valley and along the Alabama River has been dealt with in a number of studies; the most significant of them—Verner W. Crane, *The Southern Frontier, 1670–1732* (1956)—remains the starting point for historians of the era. Other scholars have studied various aspects of Indian-white relations in the river region, including Daniel H. Thomas, *Fort Toulouse: The French Outpost at the Alabamas on the Coosa* (1989), with its excellent introduction by Gregory A. Waselkov; Jay Higginbotham, *Old Mobile: Fort Louis de la Louisiane, 1702–1711* (1977); John R. Alden, *John Stuart and the Southern Colonial Frontier: A Study of Indian Relations, War,*

Trade, and Land Problems in the Southern Wilderness, 1754–1775 (1944); James H. O'Donnell III, *Southern Indians in the American Revolution* (1973); and most recently Kathryn E. Holland Braund, *Deerskins and Duffels: Creek Indian Trade with Anglo-America, 1685–1815* (1993). William Bartram's *Travels* (1791; reprint, 1958) remains required reading for any student of the period.

These works lead naturally into the post-revolutionary developments along the rivers, when the United States became a major participant. John Walton Caughey's *McGillivray of the Creeks* (1938) remains an excellent treatment of that important figure, while C. L. Grant's edition of *Letters, Journals, and Writings of Benjamin Hawkins* (1980) is the best source on the American agent. Additional insight into the era can be found in Florette Henri, *The Southern Indians and Benjamin Hawkins, 1796–1816* (1986), and William S. Coker and Thomas D. Watson, *Indian Traders of the Southeastern Spanish Borderlands: Panton, Leslie & Company and John Forbes & Company, 1783–1847* (1986). The Creek War marked a turning point in the development of the river region. Pickett's *History of Alabama* and H. S. Halbert and T. H. Ball's *The Creek War of 1813 and 1814* (1895) are both interesting and, in many cases, credible accounts of this struggle. Both relied to some degree on accounts from participants (or those who knew them) and are particularly valuable for that reason. Another interesting evaluation of the period is contained in Benjamin W. Griffith, *McIntosh and Weatherford, Creek Indian Leaders* (1988); however, Frank Lawrence Owsley, Jr., *Struggle for the Gulf Borderlands: The Creek War and the Battle of New Orleans, 1812–1815* (1981), is clearly the best work on the subject. Owsley not only covers the war along the rivers but also treats the conflict within the context of the greater struggle for control of the region.

The flood of immigration that led to statehood in 1819 and the subsequent development of the river region has produced a number of important books that have been helpful in understanding the role the rivers played in Alabama's early years. Any student of this era should begin with Thomas P. Abernethy, *The Formative Period in Alabama, 1815–1828* (1922), which, despite being nearly three-quarters of a century old, remains the most important book on frontier Alabama yet written. Also helpful are Charles S. Davis, *The Cotton Kingdom in Alabama* (1939), and Weymouth T. Jordan, *Ante-bellum Alabama: Town and Country* (1957). How federal policies and programs helped bring immigrants into the territory and the state is described in Henry deLeon Southerland and Jerry Elijah Brown, *The Federal Road through Georgia, the Creek Nation, and Alabama, 1806–1836* (1989), while the political maneuvering that went on to locate the seat of government on the Alabama River is covered in William H. Brantley, Jr., *Three Capitals: A Book about the First Three Capitals of Alabama: St. Stephens, Huntsville & Cahawba, 1818–1826* (1947). Essential to understanding the politics of antebellum Alabama is J. Mills Thornton III, *Politics and Power in a Slave Society: Alabama, 1800–1860* (1978).

Primary accounts of the rivers and their people are more available in the late eighteenth and early nineteenth centuries, and many of these have been collected in Lucille Griffith, *Alabama: A Documentary History to 1900* (1972). In addition, there are Wilber R. Jacobs, ed., *The Appalachian Indian Frontier: The Edmond Atkin Report and Plan of 1755* (1967); William Bartram's *Travels;* Louis

LeClerc Milfort, *Memoirs; or, A Quick Glance at my Various Travels and my Sojourn in the Creek Nation* (1972), edited by Ben C. McCary; John Pope, *A Tour Through the Southern and Western Territories of the United States of North America; the Spanish Dominions of the River Mississippi, and the Floridas; the Countries of the Creek Nations, and Many Uninhabited Parts* (1971); and John Spencer Bassett, ed., "Major Howell Tatum's Journal, while acting Topographical Engineer (1814) to General Jackson, Commanding the Seventh Military District," *Smith College Studies in History* (1921–22). Also helpful in assessing events that took place in the river valley were Thomas S. Woodward, *Woodward's Reminiscences of the Creek or Muscogee Indians* (1859); J. F. H. Claiborne, *Life and Times of General Sam Dale, the Mississippi Partisan* (1860); A. B. Meek, *Romantic Passages in Southwest History* (1857); and Rev. T. H. Ball, *A Glance into the Great South-East, or, Clarke County, Alabama and its Surroundings, from 1540 to 1877* (1882).

Alabama's antebellum era was highlighted by the arrival of the steamboat, which in turn magnified the importance of the rivers as transportation arteries and of river towns as economic, social, and political centers. Insight into this era and the role river travel played can be found in Mel A. Frazier, *Early History of Steamboats in Alabama* (1907); James Fleetwood Foster, *Ante-Bellum Floating Palaces of the Alabama River and the "Good Old Times in Dixie"* (1904); Robert O. Mellown, "Steamboat Travel in Early Alabama," *Alabama Heritage* (1986); George Vernon Irons, "River Ferries in Alabama Before 1861," *Alabama Review* 4 (1951); and Thomas L. French, Jr., and Edward L. French, "Horace King, Bridge Builder," *Alabama Heritage* (1989). *Lloyd's Steamboat Directory and Disasters on the Western Waters* (1856) contains valuable information on many of the boats that traveled the Alabama and Coosa. Also shedding light on the river region during this period is Harriet E. Amos, *Cotton City: Urban Development in Antebellum Mobile* (1985); Donald E. Collins, "A Georgian's View of Alabama in 1836," *Alabama Review* 25 (1972); Fletcher M. Green, ed., *The Lides Go South . . . And West* (1952); Lester B. Shippee, ed., *Bishop Whipple's Southern Diary, 1843–44* (1968); and Caroline Gaillard Hurtel, *The River Plantation of Thomas and Marianne Gaillard, 1832–1850* (1959). Many of the essays in Jerry Elijah Brown, ed., *Clearings in the Thicket: An Alabama Humanities Reader* (1985) were valuable.

The arrival of the steamboat also elevated the status of river residents and made them the subject of attention that their numbers might not have otherwise merited. During this era the state attracted many visitors, some of them professional travelers, and these sojourners recorded their impressions of a plantation culture emerging from the frontier. Not surprisingly, the steamboat was the mode of travel they frequently chose, and when setting down the record of their journey, they left us a vivid picture of life on and along the rivers. Visitors from the British Isles like James Silk Buckingham [*The Slave States of America* (1842)], George W. Featherstonhaugh [*Excursion through the Slave States* (1844)], Basil Hall [*Travels in North America in the Years 1827 and 1828* (1829)], his wife Margaret Hunter Hall [*The Aristocratic Journey: Being the Outspoken Letters of Mrs. Basil Hall, Written during a Fourteen Months' Sojourn in America, 1827–1828* (Una Pope Hennessay, ed., 1931)], Philip Henry Gosse

[*Letters from Alabama, (U.S.) Chiefly Relating to Natural History* (1859)], Thomas Hamilton [*Men and Manners in America* (1833)], Charles Lyell [*A Second Visit to the United States of North America* (1849)], Harriet Martineau [*Society in America* (1837)], Tyrone Power [*Impressions of America, During the Years 1833, 1834, and 1835* (1836; reprint, 1971)], and James Stuart [*Three Years in North America* (1833)] all added their unique perspectives to accounts of the rivers and river culture. A[uguste] Levasseur recorded the visit of the aging hero of the Revolution in *Lafayette in America in 1824 and 1825; or, Journal of a Voyage to the United States* (1829), while Albert C. Koch brought the insights of a scientist to his observations in *Journey Through a Part of the United States of North America in the years 1844 to 1846* (Ernest A. Sadler, ed., 1972). Reports by John H. B. Latrobe [*Southern Travels: Journal of John H. B. Latrobe, 1834* (Samuel Wilson, Jr., ed., 1986)], Frederick Law Olmsted [*A Journey in the Seaboard Slave States, with Remarks on their Economy* (1856)], and John S. C. Abbot [*South and North; or, Impressions Received During a Trip to Cuba and the South* (1860)] were also helpful in recreating life along the streams that drained central Alabama.

Local accounts were critical to this analysis of the river region, both before and after the Civil War. W. G. Robertson, *Recollections of the Early Settlers of Montgomery County and their Families* (1892), contains many first-hand reflections on the people who farmed and planted around the city that became the capital. An equally valuable (and equally romantic) treatment of life downstream is Anna M. Gayle Fry's *Memories of Old Cahaba* (1908), while a more candid account of town life can be found in John Hardy's *Selma: Her Institutions and Her Men* (1879). These should be read along with some of the better local histories now available. Important among them are Rhoda Coleman Ellison, *Bibb County, Alabama: The First Hundred Years, 1818–1918* (1984), George E. Brewer, *History of Coosa County, Alabama* (1990), Alston Fitts III, *Selma: Queen City of the Blackbelt* (1989), Walter M. Jackson, *The Story of Selma* (1954), Clanton Ware Williams, *The Early History of Montgomery, and Incidentally of the State of Alabama* (1979), Wayne Flynt, *Montgomery: An Illustrated History* (1980), and Elizabeth Porter, *A History of Wetumpka* (1957). Also helpful in locating towns that rose and declined during this period is W. Stuart Harris, *Dead Towns of Alabama* (1977).

Central to these studies, just as it was central to life in the river region, was the institution of slavery. Almost all the books on the river region include observations on black laborers and their white masters; however, few of them attempted to assess conditions from the perspective of the slaves themselves. For this evaluation, one should consult George P. Rawick, ed., *The American Slave: A Composite Autobiography* (1941), which contains slave narratives compiled under the auspices of the WPA during the New Deal era. An easily accessible collection of some of the most significant narratives is that of E. A. Botkin, ed., *Lay My Burden Down* (1945).

Walter L. Fleming's *Civil War and Reconstruction in Alabama* (1905) covers the course of the conflict in the Alabama-Coosa-Tallapoosa-Cahaba valleys; however, anyone seeking to understand fully the impact of the war on the river region should consult Malcolm M. McMillan, *The Alabama Confederate Reader*

(1963), and James Pickett Jones, *Yankee Blitzkrieg: Wilson's Raid Through Alabama and Georgia* (1976). Also important are Brian Steel Wills, *A Battle from the Start: The Life of Nathan Bedford Forrest* (1992); William O. Bryant, *Cahaba Prison and the Sultana Disaster* (1990); Arthur W. Bergeron, Jr., *Confederate Mobile* (1991); Thomas C. DeLeon, *Four Years in Rebel Capitals* (1890); and William Howard Russell, *My Diary, North and South* (1863).

Politics in postwar Alabama is covered ably in Jonathan M. Wiener, *Social Origins of the New South: Alabama, 1860–1885* (1978); Sarah Woolfolk Wiggins, *The Scalawag in Alabama Politics, 1865–1881* (1977); Allen Johnston Going, *Bourbon Democracy in Alabama, 1874–1890* (1951); William Warren Rogers, *The One-Gallused Rebellion: Agrarianism in Alabama, 1865–1896* (1970); and Sheldon Hackney, *Populism to Progressivism in Alabama* (1969). Also interesting is Edward King, *The Great South* (1875). Highlighting this era, as far as the rivers were concerned, were the first serious efforts to open the Coosa to navigation. Maj. Thomas Pearsall, *Report of the Survey of the Coosa River, Made Under Authority of the State* (1868), describes the problems that would be faced. Development along the Coosa and the rise of Gadsden are covered in *A History of Etowah County* (1968), which was compiled by that county's centennial committee, and in Hughes Reynolds, *The Coosa River Valley from De Soto to Hydroelectric Power* (1944). Also useful were William Elejius Martin, *Internal Improvements in Alabama* (1902), Saffold Berney, *Hand-Book of Alabama* (1892), Jesse Richardson, ed., *Alabama Encyclopedia* (1965), and *Alabama: A Guide to the Deep South, Compiled by Workers of the Writers' Program of the Work Projects Administration in the State of Alabama* (1941).

Newspapers have been of particular value throughout the study. Publications from Montgomery, Selma, Wetumpka, Gadsden, Camden, Cahawba, Claiborne, and Mobile carried not only reports of steamboat arrivals and departures, but also often described the boats in detail. There were frequent accounts of accidents, wrecks, and disasters like the one that befell the *Orline St. John*. After the Civil War, these accounts continued to appear. Later in the century, as railroads began to replace steamboats, river folks were moved to tell about their earlier experiences, and Alabama newspapers published these accounts with obvious delight. Many of these appeared as letters or interviews, but some were published in columns by Peter Brannon, Atticus Mullin, Isaac Grant, C. M. Stanley, and Will I. Martin. Through the efforts of writers such as these, river legend and lore were spread and preserved.

Industrialization of the river region began before the Civil War, as Dwight M. Wilhelm relates in *A History of the Cotton Textile Industry of Alabama, 1809–1950* (1950). The rise of Prattville is described in Randall M. Miller, "Daniel Pratt's Industrial Urbanism: The Cotton Mill Town in Antebellum Alabama," *Alabama Historical Quarterly* 34 (1972), while the development of Tallassee is covered in Virginia Noble Golden, *A History of Tallassee for Tallasseans* (1949). Life for Alabama's mill people is described with clarity and sensitivity by J. Wayne Flynt in *Poor but Proud: Alabama's Poor Whites* (1989). However, it was the rise of the Alabama Power Company that moved the Coosa and Tallapoosa Valley (and some might say Alabama itself) into the twentieth century and changed the rivers forever. Unfortunately, most books relating to the Alabama Power Company fall into the category of "court biographies" and inside accounts. I do not suggest that they are not valuable, but they must be read with their pro-company slant in mind. The most important of these is Thomas W. Martin's own *Forty Years of Alabama Power Company, 1911–1951* (1952) and his *The Story of Electricity in Alabama since the Turn of the Century* (1952). William M. Murray, Jr., in *Thomas W. Martin: A Biography* (1978), drew heavily on these accounts. Also helpful, especially for its information on William Patrick Lay, is John R. Hornaday, *Soldiers of Progress and Industry* (1930). Until some scholar can combine material from the files of Alabama Power with the rich oral tradition that survives in the Coosa and Tallapoosa valley, however, the story of the most important company in the development of the state will remain untold.

Oral history has been an important part of this study. The acknowledgments list the many people who shared their stories with me. One of the lessons learned while searching out people who know the rivers and river lore is just how much is lost with each passing. This was especially true in efforts to try to recreate life along the rivers in the 1930s. Newspapers, with stories based on interviews with local "characters," have helped fill some of this gap, as have "life histories" written under the auspices of the Alabama Writers' Project. Some of these were collected in James Seay Brown, Jr., ed., *Up Before Daylight: Life Histories from the Alabama Writers' Project, 1938–39* (1982), and others are in the WPA materials, Manuscript Division, Alabama State Department of Archives and History. Providing a broad context for these "histories" and for the oral accounts I was able to collect was the work of Carl Carmer, Clarence Cason, and H. C. Nixon. As acknowledged elsewhere, these books represent some of the best writing of their kind, and they proved essential to my understanding of Alabama and its people.

The community of Gee's Bend figured heavily in my efforts to describe life along the Alabama and the changes through which the region has gone. The articles by Rev. Renwick C. Kennedy in *Christian Century* are first-hand accounts of what took place in the Bend in the 1930s, while the study of Wilcox County carried out by sociologist Morton Rubin and published in 1951 as *Plantation County* provided the context for developments there. Also consulted were Kathryn Tucker Windham "They Call It Gee's Bend," an unpublished paper in the Tutwiler Collection of the Birmingham Public Library; John Temple Graves II, "The Big World at Last Reaches Gee's Bend," *New York Times Magazine*, August 22, 1937; and Nancy Callahan, *The Freedom Quilting Bee* (1987). Insight into Wilcox County after the paper mill at Camden and the Corps of Engineers dam at Miller's Ferry were built came from a variety of sources, including Bob Alderman, *Down Home* (1975). General accounts of Alabama politics during this era include William D. Barnard, *Dixiecrats and Democrats: Alabama Politics, 1942–1950* (1974).

Surprisingly, there are few accounts that deal directly with the development of the Alabama River System. James E. Larson's *Alabama's Inland Waterways* (1960) is valuable from the administrative standpoint, while D. Gregory Jeane, *Evaluation of Engineering Cultural Resources: Lock No. 3, Coosa River, Alabama* (1981), is useful in understanding efforts to make that stream navigable.

Information supplied by the Coosa-Alabama River Improvement Association located in Montgomery helped a great deal, as did the U.S. Army Corps of Engineers assessments, *Waterborn Commerce of the United States*, for various years. Despite these yearly publications, commerce records for the Alabama are sketchy and are nonexistent for the Coosa.

Equally difficult to come by, much less assess, is information on the ecological changes in the streams. At the turn of the century Herbert H. Smith studied the mollusk life in the Coosa, and nearly fifty years later Calvin Goodrich wrote of how it had been threatened by dams and industrialization. However, only within the last two decades has serious attention been paid to the streams and the dangers they face. The subject is a passionate one for all sides, and publications from each hint strongly of propaganda for a particular position. To date, the best overall assessment of the rivers in their current state is the series published in the *Alabama Journal*.

In the final analysis, the greatest source of material on the rivers came from the writings of a group of amateur historians who loved the streams and who put their feelings into books and articles. Marvin B. Small of Gadsden was the chronicler of the Coosa, and his stories have memorialized that river for generations to come. Harold Rozelle came back to his home near Lincoln in the late 1940s, ran a ferry on the Coosa, and recorded his experiences in *Drift on the River* (1988). Viola Goode Liddell sprinkled river tales throughout her memoirs *With a Southern Accent* (1948) and *A Place of Springs* (1979), as did Mattie Lou Teague Crow in her *History of St. Clair County (Alabama)* (1973) and Kathryn Tucker Windham in her chapter on the Cahaba in *Rivers of Alabama* (1968). But the dean of the river writers was Bert Neville of Selma. A lifelong collector of river material and a friend of river men on every stream in the state, he published small volumes crammed with pictures, maps, articles, and lists. Among those most valuable in this study were *Directory of River Packets in the Mobile-Alabama-Warrior-Tombigbee Trades (1818–1932)* (1962), *Directory of Steam—Some Motor—Towboats and U.S. Engineer Department Vessels on the Mobile-Alabama-Tombigbee-Warrior Rivers (1881–1947)* (1964), and *Steamboats on the Coosa River in the Rome, Georgia-Gadsden-Greensport, Alabama Trades (1845–1920's)* (1966). When Bert Neville died, many of his papers were destroyed. Some, however, were saved, and today they are in the State Archives in Montgomery.

In the final analysis, the greatest sources were the people of the rivers. There is a wealth of oral history and tradition waiting to be explored. This book only scraped the surface. One can only hope that others will recognize the potential there and give it the attention it deserves.

Index

ABOUT THE AUTHOR

Harvey H. Jackson III is Head of the History Department at Jackson-ville State University, Alabama, and he lectures on river history throughout the state. He attended Marion Military Institute, received his bachelor's degree from Birmingham Southern College, his master's from The University of Alabama, and his doctorate from the University of Georgia. Among his many publications are *Oglethorpe in Perspective: Georgia's Founder After Two Hundred Years* (coeditor and contributor), *Hansell & Post: From King & Anderson to Jones, Day, Reavis & Pogue, 1890–1990* (author), *The Mitcham War of Clarke County, Alabama* (coauthor), *Georgia: Empire State of the South* (coauthor), *Lachlan McIntosh and the Politics of Revolutionary Georgia* (author), *Forty Years of Diversity: Essays on Colonial Georgia* (coeditor and contributor), and *Georgia Signers and the Declaration of Independence* (coauthor). His journal articles have appeared in *William and Mary Quarterly, Journal of Southern History, Alabama Review*, and *Georgia Historical Quarterly*.